Fighters for Freedom

Fighters for Freedom

THE HISTORY OF ANTI-SLAVERY ACTIVITIES

OF MEN AND WOMEN ASSOCIATED WITH

KNOX COLLEGE

By Hermann R. Muelder

New York   1959

COLUMBIA UNIVERSITY PRESS

Copyright © 1959 Columbia University Press, New York

Library of Congress Catalog Card Number: 59-9320

Published in Great Britain, Canada, India, and Pakistan
By the Oxford University Press
London, Toronto, Bombay, and Karachi

Manufactured in the United States of America

94266
AUG 29 1959

E
445
I3
M94

To Annie

Acknowledgments

A WORK SUCH AS THIS draws heavily upon the treasury of scholarship and depends upon the unrewarded cooperation of scores of men and women with interest in scholarly labors. How deeply the author is indebted to the previous studies of others is readily apparent from the bibliography, and he has been able to come by this store of resources for research only through the services of librarians, curators, or custodians of records in many places. The help of staff members was both encouraging and useful upon the occasion of visits to collections at: Oberlin College, Berea College, Syracuse University, University of Minnesota, University of Wisconsin, Chicago Theological Seminary, Newberry Library, Chicago Historical Society, the Public Library of Chicago, Illinois, the Public Library of Milwaukee, Wisconsin, the Public Library of Peoria, Illinois, the Public Library of Burlington, Iowa, the County Court of Knox, Illinois, and the County Court of Warren, Illinois. The greatest debt has been incurred by innumerable calls upon the facilities and for the assistance of the staff at the Galesburg Public Library and the Knox College Library.

Privileges appertaining to the community of scholars also have been extended to the author from: McCormick Theological Seminary, Olivet College, University of Chicago, University of Michigan, and the state historical societies of Illinois, Iowa, Kansas, and Missouri; also from the Historical Society of Quincy and Adams County, Illinois, the Library of Congress, and the

Congregational Library of the American Congregational Association of Boston, Massachusetts.

Several colleagues on the faculty of Knox College have been helpful at some stage of the research or writing. Far the greatest obligation is to Dr. John L. Stipp and Mr. Benjamin B. Richards for their care and candor in correcting and criticizing the entire manuscript.

Completion of the research was made possible by relief from teaching duties provided by a grant from the Social Science Research Council, and final preparation of the manuscript was facilitated by research funds from Knox College.

                                        HERMANN RICHARD MUELDER
Knox College
November, 1958

Contents

Maps and Illustrations

Prologue

What Lawrence is to Kansas, Galesburg has been to Illinois. The
activity and energy of its citizens, and their advocacy of right
principles and free institutions, when those principles were unpopular, made it envied and hated of its neighbors, and gained
for it the title of Abolition Hole.[1]

THIS WAS THE ASSERTION of a writer in the *Pantagraph*
of Bloomington, Illinois, made twenty years after Galesburg
was settled and after Knox College, for which the town had
been planned, was chartered. The reputation the college town
had in Bloomington prevailed elsewhere; in Peoria it was
known as "the Abolition nest," [2] in Quincy as "the little nigger
stealing town . . . a nest of nigger thieves." [3] At the time of
the Lincoln-Douglas debates the representatives of the St. Louis
Missouri Republican called Galesburg "the chief city of the
Abolitionists" in Illinois,[4] while the Chicago *Times* in several
communications referred to it not only as a "stronghold" of
Black Republicanism,[5] but also as the "center of abolitiondom
in this state" [6]—"notoriously known to be the very hotbed of
abolitionism in Illinois." [7]

That in later years this reputation should generally have
been lost abroad and largely forgotten at home may partly be
owing to the fact that Galesburg, though conspicuous in the

[1] Quoted in the Galesburg *Free Democrat*, Sept. 16, 1857.
[2] *Ibid.*, Feb. 23, 1854.   [3] *Ibid.*, Nov. 27, 1856.
[4] Sparks, *The Lincoln-Douglas Debates of 1858*, p. 376. This reference is to the
issue of Oct. 11, 1858.
[5] *Ibid.*, p. 380; issue of Oct. 9, 1858.   [6] *Ibid.*, p. 386; issue of Oct. 13, 1858.
[7] *Ibid.*, p. 382; issue of Oct. 12, 1858.

anti-slavery crusade when unrewarded courage was required, became obscure when victory had supplied spoils for the career politicians. That the influence of a Yankee settlement and a frontier college should be so far forgotten is no stranger than that twentieth-century researchers should need to demonstrate the significance of Theodore Dwight Weld. Though many of the builders of Knox College unselfishly devoted themselves to the abolitionist cause, they never collected the dividends of widespread popularity in secular affairs.

At a time when much of the older historical analysis of the anti-slavery movement is treated as legend,[8] it is a worthy labor of scholarship to examine the nature of the contribution which the Galesburg colony made to that humanitarian movement that hastened the freeing of the American Negro. The place of Knox College in that abolitionist agitation may at the outset be briefly suggested by noting that an academic genealogy places it as a daughter of Oneida Institute and a sister to Lane Seminary and Oberlin College. This trio of kindred schools and their role in the anti-slavery drama were given the lime-light in the field of historical literature by the publication of the Weld and the Birney letters. The relation of these schools to Knox and its share of the anti-slavery impulse are described in the following pages. Here again the student of American history encounters the founders and faculty of Oneida Institute, several of the Lane Rebels, some of the famous Beechers, and once more observes that fervor with which Finney's evangelism fired other zealots to an espousal of human reforms.

The story of what took place at Galesburg deserves to be re-told, not merely as an historical annotation to a more widely known tale, but in its own right. These were the contributions of Knox College and its founding colony: they furnished leadership in the establishment of anti-slavery organizations in Illinois and in the formation of the first abolitionist political party in that state; they were central to the operation of the Underground Railroad; their leaders pressed the sinful aspect

[8] Dexter, "The Legend of William Lloyd Garrison," *Social Studies*, XXX (Feb., 1939), 56–60.

of slavery on the tribunals of the Presbyterian denomination, thereby loosening the bonds of union with Congregationalists and intensifying the sectional religious differences in the nation; they affected the opinion of an unfriendly neighboring population largely of Southern extraction and influenced the attitude of the numerous pioneer Swedish communities; they educated a number of very active abolitionist agitators; and they sent out a second generation of colonists to the new frontier of the 1850s.

PART ONE

Origins

❧ I ❧

"Psychic Highway"

This is the uneven and rolling land that was the American idea-frontier of the nineteenth-century when outraged New Englanders (once rebels dreaming of freedom) pushed their newer visionaries westward to a less hostile environment. . . . So many of them have felt the presence of supernatural beings who thread the mist-hung valleys, stride the hills, that there is a wide belt, a kind of psychic highway, across the state that is enchanted as are few landscapes.[1]

ONLY IN THE VILLAGE of Western during the mid-autumn of 1825 were there signs of the anxiety that by winter-time would pervade Oneida County. Most people in western and central New York were eagerly anticipating the completion of the Erie Canal. To carry the message that it was finished, cannon were stationed along its course from Buffalo to New York. The towns along the route vied with each other in planning processions and preparing banquets with which to welcome the flotilla that on October 26 formally demonstrated that the waterway from the Great Lakes to the Atlantic was open. Small talk as well as big speeches predicted the most bountiful benefits.

But a man on the banks of a new canal might also be standing at the abyss of everlasting hell, and what would it profit him to gain all America if he lost his own soul? As the festivities wore off there was more and more talk, anxious talk, about the "protracted meeting" at Western, where the new preacher, Charles Grandison Finney, was leading a religious

[1] Carmer, *Dark Trees to the Wind*, pp. 7–8.

revival and was revealing his powers as an evangelist. Since late in September he had paused at the request of his religious mentor, George Washington Gale, to preach awhile in the village church that Gale, feeble from dyspepsia, could only partly minister.[2] Soon the most astonishing reports came out of Western, how the village and countryside were overcome with religious conviction and how scores were "converted."

The "Great Revival," though it was still some time before men called it such, had begun. Other towns in Oneida County begged for Finney's preaching, until the calls far exceeded those he could answer.[3] But other evangelists also found how white were the fields to the Lord's harvest, settled ministers discovered new and unexpected powers of evangelism, and young converts proved to have the talents by which religious anxiety could be developed in others and then transformed to enthusiasm. By the spring of 1826 the counties all along the canal were affected, and the entire northeastern part of the nation was showing its concern. From week to week the religious journals of Boston and elsewhere presented "glowing accounts of the wonderful outpourings of the Holy Spirit." [4]

Thus it happened that a "psychic highway" appeared alongside the Erie Canal. During the dozen years still remaining until the Panic of 1837, while the canal would make New York City the economic metropolis of the nation, the Great Revival would strengthen the position of the city as the center of philanthropy for religion and reform. Westward the canal would carry thousands of settlers from New York and New England to northern Ohio, Indiana, and Illinois—settlers who would change the cultural complexion of those states, in which previously people from the South had been predominant. And most of these Yankees and New Yorkers who came by way of the canal carried along with their worldly effects a burden of spiritual, moral, and social convictions acquired during the Great Revival.

[2] George Washington Gale, "Autobiography" (typed copy of MS in Knox College Library, Galesburg, Illinois), p. 204.
[3] Finney, *Memoirs*, pp. 140–53.
[4] Charles Beecher, ed., *Autobiography of Lyman Beecher*, I, 89.

The country in which the Great Revival originated and blazed with the greatest intensity was known as the Burned-over District. It comprised the part of New York west of the Catskill and Adirondack mountains. The revival that began at Western in 1825 was merely the culmination of a quarter century of lesser revivals that had burned, smoldered, and flamed over one part or another of the newly settled country.

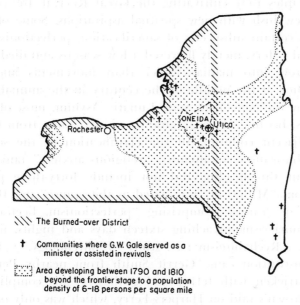

\\\ The Burned-over District

✝ Communities where G.W. Gale served as a
   minister or assisted in revivals

Area developing between 1790 and 1810
beyond the frontier stage to a population
density of 6-18 persons per square mile

The Burned-over District of New York

More than any other American frontier, that of western New York had experienced fervent revivalism. "Emotional religion was thus a congenital regional characteristic, present at birth and developed throughout the youth of the section."[5] The settlers were predominantly Yankees who departed from the thin soils of New England but carried with them to their new homes that extraordinary "fertility of projects for the salvation of the world" which Emerson noted in the New England of that time. Visionaries usually found that in the Burned-over

[5] Cross, *Burned-over District*, p. 4.

District they gathered followers more easily than elsewhere, and not a few of their heady enthusiasms were generated in this area itself.[6]

Even before the Great Revival the area had been seeded with a number of religious and social eccentricities, though none that grew to the stature of Mormonism and Millerism in that section later. During the decade after 1825, when Finney and his disciples were cultivating the Great Revival, the countryside grew lush with new spiritual aspirations. Some of these, such as certain subspecies of sanctification, perfectionism, and spiritual wifery, merely flowered a few seasons and died. Often they grew into manias rather than movements and were catalogued at the middle of the century in the annual report made by the New York State Lunatic Asylum, most of whose patients, because of geographic proximity, came from Oneida and adjacent counties. In the classification of the so-called "probable causes" of insanity, "religious anxiety" ranked second, but this heading did not include forty-three patients for whom "Millerism" was stated as the "cause" nor the miscellany of "causes" comprising "perfectionism, license question, Fourierism, preaching sixteen days and nights, mesmerism, . . . Rechabiteism . . . study of phrenology."[7] To this same institution came Gerrit Smith from nearby Peterboro when stricken with terror and guilt over his complicity in John Brown's raid on Harpers Ferry, which was only one of a series of "causes" he had supported during thirty years of reforming, most of them, such as vegetarianism, dress-reform, "indigent-females," Sabbath-keeping, anti-tobacco, and the like, much less serious in their consequences.

The historical significance of the Burned-over District derives, however, from religious phenomena of greater permanence. Indeed, a feature distinguishing the Great Revival from other waves of religious emotionalism in our history was its greater lasting power. More of the "leading minds" in communities were affected by it, the number of apostates was smaller, and the effect on the "moral state" of communities

[6] *Ibid.*, chapter 3.
[7] Jones, *Annals and Recollections of Oneida County*, pp. 593–600.

was more general.[8] It resulted in a kind of "practical" Christianity.[9] Finney taught that conversion meant a change in the individual from self-interest to unselfish benevolence. As part of his evangelistic technique he learned that to make men anxious about their souls it was quite as effective to discourse at length upon particular evils in our society as to arouse them by extravagant descriptions of the parlous state of the sinful individual.[10] Consequently the emotional energies released by the revival were readily transformed into humanitarian enterprises.[11] Dozens of benevolent societies sprang up, not merely to carry the torch for missions, Sunday Schools, religious tracts, and the like, but also to promote causes such as peace, prison reform, education, abolition of imprisonment for debt, temperance, and the emancipation of slaves. The coordination of such benevolent societies with religious fervor was especially facilitated when Finney transferred his evangelistic headquarters to New York City after 1830, and worked in conjunction with those merchant-princes, philanthropists, and promotors of reform, Arthur and Lewis Tappan.[12] New York City became more or less the administrative center of a "benevolent system" based on the interlocking of the personnel of a number of national societies. By the early forties, when the "benevolent system" was fully formed, a dozen organizations would hold their "national anniversaries" during a single week in May, and the New York *Evangelist* would daily issue a small sheet giving a full report of the proceedings of each society for the benefit of those who, perforce, could attend only one or two a day.[13] Leadership and coherence were given to the activities of these societies by Congregationalists and

---

[8] Asa Mahan, *Autobiography*, p. 222.   [9] Roy, *Memorial Addresses*, pp. 2–3.
[10] Cross, *Burned-over District*, pp. 165–66.
[11] Stanton, *Random Recollections*, p. 51.
[12] *Letters of Theodore Dwight Weld, Angelina Grimké Weld, and Sarah Grimké, 1822–1844*, I, vi. Hereafter referred to as *Weld Letters*.
[13] Between May 8 and May 13 of 1842, in addition to several New York state societies, the following held their anniversaries in New York City: American Seaman's Friend Society, American and Foreign Anti-Slavery Society, American Sunday School Union, American Tract Society, American Home Missionary Society, American Female Reform Society, American Bible Society, American Education Society, American Board of Commissioners for Foreign Missions (New York *Evangelist*, May 5, 1842).

New School Presbyterians whose interdenominational agencies were the core of the system. It was in the Burned-over District that these two denominations were most thoroughly blended, and in the hybrid churches of that area that Finney's evangelical fervor was most effectively combined with the zeal for reform.

The first of the "causes" in the Burned-over District to make a serious impact upon secular affairs was the anti-Masonic movement.[14] Less widely appreciated at the time but more enduring were certain educational developments that came out of the area. But if the movement with the greatest influence upon our national history is to be selected from these moral and religious crusades, then the anti-slavery agitation must be chosen. Though abolitionism as a doctrine originated at this time in New England, the leadership in the movement was appropriated by the Burned-over District. To appreciate this activity it is necessary to have some understanding of the social structure of the region.

Utica and Rochester were the chief centers of the areas marked by enthusiasms. Before leaving on the itinerary that left him established as "the Evangelist" in New York City, Finney had crowned his labors for western New York with a six months' revival in Rochester that in its extent and intensity matched the revival with which he had shaken the foundations of Utica in Oneida County five years before. Utica and Rochester each dominated a trading area that had developed beyond the frontier stage and was approaching agrarian maturity, and such areas, it has been noted, were those in which "isms" flourished the most. Another possible economic factor in explaining the roles of Utica and Rochester in the religious revival is that Finney arrived in both places at a time when the boom brought on by building a section of the canal had declined, and the townspeople had reverted to more thought upon their religious condition and to concern about "sin," a commodity that moved with considerable facility along the canal.[15]

During this generation, however, Utica, which had first grown

<hr>

[14] Cross, *Burned-over District*, chapter 6.   [15] *Ibid.*, pp. 59, 75–76.

to urban proportions, maintained its lead over Rochester. The former shared with neighboring Rome the commerce of the tract comprising Oneida and Madison counties and extending north and south to the state boundaries. For the country west of the Hudson River, Utica led in manufacturing. It was then the customary meeting place in western New York for political and religious convocations, even for state-wide groups, such as the convention that met in 1835 to organize the state anti-slavery society. Here were also the printing establishments that ran off the reports, broadsides, and pamphlets promoting new "causes"; for a decade, in fact, Utica led upstate New York in its book trade.[16]

Well before there was a canal, Utica and Oneida County had been the center of an organization, the Female Missionary Society of Western New York, that sent out itinerants who called the sinners of this area to repentance. Finney and his mentor, Gale, were both supported at the start of their careers by this body.[17] After the Great Revival began, Finney and several other evangelists of the Burned-over District received the subsidies of a specially organized "Oneida Evangelical Society" that attempted to pay each cooperating preacher six hundred dollars from a fund derived by pooling the receipts of the itinerants with contributions from the wealthy men of Utica.[18] By 1829, though its population was still less than 8,000, Utica may have been contributing as much as $70,000 for religious causes,[19] and at nearby Peterboro, Oneida County's great landowner, Gerrit Smith, having served a year as president of the Western Sunday School Union, had begun his long career as a philanthropist.[20]

On traditional religious lines the most important organization was the Oneida Presbytery, to which belonged the churches in which the Great Revival began. Finney himself was a regular member of the Oneida Presbytery from 1826 until 1832, when he became a member of a New York City presbytery.[21]

[16] *Ibid.*, p. 64.   [17] G. W. Gale, "Autobiography," pp. 78–79, 205.
[18] Cross, *Burned-over District*, p. 187.   [19] *Ibid.*, p. 153.   [20] *Ibid.*, p. 129.
[21] *Minutes of the Presbyterian Church in the United States of America, A.D. 1836* (Philadelphia, 1836), pp. 317–18.

Jedediah Burchard, next in popularity to Finney as an evangelist, also became a member of this Oneida body,[22] as did George Washington Gale, who had prepared them both for the ministry.

Much of the impact that the Oneida communities made upon the nation came from a far-flung dispersal of personnel that occurred during the decade after the revival began. Theodore Dwight Weld, who had been converted by Finney at Utica and educated under Gale at Whitesboro, had become the most famous reforming itinerant of the nation. Finney, after an exhausting decade, was teaching theology at Oberlin in Ohio, where one of his followers, Asa Mahan, licensed by the Oneida Presbytery in 1827,[23] had gone as president following an eventful pastorate in Cincinnati. Among their students was a particularly notable group of young converts known as the Lane Rebels, many of whom had been previously identified as the "Oneidas." By 1840 several of these had appeared in Illinois, where they renewed contacts with their former teacher, Gale, who was leader of a colony from Oneida County that was establishing a revivalistic, reform-minded college town. The man slated to become president of that college, Hiram Huntington Kellogg, was also of the Oneida Presbytery [24] and had been one of the auxiliary evangelists under Finney's leadership, ministering to half a dozen towns in Oneida and the counties immediately west.[25] When the American Anti-Slavery Society sent an agent out to Illinois to maintain more regular connections with these men and others, it chose a former licentiate of the Oneida Presbytery, the Reverend John Cross.[26] Antislavery meetings in Illinois were to a considerable extent reunions of these men and other alumni of the Burned-over District.

This western expansion of the reforming influence from the Burned-over District in general and from the Oneida

---

[22] Fletcher, *History of Oberlin*, I, 11–13.   [23] *Ibid.*

[24] *Minutes of the Presbyterian Church, 1836*, pp. 317–18.

[25] H. H. Kellogg to Finney, May 20, July 6, 1826; Oct. 15, Sept. 2 and 3, 1827; March 26, April 28, 1828; Sept. 26, 1829. Gale to Finney, Sept. 26, 1827; Laura Fish to Mrs. Lydia Finney, Aug. 6, 1826; Sarah Brayton to Mrs. Finney, April 25, 1827, Finney Papers, Oberlin College Library.

[26] *Minutes of the Presbyterian Church, 1836*, pp. 317–18.

locality in particular forms the main theme of this book. As the historian of Oneida County remarked, while the events of the Great Revival were still fresh in men's memories: "The influences of this revival have been likened to the waves formed by casting a pebble upon a sheet of water, pressing forward, wave forming wave, until they strike the farthest shore; so many of the inhabitants of the western prairies, and granite bound New England, yet bless God that they lived in 'these' days." [27]

[27] Jones, *Annals and Recollections of Oneida County*, p. 390.

❧ II ❧

Mentor of the Great Revival

How is the world to be converted unless we have men—ay men—
men who can endure hardness, men of fearlessness—men of a
apostolic spirit? Men of this stamp are needed by thousands, and
the world is dying for them. . . . Little did we think talking
over this subject what was to grow out of the little experiment
it was then thought best to make in Western. . . . It will be to
the moral world what the lever of Archimedes, could he have
found a fulcrum, would have been to the natural.[1]

NO ECSTASY MARKED the conversion of George Washington Gale. Though this was the sign of salvation that he anticipated for himself and hoped for in others, his own conversion
was calmer, less intense. There was the long period of intermittent and increasing anxiety, of shame, grief, and fear; there
was the conviction of sinfulness, the sense of his own inadequacy
to purge himself, and the search in the Scriptures and at religious meetings for the assurance that he was redeemed.
Eventually he was calmly confident that he had undergone an
inward change, a regeneration or "change of heart." But in
between there did not occur, as in the case of his own convert
and student Finney, a crescendo of hours of extreme emotional
disturbance with trembling, weeping, sleeplessness, and a central climax of oblivion followed by release, by a glow of warmth,
by joy. Gale, however, believed in the necessity of some sort
of strong individual religious experience and the efficacy of
such an experience in altering the personality of the individual.

[1] From letters of Gale to Finney, Jan. 21, Jan. 29, Dec. 3, 1830, Finney Papers,
Oberlin College Library.

The variety of emotional experience associated with conversion intrigued him; several are related with harrowing detail in his autobiography. And like most contemporary clergymen in the Burned-over District, he measured success largely by counting converts.[2]

The field of Gale's own ministry was located mostly north of Oneida County in the new settlements near the eastern end of Lake Ontario.[3] He was sent to this area in 1817 by the Female Missionary Society of Western New York, the seat of which was in Utica. To this area he returned as a missionary when his seminary studies at Princeton were completed, and here in 1819 he settled as pastor at Adams. Five years of ministry were marked by more and more religious excitement and mounting revivalism, concluding in a last year of almost incessant labors. During many weeks there were daily meetings, both in the afternoon and evening, with visits to the "hopeful" in between.[4] This trial of Gale's health was too severe, for he was a small man, slight of build, even frail, inclined to be sickly; he frequently found that food did not agree with him.[5] In 1824 he gave up his pastorate in Adams and retired—as it proved, permanently—from the regular ministerial profession, though not from occasional preaching.

Gale already had discovered the role, however, in which he was to make his greatest contribution, that of mentor for others who were better equipped than he to act on pulpits and platforms, to move people in the mass. Gale's talents for persuasion seem to have been considerable, but they were not forensic and derived rather from certain personal traits of graciousness in social intercourse, dignity, interest in people, and keen observation of their personalities and their relationships with others. He was motivated by a blend of idealism, practicality, and genuine piety that commanded respect from individuals even though it might not excite audiences.

The two leading evangelists of the Great Revival were both

[2] George Washington Gale, "Autobiography."
[3] *Ibid.*, pp. 78–79, 86, 100, 109 ff.   [4] *Ibid.*, pp. 100–9.
[5] Calkins, *They Broke the Prairie*, pp. 37–39.

prepared for the ministry and were introduced to formal professional standing under Gale's personal guidance. The first
of these was Jedediah Burchard,[6] a young man whom Gale
discovered at Adams. Burchard's aspirations to the ministry
had been rebuffed by a presbytery in eastern New York, but he
had remained active in religious affairs and even did some
preaching in the newly settled country near Adams, for which
he was reproved by Gale's ministerial colleagues. Gale observed,
however, that the vivacity, impulsiveness, fascination for others,
and fondness for society that made Burchard suspect to the
ministerial profession were aspects of character of a very high
order for a preacher. He noted Burchard's powers as a conver-
sationalist, his skill at storytelling, his capacity of impersona-
tion, his retentive memory, and his facility at oral rhetoric. To
give him counsel and training Gale arranged that Burchard
should live with him for several weeks and assist him in the
conduct of religious services under Gale's immediate tutelage.
Convinced that the young man's ability warranted a relaxation
of the usual requirements for the ministry, Gale presented him
to a Congregational association which would not be so inflexible
about its rules as a presbytery. Burchard was given a license to
preach for one year with the understanding that during that
time he study under Gale, a license that was renewed by a
still dubious association for two years. By that time the Great
Revival was under way and Burchard had become a preacher
of such power and popularity as to overwhelm, if not to silence,
his critics.[7]

One day when Burchard and Gale were returning from
one of their pastoral visits, Gale remarked that there was a
young man in town of considerable influence who stood in
the way of the conversion of others, and that if he could be
converted the "spell" would be broken. This young man was
quite friendly with Gale, respectful of religion, and even served
as choirmaster in Gale's church, but he distressed his pastor
by making light of the revival and by flippant remarks about

---

[6] Cross, *Burned-over District*, p. 188.
[7] G. W. Gale, "Autobiography," pp. 134–42.

certain special meetings that were part of a revival routine. The scoffer, Charles Grandison Finney, explained that he did not go to the schoolhouse for prayer meetings because of the fleas, and called the "meetings of inquiry," at which Gale went from one person to the other conversing in low tones, "whispering meetings" or "Bucktail" conferences.

Came one autumn evening, however, when Finney surprised Gale by appearing when one of these "Bucktail" conferences was in progress. Gale left a weeping penitent with whom he was "whispering" at the time, went to the newcomer, took him by the hand, and looked him straight in the eye.

"You have come in here, I presume as a spy; you want to get something to make sport of."

But Finney's face was solemn. "No, Mr. Gale," he said, "I have not; I am willing now to be a Christian."

They sat down together.

"Do you think," asked Finney, "there is any hope in my case?" [8]

Brusquely Gale told him that if he were converted it would be something very similar to God's exercise of miraculous powers. The congregation knelt to pray, Gale at Finney's side, the latter trembling so that he thought the house shook. With this beginning, Finney entered upon three days of religious hysteria, the events of which Gale must have related a good many times, for he preserved them in his memoirs with all the vivid detail and the obvious pride with which a midwife would narrate her most famous delivery.

The experience was in all truth a turning point in Finney's life.[9] During the winter Gale took the young convert into his home to begin preparation for the ministry by general studies in literature, the classics, and philosophy, for Finney's education approximated only what a student should have on entrance to college. This was considerable hospitality on the part of the

[8] *Ibid.*, pp. 143–52, 165, 174.

[9] Finney's account of his relation to Gale is found in Finney, *Memoirs,* pp. 6–60. These relations are also described by a member of the Galesburg colony: E. P. Chambers, "Reminiscences of Early Days," Knox County Historical Society Papers, Knox College Library.

Gales, for they had only recently found adequate housing in a brick building vacated by a bank; Mrs. Gale was expecting a baby soon, and Gale himself was never quite well for very long at a time. It is true that Gale raised money in the neighborhood to pay for Finney's board and room, but the list was headed by a six months' subscription by Gale himself.

The following summer, at Gale's advice, Finney placed himself under the care of the presbytery, which prescribed a course of theological studies. The actual tutelage was in Gale's home and at Gale's hands, and the instruction was accompanied by active assistance in ministerial labors, for which Gale could well be grateful, inasmuch as his stomach gave him more and more distress and at times he was able to keep going only with dosages of laudanum. For about two years the two men studied and worked together, until the master, too feeble to continue his preaching, turned over the church to his apprentice— Gale having persuaded the presbytery to license Finney six months ahead of schedule. And when the church at Adams shortly found its own prophet without honor, Gale applied to the Utica Female Missionary Society and got his protégé a commission as a home missionary.[10]

Later in the year 1824 the Gales closed up their home in Adams, and Gale set out on a long journey as far south as Virginia in pursuit of better health. Upon his return in 1825 the Gales settled on a small farm at Western in Oneida County. Here in the fall Finney stopped with his wife and baby, while on his way back to north-central New York, after a visit with his wife's parents at nearby Whitesboro. This call at the Gale home was extended into a visit of nearly three months, for Gale persuaded Finney to preach a few Sabbaths in the church at Western and from this preaching an astounding religious excitement developed. With Gale helping as he could the delirium developed into the opening stage of the Great Revival.[11] As Finney carried the fire to other towns in Oneida

[10] G. W. Gale, "Autobiography," pp. 174–205; Cross, *Burned-over District*, pp. 151–53.

[11] Finney, *Memoirs*, p. 153.

County that winter, Gale gave some occasional assistance. At
Rome, which had been veritably prostrated by Finney's evangelism, Gale was called to assist with the examination of about
200 candidates for new membership; on that occasion he bap-
tized in succession sixty-four persons, of all ages! [12]

What Gale had done for Finney and Burchard, at the very
dawn of the Great Revival, he now set out to do for the great
number of their young converts, many of whom desired to enter
the ministry but lacked the means to obtain proper schooling.
Early in the spring of 1826 he took seven of these young men
into his home, provided them their board, lodging, and washing, solicited books for them, and gave them instruction. He
used as a schoolroom a small building nearby that had formerly
been a physician's office. The students in return were required
to work three and a half hours a day on Gale's small farm, to
tend his garden, and to cut fuel. By autumn, after the students
had gathered the crops and departed to teach during the winter,
it was evident that the enterprise had been a decided success,
and Gale was certain that he had devised a method for solving
the general problem of education for young men without
means, as well as a method for meeting the special necessity
of the zealots produced by the revival.[13]

A difficulty Gale had with these young men illustrates the
fanaticism that gave the Great Revival a bad name in conservative religious circles, though it helped make the students
effective agitators for reforms during the succeeding decade.
They had assumed not only some of the more unconventional
mannerisms of Finney but also the even more extreme histrionic
devices of "Father" Nash, an evangelist who up to this time
had been with Finney a great deal. Among these practices was
that of loud, fervent, and fluent prayers, which publicly named
"cold" Christians and impenitent sinners. One or two of the
zealots would attend the numerous prayer meetings around
town that had been started during the excitement of the preceding winter, and at these meetings the students would describe in their prayers what they conceived to be the character

of certain individuals. Some of these descriptions were quite slanderous. Back in their own schoolroom the students sometimes experienced what they called, after Nash, "spiritual travail," during which they prayed so loud for certain souls that people going down the street would stop and ask what was the matter.

Excesses such as these threatened for a time to split even the liberal or New School party of the Presbyterian denomination. Had this occurred the Great Revival as such would have been circumscribed, and the impulse which it gave to abolitionism and the other reform agitations of the next dozen years might have been badly weakened. Even the ministers of the Burned-over District were sometimes disturbed over the "New Measures." Finney himself reported to Gale that the pastor of the Rome church was frightened: "Last night after the meeting some of the young people wrung their hands and fell upon each others' necks. We had to send them home." [14] But to the pastors of this area such episodes were not so novel as they were in more staid and conservative New England. The former were convinced that, as a whole, the revival was a work of overwhelming good, and believed that Finney should not be blamed for the disorderly religious activities of followers in whose less skillful hands the New Measures were sometimes crudely used. Finney was taken into the Oneida Presbytery in September of 1826. The clergy of this body answered the mounting criticisms from New England by correspondence and by a published description of the revival. They met Finney's detractors in conferences, first at Albany and then at New Lebanon. In these negotiations Gale took a very active part, although the most active agent on Finney's side seems to have been the Reverend John Frost of the church at Whitesboro.[15] Though it was not possible immediately to reconcile all differences, an open break was averted and with time a moderation of Finney's techniques, combined

[14] *Ibid.*, p. 212.

[15] The New Measures controversy is discussed in Charles Beecher, ed., *Autobiography of Lyman Beecher*, II, 91–108; Gale to Finney, March 14, June 6, Sept. 6, 1837, Finney Papers, Oberlin; Finney, *Memoirs*, pp. 188–89; G. Frederick Wright, *Charles Grandison Finney*, p. 85.

with the growing strength of evangelism outside the Burned-over District, effected an accommodation.[16] Within three years Dr. Lyman Beecher, chief spokesman for the New Englanders, found himself joined in a common venture with the Finneyites and "Oneidas."

Meanwhile the Oneida Presbytery had been persuaded by Gale to embark upon an educational enterprise. The combination of schooling and farm labor at Western had proved so successful that Gale approached the Reverend John Frost of Whitesboro and other of his ministerial friends with the proposal that he be given aid in establishing a regular school on the same design. Frost, who had been a particularly close friend of Gale's since the days when Frost had been his teacher at Middlebury Academy, entered actively into the scheme during the fall of 1826.[17] At the winter session of the Oneida Presbytery their plan for a manual labor school was approved. On February 14, 1827, a public meeting in Utica organized the "Oneida Academy," later incorporated as the "Oneida Institute of Science and Industry." [18] Its primary object was to educate young men who intended to become ministers, although other young men of good moral character would also be admitted; all were to be required to do manual labor. Gale and Frost were appointed agents to raise funds.[19]

The largest contributions came from Utica, as did the leading officers of the original board of trustees; [20] the project was mainly supported from Oneida County and its immediate vicinity, but assistance was also received from New Measures clergymen and lay followers of Finney elsewhere in the state. During the school's first three years of operation almost eight hundred persons from over sixty communities in fourteen counties had subscribed their support. Many of the donations

[16] Cross, *Burned-over District*, pp. 151–65.
[17] G. W. Gale, "Autobiography," pp. 226–28.
[18] Lamb, "George Washington Gale" (Unpublished Ed.D. dissertation, Syracuse University, 1949), pp. 105–6; Coates, "From George Gale to Arthur Morgan," *Educational Review*, LXXII (June 19, 1926), 53–55.
[19] *First Report of the Trustees of Oneida Institute of Science and Industry, March 1828*, pp. 1–2.
[20] Lamb, "George Washington Gale," pp. 107 ff.

were modest gifts of materials, such as siding, stone, glass, nails, masonwork, etc.; [21] Finney's father-in-law, for example, gave a thousand feet of hemlock lumber.[22] A site was selected on a farm within view of the Erie Canal near Whitesboro; Gale moved to this location, and in the second week of May, 1827, the school got under way.

[21] *Second Report of the Trustees of Oneida Institute of Science and Industry, Whitestown, March 20, 1830,* pp. 22–28.
[22] Cross, *Burned-over District,* p. 149; Fletcher, *History of Oberlin,* I, 38–39.

✣ III ✣

Manual Labor for the Millennium

The hobbies of Oneida Institute furnished what became the horses on which politicians afterward complacently rode to place and power.[1]

ONEIDA INSTITUTE, which began as a sort of training school for young evangelists, developed into a hotbed of young radicals. The one thing which the school never lacked during Gale's regime was students. The seven or eight who began the first term in May, 1827, had become twenty by the end of the term, and already thirty had been turned away. This was typical of the situation for the next decade. A wing was built to the original two-story farmhouse, and the next year thirty-five students were taken, but fifty were turned away.[2] New three-story wooden buildings were constructed, three in all by 1836, but they were never enough. In 1830 sixty students were registered but 500 were turned down,[3] and in the fall of 1832 Gale reported to Finney that he was refusing applications at the rate of two or three a day. Even Finney, who in 1827 might recommend a man with assurance of immediate admission, was told by Gale in 1832 that a Finney candidate would have to wait his turn, for the trustees had ruled that young men must be taken in the order of application.[4]

Among these students there developed a remarkable *esprit*

[1] Grinnell, *Men and Events of Forty Years*, p. 31.
[2] Lamb, "George Washington Gale" (Unpublished Ed.D. dissertation, Syracuse University, 1949), pp. 120–26.
[3] *American Annals of Education and Instruction*, I (Feb., 1831), 84.
[4] Gale to Finney, Sept. 6, 1827; Gale to Finney, May 20, Oct. 20, 1832, Finney Papers, Oberlin College Library.

de corps. Much of this derived from their common experience
in the Great Revival and the intellectual milieu of the Burned-
over District. Strong group feeling and continuing zeal for the
Institute and its causes also grew out of the operation of the
manual labor system. Students were expected to pay for their
board by working from three to four hours on the college farm
or in its shops at carpentry, blacksmithing, making joiners'
tools, making chairs and wagons and harness. At first this work
was done in two short periods at the very beginning and the
very end of the day, but it was later found more efficient to
concentrate it all in the middle of the afternoon. The students
worked together in classes, each in charge of a student monitor,
who was responsible to the farmer who managed the enterprises.[5] One of the student monitors, Theodore Dwight Weld,
who was in charge of the milking class, especially won the
loyalty and admiration of his schoolmates. Living quarters
were plain and crowded, comprising, as Gale put it, a "prophet's
chamber" with a bed, stool, and a pitcher of water. "Good
moral character and respectable talents" were not enough to
make a good "Oneida Institute man"; he must be one who
would "imbibe the spirit of the body of the students," adopt
the system of the school "from principle," and submit to the
"self-denial and duties" of the Institute.[6]

During the summer of 1829 the Institute was visited by the
editor of the *Journal of the American Education Society*. He
reported, "I can say with truth, that I have rarely seen a company of young men in any institution, more healthy, vigorous,
or cheerful." [7] Two years later the wealthy New York merchant
and philanthropist, Lewis Tappan, visited his two sons who
were at the school and proudly told his brother how his older
son got up at four o'clock every morning to swill the fourteen
pigs in his charge. The students, he asserted, "live simply and

[5] The best account of the operations of Oneida Institute is in a letter, Gale to
H. Norton, Sept. 1, 1832, published in the New York *Evangelist*, Oct. 13, 1832;
see also articles in the July 21 and Nov. 10, 1832, issues of the *Evangelist*; *American Annals of Education*, Feb., 1831, p. 84; July, 1832, pp. 350–51.

[6] Gale to Finney, May 20, 1832, Finney Papers, Oberlin.

[7] Lamb, "George Washington Gale," p. 127.

happily. . . . I was delighted to see young men, who a few hours previous were reaping, mowing, milking etc. come onto the platform before a large assembly and deliver their compositions in Latin and English orations, poems, colloquies etc. with ease and dignity." [8]

Some of the excellent spirit in the student body was no doubt due to the awareness that they were participating in an experiment. In January, 1829, Weld and Horace Bushnell, comprising a committee on behalf of the students, wrote a letter to the trustees affirming the practicability of the plan of the institution as formulated by Gale and declaring that the manual labor was not excessive, did not hinder their intellectual development, and made them "hardy, enterprising, and independent." [9] When a barn was needed Weld got permission to cut timber from a neighbor's wood lot, and led a crew which cut the wood, rafted it to the Institute, and built the barn and several sheds.[10] During the winter of 1829–30 eleven students, without solicitation, subscribed two hundred and forty dollars to the school, which money they raised by such work as quarrying stone, threshing grain, cutting wood, and teaching school.[11]

It was to be expected that these students would have decided notions of their own about the school's responsibilities to themselves, about its teachers, and about its curriculum. One of the first signs of this attitude was a proposal for a practical short cut for training ministers in the ancient languages. As early as 1829 the Reverend John Frost was discussing the advisability of giving priority to Hebrew over Latin as a scriptural language.[12] By July of 1833 this had become a fixed determination on the part of several students who wrote to Finney for support on this issue, their spokesman being a Finney convert who before entering Oneida Institute had been for six years a midshipman in the United States Navy.[13] The Lord Jesus, they pointed out, "took ignorant men [who] studied 3½ years with

---

[8] Benjamin P. Thomas, *Theodore Weld*, p. 19.
[9] Lamb, "George Washington Gale," p. 123.
[10] Benjamin P. Thomas, *Theodore Weld*, p. 20.
[11] Lamb, "George Washington Gale," p. 129.   [12] Ibid., pp. 126–27.
[13] Weld to Gerrit Smith, Aug. 6, 1839, *Weld Letters*, II, 780–81.

him learning practical lessons, and practicing what they learnt."
At Oneida Institute it was "just the reverse now," for in a
course of five years all too much time was wasted "plodding
through these 'prophane and old wives fables' " in Latin and
Greek.[14] The fact that adequate training in theology was never
provided at Oneida Institute, despite Gale's strong efforts to get
an outstanding teacher, resulted, as will be seen, by 1833 in a
removal of the first and finest crop of "Oneidas" to Cincinnati.

Though the most lasting impact of Oneida Institute was made
by the migration of much of its personnel, students, faculty,
and patrons to the West during the middle thirties, it had before that time exerted great influence on the educational institutions of the nation by supplying the model for manual
labor schools throughout the country. Though the school in
Whitesboro may have missed the accident of priority by a few
months, it is certain that the project was original with Gale.
A doctrine of manual labor in his case followed the practice of
it, and was not merely the application of some educational
theory he might have picked up in his reading. Manual labor
education was the natural outgrowth of his tutoring of aspirants
for the ministry, which had been going on more or less without
interruption since he had taken Burchard and then Finney
under his tutelage. Manual labor was first combined with such
instruction on his farm at Western during the summer of 1826,
and developed directly into Oneida Institute. The reading of
contemporary periodicals leaves no doubt that though the
parallel and independent invention of similar enterprises may
have occurred elsewhere, it was Gale's experiment that received
the primary attention of commentators on the new idea and
Oneida Institute that was directly copied by many imitators.
The academicians quickly uncovered many earlier suggestions
of manual labor theory and even some foreign prototypes, but
the actual working of the American experiment at Whitesboro
was that most carefully described and closely followed in the
educational periodicals.[15]

[14] Charles Stewart Renshaw and "2 others" to Finney, July 15, 1833, Finney
Papers, Oberlin.
[15] Coates, "From George Gale to Arthur Morgan," *Educational Review,* LXXII

The extremely optimistic philosophy of manual labor in education captivated many minds. Carried away by the success of his school during the early years at Whitesboro, Gale wrote to Finney that it was an "impulse to a system of education that is to introduce the millennium. . . . I am not extravagant. If you and I live twenty years longer, or half that, we shall see it. Little did we think when talking over this subject what was to grow out of the little experiment it was then thought best to make at Western." [16] Gale's enthusiasm was shared for a time in many hearts. The great Lyman Beecher also regarded manual labor in education as a "millennial enterprise," declaring with tears in his eyes that if there were anything in his life that would make him want to live it over again it was his being instrumental in training a corps of "manual labor young men and then leading them forth against the infidelity and wickedness of the world." [17]

The scheme of joining manual labor with education suited well the spirit of benevolence and rising democracy of this Jacksonian era. It was a system that promised to equalize opportunity for rich and poor without the evil of charity and without weakening the important sense of self-dependence in young men. Health and bodily vigor, often impaired by exclusive attention to study, were preserved and developed, and future ministers were toughened to endure the hardships of the frontier. Moral character, diligence, and self-reliance were stimulated. That mutual regard and sympathy between different strata of society essential to a democratic state was

---

(June 19, 1926), 53–55; Anderson, "The Manual Labor School Movement," *Educational Review*, XLVI (Nov., 1913), 369–86; Lamb, "George Washington Gale," pp. 100–4, 111–12; *American Annals of Education*, I (Feb., 1831), 82, cites a possible manual labor school in Maine in 1825; from Aug., 1830, to Oct., 1831, the *American Annals of Education* ran a series of articles on the Fellenborger Institution at Hofwyl, Switzerland. A Prussian example was given in Aug., 1830, p. 367; an English case was described in Jan., 1832, pp. 42–47. Kellogg, *Education for the People*, p. 12, discusses Oneida Institute as a model for imitators. Close following of affairs at Oneida Institute is evident in the *American Annals of Education*, I (Aug., 1830), 366; I (Feb., 1831), 84; I (June, 1831), 281; II (July 1, 1832), 350–51; and in the *American Quarterly Register*, II (Nov., 1829), 112–13.

[16] Gale to Finney, Jan. 29, 1830; Dec., 1830, Finney Papers, Oberlin.

[17] Conversation reported, Calvin Waterbury to Weld, Aug. 3, 1832, *Weld Letters*, I, 81.

fostered by the discipline of mutual manual labor for all students. And finally there was the argument that helped to bind the manual labor leaders to the anti-slavery movement, namely, that this educational innovation helped to make manual labor respectable.[18]

The doctrine of manual labor appeared in a number of large-scale educational proposals. The governor of Pennsylvania proposed it for teachers' seminaries; the chief magistrate of Georgia recommended its introduction into the schools of that commonwealth.[19] A resolution offered in the United States Senate in 1836 proposed that the Committee on Public Lands be instructed to look into the expediency of making a grant of lands in each of the new states to one or more colleges which should operate on the manual labor plan.[20] In Boston, in 1832, a number of men, including John Tappan and Lyman Beecher, planned to use the scheme as a means of reforming juvenile lawbreakers.[21] News items in the *American Annals of Education* from 1829 through 1838 furnish some basis for estimating the extent of the movement among academies and colleges. By the end of 1829 at least seven manual labor schools were operating. During the next nine years manual labor was adopted by at least thirty-five institutions, although this list, it is known from other sources, does not include many that never came to the attention of this publication. So far as the number of schools adopting the idea is concerned, the growth seems to have been most rapid between 1831 and 1834.

The astonishing speed with which this educational novelty

[18] A summary extracted from various sources, the chief being: *Second Report of the Trustees of the Oneida Institute*, pp. 8–22; "Proceedings of the American Lyceum, May 3, 4, 6, 1833," *American Annals of Education*, III (Aug., 1833), 346–60; "First Annual Report of the Society for Promoting Manual Labor in Literary Institutions, Including the Report of General Agent Theodore D. Weld," Jan. 28, 1833, *ibid.*, III (June, 1833), 243–46; Franklin Y. Vail to the directors of the Presbyterian Education Society, Cincinnati, March 13, 1832, *American Quarterly Register*, May, 1832, pp. 343–45; address by Edward Beecher at the first annual meeting of the Illinois branch of the American Education Society reported in *ibid.*, Feb., 1833, p. 268; "A Few Thoughts on Education," *Illinois Monthly Magazine*, I (Dec., 1830), 111–12.

[19] *American Annals of Education*, IV (Jan., 1834), 50–51.

[20] *Ibid.*, VI (March, 1836), 134.   [21] *Ibid.*, II (March, 1832), 127–29.

spread throughout the country was due considerably to the promotion of a number of new educational organizations that were in turn part of that larger "benevolent system" then taking shape in the Northeast. In fact, the story of how Oneida Institute became part of a national manual labor movement specifically demonstrates the process by which the Great Revival merged with social reforms, to which it then gave the chief impetus. That process is illustrated by the steps through which George Washington Gale, preacher and evangelist, became involved as an "educator" in several new educational societies. As already mentioned, in 1829 Oneida Institute was visited by an officer of the American Educational Society, an interdenominational organization dominated by Congregationalists and Presbyterians, and in the fall it received his published endorsement. About a year later, in October, 1830, the Utica courthouse was the scene of a "Convention of the Friends of Education," Gale and Frost attending. Gale was appointed to the committee of correspondence, along with such notables as Eliphat Nott, president of Union College, and Gerrit Smith.[22] After the discussion of several educational reforms, another meeting was called for the following January in the same place; at this time the New York State Lyceum was organized.[23] This body in turn called a meeting of other state lyceum groups and friends of education to meet the next May (1831), and this convention organized the American Lyceum. Though Gale was not present at this last meeting, he was scheduled to speak at the first anniversary of the American Lyceum on the proposition "Ought Manual Labor Schools to Be Encouraged, and Upon What General Plan?"[24] At the annual meeting of the American Lyceum in 1833, John Frost was present, and since manual labor was one of the four main topics of discussion, he gave a history of Oneida Institute and a description of its condition and prospects.[25]

[22] Lamb, "George Washington Gale," pp. 134–35.
[23] Fletcher, *History of Oberlin*, I, 341–42.
[24] Lamb, "George Washington Gale," p. 141.
[25] *American Annals of Education*, II (July, 1832), 350–51; III (Aug., 1833), 346–60.

Many of the members of the American Lyceum appeared
again in the American School Agents Society, which was formed
at Andover, Massachusetts, on July 13, 1832,[26] with the objectives of exciting public attention to the importance of "practical education," of leading the young to appreciate their ability
to educate themselves, of carrying to every child the benefits of
"Infant School" instruction, of procuring funds to educate
young men teachers, especially for the Mississippi Valley, of
promoting teaching as a profession—in short, of acting as a
"Lay Education Society . . . which shall supply destitute
portions of our own and other countries with the blessings that
follow in the train of our Free Schools." To achieve this am-
bitious program, especially in the South and the West, auxiliary
associations, new teachers' seminaries, agents, and lecturers
were to be used. In the most needy regions it was planned to
form "circuit schools." [27] Corresponding secretaries were appointed for twenty states, Gale filling that office for New
York.[28] Membership in the School Agents Society overlapped
that of the American Educational Society and this group in
turn intermeshed with the Presbyterian Educational Society,
which by this time was giving some aid to a few students at
Oneida Institute. In 1833 a new auxiliary agency to the Presbyterian organization was established at Utica, on the board of
which Gale was a member.[29]

Meanwhile still another educational society with manual
labor as its particular specialty had come into existence. This
Society for Promoting Manual Labor in Literary Institutions
was so much at the very focus of the reforming clique in New
York City and so intimately tied up with the expansion of the
anti-slavery movement that it must be discussed in connection
with the origins of abolitionism.

[26] *Ibid.,* II (Aug., 1832), 422.
[27] *Ibid.,* II (Sept., 1832), 443–45; III (Sept., 1833), 418–22; IV (Nov., 1833),
524–30.
[28] *Ibid.,* III (Aug., 1832), 422.
[29] "Journal of the American Education Society," *American Quarterly Register,*
VI (Feb., 1834), 213.

❧ IV ❧

Oneida Institute and Abolitionism

I have here met congenial minds. I have rejoiced in sympathies
delightful to the soul. Heart has beat responsive to heart, and
the holy work of seeking to benefit the outraged and despised
has proved the most blessed employment.
But now we must retire from these balmy influences, and breathe
another atmosphere. The chill hoar frost will be upon us. The
storm and tempest will rise, and the waves of persecution will
dash against our souls. Let us be prepared for the worst. Let us
fasten ourselves to the throne of God as with hooks of steel.[1]

IN HIS OLD AGE John Greenleaf Whittier recalled that a
speech by the president of Oneida Institute was "the most
powerful and eloquent speech to which I have ever listened." [2]
The quotation standing at the head of this chapter comes from
the concluding paragraphs of that speech. The time was December, 1833; the place, Philadelphia; the audience, threescore
plainly dressed men, mostly rather young, some middle-aged,
a few older.[3] The occasion was the conclusion of the convention that organized the American Anti-Slavery Society. A committee had vainly sought in Philadelphia some distinguished
citizen of high social standing to preside at the convention.[4]
As the committee left the front door of one such gentleman
who had refused, Beriah Green, turning to his colleagues Whittier and Lewis Tappan, said in a sarcastic tone: "If there is not

---

[1] From the speech by Beriah Green at the conclusion of the convention organizing the American Anti-Slavery Society.

[2] Whittier, "The Anti-Slavery Convention of 1833," *Old South Leaflets,* Vol.
IV, No. 81, p. 10.

[3] *Ibid.,* p. 4.   [4] *Ibid.,* p. 3.

timber amongst ourselves big enough to make a president of, let us get along without one, or go home and stay there until we have grown up to be men." [5]

Beriah Green became president of the convention. For three months he had been the new head of Oneida Institute, which could give him assurance that he would be "untrammeled" in his abolitionism, a doctrine that had gotten him into trouble on the faculty of Western Reserve College the preceding spring.[6] Now with the secretaries, Tappan and Whittier, on either side, he presided over the miscellany of "delegates" that founded a national abolitionist society.

Students at Oneida Institute had organized the first abolitionist society in New York in June, 1833,[7] and three of them soon after had written to Finney of their impatience to spend a "year or so," before entering upon a regular missionary assignment, preaching "abolition—Emancipation from sin and slavery." [8] Though it was about this time that Green accepted the presidency of Oneida Institute, this student movement occurred at least two months previous to his arrival on the scene, so that the abolitionizing of the school was due not to him or any other "outsider" but to the students themselves. The details of this "conversion" are of considerable significance because of the "extracurricular" activities of these students during the next few years.

It began in what was called the "gravel debate." Because most of the students were too poor to pay their road tax, they reported in a body to the pathmaster for actual labor, and were sent along with some of the townsmen to shovel gravel from a creek. There were not enough teams to keep the shovelers busy; and "as it was an all pervading sentiment of that institution that no moment should ever be left unoccupied, and that every-

[5] May, *Some Recollections of Our Anti-Slavery Conflict*, p. 83.
[6] Elizur Wright to Weld, Hudson, Ohio, Sept. 5, 1833, *Weld Letters*, I, 114–17.
[7] See founding dates for societies listed in *Third Annual Report of the American Anti-Slavery Society*, 1836, p. 94. See also *Weld Letters*, I, 18, note.
[8] Charles Stewart Renshaw and "2 others" to Finney, Oneida Institute, July 15, 1833, Finney Papers, Oberlin College Library.

thing in heaven and earth, and under the earth, needed a new discussion, they extemporized a debating society there on the gravel" with one of the citizens as chairman.[9] Emancipation as opposed to colonization of slaves was chosen as the subject, and several students volunteered to support the former and less popular side. One of these students, it turned out, was well read in the Garrisonian literature on immediate emancipation, and spoke so forcefully as to astound both his schoolmates and the citizenry. They called on him for proof, and he replied, just as this debate was stopped by the village bell ringing for noon, "Go to the reading room, and in the *Liberator* and first report of the New England Anti-Slavery Society, you will find all I have said confirmed." [10]

Though the reminiscence which reports this episode perhaps oversimplifies the process by which Oneida Institute turned toward abolitionism, the essential features of the narrative are probably true: a group of unusually mature, self-reliant, and earnest young men, sensitized to "reform" issues in the Burned-over District, were provoked by a student debate to a closer study of Garrison's powerful polemics and were quickly convinced that the "fanatic" was right. An anti-slavery society was organized and prospered, while the more moderate colonization society at Oneida languished and in less than a year died.[11]

The conjunction of the manual labor movement with abolitionism on a national scale can be rather clearly observed in the work of the Society for Promoting Manual Labor in Literary Institutions, organized in July, 1831, in New York City. Support for this project came particularly from the Tappan brothers, who were brought close to the Oneida Institute by way of Finney (who lived in Arthur Tappan's home) and by way of the two sons of Lewis Tappan who attended that school.[12]

[9] Hammond, "The Gravel Debate," *Advance Supplement,* April 28, 1870.
[10] *Ibid.*   [11] *Ibid.;* Fletcher, *History of Oberlin,* I, 146–47.
[12] Benjamin P. Thomas, *Theodore Weld,* pp. 19–25; Tappan to Weld, Oct. 25, 1831, *Weld Letters,* I, 50–52. Account books of George Washington Gale (MSS, Knox College) have entries for the Tappan boys and also one for a bill from "Mr. Tappan" for thirty dollars for printing pamphlets, dated January, 1832.

Gale became a member of the board of managers, and his most outstanding student, Theodore Dwight Weld, became the General Agent.[13] At the very time that the inner circle of pious and wealthy gentlemen of New York City were espousing this cause they were also turning to Garrison's doctrine of immediatism, as opposed to colonization,[14] though it was to be two years before national organization of the abolitionists occurred.[15] Meanwhile it is interesting to note that Garrison had taken up the idea of manual labor and had gone to Europe to collect funds for a manual labor school for Negro youth which was being projected by the abolitionists in New England.[16]

The selection of Weld as General Agent of the Society for Promoting Manual Labor in Literary Institutions brought into the directorate of the "benevolent system," straight from the Burned-over District, a young enthusiast with considerable experience as evangelist, lecturer, and agent. He had been converted by Finney in 1825 and had become a member of the "Holy Band" of assistant revivalists.[17] Already in March, 1827, he was in direct contact with Gale,[18] though he did not enter Oneida Institute until the next fall, at which time he brought with him more than a score of the young men who had come under the influence of his evangelism.[19] During part of the three years he spent at Oneida Institute he boarded with the Gales, and during the first long winter vacation he did Gale's chores.[20] Though Weld's relations with the head of the school may not have approached the fervent friendship he enjoyed with Finney, "my dear father in Christ," [21] their association was

[13] *American Annals of Education*, I (Aug., 1831), 396–97; II (Jan., 1832), 92.
[14] Fletcher, *History of Oberlin*, I, 183.
[15] A New York City Anti-Slavery Society was not organized until October, 1833, four months after the Oneida Institute society was founded.
[16] W. P. Garrison and F. J. Garrison, *William Lloyd Garrison*, I, 325–30, 337, 443, 494.
[17] *Weld Letters*, I, xxi.
[18] Gale to Finney, Utica, March 4, 1827, Finney Papers, Oberlin.
[19] *Weld Letters*, I, xxi.
[20] George Washington Gale, "Autobiography," p. 233.
[21] Weld to Finney, April 22, 1828, *Weld Letters*, I, 14–18.

intimate enough for Gale to open Weld's mail.[22] Weld was appointed monitor of the milking class and led the students in the building of a barn for the livestock.[23]

Like many of his fellow students, Weld used his spare time, as on Sundays, preaching in the neighborhood or otherwise serving moral causes, and during vacations he lectured for the American Temperance Society.[24] These talents Gale put to work, sending Weld out to raise funds—to exploit such promising sources as Rochester after Finney had excited it by a rousing revival.[25] His father became concerned that Weld would not finish his ministerial training and advised him to "give up the externals of Oneida Institute to Mr. Gale, Mr. Frost, etc." [26] Among the students Weld exerted a tremendous influence, as he himself realized,[27] for on one occasion Weld had to pacify his schoolmates who were in "high dudgeon" over Gale's failure adequately to acknowledge how much Weld did for their school.[28] His leadership over these young men was soon to have important national consequences in the expanding of abolitionism.

Weld's responsibilities as General Agent of the Society for Promoting Manual Labor in Literary Institutions were by their nature expansionistic. Beginning in the autumn of 1831 he traveled and lectured in Ohio, Indiana, Illinois, Missouri, Kentucky, Tennessee, and Alabama, visting most of the manual labor institutions,[29] collecting information from which sound policies of manual labor in education could be formulated, determining the adaptability of the new educational scheme to the West, and looking for a site where a great model manual

[22] Finney to Weld, March 27, 1828, *ibid.*, I, 10–11.
[23] Communicated by Weld to Charles Beecher, in Charles Beecher, ed., *Autobiography of Lyman Beecher*, II, 313.
[24] Benjamin P. Thomas, *Theodore Weld*, p. 20; *Weld Letters*, I, xxi.
[25] Gale to Finney, Jan. 21, Jan. 29, Dec. 16, 1830, Finney Papers, Oberlin.
[26] Elizabeth and Ludovicus Weld to T. D. Weld, Jan. 16, 1830, *Weld Letters*, I, 30–33.
[27] Weld to Angelina Grimké, March 12, April 15, 1838, *ibid.*, I, 592.
[28] Weld to Finney, March 12 [1831?], *ibid.*, I, 40–41.
[29] Weld's statement in Charles Beecher, ed., *Autobiography of Lyman Beecher*, II, 313–15.

labor institution might be established to the best advantage.[30]
Weld, however, mixed his manual labor agency with other
benevolent interests; he did a good deal of temperance lecturing and "conversed freely, wherever he had a chance, with
young men on the subject of slavery." [31] Not the least important
of the results of Weld's travels was the establishment of lines
of communication in the West among a large number of enthusiastic young men who by Weld's influence or otherwise
were converted to "reforming" causes.

The assimilation of abolitionism into the benevolent system
created considerably more irritation than did the addition of
other reforms. Where evangelism might meet with indifference,
where the manual labor idea encountered doubt, and where
temperance received ridicule, immediate emancipation provoked angry violence; the grapes of wrath were being stored.
Even at the reformers' citadel in Utica was this true. When a
call went out for a convention to meet in Utica on October 21,
1835, to organize a New York State Anti-Slavery Society, three
mass meetings were held to denounce the disgrace to the city
and to warn the "deluded fanatics" and "incendiaries" that all
means would be used to keep churches, schools, and courthouse
closed to them. Six hundred abolitionists from all parts of the
state nevertheless persisted in answering the convention call.
Early in the morning of the scheduled day, cannon were fired,
and thousands flocked to Utica from the neighboring area. A
hostile mass meeting occupied the courthouse to keep the delegates from assembling there as scheduled, and when the latter
met in a Presbyterian church, a mob, led by "gentlemen of
property and standing," broke into the church and forcefully
prevented the meeting from continuing its business.[32]

[30] Benjamin P. Thomas, *Theodore Weld*, p. 25, *American Annals of Education,* I (Aug., 1831), 396–97; II (Jan. 15, 1832), 92–94; III (Jan. 28, 1833), 243–
46; III (April, 1833), 187.

[31] Charles Beecher, ed., *Autobiography of Lyman Beecher*, II, 313–15.

[32] Accounts of the Utica riot: Jones, *Annals and Recollections of Oneida County,*
pp. 551–55; *Third Annual Report of the American Anti-Slavery Society, Held
in the City of New York on the 10th of May, 1836,* pp. 63–65; Stanton, *Random
Recollections,* pp. 51–52.

The chief effects of such mob violence were likely to be favorable to the cause of the abolitionists,[33] who skillfully made most effective propaganda of any persecution.[34] Far from keeping abolitionism out of Utica, its citizens saw the city become an anti-slavery headquarters that ranked next to New York City and Boston in importance.[35] No small factor in making Utica

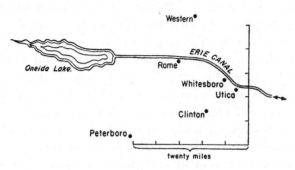

The Oneida Institute Neighborhood

so significant in anti-slavery circles was the nearness of Gerrit Smith's home at Peterboro in Oneida County. It was at his house that the anti-slavery convention reconvened after the mob drove it out of Utica in October, 1835. The episode in fact had caused Smith definitely to commit himself to this reform, about the "measures" of which he had been previously doubtful,[36] and he became the most generous of all the donors

[33] Jones, *Annals and Recollections of Oneida County*, p. 555.

[34] British and Foreign Anti-Slavery Society, *Minutes of the General Anti-Slavery Convention*, London, 1840, pp. 316–17.

[35] Stanton, *Random Recollections*, pp. 65–66. "In surveying the anti-slavery field up to this time 1840, two centres of activity are preeminent: Boston, the fountain of the agitation, the home of the *Liberator;* and New York, the seat of the parent society, the home of the *Emancipator*. Remark, also, Utica, the seat of New York State Society, and home of Goodell and his *Friend of Man;* home, likewise, of Alvan Stewart, whose nearly successful effort to commit the American Society to the doctrine of Federal control over slavery in the States was recorded in the last chapter. Not far to the west at Peterboro, lives Gerrit Smith, anxious, as we have seen, to convert the moral basis of anti-slavery into a political one; and still beyond, in Rochester, lives Myron Holley" (W. P. Garrison and F. J. Garrison, *William Lloyd Garrison*, II, 259).

[36] See the account of the Utica riot by May, *Some Recollections of Our Anti-Slavery Conflict*, pp. 162–70; Harlow, *Gerrit Smith*, pp. 121–24.

to the American Anti-Slavery Society, to the New York State Anti-Slavery Society, and to other abolitionist groups.[37]

Of this abolitionist machine, as fully assembled, Oneida Institute was an important component. It received the special endorsement of the American Anti-Slavery Society at its first anniversary [38] and of the New England Anti-Slavery Society, particularly because it was the first of the manual labor schools to admit Negroes.[39] Oneida Institute shared with abolitionism the patronage of the Tappans [40] and Gerrit Smith. In addition to very substantial contributions of money and land to the school beginning in 1827,[41] Smith helped needy students there [42] and frequently came over to address the student body.[43] The president of Oneida Institute, Beriah Green, remained to the end a prominent leader in the American Anti-Slavery Society, at the anniversaries of which he regularly appeared, usually with one or two other delegates sent from the Oneida Institute Anti-Slavery Society,[44] and sometimes with still others

[37] Quarles, "Sources of Abolitionist Income," *Mississippi Valley Historical Review*, XXXII, 63–64.

[38] *First Annual Report of the American Anti-Slavery Society*, 1834, p. 43.

[39] Coates, "From George Gale to Arthur Morgan," *Educational Review*, LXXII (June, 1926), 53–55. This was true at least as early as the term for 1835–36; *Proceedings of the New England Anti-Slavery Convention Held in Boston, May 24, 25, 26, 1836*, pp. 49–54, 59. Other Negro students at Oneida Institute are specifically mentioned in the *Weld Letters*, I, 445–46, and II, 811–12; and in May, *Some Recollections of Our Anti-Slavery Conflict*, p. 292. In 1840 there were twenty "coloured" students at Oneida Institute; British and Foreign Anti-Slavery Society, *Proceedings of the General Anti-Slavery Convention, London, 1843*, p. 86.

[40] Barnes, *Anti-Slavery Impulse*, p. 38.

[41] Frothingham, *Gerrit Smith*, p. 100; May, *Some Recollections of Our Anti-Slavery Conflict*, p. 325.

[42] There are frequent references to such aid in the Gerrit Smith Papers, Syracuse University.

[43] Grinnell, *Men and Events of Forty Years*, pp. 32–33. Already in 1830 Gerrit Smith was talking about a manual labor school for young Negroes at Peterboro, and in 1834 it was actually established. Its head was C. Grant from Whitesboro, a brother of Innes Grant, professor of languages at Oneida Institute and one of the members of the faculty of that school who later followed Gale west to Knox College. The Peterboro school continued only through the summer of 1836, when possibly because of the hard times it was given up. Smith had been urged to merge it with the preparatory department of Oneida Institute. Harlow, *Gerrit Smith*, pp. 61–62; *American Annals of Education*, IV (Oct., 1834), 481; *Letters of James Gillespie Birney, 1831–1857*, I, 355. Hereafter referred to as *Birney Letters*.

[44] American Anti-Slavery Society: *First Annual Report*, pp. 12, 34, 38; *Second*

from the society at Whitesboro, which town by 1838 also had a "Female Anti-Slavery Society" and a "Juvenile Anti-Slavery Society." [45]

The notoriety of Oneida Institute as a haven for the "foul abomination" of abolitionism [46] brought it considerable hostility from moderate men as well as from pro-slavery protagonists. At the time of the Utica riots the doors of the school were several times guarded by the students.[47] In the New York Senate it was proposed in March, 1836, that because Oneida Institute had become a "hot-bed of sedition" the support of the Committee on Literature be withdrawn from the school. A meeting in Utica to protest this proposal attracted 150 supporters and was addressed by Gerrit Smith; resolutions for academic freedom were adopted and five thousand dollars were pledged to the school's support.[48] Though nothing came of this threat in the legislature to penalize Oneida Institute, it was later charged that the State Regents, "to punish radical innovation," denied to the school's trustees the power to confer degrees.[49]

Beriah Green reaped to the full the crop of radicalism that he had found already planted at Oneida Institute when he assumed its presidency in the fall of 1833. As if anti-slavery activities did not make the school peculiar enough, he at once struck out Latin in favor of Hebrew, thus carrying out the shift to a "practical" and away from a "classical" curriculum that had been agitated for before he became president.[50] It is not surprising that a young man doubtful about the ordinary morals of Yale and the conservatism of its courses should be persuaded to change his plans and go to Oneida Institute.[51] Half a century later an "Oneida" who had made just such a

Annual Report, pp. 29, 85; *Third Annual Report*, pp. 20, 22, 24, 94; *Fourth Annual Report*, pp. 133, 135; *Fifth Annual Report*, pp. 142, 144.
[45] American Anti-Slavery Society, *Fifth Annual Report*, p. 144.
[46] "Colleges," *Western Monthly Magazine*, April, 1836, p. 224.
[47] Lamb, "George Washington Gale," p. 158.
[48] Harlow, *Gerrit Smith*, pp. 224–25.
[49] Grinnell, *Men and Events of Forty Years*, p. 31.
[50] Green, *Miscellaneous Writings*, pp. 243–45, 250–51.
[51] Grinnell, *Men and Events of Forty Years*, pp. 23, 28–29.

choice (and went on to become one of an astonishingly large number of alumni who helped found reform-minded college-colonies in the West) wrote this catalogue of his Oneida school-mates: a "motley company"—wards of rich reformers; an emancipator's boys from Cuba; some mulattoes taken from their "sable mother" and sent to the school under an alias; a "high-tempered" Spaniard; an Indian with an inelegant name; "black men" who had served as sailors; a city hackman; "the purest Africans escaped from slavery"; sons of the American radicals; "enthusiasts"; plowboys and printers; "also real students of elegant tastes." Oneida Institute was then perhaps "too far ahead of the times," but whatever the value of its "experiments," it was "the home of freedom" and "its pupils were trained for practical men in the coming struggles of the Republic." [52]

During the mid-thirties, while Oneida County was quivering with the excitement over abolitionism, the founder of Oneida Institute, G. W. Gale, was recruiting a colony to found a new manual labor school on the Western frontier. This too would be a radical instrument of reform. Though Gale was not so extreme a zealot as Green, all of the radical elements that ripened so notoriously after Green took over had already taken form under Gale's administration. It is true that Green's reckless jabs against those who were slow to accept abolitionist measures weakened the very foundations on which Oneida Institute had been built; the Oneida Presbytery was strained by internal tensions; the Whitesboro church was split wide open.[53] After the school failed in 1841, Gale was inclined to blame Green's reckless administration as one of the causes.[54]

As the Oneida Institute had grown from an experiment to a promising venture it had become less and less merely Gale's affair. Originally not only the management of the school's business and the administration of its instruction but also much

[52] *Ibid.*, pp. 24–31.
[53] Coates, "From George Gale to Arthur Morgan," *Educational Review,* LXXII (June, 1926), 53–55; Jones, *Annals and Recollections of Oneida County,* pp. 811–12.
[54] G. W. Gale, "Autobiography," p. 232.

of the actual teaching was Gale's responsibility. At the same time Gale also was involved in "promoting" the school and the cause of manual labor in general. As the school prospered, additional faculty took over more and more of the teaching load, a steward assumed direct management of farms and shops, and in the spring of 1832 Gale and others interested in the school's welfare were looking for a "principal or president of the right stamp" [55] to take over the educational direction of the college. Gale announced in the fall that he had retired from the teaching departments in order that a "principal teacher" with better health and qualifications might take his place. He explained that in his teaching he had been embarrassed by his duties in the business affairs of the school, which department the trustees wanted him now to make his particular responsibility.[56] Green, the new principal, was not found until the following summer,[57] however, and did not take over until September, 1833; meanwhile "Father Gale," as a student put it, was still "chief cook and bottle-washer." [58] Though Gale was making business arrangements for Oneida Institute as late as December, 1833,[59] a number of new appointments by the trustees had gradually transferred even these duties to other men.[60] By the beginning of 1834 Gale was already planning a college-colony to go West,[61] and he was now free to give all his energies to this enterprise.

A westward impulse had always been latent in the manual labor movement; at the very outset, in selecting a site for Oneida Institute, Gale and Frost had first looked westward, go-

[55] Gale to Finney, May 20, 1832, Finney Papers, Oberlin.

[56] Gale to H. Norton, Oneida Institute, Sept. 1, 1832, in the New York *Evangelist*, Oct. 13, 1832.

[57] Charles Stewart Renshaw and "2 others" to Finney, July 15, 1833, Finney Papers. The Reverend William T. Hamilton declined the "presidency" of Oneida Institute according to the New York *Evangelist* of Dec. 1, 1832.

[58] S. W. Streeter to Weld, Aug. 3, 1832, *Weld Letters*, I, 82–83.

[59] Gale MSS, Knox College, contain a business contract for Oneida Institute signed by Gale on Dec. 1, 1833.

[60] Lamb, "George Washington Gale," pp. 151–52.

[61] According to his oldest son, William Selden, in an article saved in George Churchill's Scrapbook No. 2, p. 13 (Knox College Library), Gale in 1833 planned to locate a town and college in Michigan.

ing as far as northeastern Ohio.[62] One of the chief purposes of
manual labor education was to provide young ministers able
to endure the hardships of, and willing to go to, the frontier.
Weld's agency for the Society for Promoting Manual Labor in
Literary Institutions was mainly expended beyond the mountains and was in part devoted to locating a site for a manual
labor school to serve that area. By the end of 1832 many of
Gale's students were migrating to a school established in Cincinnati for that purpose. The idea of frontier colonies had
become part of the intellectual climate of the Burned-over
District, and Gale's new college company was only one party in
the westward migration of Oneida apostles.

[62] G. W. Gale, "Autobiography," p. 226.

PART TWO

Migration

V

Oneida Moves West

But what will become of the West, if her prosperity rushes up to
such a majesty of power, while those great institutions linger
which are necessary to form the mind, and the conscience, and the
heart of that vast world. It must not be permitted. And yet what
is done must be done quickly; for population will not wait, and
commerce will not cast anchor, and manufactures will not shut
off the steam nor shut down the gate, and agriculture, pushed by
millions of freemen on their fertile soil, will not withhold her
corrupting abundance.

We must educate! We must educate! or we must perish by our own
prosperity.[1]

THE METROPOLIS OF THE WEST in 1831 was Cincinnati, a rapidly growing city of 30,000 that had more than
doubled its population since 1822, when a traveler still saw it
as a "great slash in the wilderness." [2] Located in the extreme
southwestern corner of the state of Ohio, on the great bend
where the Ohio River turned sharply to a more southerly
course, Cincinnati had become the chief mart for the goods
and ideas circulating in the vast territory that had been settled
since the opening of the century. Lyman Beecher wrote his
daughter in 1830 that it was "the London of the West."

One of the many lines of traffic converging at Cincinnati by
1831 can be traced back to the very heart of the Burned-over
District. Late in August of that year the newly organized Sixth
Presbyterian Church received as its first pastor the Reverend

[1] Lyman Beecher, *A Plea for the West*, pp. 31–32.
[2] Brown, *Historical Geography of the United States*, p. 233.

Asa Mahan, who came fresh from the Rochester phase of the Great Revival, in which he had been associated with the great Finney himself.[3] Mahan had been licensed to preach by the Oneida Presbytery in 1827, at a special session attended by Gale.[4]

The Sixth Presbyterian Church had only fifteen to twenty members who worshiped in a plain hall,[5] but under Mahan's ministry this group developed into the congregation that was most influential in the reform agitations of the next dozen years. In April of 1831 this little group of "New School" Presbyterians had withdrawn from the congregation of the Reverend Joshua L. Wilson, the dominant ecclesiastical personage in Cincinnati, but a leader of the Old School.[6] The seceders adopted "the principle of no fellowship or communion with slaveholders" and believed their church was the first in the nation to be organized on this basis.[7] One of the original elders of this church was William Holyoke, a leading Presbyterian layman [8] and a well-to-do coachmaker, whose wife was a cousin of John Greenleaf Whittier.[9] Frequently associated with Holyoke in reform activities were two other charter members, John and James Melendy.[10] These three purchased and held the title of the brick building in which the church met, and each of them contributed a thousand dollars a year to Mahan's salary and other expenses.[11] When the inevitable clash occurred between Mahan and the conservative Wilson, it was Holyoke who, with an associate in the Sixth Presbyterian Church, brought charges in the presbytery against Wilson for "un-

[8] Fletcher, *History of Oberlin*, I, 44.
[4] Gale to Finney, June 6, 1827, Finney Papers, Oberlin College Library.
[5] Asa Mahan, *Autobiography*, pp. 163–64.
[6] Fletcher, *History of Oberlin*, I, 44–47.
[7] Holyoke, "A Historical Sketch," Galesburg *Republican Register*, July 7, 1911.
[8] Holyoke was on the board of the Central Committee of Agency for Home Missions in the Western States, the office of which was located in Cincinnati. This was an auxiliary body of the American Home Missionary Society (A.H.M.S.), created to assist Western congregations unable to support themselves (*Home Missionary and American Pastors' Journal*, III [April, 1831], 242).
[9] Perry, *Knox County*, II, 1145.
[10] Luella Wright, *Peter Melendy*, pp. 37–39; Fletcher, *History of Oberlin*, I, 44–47.
[11] Holyoke, "A Historical Sketch," Galesburg *Republican Register*, July 7, 1911.

christian conduct" in slandering Mahan in the press.[12] Before
the new congregation was a year old, its leaders had twice
begged Finney to come to Cincinnati to conduct a revival, the
second appeal being written by Mahan and signed by twelve
Cincinnati ministers and fifteen leading laymen, one of whom
was Holyoke.[13]

Soon after arriving in Cincinnati, Mahan was elected to the
board of trustees of Lane Theological Seminary [14] and Wilson
immediately resigned.[15] This Cincinnati institution had originated in a gift of $4,000 for a theological school made by
Ebenezer Lane and his brother in February, 1829. During the
academic year of 1829–30 it had three or four students. The
Lanes insisted that it be conducted on the manual labor plan,[16]
and as a consequence the solitary faculty member visited
Oneida Institute. He reported to Cincinnati that the plan
worked very well; in January, 1831, Gale was asked to recommend a steward for the seminary farm and in February the
Lane trustees appointed the man he recommended. At that
time Lane Seminary was in a state of suspended animation, for
its only faculty member had resigned. A source of renewed
life for the school was, however, already indicated by the presence of two former students from Oneida Institute who were
permitted by the trustees to live in the unused seminary building.[17]

This was the condition of Lane when Weld arrived in Cincinnati early in 1831 on his agency for the Society for Promoting Manual Labor in Literary Institutions. He saw in the
faltering enterprise of Lane the opportunity to develop a manual labor school that would serve as a national model, a project
for which he had been instructed to discover a site by the Tap-

[12] Fletcher, *History of Oberlin*, I, 44–47.   [13] *Ibid.*, I, 48.
[14] Asa Mahan, *Autobiography*, p. 172; *Catalogue and History of the Foundation
and Endowment of the Lane Theological Seminary*, p. 25.
[15] Fletcher, *History of Oberlin*, I, 51.
[16] Manual labor features of Lane Seminary are noted in *American Annals of
Education*, I (Aug., 1830), 367; II (June, 1832), 290; IV (April, 1834), 162–63. See
also *American Quarterly Register*, May, 1832, pp. 343–45. The early history of
Lane is reviewed in Charles Beecher, ed., *Autobiography of Lyman Beecher*, I,
249–53.
[17] Fletcher, *History of Oberlin*, I, 49–51.

pans.[18] His selection of Lane rather than another of the many institutions he visited may very well have been influenced by the presence of his Oneida schoolmates and by his association with Mahan. He joined the latter in making a supplication to Finney to leave the seaboard cities and come to Cincinnati, for as Weld wrote, "Here is to be the great battle field of the world, here Satan's seat is. A mighty effort must be made to dislodge him soon or the West is undone." [19]

Arthur Tappan accepted Weld's endorsement of Lane and promised an income of thirty thousand dollars if Dr. Lyman Beecher would accept the leadership of the seminary.[20] The distinguished divine became president in October, 1831, but he did not settle on the scene until more than a year later. Meanwhile Weld made Lane his own project, counseling with the trustees about faculty appointments, and using his continued travels for the manual labor society and his extensive acquaintances to urge young men to come to Lane. He might possibly have had a teaching appointment himself,[21] but preferred instead to become one of the students, to complete along with his Oneida classmates that study of theology which had never been adequately provided at Oneida Institute.[22]

During 1832 he persuaded a considerable party of students from Oneida Institute to come to Cincinnati, and while he was absent lecturing, and before Beecher arrived in the fall, the Yankee students from New York ran the school through Asa Mahan.[23] Many of the student-migrants from New York knew Mahan either personally or by reputation before they arrived in Cincinnati; and they connected themselves quite naturally with his new congregation, in the affairs of which they took a very active part. This, if nothing else, made Mahan's role as trustee very influential.[24]

By December, 1832, when Beecher was inaugurated, ninety students had already arrived, but the emigration from the

[18] Benjamin P. Thomas, *Theodore Weld*, p. 41.   [19] *Ibid.*, p. 34.
[20] *Ibid.*, p. 43.   [21] Stanton to Weld, Aug. 3, 1832, *Weld Letters*, I, 83–87.
[22] Benjamin P. Thomas, *Theodore Weld*, p. 42.
[23] Fletcher, *History of Oberlin*, I, 54.
[24] Asa Mahan, *Autobiography*, p. 172.

East was still not complete. One of Weld's lieutenants, Henry Brewster Stanton,[25] returned to Rochester in the spring, promising to recruit in that area as well as to visit Oneida Institute and "find others whose eyes are turned Westward."[26] While in that locality Stanton joined Weld, who had been visiting his father (then residing near Oneida Institute), and with several other Finneyites they traveled to French Creek on the Allegheny where they bought a boat for six dollars and floated downstream to Pittsburgh. "We had good times," Weld recalled, "discussing anti-slavery, and stopping occasionally to get supplies, to hold prayer meetings, or find a place to sleep, if we could not, we got along in our boat." At Pittsburgh they took deck passage to Cincinnati, paying their way by helping "wood," and "finding" for themselves and sleeping on deck.[27] With Weld's arrival early in June to settle down as a student, the real leader of the student body was on hand; and Weld might well be proud of his handiwork, for the theological class was the largest that had ever been assembled in America.[28]

Lane Seminary was clearly "Oneida moved west." By 1834 twenty-four of the students had formerly been at Oneida Institute, and they were the integrating core of a student body largely derived from New England and the Burned-over District. One of the "Oneidas" taught elementary courses in the seminary, another was student monitor-general, and still another served on the committee of three supervising the printing

[25] Stanton, *Random Recollections*, p. 42; Stanton to Weld, Aug. 3, 1832, *Weld Letters*, I, 83–87.
[26] Fletcher, *History of Oberlin*, I, 55.
[27] Related by Weld in Charles Beecher, ed., *Autobiography of Lyman Beecher*, II, 313–15. This party was not the first to use this means of coming to Lane. The New York *Evangelist* for October 13, 1832, reprinted from the Cincinnati *Journal* an anecdote that "happily exhibits the effect of the Manual Labor system upon the character of young men." It told how two pious students from Oneida Institute, instead of taking the stage to Cincinnati at a cost of $20, had earned that amount by traveling downriver to their destination, on the way introducing "the gospel among their new class mates on the raft." The editorial comment was, "Why cannot many of the young men at Whitesborough in this way transport themselves to Lane Seminary for the completion of their studies?"
[28] Barnes, *Anti-Slavery Impulse*, p. 46. Already before Weld had enrolled as a student the seminarians had looked to him to use his influence with the trustees over matters that made them uneasy; Stanton to Weld, Aug. 3, 1832; Weed to Weld, Aug. 2, 1832, *Weld Letters*, I, 83–87, 78–80.

shop.[29] At no other time in the history of American theological training has so remarkable a group of seminarians been gathered together.[30] Thirty were over twenty-six years of age and nine were past thirty; six were married; one had practiced medicine for ten years; twelve had already served as agents of benevolent societies! Such men had minds of their own, and already in the month of Beecher's inauguration it was noted that some of the trustees were "of the opinion that the Oneida Boys had conspired to overthrow Lane Seminary." [31] Beecher conceded that Weld was a genius, but complained that the students "thought he was a god" who in their estimation was the president of the school.[32]

Arthur Tappan's satisfaction with the project at Cincinnati was much increased when he learned that a large number of the students of Oneida Institute had decided to complete their theological studies at Lane.[33] The New York abolitionist headquarters would then have two academic strongholds securely in their possession, for they knew that Weld intended "to improve the excellent opportunity to introduce anti-slavery sentiments." [34] Though Weld had not been able to attend the Philadelphia meeting that organized the American Anti-Slavery Society in December, 1833, he was appointed one of the first four agents.[35] Significantly the device used to commit Lane to abolitionism was a student debate, the same means by which Oneida Institute had already been converted from the principle of colonization to the doctrine of immediate emancipation. The Oneida "gravel debate" occurred about the time that Weld left the Whitesboro neighborhood to enroll at Lane. From the time he arrived in Cincinnati in June, 1833, to

[29] Fletcher, *History of Oberlin*, I, 55–57; Benjamin P. Thomas, *Theodore Weld*, p. 49.
[30] The group was described by Weld in the *Second Annual Report of the American Anti-Slavery Society*, 1835, pp. 41–42.
[31] C. Waterbury to Weld, Dec. [?], 1832, *Weld Letters*, I, 93–94.
[32] Charles Beecher, ed., *Autobiography of Lyman Beecher*, II, 321.
[33] Tappan, *Life of Arthur Tappan*, p. 225.
[34] Reminiscence by Weld in Charles Beecher, ed., *Autobiography of Lyman Beecher*, II, 313–15.
[35] Fletcher, *History of Oberlin*, I, 150.

February, 1834, he worked individually among the students to "complete the preparation for a final discussion." The Oneida debate had probably been a more spontaneous event, for the Lane debate was the culmination of rather careful indoctrination and was more like one of the protracted meetings used by evangelists to get a revival going. That was a rather trustworthy technique, however, and the result was no less overpowering because it was so carefully calculated. For eighteen evenings, seventeen speakers held forth.[36] Though knowledge of the subject by most of the students was "short and crude," Weld had studied the subject thoroughly and his speech impressed a classmate as a "thesaurus, giving the origin, history, effects, both upon the despot and the victim, of slavery." [37]

When the "debate" was over, all but one of the students voted to repudiate the mild doctrines of the American Colonization Society. A student abolitionist society was then formed with William T. Allan from Alabama as president.[38] Moreover, the students entered upon certain extracurricular activities on behalf of the Negro as if their work "was to be done and finished while the sun and moon endured." [39] To "elevate" the Negroes of Cincinnati they established a lyceum, a circulating library, Sabbath schools, Bible classes, and a regular evening school; and several students went out lecturing.

When the American Anti-Slavery Society met for its first anniversary in New York City on May 6, 1834, a student delegate from the new anti-slavery society of Lane Seminary gave an account of the stirring debate and its consequences in making abolitionist converts. It is indicative of the academic content of the abolitionist crusade at this stage that two of three set speeches in the opening session were made by the president of Oneida Institute and by a student from Lane. At the second session still another Lane student was one of the

[36] *Ibid.*, I, 150–56.
[37] Lyman, "Lane Seminary Rebels," in *The Oberlin Jubilee, 1833–1883*, pp. 60–74.
[38] Fletcher, *History of Oberlin*, I, 150–56.
[39] Lyman, "Lane Seminary Rebels," in *The Oberlin Jubilee, 1833–1883*, pp. 60–74.

chief speakers, and a substantial part of the first annual report of the national society was devoted to the Cincinnati seminary.[40]

But at the very time that Lane was in the limelight at New York, denunciation of the young radicals mounted, and many voices insisted that they be suppressed. Their agitation for immediate freeing of the slaves and their activities among Negroes had inevitably provoked strong hostility in a city that was one of the main gateways between the North and the South. In May, the *Western Monthly Magazine,* published in Cincinnati, directed an article against the doings of the Lane students.[41] Even Elijah P. Lovejoy, in June, issued an editorial in St. Louis expressing the fear that they would excite bitterness, and referred to the "overstrained and highly wrought picture that was presented at Lane Seminary by some zealous and heated young men, under the temptation that it would make a good speech." [42] An immediate outbreak of violence in Cincinnati was probably averted by the onset of the summer vacation and the dispersal of the faculty and most of the students. President Beecher himself left the city to attend the New York anniversaries of the benevolent system. Though he assured the Tappans that free discussion would be preserved at Lane, the issue was soon taken out of his hands. At the anniversaries he discovered that college circles were highly excited by the Lane debate and feared that similar events might disturb other campuses, most of which had as yet little anti-slavery sentiment and some of which had considerable pro-slavery feeling.[43] To avert such a threat the college presidents and other college spokesmen who had come to the anniversaries met in conference and agreed unanimously that "the times imperiously demanded that all agitation should be suppressed."

[40] *First Annual Report of the American Anti-Slavery Society,* 1834, pp. 6, 12, 23, 44–45.
[41] *Western Monthly Magazine,* II (May, 1834), 266–73.
[42] Joseph C. and Owen Lovejoy, *Memoir of the Rev. Elijah P. Lovejoy,* p. 120.
[43] Barnes, *Anti-Slavery Impulse,* p. 70 and p. 228, note.

When copies of these resolutions reached the executive committee of the Lane board of trustees, they started action to abolish the students' anti-slavery society, to suppress their work among the Cincinnati Negroes, and to expel Weld and William T. Allan, whose presidency of the student organization was all the more notorious for the fact that he was a Southerner. Mahan protested vehemently against these repressive measures, but on the board only William Holyoke and John Melendy voted with him in support of the students' freedom.[44] These two elders of the Sixth Presbyterian Church stood by their pastor "through all the 'firey trials' through which" Mahan passed,[45] which in the Cincinnati of that day was like Shadrach, Meshach, and Abednego standing in the burning furnace.

The Lane students rebelled. Upon their return at the opening of the autumn term they refused, almost to a man, to re-enter the seminary. Fifty-one of them signed "A Statement of the Reasons Which Induced the Students of Lane Seminary to Dissolve Their Connection with That Institution." Over one fourth of these signers were from Oneida Institute, and most of the rest from other localities in the Burned-over District.[46] Mahan had vainly pleaded with Beecher to cut short his protracted absence from Cincinnati and to deal with the troubles brewing for him at the seminary, but when the president did return the damage was irreparable. By the time he had persuaded the trustees to withdraw the offensive gag-rules it was too late, for the Lane Rebels had already established themselves in Cumminsville, near Cincinnati, and had organized a self-conducted seminary of their own.[47] Thus, as Mahan put it, "in an incredibly short time" there were two institutions, one "full of students, but without endowments and without faculty," and

[44] *Ibid.;* Lyman, "Lane Seminary Rebels," in *The Oberlin Jubilee, 1833–1883,* pp. 64–65.
[45] Asa Mahan, *Autobiography,* pp. 179–80, 191–92; Holyoke, "A Historical Sketch," Galesburg *Republican Register,* July 7, 1911.
[46] This document, twenty-eight pages long, was published in Cincinnati in 1834.
[47] Benjamin P. Thomas, *Theodore Weld,* p. 162; Barnes, *Anti-Slavery Impulse,* pp. 71–73.

one "with large but empty buildings, an ample endowment, and able faculty, but practically without students." [48]

During the winter some of the Rebels scattered, but the leaders and a nucleus of "Oneidas" kept much of the group together and this faithful company was joined by three more students from Oneida Institute.[49] They could count on Mahan and Holyoke for advice and some assistance,[50] friends in Cincinnati gave them shelter, and a young lawyer, Salmon P. Chase, persuaded his brother-in-law to let them use a large, roomy house. One of the Oneida boys wrote to Whitesboro and to New Hartford for funds and learned that the women of those New York towns would raise money to help carry on the Negro schools. And through Weld they had a life line to the philanthropy of the loyal Tappans, who immediately were planning another seminary where free speech would be assured.[51]

The next move of the Lane Rebels was to unexpected quarters. One day a group of them who called at Mahan's home met there the Reverend John Shipherd,[52] who was desperately seeking help for Oberlin Institute, which after a year of operation was tottering and near collapse. For the more or less orphaned Lane Rebels the meeting was providential—but so it was for Oberlin also; as Shipherd rejoiced: "I believe God has here put my hand on the end of a chain, linking men and money to our dear Seminary in such a manner as will fill our hearts with gratitude and gladness when it is fully developed." [53] He appreciated the fact that the addition of the Lane Rebels would be followed by the Tappans' loyalty, as well as their money.[54]

Shipherd was entrepreneur of a social project destined to in-

[48] Asa Mahan, *Autobiography*, pp. 183–84.

[49] Fletcher, *History of Oberlin*, I, 165–66.

[50] S. Wells to Weld, Jan. 8, 1835, *Weld Letters*, I, 191–93; Holyoke, "A Historical Sketch," Galesburg *Republican Register*, July 7, 1911.

[51] Barnes, *Anti-Slavery Impulse*, pp. 74–77.

[52] Asa Mahan, *Autobiography*, p. 191.

[53] Fletcher, *History of Oberlin*, I, 169.

[54] The story of the transfer of the Lane Rebels to Oberlin is related in *ibid.*, chapters 14 and 15; also in Barnes, *Anti-Slavery Impulse*, chapter 7.

spire the enthusiasm of the most spiritual of the student radicals. He shared with them a profound respect for Finney, whom he had unsuccessfully summoned to northeastern Ohio, where Shipherd had settled in 1831 as a missionary pastor.[55] About the time that the "Oneidas" had begun their migration to Cincinnati, Shipherd dreamed of settling a colony of "right spirits" in northeastern Ohio and rode from town to town in New York and New England to gather men and women who would subscribe themselves and their wealth to his plan of a village where each member would "consider himself a steward of the Lord, and hold only so much property as he can advantageously manage for the Lord." All should live with "Gospel simplicity" of dress, diet, house, and furniture, none should hoard anything for old age or their children, and yet each colonist should work hard in order to give to the needy and to save as much as possible to support the educational enterprises that were to distinguish the village. "From the four winds," from "the vain amusements and strong temptations of the world," should come "multitudes" to be instructed for the ministry, for missionary labors, for schoolteaching. Only thus could the "dark Valley" of the Mississippi be saved from Mammon, the Gospel keep pace with the increase of the population, and the millennium ever cheer our "benighted world." [56] According to Shipherd's vision the schools were to be conducted on the manual labor plan, about which he conferred with Gale himself at Oneida Institute.[57] Odd though Shipherd's prospectus must have seemed at a time when more worldly schemes were proffered by the score, some subscribers were found. The settlement of Oberlin began in April, 1833, and the Oberlin Institute opened the following December.

The oddities of Oberlin are important because some of them became the conventionalities of the next generation. Notable was the unusual attention paid to women, for whom, as well as for the men, there should be a manual labor education. This was a novelty, though the idea was already being demonstrated

[55] Fletcher, *History of Oberlin,* I, 76–79.
[56] *Ibid.,* I, 88–89.   [57] *Ibid.,* I, 117.

back in Oneida County, where Gale's friend, the Reverend
H. H. Kellogg, was operating a Young Ladies' Domestic Seminary successfully on the manual labor plan.[58] At Oberlin, however, both gentlemen and ladies were part of the educational
scheme. The plain living that Shipherd desired for his community is evident in the announcement that while board was
only eighty cents a week for students having "vegetable food,"
it was twelve cents more for those who got "animal food twice a
day." [59]

The school at Oberlin was still only a rickety venture when
Shipherd, on his way to the East, learned about the unexpected
developments at Lane Seminary, and through Mahan met the
Rebels and negotiated with them and their influential patrons
a deal that marks the real foundation of Oberlin College.[60]
The Lane Rebels would come to Oberlin, the Tappans would
give it munificent assistance, but as a concession to these parties
certain alterations must occur in the Oberlin faculty. John
Morgan—an Oneida County man who had been at the manual
labor school developed in Rochester during the Finney revival
there, who had become a teacher at Lane, but who had been
peremptorily discharged by the Lane trustees as part of the
purge of abolitionism—must be added to the Oberlin faculty.
Asa Mahan, it was proposed, should become president of Oberlin; after discussing the matter with Holyoke and Melendy, his
elders and stand-bys, Mahan accepted.[61] Finney, no less, must
become professor of theology.

To assist in capturing Finney and to confirm commitments
with the Tappans and other philanthropists, Mahan accompanied Shipherd to New York City.[62] The arrangements were
made with considerable dispatch and were accepted by the
Oberlin trustees. More opposition was encountered when the
Lane Rebels and their nominees for the faculty insisted that

[58] Calkins, *They Broke the Prairie*, pp. 47–48.
[59] *American Annals of Education*, IV (May, 1834), 242–43; VI (April, 1836),
186–87.
[60] Fairchild, *Oberlin*, pp. 51–52, 54, 66, 336; *Weld Letters*, I, 69–71.
[61] Asa Mahan, *Autobiography*, pp. 191–92.
[62] Fletcher, *History of Oberlin*, I, 172.

students be received irrespective of color. Assurance from the proprietors of Oberlin was essential on this issue not only as a matter of principle but as a test of the freedom of students and faculty from such trustee interference as had occurred at Lane.[63] On this point, as Morgan wrote to Weld, there could be no doubt as "to the course you and the (hat off!) *Oneidas* will take," and fortunately the trustees were "straightened" on the matter [64] and the necessary guarantee given. During the spring of 1835 the Lane Rebels came to Oberlin and its boom times began.

Oberlin reassembled three of the forces recruited during the Great Revival [65]—the repulsed and partially dispersed detachment commanded by Weld and Mahan at Cincinnati, the *avant-garde* in New York City where Finney had been about to retire from exhaustion, and the militant reserve that still centered about Oneida Institute. Directly and indirectly it was from Oneida Institute that Oberlin was mainly derived. In addition to the "Oneidas" who comprised one third of the Lane Rebel party, many other young men came directly from the Whitesboro school to Oberlin. For example, of the ninety listed in the secondary department of Oneida Institute in 1834, twenty later studied at Oberlin, and only two of these had come there by way of Lane.[66] Institutional features of the mother school reappeared in the characteristics of its daughter, in the operation of the manual labor scheme, in a curricular "de-emphasis" of classics, in a seriousness of the school spirit of the student body, and, most significant of all, in an ardor for reform.[67] As the historian of Oberlin expresses it, Lane's radicalism came from a transfusion from Oneida, and Oberlin's chiefly from both." [68]

Weld never joined Oberlin College formally, but a few weeks

[63] *Ibid.*, I, 168–78.

[64] John Morgan to Weld, Jan. 13, 1835, *Weld Letters*, I, 197–99.

[65] Hammond, "The First Decade," in *The Oberlin Jubilee, 1833–1883*, pp. 192–206.

[66] Fletcher, *History of Oberlin*, I, 183–85.

[67] Fletcher, "Oneida and Oberlin," *Town Topics of the Mohawk Valley*, Nov., 1931.

[68] Fletcher, *History of Oberlin*, I, 242.

before the close of the first full term after the arrival of the
Lane Rebels he came to deliver more than a score of lectures
on slavery.[69] He was now fully committed to an agency for the
American Anti-Slavery Society and his former classmates were a
valuable resource upon which he expected to draw for abolitionist workers. Already in August of 1835 he summoned
thirteen of them to Cleveland for two weeks' instruction, preparatory to sending them out to abolitionize Ohio. Soon after
that he conducted an "abolition school" in Oberlin itself. The
national anti-slavery organization called on this corps of radicals for more and more agitators,[70] until thirty of the Lane
Rebels were acting as its agents. In fact, until 1837 they comprised the bulk of the field workers of the abolition movement.[71]

In the flaming evangelism of these young men the leaders of
the American Anti-Slavery Society finally found the brand that
would spread the fire of immediate emancipation. Journalism,
pamphleteering, and the lectures of the small number of earlier
agents from the East had not been very effective. These measures had not sufficed to persuade individual men of the right-
ness of immediate emancipation. The cause must, like the other
projects of the benevolent system, be sustained by local societies
in local church communities. Then, like the temperance or missions movements, it would truly fulfill its intention to be "one
of the sisterhood of Christian charities." [72] Instead of elaborate
arguments about the social consequences, the ethical aspect,
and the political complications of slavery, it was more effective
to convert men by evangelical techniques to the simple conviction that slavery was a sin—to be dealt with like all other sins.
The national society decided at its 1836 anniversary to reduce
its printed propaganda and rather to expand Weld's band of
abolitionist agents to a group of "Seventy," like unto that
earlier company whom the Lord himself had appointed and

[69] Fairchild, *Oberlin*, p. 75.
[70] See the list, p. 37, *Third Annual Report of the American Anti-Slavery
Society*, 1836.
[71] Barnes, *Anti-Slavery Impulse*, p. 77.   [72] *Ibid.*, p. 63.

sent "before his face into every city and place," saying unto them:

The harvest is great, but the laborers are few. . . . Behold I send you forth as lambs among wolves. . . . Into whatsoever city ye enter and they receive you not, go your ways out into the street of the same, and say, "Even the very dust of your city, which cleaveth on us, we do wipe off against you. . . . It shall be more tolerable for Tyre and Sidon at the judgement, than for you."

Weld selected the "Seventy" with the aid of Whittier and of Henry B. Stanton, a Lane Rebel. The anti-slavery movement and the Great Revival had now become one "in method and in objective." Abolitionism was now "as a whole what it had long been in larger part, an aspect of the Great Revival in benevolent reform." [73]

At the very time Weld was recruiting his "Seventy," his former teacher, Gale, was grouping in the Burned-over District his college-colony for Illinois around a nucleus of former faculty, students, and patrons of Oneida Institute. By moving farther west to Illinois, this company and other exponents of the Great Revival infiltrated the extreme right flank of free territory, an accomplishment which the "Seventy" were not able to encompass in their tremendously successful campaign.[74] By the summer of 1836 Gale's colony was on its way to the Illinois frontier, where its town and church and college were to serve as the chief rallying point for abolitionists, including several Lane Rebels, the Holyokes, and a worthy successor to Mahan in the pulpit of the Sixth Presbyterian Church in Cincinnati.

[73] *Ibid.*, p. 107.
[74] In this they fell short of Weld's original plan (*ibid.*, p. 106).

☙ VI ☙

Gathering of the Galesburg Colony
1835–1840

Many persons who emigrate from older to younger states set out
with the spirit of reformers. . . . If a colony of backwoodsmen
should settle in Massachusetts, and resolutely determine to raise
nothing but corn and tobacco, to wear blanket coats and leggins,
and to make stump speeches, there would be a sad outcry about;
yet they would do no greater violence to the feelings of that
people, than a colony coming from the East, who should per-
tinaciously resolve upon planting all their own customs among
us, would do to ours.[1]

FUGITIVES FROM MISSOURI

INTO THE GREAT MIDDLE BEND of the Mississippi
River the broad belly of Illinois bulges westward against the
northeastern corner of Missouri. At Quincy, on the Illinois
side, one crossed from the borderland of "Yankee" and
"Hoosier" into country that by the token of slavery was in-
dubitably Southern. When the exploring committee for the
Galesburg colony came to the government office at Quincy in
the fall of 1835 to purchase lands in the name of the proposed
college, they crossed the river to Palmyra, Missouri, to visit with
two former Oneida Institute students who were continuing
their studies at a newly established manual labor institute,
Marion College.

The founder of Marion College, Dr. David Nelson, was
already famous in Presbyterian circles for his dramatic con-

---

[1] "Emigration," *Illinois Monthly Magazine,* I (1831), 417–20.

version from a skeptic into one of the most powerful camp meeting preachers of the West.[2] His career in Kentucky and Tennessee had touched upon some of the same liberalizing influences that appeared in the life of Birney,[3] and before Nelson removed to Missouri in 1829 he had freed his slaves. Nelson adopted even more advanced anti-slavery principles under the influence of Weld during the latter's tours [4] for the manual labor society in 1831 and 1832, tours which took him to St. Louis and on a six-hundred-mile journey through Missouri.[5] Weld's first appearance in St. Louis followed closely upon a religious revival there during which Nelson had converted Elijah P. Lovejoy. The mutual influence of these three men at this time [6] was profoundly to affect the beginnings of abolitionism in Missouri' and Illinois and also in Iowa, for it was Nelson who aroused a missionary of the Yale Band, Asa Turner, stationed at Quincy before moving to Iowa, to more concern about slavery reform.[7]

At the time of Weld's travels to Missouri Nelson was founding Marion College on a manual labor basis.[8] While in the East in 1835 raising money to finance the 4,000 acres purchased for the college, Nelson again encountered Weld and returned with a commission as agent for the American Anti-Slavery Society. Meanwhile Marion College had started operations in 1834.[9]

Among the earliest students at Marion College were Henry

[2] Gallaher, "Recollections of Dr. David Nelson," *The Western Sketch Book*, pp. 369–92; Gilbert H. Barnes's article on Nelson in the *Dictionary of American Biography*.

[3] *Birney Letters*, I, xiii.

[4] Richardson, "Dr. David Nelson and His Times," *Journal of the Illinois State Historical Society*, XIII (Jan., 1921), 433–63.

[5] Benjamin P. Thomas, *Theodore Weld*, pp. 33–35; *Weld Letters*, I, 69, 75–78.

[6] Merkel, "Abolition Aspects of Missouri's Anti-Slavery Controversy, 1819–1865," *Missouri Historical Review*, XLIV (April, 1950), 242.

[7] Magoun, *Asa Turner*, p. 155. According to Turner, who knew Nelson well, Nelson heard Weld discourse upon the "second table of the law" in 1831 and was led to say that "he would live on roast potatoes and salt before he would hold slaves" (*ibid.*).

[8] Every student was required to cultivate one acre of garden and harvest nine acres of timothy (Alton *Observer*, Feb. 16, 1837).

[9] Merkel, "Abolition Aspects of Missouri's Anti-Slavery Controversy," *Missouri Historical Review*, XLIV (April, 1951), 246.

Ferris and Sherman Williams, who had come by way of New
Orleans from their homes in Russia, New York. Both were
former Oneida Institute students who were preparing for the
ministry and both were members of families interested in the
Galesburg colony; both had come directly under the influence
of the Reverend ("Father") John Waters, who was one of the
ministers promoting that enterprise. How they happened to
come all the way to Marion College is not apparent; possibly
they were attracted by the speculative features that were associated with the Marion College project, for both young men
had some means.[10]

Of the two students, Ferris was undoubtedly less deeply dedicated to a religious career.[11] One of the members of the Galesburg exploratory committee that visited Marion College in the
fall of 1835 was Henry's father, Silvanus Ferris, a distant relative of Gale's and chief financial backer of the colony. The elder
Ferris was also buying land in the locale of the Galesburg site
for himself and the members of his large family, all but one of
whom migrated to Illinois with the colony.[12] Henry decided to
go to the newly purchased land in Knox County and was on the
site of the proposed village by November 1, 1835, the first actual
resident,[13] and spent the winter in the grove north of the
prairie-purchase cutting logs that would be needed to build
temporary homes when the first immigrants arrived in the
spring.[14]

[10] Gettemy, "A Memoir of Silvanus Ferris, 1773–1861," MS in the Knox College
Library. The Reverend John Waters was a missionary with a commission including Russia, New York, in 1832 and 1833. He reported a revival for 1832, no
doubt the same one to which Sherman Williams refers in a letter cited later in
this chapter (American Home Missionary Society: *Sixth Annual Report*, 1832, p.
42, and *Seventh Annual Report*, 1833, p. 45). Henry Ferris arrived in Missouri in
1833 and attended Marion College one year according to a biographical sketch in
Chapman, *Portrait and Biographical Album of Knox County*, p. 693.

[11] The young lady whom he later married wrote in July, 1836, that though he
kept up with his studies she doubted that he would become a minister (Elizabeth
Hudson, Knoxville, Ill., to Marie Hudson, New York Mills, New York; MS, Knox
College Library).

[12] Calkins, *They Broke the Prairie*, pp. 56–63.

[13] Churchill, "Galesburg History," MS, Knox College Library.

[14] In the early records of the college Henry Ferris is listed as taking 160 acres
for $960 ("Blotter A," Knox College Library).

Sherman Williams, who seems to have been a restless person, must have been tempted to accompany his friend on the new venture, but he was not so foot-loose, having a family and possessing property acquired in the Palmyra neighboorhood.[15] Williams manifested to a marked degree the inner tensions between godly aspirations and earthly limitations engendered within many a convert of the Great Revival. These tensions are set forth in detail in a letter which Williams wrote to Finney from Palmyra in May, 1835. He portrayed himself as an only son who had been overly indulged by his parents because of his poor health. Married before he was of age and apparently having settled down to farming, he was unwillingly but deeply converted by the preaching of "Father" Waters in Russia, New York, and resolved to become a missionary. Illness and disinclination to studies cut short his educational preparation at Oneida Institute, but Gale, Waters, and others nevertheless supported him in an application for a teaching mission in the South Sea islands. This was refused, partly because the Williamses were now encumbered by a baby and partly because husband and wife were rather sickly. In pursuit of better health Williams traveled to the South, spent some time in New Orleans, and then with Henry Ferris went up the river to Marion College and started to school again, hoping to find some kind of religious vocation in this western country. The urgings of his father, mother, and sister caused him to settle down again to farming, which he soon regretted, for, as he explained to Finney, he could find no peace of mind. The particular purpose of his autobiographical letter to the famous evangelist was to ask his advice about the feasibility of his living on a mission station somewhere at his own expense until it could be determined by the mission directors whether or not his health would permit him to function effectively in the role of missionary.[16]

Williams's next move was determined by a Missouri mob.

[15] Churchill, "Galesburg History."
[16] Sherman Williams, Palmyra, Mo., to Charles G. Finney, May 22, 1835, with a note added by A. C. Garratt (Finney Papers, Oberlin College Library).

Apparently even before Henry Ferris left Palmyra for the Galesburg purchase, there had been some trouble with Missourians over the abolitionism of the former Oneida students.[17] By the spring of 1836 reports about the anti-slavery activities at Marion College were arousing resentment as far away as St. Louis.[18] Hostility around Palmyra converged in May upon Williams and a close friend, A. C. Garratt, superintendent of the college farm, because, it was said, they excited slaves to rebellion with incendiary pamphlets. When a mob found a box of anti-slavery tracts in Williams's corncrib, they threatened to burn these missionaries of abolitionism along with their books, or at least to tar and feather them, give them 150 lashes, and then banish them from the state. Williams talked the mob into letting them off with the banishment, and he with his family fled by night across the river to the vicinity of Quincy.[19] A few days later Dr. Nelson also had to take refuge in the same locality. Williams bought land the next month from the college in the Galesburg settlement,[20] where he brought his family the following winter.[21] Two years later he was joined by his parents and his sister, who became the second wife of George Washington Gale.[22]

COLONISTS FROM ONEIDA COUNTY AND ELSEWHERE
IN NEW YORK

Migrants coming directly from New York began to arrive in June, 1836, and altogether seven companies, each numbering twenty to forty persons, came to the colony lands during 1836 and 1837.[23] The largest number of these settlers came

---

[17] Gettemy, "Memoir of Silvanus Ferris," p. 217.

[18] Martineau, *Retrospect of Western Travel*, I, 32–34.

[19] *Fourth Annual Report of the American Anti-Slavery Society*, 1837, p. 80; contemporary Marion and Quincy newspaper accounts are reported in Asbury, *Reminiscences of Quincy, Illinois*, pp. 64–68.

[20] "Blotter A," MSS, financial records of Knox College.

[21] Churchill, "Galesbury History"; Perry, *Knox County*, II, 236.

[22] *Herald of the Prairies*, April 4, 1849; the second Mrs. Gale (Esther Williams Coons Gale) was one of the early converts of the Great Revival (Peoria *Register and Northwestern Gazetteer*, Jan. 6, 1843).

[23] Calkins, *They Broke the Prairie*, chapter 3.

from Oneida County and most of the others from adjacent counties in New York state, from localities in which the ministerial leaders of the colony, Gale, Waters, and Hiram Huntington Kellogg, had preached. Since most of these New Yorkers had previously contributed to Oneida Institute, this was the second time they were supporting an educational scheme of which Gale was the leader.[24] Waters and Silvanus Ferris had subscribed generously to Oneida Institute [25] and now were major investors in the new venture; Waters was one of the three men who had first promised a thousand dollars to the Galesburg enterprise; Ferris used his credit to borrow money for the purchase of the more than ten thousand acres whose rise in price was to finance the development of the college. The Reverend John Frost, Gale's chief assistant in the founding of Oneida Institute, also helped to get the new project under way, and members of his family later settled in the colony. Two of the teachers in the New York school, besides Gale, settled in Galesburg and were on the original faculty of Knox College.[26]

Other migrants from the Oneida locality, though not part of the colony itself, were associated with former neighbors in the development of the college. When Nehemiah West set out from Galesburg in the winter of 1836–37 for Vandalia to get a charter for Knox Manual Labor College, he took with him a politician from nearby Knoxville who during the height of the Great Revival had been attending college at Clinton in Oneida County.[27] The first trustees under this charter included, along with the leaders of the colony, two other former Oneida County men who had settled in this part of Illinois; one was a merchant and landholder living about twenty-five miles away at Mt. Sterling; another was a physician and land speculator,

[24] G. W. Gale to the editor, Galesburg *Free Democrat*, Aug. 11, 1857.

[25] *First Report of the Trustees of Oneida Institute.*

[26] Nehemiah Losey had been principal of the juvenile branch of Oneida Institute (Peoria *Register and Northwestern Gazetteer*, Dec. 15, 1838). Innes Grant was professor of languages at Oneida Institute.

[27] James Knox, later a trustee of the college (Chapman, *History of Knox County*, pp. 686–87).

George H. Wright, who resided in the next county to the west.[28] Contemporaneous with the settling of Galesburg, several other Oneida families occupied farms farther east and north in Knox County, starting a community that was clearly a by-product of Gale's colonizing. Here eventually a town bearing the name of Oneida developed.[29]

REFORMERS FROM VERMONT AND RADICALS FROM CINCINNATI

During the first summer Galesburg attracted two parties of settlers from outside the state of New York who made substantial contributions to both the material and the spiritual resources of the community. The leaders of both groups were immediately elected to the board of trustees of the college. One of these parties was from Vermont; the other from Cincinnati. The foremost figure in the group of five families from Vermont was "Colonel" Matthew Chambers, who was deeply interested in "every department of social and moral reform." The decision of these Vermonters to join the colony from New York was influenced by their "attachment" to the great reform movements.[30]

The Cincinnati group consisted of the large family of William Holyoke, who first learned of Gale's plan in July, 1836, from a company of the colonists who stopped at Cincinnati to have a stern wheel attached to the canal boat in which they were traveling from New York to their new Illinois home. While waiting in their boat they learned of threats against them because of their notoriety as abolitionists,[31] and the women took refuge on shore. Holyoke was persuaded by the

---

[28] Robinson, ed., *Historical and Biographical Record of Monmouth and Warren County, Illinois*, II, 311; Moffat and Rogers, *History of Warren County*, p. 706.

[29] Isaac Wetmore Papers, Knox College Library; Oneida as a town resulted from the coming of the railroad in 1854. The middle fifties witnessed several additions to this community from Oneida County, New York (Perry, *Knox County*, II, 34, 485, 634–35, 666).

[30] Statement by Matthew Chambers in Appendix L, *Rights of Congregationalists in Knox College*, pp. 69–71; Edward Beecher, [Funeral] *Sermon and Obituary* [of Matthew Chambers, 1869], pp. 6–8.

[31] During July, 1836, Cincinnati was disturbed with mob violence against the abolitionists' press in that city (*Birney Letters*, I, 342–57).

leaders of this company to cast his lot with their enterprise; he followed them by steamboat to look over the colony site, was impressed by what he found, and migrated to Galesburg with his family the following spring.[32]

Holyoke's coming established a direct connection with the militant abolitionist group in Cincinnati that was to have important consequences in the early history of the town. His activity as a founder and elder of the anti-slavery Sixth Presbyterian Church in Cincinnati, his close friendship with Asa Mahan, his membership on the Lane board of trustees, his support of the Lane Rebels, have already been noted. He was associated with these student insurgents in the convention that in April, 1835, organized the Ohio Anti-Slavery Society at Putnam, despite a hostile mob.[33] And one of his daughters married a Lane Rebel, Lucius H. Parker, who also later joined the Galesburg settlement.

Parker was one of the Lane students who stemmed from the Rochester phase of the Great Revival.[34] He had traveled to Cincinnati in the company of eight enthusiasts led by Weld himself, and with the latter he entered Lane in June of 1833.[35] With several other seminarians he worked in Holyoke's carriage shop.[36] Along with the other Rebels he withdrew from Lane in the autumn of 1834, and later was one of those who signed the "Declaration of Sentiments and Plan of Operations" issued by the Putnam anti-slavery convention of April, 1835. On August 31, 1836,[37] he married a daughter of Holyoke,

---

[32] Avery, "Canal Boat," MS in Knox College Library; Holyoke, "A Historical Sketch," Galesburg *Republican Register*, July 7, 1911; Joseph Holyoke to George Churchill in *Semi-Centennial Celebration, First Church of Galesburg*, pp. 69–76; Samuel G. Holyoke, "Sketch of Log City," in Calkins, ed., *Log City Days*, pp. 71–72.

[33] *Proceedings of the Ohio Anti-Slavery Convention Held at Putnam on the 22nd, 23rd & 24th of April, 1835*, pp. 1–2, 10–11; Shepphard, "An Abolition Center," *Ohio Archaeological and Historical Publications*, XIX, 265–68.

[34] His elder brother, Joel, was a prominent member of the Finney-Tappan band promoting religious reforms in New York City, to which he had been transferred from Rochester (Fletcher, *History of Oberlin*, I, 17–18, 32–33, 54–55).

[35] *Ibid.*, I, 54–55, note; 183, note.

[36] A tradition in the Parker family related to the author by Mrs. J. A. Peterson of Galesburg, Illinois.

[37] Perry, *Knox County*, II, 1145.

and apparently might have accompanied the Holyoke family to Galesburg the following spring had his wife not been pregnant.[38] Instead the Parkers moved to Oberlin, where Lucius was graduated from the seminary in 1838, and it was not until after a pastorate in Erie, Pennsylvania, that he heeded the argument of Mrs. Holyoke that he turn his face from the East to the West, where there was much to do.[39] In the summer of 1843, while he was visiting in Galesburg, the trustees of the colony church urged Parker to become their pastor, which he did early the following summer.[40] This pastorate was followed by many years of service as a home-missionary with headquarters in Galesburg. His aggressive espousal of Congregationalism and abolitionism and his importance as a founder of churches in central Illinois will be apparent in the succeeding pages.

EVANGELISTS

What the colony never lacked in its early years was evangelistic preaching. Besides Gale there was the venerable Reverend John Waters, who, though retired from a regular ministry even before leaving New York,[41] was often sought after for revivalistic services for short periods.[42] He continued his intermittent evangelistic missions after he came to Illinois, and despite his age might drive fifty miles or more across open

[38] Mrs. William E. Holyoke to Mrs. Elizabeth Parker, Whiteford, Ohio; MS letter in the possession of a descendant, Mrs. J. A. Peterson, Galesburg, Illinois.

[39] *Ibid.*

[40] "Minutes of the Society of the First Presbyterian Church of Galesburg, Ill.," Aug. 14 and 21, Dec. 11, 1843 (MSS, Knox College Library); Gale, *Articles of Faith and Covenant*, p. 10.

[41] Waters was pastor for one year in Augusta, Oneida County, in 1831, during which time a very successful revival occurred. During the first half of 1831 he helped supply a church in Rome (Jones, *Annals and Recollections of Oneida County*, pp. 105, 392). He had a three months' commission as missionary in Herkimer County in 1832, being supported by an agency with headquarters in Utica of which Gerrit Smith and John Frost were members. This commission was extended for twelve months in 1833 and covered Herkimer and Oneida counties, where he reported a successful revival (American Home Missionary Society: *Sixth Annual Report*, 1832, p. 42; *Seventh Annual Report*, 1833, p. 45). The places referred to lay in the area whence came the bulk of the Galesburg colonists.

[42] Jane Waters Johnson to M. L. Comstock, May 19, 1887, *Semi-Centennial Celebration, First Church of Galesburg*, pp. 148–50.

prairie to assist in protracted meetings. To a younger minister who met this "lovely gray headed patriarch" on one of these extended journeys, "Father" Waters explained, "I have come out here to stir about a little, to awaken the church to feel for souls and die. I have come here to die in a little while, but I want to work while I live." [43]

During the first winter Waters and Gale were assisted in refreshing the zeal of the settlers by the Reverend John T. Avery, who came to visit his brothers and sisters. Avery had ascended to eminence as an evangelist by the familiar steps of conversion under Finney, of membership in his Holy Band, and of studies under Gale at Oneida Institute. He successfully renewed in the log-cabin village in Illinois the Great Revival that he had helped to promote in New York.[44]

Two winters later, the even more notorious evangelist, Horatio Foote, conducted daily revival meetings for several weeks.[45] A minister from Peoria, the Reverend Jeremiah Porter, who joined in the effort for twelve days, recorded that never had he seen "so large a church wrestling so unitedly and importunately & for such a length of time" and that the "days were like so many Sabbaths." [46] Foote was unanimously invited to become minister of the colony church, a position that he filled for more than a year.[47] He had been one of Finney's apostles in the opening stage of the Great Revival in Oneida County and had attracted throngs to his preaching. He went along with some of the unconventional excitements and notions of that time to a point where he was suspected of fostering a perfectionist cult akin to John Humphrey Noyes's Oneida Community. There is no evidence that he adopted any heterodox matrimonial doctrines, but his career in New York ended in 1837 "when his presbytery renounced him after he seduced a girl

---

[43] Jeremiah Porter, "Journal," June, 1837 (MSS, Chicago Historical Society).

[44] *Semi-Centennial Celebration, First Church of Galesburg*, pp. 38, 40, 62; Calkins, *They Broke the Prairie*, p. 99. The Reverend J. T. Avery was again in Galesburg in July, 1841 (Peoria *Register and Northwestern Gazetteer*, July 9, 1841).

[45] *Semi-Centennial Celebration, First Church of Galesburg*, p. 41.

[46] Jeremiah Porter, "Journal," Feb., 1839.

[47] "Minutes of the Society of the First Presbyterian Church of Galesburg, Ill." (MSS, Knox College Library), March 5, 1839; March 9, April 25, 1840.

taken into his home to rear." [48] If this scandal reached Illinois, he either refuted it or justified himself, for there seems to have been no stain on his reputation, and after his Galesburg ministry he held a prominent pastorate in Quincy for many years.[49] He became a trustee of Knox College in 1845.

MISSIONARIES AND AGITATORS

According to Gale's "Circular and Plan," devised in 1834 as a prospectus for a college-colony, the community of Galesburg was obligated to capture the Mississippi Valley for a pure gospel and for civil liberty. In fulfillment of this compact the colony leaders immediately assumed responsibility for missionary work in their salient of the borders of Zion. "Father" Waters, Gale himself, two young men preparing for the ministry, and the faculty of the college and academy gave themselves to this duty as they were able, but the field was too wide for part-time laborers. During the summer of 1839, while Gale was back in New York, he reviewed with the officers of the American Home Missionary Society the critical needs of "our section of the country," describing it as an area sixty miles square in Illinois and stretching beyond that into Iowa "as far as there are settlements." The Galesburg church, the only one able to support itself, contributed liberally to the mission cause, but the donations were in produce, for cash was hard to come by on the frontier.[50] Gale received assurance from the officers of the national organization that some subsidization would be available, but the procurement of the missionaries themselves apparently fell on his shoulders as the virtual director of mission work in the upper half of the Military Tract,[51] the section of land between the Illinois and Mississippi rivers.

[48] Cross, *Burned-over District,* pp. 191–96.

[49] A biographical sketch of Foote, inaccurate in part, is found in Collins and Perry, *Past and Present of the City of Quincy and Adams County,* p. 600.

[50] Gale to Charles Hall, Dec. 18, 1840, and Nov. 29, 1841, A.H.M.S. Papers, Chicago Theological Seminary; the leadership of Gale and Waters in missionary work on this segment of the frontier is apparent in the assignment given them at the first meeting of the Knox Presbytery, Galesburg, Nov. 7, 1838, "Records of the Presbytery of Knox" (MS, Knox College Library), p. 4.

[51] Gale became chairman of the committee on missions in the meeting on September 12, 1839, of the Knox Presbytery. The duties of this committee in-

A former student of Gale's at Oneida Institute was the first man recruited for this particular mission field. This was John J. Miter, who had been one of the "Oneidas" at Lane Seminary [52] and whose name headed the list of signatures appended to the statement in which the Lane Rebels vindicated their withdrawal from that school. After the "rebellion" he served, like so many of that group, as an anti-slavery agent, and in 1836 he was licensed to preach by the Oneida Presbytery of New York.[53] In 1837 he came to northern Illinois,[54] where he served briefly at the First Presbyterian Church of the village of Chicago.[55] Early in 1838 he moved to the Galesburg neighborhood and ministered to the tiny congregation that had existed at Knoxville since 1835.[56] The Knox Presbytery ordained him as an "evangelist," Gale and Waters officiating.[57] Before the end of the month the elders of the Knoxville church, one a member of the Galesburg colony and another the former steward of Oneida Institute, applied for a subsidy for Miter from the American Home Missionary Society; [58] Gale certified his protégé's good standing to that body.[59] Miter received his commission from the national society and entered upon more than three years of labor, with Gale continuing his former role as teacher and adviser.[60]

cluded the procuring of missionaries ("Records of the Presbytery of Knox"). Gale remained the chairman of this committee at least into 1843 (ibid., Oct. 11, 1842, p. 92).

[52] Weld Letters, I, 83, 241.

[53] Minutes of the General Assembly of the Presbyterian Church of the United States of America, 1836, pp. 317–18. He was still a licentiate of the Oneida Presbytery in 1837.

[54] Peet, History of the Presbyterian and Congregational Churches and Ministry in Wisconsin, p. 67.

[55] An Account of the Fiftieth Anniversary of the Organization of the First Presbyterian Church, Chicago, pp. 28–29.

[56] Ephraim Noel to corresponding secretary, A.H.M.S., Aug. 17, 1835, Knoxville, Illinois; Robert Stewart to Absolom Peters, Oct. 28, 1835, Canton, Illinois; Noel to corresponding secretary, Feb. 18, 1836, Knoxville, Illinois; A.H.M.S. Papers.

[57] Peoria Register and Northwestern Gazetteer, April 21, 1838.

[58] Matthew Chambers, Brainerd Orton, Samuel Metcalf, to Charles Hall, April 30, 1838, A.H.M.S. Papers.

[59] Gale to the secretary, A.H.M.S., Aug. 22, 1838, Galesburg, Ill., A.H.M.S. Papers.

[60] Chambers, "Reminiscences of Early Days," MS of paper read to the Knox

Miter foresaw that the great valley of the West was fraught with a future tremendous for the nation as well as for itself, and he burned with a consuming zeal to "save" it. From his headquarters in Knoxville he went out to found and to serve new churches, and by 1840 was going to three of them regularly, ten, fifteen, and twenty-five miles away. Constantly he responded to other calls from the "groves" of this section of Illinois, and westward he did considerable work in Warren County and on one trip went as far as Iowa.[61] His evangelism covered the full range of benevolent causes that had been integrated during the Great Revival, for he lectured on "temperance, moral reform, and anti-slavery," and within less than a year was instrumental in the founding of county temperance societies both in Knox and Warren counties.[62] His anti-slavery agitation, carried on despite the riotous hostility of Hoosier neighbors in Knoxville,[63] was very important during these formative years of abolitionism in Illinois and will be noted more fully later. Three years after he received his missionary commission he confidently asserted: "The Galesburg Colony in conjunction with this church [Knoxville] is producing a decided and happy change for miles around us on fundamental questions pertaining to the world's renovation." [64]

During the summer of 1840 part of the field traversed by Miter was taken over by Samuel Guild Wright, who for years thereafter ministered in small churches that did not become self-supporting until the middle fifties; [65] and for a dozen years

County Historical Society. The Chambers family were very close to Miter. Matthew Chambers, the head of the family, though a member of the Galesburg community, where he was to be a grocer, had temporarily established himself in Knoxville.

[61] Miter to Charles Hall, Jan. 9, May 4, July 1, 1839; Miter to Milton Badger, Nov. 26, 1840; Gale to Hall, Dec. 18, 1840, and Miter's addition to that letter dated Dec. 25, 1840; Gale to Hall, Nov. 29, 1841; A.H.M.S. Papers. At least one Iowa church, at Marion, Lynn Co., "Ioway" Territory, was received into the care of the Presbytery of Knox on Oct. 13, 1840 ("Records of the Presbytery of Knox," p. 40).

[62] Miter to Charles Hall, Jan. 9 and July 1, 1839, A.H.M.S. Papers.

[63] An article by E. P. Chambers in Scrapbook No. Six, p. 6, Galesburg Public Library.

[64] Miter to Milton Badger, July 14, 1841, Knoxville, Illinois, A.H.M.S. Papers.

[65] Galesburg *Free Democrat*, Feb. 16, 1854.

he averaged over three thousand miles of driving from charge
to charge.[66] Wright had come from New Hampshire in the
early thirties as a young man and had settled in Fulton County,
just south of Knox County.[67] When he was already in his late

[66] Illinois Society of Church History, Congregational, *Historical Statement and
Papers*, p. 32.
[67] Shallenberger, *Stark County*, pp. 218–19.

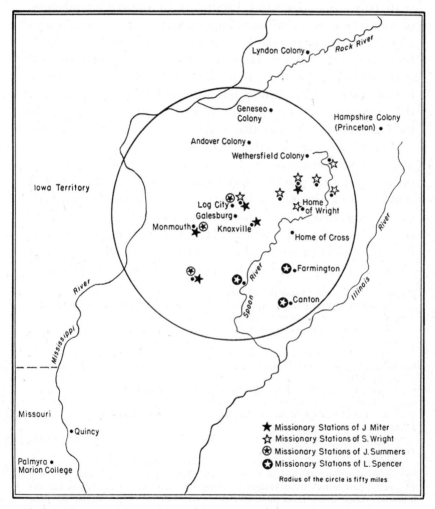

The Mission Field Centering in Galesburg, 1837–1843

twenties he decided to become a minister, and after some study under a clergyman at Farmington [68] he entered Lane Seminary in the fall of 1837 and persisted in this course until 1840, despite sickness and the death of his wife.[69] He was licensed to preach by the Cincinnati Presbytery, which at that time included Jonathan Blanchard, of whom Wright was later to see a great deal at Knox College.[70]

In July, 1840, the Knox Presbytery committee on missions, of which Gale was chairman, appointed Wright as a missionary and directed him to take his station five miles north of Galesburg at Henderson, or "Hoosier Town," as Wright discovered it was called. In October, 1840, Wright passed his examination before the Knox Presbytery and was ordained, Miter preaching the ordination sermon.[71] After Wright had been active in the field for about six months, Gale applied for assistance for Wright from the American Home Missionary Society and Miter, in his own postscript to Gale's letter, endorsed the application, stating that the churches where Wright had preached spoke well of him.[72] Late in 1841 Wright was advised by Gale to shift his mission labors more to the east,[73] and Stark County became his main responsibility. He established residence there, near the southern county line at what was locally designated "Niggers Point." [74] From the outset anti-slavery labors were

[68] Jeremiah Porter, "Journal," March 18, 1839.

[69] Wright to Milton Badger, April 20, 1842, A.H.M.S. Papers; *Lane Theological Seminary General Catalogue, 1829–1899*, p. 28.

[70] [New School] *Minutes of the General Assembly of the Presbyterian Church, 1840*, p. 55.

[71] "Records of the Presbytery of Knox," p. 41. Wright had already been "a candidate for licensure" in this presbytery before completing studies at Lane (*ibid.*, April 1, 1839, p. 10).

[72] Gale to Charles Hall, Dec. 18, 1840 (Miter's addition is dated Dec. 25, 1840); Gale to Hall, Nov. 29, 1841; Wright to Milton Badger, March 18, 1841, Henderson, Ill., A.H.M.S. Papers; Samuel G. Wright, "Journal," Book A, Knox College Library.

[73] Wright to Badger, Dec., 1841, "near Rochester," postmarked French Creek, Peoria County, A.H.M.S. Papers.

[74] McKenzie, "Congregational Church at Toulon, Illinois, 1846–1921," *Journal of the Illinois State Historical Society*, XIII (Jan., 1921), 504–37. The A.H.M.S. Papers contain letters from Wright covering his early missionary labors for the following dates, other than those already cited: Sept. 23, 1841; March 19, June 21, Sept. 22, 1842; Dec. 30, 1843; April 4, Dec. 24, 1844. There is also a MS

part of his ministry,[75] and he became the leading abolitionist of the county.[76] In these religious and reforming activities he was frequently assisted by the leaders of the Galesburg colony, where he often visited, and in 1849 he became a trustee of Knox College.

The shift of Wright to the area northwest of Galesburg was part of a redistribution of personnel occasioned by Miter's departure for Milwaukee late in 1841 [77] and by the arrival during the summer of another missionary, John Summers, who, Gale informed the American Home Missionary Society, came "from the East at our request." Summers's sphere of operations included Wright's former station at Henderson, but lay mainly to the west, where he followed up the labors previously begun by Miter in Warren County.[78] Summers, who came from Whitesboro, New York, primary source of the Galesburg colony, settled in the latter during the winter of 1841–42.[79] According to Wright he was an "ultra-radical" of the denunciatory type, a "fire-brand" who started blazes where there was already "quite enough disorganizing combustible material." [80]

To the south of Galesburg, the colony supplied missionary help at first through the ministry of "Father" Waters [81] and later through the Reverend Levi Spencer. Born and reared just

"Journal" of Samuel Guild Wright covering these and succeeding years in the Knox College Library.

[75] In his report for March 18, 1841, to the A.H.M.S. Wright reports under "Benevolent objects" contributions of $15 for the anti-slavery society.

[76] Shallenberger, *Stark County*, pp. 218–19; Samuel G. Wright, "Journal"; see illustrative entries for Aug. 22, Sept. 14, 1842, and Feb. 6, May 22, Aug. 14, 1843.

[77] Miter became pastor of the Milwaukee Congregational Church in Nov., 1841 (Peoria *Register and Northwestern Gazetteer*, May 27, 1841).

[78] Gale to Hall, Nov. 29, 1841; Wright to Badger, March 19, 1842; A.H.M.S. Papers; "Records of the Presbytery of Knox," Oct. 18, 1841, pp. 73–74.

[79] Samuel G. Wright, "Journal," Feb. 7, 1842; other references to Summers in this source may be found in entries for Nov. 8 and Dec. 3, 1841; March 7, 1842; April 10 and May 1, 1843.

[80] Wright to Badger, July 3, 1844, A.H.M.S. Papers. Wright thought Summers had been in the "Independent" Whitesboro Association, though his direct accreditation to the Presbytery of Knox was from ministers of the Methodist Protestant Church of Philadelphia ("Records of the Presbytery of Knox," Oct. 18, 1841, pp. 73–74).

[81] Jeremiah Porter, "Journal," entries for the summer months of 1837–39.

north of Oneida County, New York, Spencer had pursued a
career as constable, law student, and teacher, when he was
converted by Horatio Foote. Early in the year that the Galesburg colony began settlement in Illinois he married into one
of the migrating families and soon after was persuaded to
follow his wife's kinsfolk on their pioneering venture. Immediately after his arrival in Galesburg he entered actively
into anti-slavery work, into lay evangelism, and into studies
at the Knox Academy. He was licensed by the Knox Presbytery
in 1841 and spent much of that year assisting Wright in his
missionary activities.[82] With Gale's endorsement he received
a commission from the American Home Missionary Society to
work in the settlements around Canton,[83] where he was ordained in July, 1842, as an "evangelist," President H. H.
Kellogg of Knox College preaching the ordination sermon, with
Gale and Wright also participating in the ceremony.[84] It is
indicative of Spencer's radicalism that he soon persuaded his
Canton church to change from the Presbyterian to the Congregational polity because the former was not absolutely free of
slavery connections. Ellisville and Farmington were other places
he ministered to in the Canton area, in which he remained
until 1844 when he went on to other pastorates in central Illinois and to an aggressive role as anti-slavery agitator.[85]

For a brief period some preaching in the southwestern part
of Knox County was done by the Reverend John Cross, though
his duties were at first those of anti-slavery agent and it is in
this function that his association with the Galesburg colony

[82] Samuel G. Wright, "Journal," entries for March to Oct., 1841.

[83] Levi Spencer to secretary, A.H.M.S., Jan. 2, 1843, Canton, Illinois; Spencer
to Badger and Hall, April 18, 1843. This last letter contains a postscript by
Gale.

[84] The preceding month (June) Hiram Marsh, a member of the Galesburg
colony and the Knox faculty, had also been ordained as an evangelist, with
President Kellogg preaching the ordination sermon (Peoria *Register and Northwestern Gazetteer,* July 22, 1842).

[85] Biographical sources on Spencer are: Blanchard, *Memoir of Rev. Levi
Spencer;* Bascom, *A Discourse Delivered at the Funeral of Rev. Levi Spencer,
Late Pastor of the Congregational Church, Peoria, Illinois, April 17, 1853;
Seventy-fifth Anniversary, First Congregational Church, Peoria, Ill.*

will be later discussed at length. Cross came to Galesburg from Oneida County, New York, where he had been a Congregational-Presbyterian clergyman since the early thirties,[86] as well as a neighbor and a colleague of the founders of Galesburg. In 1836 he had been selected by Weld as one of the "Seventy" to serve as an agent for the American Anti-Slavery Society,[87] and in 1838 he attended the anniversary of that organization as a delegate from one of the local societies in Oneida County.[88] He came to Illinois in the fall of 1839 as the agent of the American Anti-Slavery Society, and the executive committee of the state society, located at that time in the Galesburg colony, agreed that he might raise money in the state to support his agency.[89] Though his duties kept him on the move most of the time, he made a home for his family in Elba Township, Knox County, where they remained until early in 1843,[90] and he

[86] There is a brief biographical sketch of Cross in *History of Page County, Iowa*, p. 622. References to his ministerial labors are in Jones, *Annals and Recollections of Oneida County*, pp. 109, 135–37. He was commissioned by the A.H.M.S. for points in Oneida County in 1834 and 1835 (American Home Missionary Society: *Ninth Annual Report*, 1835, p. 21, and *Tenth Annual Report*, 1836, p. 24). He was a licentiate of the Oneida Presbytery in 1836 (*Minutes of the General Assembly of the Presbyterian Church, 1836*, pp. 317–18). Cross attended meetings of the Presbytery of Knox in 1840 and 1841 and was invited to sit as a "corresponding member" from the Whitesboro Association ("Records of the Presbytery of Knox," April 7, 1840, and Jan. 12, 1841, pp. 31–33 and 50).

[87] *Birney Letters*, I, 357.

[88] *Fifth Annual Report of the American Anti-Slavery Society*, 1838, p. 5.

[89] Executive Committee Report, "Minutes of the Illinois Anti-Slavery Society," July, 1840 (MSS, Chicago Historical Society).

[90] According to Jacob Knightlinger, who lived in the same part of the county and who had good reason to remember Cross, the latter settled in Elba Township either in 1839 or 1840, and he is credited with preaching there in 1841 (Chapman, *History of Knox County*, pp. 205, 212, 214, 503). Entries in the Wright "Journal" for Jan. 8, 1841, and Feb. 27, 1843, speak of his preaching for Wright in a nearby church in Stark County. That Cross removed to La Moille in Bureau County some time between April and early June of 1843 is established by a letter (J. Cross to Milton Badger, Nov. 12, 1844, A.H.M.S. Papers) and by the circumstance that Wright succeeded him as agent for the *Western Citizen* between June 8 and June 15, 1843, for the French Creek, Peoria County P.O., which was near the residence of Cross in Knox County (*Western Citizen*, June 8 and June 15, 1843). Wright speaks of Cross traveling with him from the northern part of Stark County to Rochester, which was near Cross's former home in Knox County ("Journal," June 20, 1843). This confirming evidence is required to clear away the confusion caused by the listing of Cross, as late as 1842, with

was very closely associated with the abolitionists of Galesburg in a variety of ways.

THE PRESIDENT OF THE COLLEGE ARRIVES

By 1840 Galesburg was a village of 321 persons, although this number did not include at least sixteen families, comprising nearly a hundred settlers, who lived on farm homesteads in the vicinity and who may properly be regarded as members of the community.[91] The worldly labors of building new homes and of breaking the prairie had not, as the foregoing paragraphs reveal, distracted the colony from its religious and reforming purposes. Indeed these had been strengthened by the appearance of other zealots coming either from Oneida Institute directly or from its offshoots at Lane and Oberlin. The chief goal, to establish a manual labor college, was a step nearer when the preparatory school was erected in 1838 [92] and was achieved in 1841 when the Reverend Hiram Huntington Kellogg arrived to take over the presidency of Knox Manual Labor College.

President Kellogg belonged to the clique of New York reformers and was a friend or acquaintance of Weld, Beriah Green, Gerrit Smith, and Alvan Stewart, all of whose talents as social renovators he admired.[93] He had been converted in the early stages of the Great Revival, and already in May, 1826, had become a fervent follower and devoted defender of Finney, whom he willingly served as an auxiliary evangelist, preaching

---

the Adams County delegation in the "Minutes" of the Illinois Anti-Slavery Society, where a Quincy P.O. is ascribed to him. This confusion of places may be explained by his status as an agent and his constant travels. He was back in New York during the winter of 1841–42.

[91] Photostatic copies of the original census returns for 1840 for Galesburg and neighboring townships, in the Knox College Library.

[92] The frame for the "preparatory school house" was raised on Aug. 6, 1838; Waters prayed and Riley Root delivered a "sentiment" to the "Galesburg Literary Academical Department" (Peoria *Register and Northwestern Gazetteer*, Aug. 18, 1838).

[93] Kellogg to Gerrit Smith, Galesburg, Jan. 10, 1843 (Gerrit Smith Papers, Syracuse University Library). Kellogg presumably attended the anniversaries of the benevolent system as early as 1829, for he was a delegate to the Presbyterian General Assembly and wrote to Finney that he planned to attend the meeting of the American Board of Commissioners for Foreign Missions.

during the late twenties in several communities of the counties where first Oneida Institute and later Knox College received support. He was in fact preaching in Gale's home town at the very time that Oneida Institute was started.[94]

Kellogg applied the manual labor idea to a Young Ladies Domestic Seminary in Clinton, Oneida County, New York, which he founded in the spring of 1833.[95] His pioneering of manual labor in a woman's school was a matter of some importance in the history of American education,[96] but at that time more excitement was engendered by Kellogg's admission of "coloured ladies" with "social and literary privileges" equal to those of the white students.[97] Because of this policy Kellogg encountered much opposition,[98] and he was excluded from the local pulpit for preaching against slavery.[99] Help came, however, from Gerrit Smith, who agreed to assume part of the expense for each indigent Negro girl whom Kellogg admitted to the seminary.[100] Kellogg was also among the radical abolitionists who early favored political action on the slavery issue. He supported the candidacy of Birney for the presidency in 1840, when the Liberty Party ran its first ticket, and was greatly

[94] Kellogg to Finney, Clinton, New York, May 20 and July 6, 1826; Western, New York, April 2 and 3, 1827; Utica, Oct. 15, 1827, and May 1, 1828; Salina, New York, April 28 and May 26, 1828; Lenox, New York, Sept. 26, 1829; Sarah Brayton to Mrs. Finney, Western, New York, April 25, 1827; Gale to Finney, June 6 and Sept. 26, 1827, from Whitesboro; Weld to Finney, April 22, 1828, Fabius, New York; Finney Papers, Oberlin College Library.

[95] Wager, ed., *Our County and Its People—Oneida County*, pp. 227–28.

[96] Calkins, *They Broke the Prairie*, pp. 47–48, discusses the direct influence of Kellogg's school upon Mary Lyon, founder of Mt. Holyoke.

[97] British and Foreign Anti-Slavery Society, *Proceedings of the General Anti-Slavery Convention, London, 1843*, p. 265.

[98] Harriet Tenney to Mary Ingall, Whitesboro, New York, May 14, 1841 (MS, Knox College Library).

[99] British and Foreign Anti-Slavery Society, *Proceedings of the General Anti-Slavery Convention, London, 1843*, p. 265.

[100] Kellogg to Gerrit Smith, April 30, 1839, Clinton, New York (Gerrit Smith Papers). When it was learned that Kellogg was to leave this school to move to Galesburg, a letter was read before the school assembly from a Negro in New York, asserting that Kellogg ought to remain because his was almost the only institution "at which colored pupils can be received on an equality with those of fairer complexions and it would be very doubtful whether it would again be established on as liberal principles and as broad a basis as at present" (Harriet Tenney to Mary Ingall, Clinton, New York, Feb. 27, 1840, MS, Knox College Library).

concerned that Birney clear himself of charges that he had violated Puritan rules against Sabbath traveling.[101]

From the very start Kellogg was a leader in the scheme to establish a colony and a college in Illinois. He was an early and a substantial subscriber to Gale's plan and Gale's chief adviser on the project, and his influence was particularly apparent in the provisions for a female seminary as part of the educational project. After the colony had moved West, he served as its agent in the East, and in 1838 he was chosen president of the college. Associated with him as one of the first faculty members of Knox Manual Labor College was Julia Chandler,[102] preceptress of the female department, who had been a teacher in Kellogg's Young Ladies Domestic Seminary in Clinton, New York.

Kellogg's coming to Illinois to perform his duties as head of Knox College was heralded in the *Genius of Liberty,* the anti-slavery organ of the state, which reviewed his farewell address at Clinton,[103] emphasizing his anti-slavery stand.[104] In his inaugural address at Knox College in February, 1842, he left no doubt that he would in his new position carry on for the anti-slavery cause. In large part an exposition of the theory of manual labor in education, the address clearly affirmed the incompatibility of that philosophy with slavery. That Knox College would not compromise with public hostility on this issue was plain from Kellogg's criticism of the suppression that had led to the notorious students' rebellion at Lane Seminary, the recent reverses and losses of which he ascribed to the denial of free discussion to the students. "Had the trustees and faculty cherished the noble band who waited with delight upon the instructions of that seminary; if they had welcomed the manly, benevolent, and god-like views which this band avowed on the slavery question; or if they had left the field open for

---

[101] Kellogg to Birney, May 5, 1860, *Birney Letters,* pp. 560–61.

[102] Peoria *Register and Northwestern Gazetteer,* Aug. 27, 1841.

[103] His seminary at Clinton was purchased by the Free Will Baptists, who later also purchased the Oneida Institute and moved the Clinton school to the latter location; "Whitestown Seminary, History of a Famous Educational Institution," Utica *Tribune,* Jan. 31, 1904; *Birney Letters,* II, 813.

[104] *Genius of Liberty,* July 24, 1841.

free discussion," Lane would have prospered more. It had "abandoned its requisition of manual labor," declared Kellogg, so that "it might carry out its subserviency to that power which declares that the laboring classes, bleached or unbleached, of any community, are only fit for slaves." [105]

The *Western Citizen,* which had meanwhile succeeded the *Genius of Liberty* as the abolitionists' organ in Illinois, gave a lengthy description of Kellogg's address as well as of the first catalogue of the new college. In a most commendatory article, the editor enjoined his readers: "Place your sons and daughters in this institution." [106] To the overwhelming majority of communities in Illinois such an appeal, if it reached them at all, would be futile, for the subscribers to the *Western Citizen,* like the patrons of Knox College, would largely be limited to families that were sympathetic to reform movements. The attraction of the college was strongest in a group of new settlements with antecedents similar to those of the Galesburg colony.

[105] Kellogg, *Education for the People,* pp. 11–12.
[106] *Western Citizen,* Sept. 2, 1842.

❧ VII ❧

Other Colonies on the Illinois Frontier

"Seeing is believing," certainly, in most cases; but in the days of the land-fever, we, who were in the midst of the infected district, scarcely found it so. The whirl, the fervour, the flutter, the rapidity of step, the sparkling of eyes, the beating of hearts, the striking of hands, the utter abandon of the hour, were incredible, inconceivable. . . . The tradesman forsook his shop; the farmer his plough; the merchant his counter; the lawyer his office; nay, the minister his desk, to join the general chase. Even the school-master, in his longing to be "abroad" with the rest, laid down his birch.[1]

GALESBURG WAS ONE of a constellation of colonies. Its star burned more brightly and longer than the others, but all of them appeared for a time in the dawnlight of northern Illinois, and shining together presented a portent of reforming religion. The position of these bodies, their individual endowments, and their relations to each other profoundly affected the fortunes of reform movements such as abolitionism. Much of the early history of the Galesburg colony can be comprehended only by an understanding of its connections with these sister communities.

Several of these colonies aspired to found educational institutions. A perpetual motion machine to make colleges was invented sometime in the middle 1830s. It was described, at the prompting of the New York philanthropists, in April, 1836, by George Whipple of Oberlin, formerly a Lane Rebel and student at Oneida Institute. Three or four "brethren" were to

---

[1] Kirkland, *Western Clearings,* pp. 4–5.

furnish money to buy a township of land, presumably at the government price of $1.25 an acre, on which a colony would be settled; lots were then to be sold at $75 to $300, and farm land at four to ten dollars an acre. After five of the thirty-six sections had been given to the college for the campus and for a college farm, there would be a cash return of $185,035. Eighty thousand dollars of this sum would be given to the new college; of the remaining hundred thousand dollars the benevolent New Yorkers would pocket not a dollar, but as soon as the township was sold, they would "purchase another and another, *until the whole western country* was supplied with the means of obtaining a good Christian education." [2]

DAUGHTERS OF OBERLIN AND ONEIDA

Translated into ledger language, this was much like the dream of the good Shipherd, when he had required the colonists of Oberlin to covenant that they would live plainly, would give all surpluses beyond personal and family necessities to spreading the Gospel through Oberlin Institute and otherwise, and would not dispose of their colony lands for personal speculation.[3] It was to Shipherd that Whipple reviewed this grand scheme of the New Yorkers to speculate for the glory of God. "Cannot you or somebody else, go soon to Illinois and make choice of an eligible tract?" [4] Soon afterward Shipherd resigned his pastorate at Oberlin, giving as one reason his interest in establishing another educational institution like Oberlin. Near present-day Lansing, Michigan, he projected a manual labor seminary and platted a city, for which some money was raised; but a very worldly catastrophe, the financial crash of 1837, ruined the scheme. At the same time he and another Oberlin man participated with a colony from the Burned-over District in another educational speculation in northwestern Indiana that was led by one of Finney's zealous converts. When the hard times were finally over, Shipherd led another colony to the area

[2] Appendix: "Colonization," in Williams, *Olivet College,* pp. 135–39.
[3] Fletcher, *History of Oberlin,* I, 88–89, 110, 114.
[4] Williams, *Olivet College,* pp. 135–39.

in Michigan where the first enterprise had collapsed, and with another Oberlin man as his chief helper he began the settlement and laid the foundations of Olivet Institute, later Olivet College. Classes began in December, 1844, four of the nine students being formerly from Oberlin.[5] Amos Dresser, Lane Rebel, onetime student at Oneida Institute, also helped in this educational venture.[6]

The remarkable tendency to institutional reproduction manifest in these activities of Shipherd also produced a colony for Illinois in which the personnel involved again exemplify the close relations of Oberlin with the Oneida locale in New York. The promoters in this case were the four Foote brothers, Horatio, Horace, Hiram, and Lucius, and a brother-in-law of Lucius, Dr. Archibald M. Catlin. Lucius had recently come to northern Ohio from a pastorate in Oneida County, having been commissioned there as a missionary in 1831 by the Central Agency for New York State, which was directed mainly by Oneida County ministers.[7] Hiram, while at Oneida Institute in 1833, had been the first president of the students' anti-slavery society, was one of the Lane Rebels, served a year as anti-slavery agitator with the "Seventy," [8] and was a student at Oberlin along with his sister. Though all the Footes reflected the influence of Finney, this was most evident in the eldest of the brothers, Horatio, who was one of the foremost followers of the great evangelist and who as Finney's assistant and companion in the Oneida meetings was one of the creators of the Great Revival.[9] Dr. Catlin practiced medicine near the border of Oneida and Herkimer counties until the middle thirties, when he migrated to the vicinity of Oberlin.[10] Horace Foote, youngest of the brothers and the only one not to become a minister, remained at the Foote homestead in Otsego

[5] *Ibid.*, pp. 6–22, 140–41.   [6] Fletcher, *History of Oberlin*, I, 202–80.
[7] *Sixth Annual Report of the American Home Missionary Society*, 1832, p. 22.
[8] *Weld Letters*, I, 18, 299, 329, 464.
[9] Cross, *Burned-over District*, pp. 194–95; Finney, *Memoirs*, p. 204.
[10] A biographical sketch of Catlin appears in *Portrait and Biographical Record of Winnebago and Boone Counties, Illinois*, pp. 243–44.

County, New York, until 1837, when he and his mother traveled to Oberlin to join the others for the Illinois venture.[11]

The Foote company proposed to establish in Illinois an educational institution like Oberlin. In 1837 Horace and Horatio went to northern Illinois and selected a promising site at the confluence of the Kishwaukee and Rock rivers, slightly below present Rockford, which was then still a tiny settlement of uncertain future. The tract the Footes wanted was still government land, but they bought a squatter's claim and Horace stayed to build cabins while Horatio returned to Oberlin to bring on the others. The first families arrived the following February and others came later. Apparently the speculation of the settlers was that their townsite might become the county seat; when that advantage fell instead to nearby Rockford in 1839, the boom of the Kishwaukee location was blasted. Only a small settlement came into being. A large building for the proposed school was begun but never completed, and the unused frame for a number of years stood to testify to the unwisdom, the misfortune, or the untimeliness of these educational missionaries and adventurers.[12] Except for Horace, the Foote brothers were soon ministering elsewhere in Illinois and Wisconsin. Individually the brothers made a considerable contribution to the causes of "reform" on the Midwest frontier and their support of the forces of "fanatical" benevolent religion did not go unnoticed.[13] Horatio took his noted revivalistic talents downstate, where already in March, 1839, he became pastor of a more successful educational venture from Oneida County, the colony of Galesburg and Knox College.[14]

[11] *Ibid.*, p. 210. Another member of the company was the Reverend Lewis Sweasy, a native of Oneida County (Kett, *History of Winnebago County, Its Past and Present*, p. 353).

[12] Church, *History of Rockford and Winnebago County, Illinois*, pp. 107–8, 109, 122–23; Kett, *History of Winnebago County, Its Past and Present*, p. 455.

[13] *Western Citizen*, Nov. 9, 1843.

[14] J. J. Miter reports Foote as conducting revival meetings at nearby Knoxville during the last week of February, 1839 (Miter to Charles Hall, May 4, 1839, A.H.M.S. Papers).

THE GALESBURG COLLEGE PLAN

Distance, diversity of environment, and a century of separating traditions have largely obliterated the memory of their common origins, but to the generation of the founders it was known that Oneida Institute, Oberlin Institute, Olivet Institute, and Knox College were alike the result of the "white heat" of the great Finney revival.[15] It was the last of these schools, Knox College, that made the most sensible effort to harness the speculative energies of the middle thirties for a new manual labor school. In 1834 George Washington Gale of Oneida Institute issued his "Circular and Plan." It too began with a pious emphasis on the obligation of Christians to devise and execute liberal plans for spreading the Gospel, especially in the West, and particularly by means of a manual labor school. The plan that Gale set forth was that subscribers provide the funds with which to locate, purchase, and begin the settlement of an entire township. The land should be purchased at the government price of $1.25, and then the subscribers be paid off by receiving land at $5.00 an acre. Though this plan speculated on an immediate 300 percent increase in the value of the land, it was not, aside from any considerations of benevolence, an unreasonable expectation that the creation of a town, the settlement of forty families, and the availability immediately of a good church and good schools, including a college, would create such a rise in land values.[16] Three of the thirty-six sections were to be reserved for the village and college grounds. The profits from village lots were to go to an academy and a female seminary. Even if the remaining 13,120 farm acres were sold at no more than the $5.00 rate, the profit would be $86,400, a handsome sum in those days with which to begin and endow a college.

Gale's plan was at once optimistic and feasible and was put

---

[15] *Semi-Centennial Celebration, First Church of Galesburg,* p. 106.

[16] Five dollars an acre for unimproved prairie land was the price asked in northwestern Peoria County in 1838, after the panic had deflated prices. Peoria County was, however, somewhat more thickly settled (Peoria *Register and Northwestern Gazetteer,* July 14, 1838).

into operation on a somewhat reduced scale. The Galesburg colony withstood the financial stress of the panic and proved to be the most successful of the several colonies planted in Illinois during this period. Fully to appreciate its character and its remarkable role in the Illinois frontier it is necessary to note several other colonies with which it was related and to examine the general exploitation of the colony idea, especially in the Military Tract.

GENESEO COLONY AND ITS LANE REBELS

The colony in Illinois that most nearly paralleled Galesburg in faithfully transplanting the seed of the Great Revival and in cultivating its variety of reforms was Geneseo. It was a direct offshoot of the crop of religious enthusiasm harvested by Finney in the Burned-over District; Finney's sermons were literally part of the baggage of the Geneseo pioneers,[17] and the Finney species of theology a distinguishing aspect of the Geneseo church.[18] Three of the Lane Rebels made this settlement their permanent home, one of them participating in its foundation.

The minister who led this colony was the Reverend Jairus Wilcox of Bergen, New York, who first suggested to his parishioners that they go to Illinois for the sake of Christ, establish a manual labor school, and foster temperance and the principle of anti-slavery.[19] Wilcox had been one of a group of young seminarians at Yale who had dedicated themselves to the religious and educational needs of the West. Although most of the group had fulfilled this covenant by going to Illinois, Wilcox instead had become a minister in western New York.[20] One of his classmates, Flavel Bascom, continued to urge him to

[17] *Proceedings of the Seventy-fifth Anniversary of the First Congregational Church, Geneseo, Illinois, September 10, 11, 12, 13, 1911*, p. 11.

[18] Typed copy of MS, "Records of the First Orthodox Church in Geneseo, Henry County, Illinois," entries Dec. 5, 1843, to June 30, 1844.

[19] Hubbard, "A Colony Settlement, Geneseo, Illinois, 1836–1837," *Journal of the Illinois State Historical Society*, XXIX (1937), 403–31; Roy, *Memorial Addresses*, pp. 2–4.

[20] The Yale Band consisted first of seven (and later of six more) seminarians. Wilcox and Flavel Bascom belonged to the second group (Rammelkamp, *Illinois College*, p. 25).

join them in Illinois,[21] and in the glow of the Great Revival Wilcox was moved to a renewal of his commitment to the farther West.

The Geneseo colony, the name of which accurately suggests the locale in New York whence it came, was organized on March 8, 1836. In May an exploring committee was sent out to locate and to buy land, to fix upon a site for a village, and to lay it out in lots, the sales from which should help establish a manual labor high school.[22] This committee had unexpected help from a Lane Rebel, James M. Allan, in finding suitable land near the northern edge of the Military Tract, in an unsettled area that was still under the jurisdiction of Knox County. Early in the autumn the colonists, in preparation for their departure, organized themselves as a church. Five families set out in September, two more left the following spring, and by the time corn was being planted in 1837 Geneseo was a community of nearly fifty persons.[23]

James M. Allan, who had helped the exploring committee locate their colony tract, was buying land for himself and members of his family.[24] The Allan family had been brought into the orbit of the benevolent system through the influence of Weld, who in 1832, while on his agency for manual labor in education, visited for a week at Huntsville, Alabama, where the elder Allan, a Presbyterian minister, was his host. Though the Reverend Mr. Allan was the owner of fifteen slaves, Weld found him sensitive to the moral arguments against slavery and ready to discuss it fully with his guest.[25] An elder in Allan's church, James G. Birney,[26] was brought into the discus-

---

[21] Kett, *Henry County, Illinois, Its Taxpayers and Voters,* p. 516.

[22] Taylor, "A History of the First Congregational Church, Geneseo, Illinois," *Journal of the Illinois State Historical Society,* XX (1927), 112–27. A manual labor school was approved by the state legislature in March, 1839. Wilcox was very active raising money for it in the East. It opened in 1840 and ceased operations as an independent school in 1858.

[23] *Ibid.,* pp. 114–15; Colby, "Historic Spots in Henry County," *Journal of the Illinois State Historical Society,* XXVIII (1936), 164–87.

[24] Hubbard, "A Colony Settlement," *Journal of the Illinois State Historical Society,* XXIX (1937), 407–8.

[25] William Birney, *James G. Birney and His Times,* pp. 106–8.

[26] Weld quoted in Charles Beecher, ed., *Autobiography of Lyman Beecher,* II, 313.

sion. He was moved at this time to commit himself to a militant position against slavery, and soon gave up a lucrative legal practice and returned to his former home in Danville, Kentucky, to labor for the cause. Another effect of Weld's stay in Huntsville was that two of the Allan sons, William T. and James M., were persuaded to go north to Lane Seminary, which Weld was promoting at that time as the model national manual labor seminary.[27]

The early training of the two Allan sons had inclined them to question the institution of slavery, but at Lane both were converted to abolitionism, which was rather more than the father had hoped for.[28] The winning of the older brother, William, to abolitionism was regarded by Weld as the turning point in the conversion of the student body into an anti-slavery organization. Weld wrote as follows to Lewis Tappan in March, 1834:

The Lord has done great things for us here. Eight months ago there was not a single immediate abolitionist in this seminary. . . . The first change was brought about in some of the first minds of the seminary, and especially in an individual of great sway amongst the students, who was from Alabama; born, bred, and educated in the midst of slavery; his father an owner of slaves, and himself heir to a slave inheritance. After some weeks of inquiry, and struggling with conscience, his noble soul broke loose from its shackles. He is now President of our Anti-Slavery Society.[29]

James also became an officer in the Lane Seminary Anti-Slavery Society, and when the school's trustees suppressed this organization and moved to expel William along with Weld as the arch leaders of the disturbance, both brothers became Lane Rebels.

William remained with the core of the radicals in the Cincinnati vicinity, joined in the migration to Oberlin, and went

[27] Barnes, *Anti-Slavery Impulse,* p. 39; *Birney Letters,* I, xii–xiii.

[28] James M. Allan, "Autobiography," clipping of a newspaper article in the possession of a descendant, Mrs. Susan Bradley of Geneseo, Illinois. The printed clipping states that the MS from which it was copied was in the possession of Mrs. James M. Allan. It is written in the first person. This and other documents used by the author through the courtesy of Mrs. Bradley will be cited hereafter as the Bradley MSS.

[29] Weld to Lewis Tappan, March 18, 1834, *Weld Letters,* I, 132.

on from there to a career as an anti-slavery agitator. James went from Cincinnati to James G. Birney at Danville, Kentucky, to deliver for the Lane Rebels 300 copies of an anti-slavery tract. Birney, the author, had not been able to issue this pamphlet because his printer was threatened with violence.[30] The Lane students procured a press, printed the article, and mailed it to ministers of all denominations and to the principal laymen in the Ohio valley.[31] At Danville, James entered Centre College along with another Lane Rebel,[32] in October, 1834; after five weeks there he wrote to his mother that though the college was not as religious in its outlook as the seminary, yet the "flame" kindled in him at Cincinnati for God's "cause" was still alive.[33]

In the summer of 1835 James went home to Alabama and discovered that his former neighbors now snubbed him as an alien.[34] They said that William was afraid to come home and that his throat would be cut if he did. His father felt that the Lane Rebels were actuated by "rank pride" and "reckless ambition," and was very pained over the particular notoriety that the older brother had acquired.[35] James's stay at Huntsville was not very agreeable,[36] and he asked his father to give him a hundred dollars with which to go to Illinois to buy some of the rich prairie land of which he had heard. He set out for Illinois in October of 1835 and spent the following winter at Carrolton, Illinois, with an aunt and her husband, the Reverend Hugh Barr, who had earlier that same year migrated from Tennessee because of aversion to slavery.[37] The following

---

[30] Benjamin P. Thomas, *Theodore Weld*, p. 83.

[31] Weld to Birney, Oct. 6, 1834, *Birney Letters*, I, 136–37.

[32] Weld to Birney, Dec. 11, 1834, and Jan. 23, 1835, *ibid.*, I, 155, 170–73.

[33] James M. Allan to Mrs. David Allan, Nov. 20, 1834, Bradley MSS.

[34] Allan, "Autobiography," Bradley MSS.

[35] William T. Allan to Weld, Dec. 15, 1834; Allan to Weld, Jan. 8, 1835, *Weld Letters*, I, 182, 190.

[36] Allan, "Autobiography," Bradley MSS.

[37] Evidence for the identification of the Barrs is that Allan in his "Autobiography" speaks of Uncle and Aunt Barr at Carrolton. He also refers to this aunt as Aunt Catherine. James's father had married a Nancy Hodge of Sumner, Tennessee. Hugh Barr had been reared in Sumner, Tennessee, and married Catherine Hodge, presumably a sister of Nancy Hodge and the aunt of James Allan. Hugh Barr came to Morgan County, Illinois, early in 1835 and settled at

spring James was visited here by his father and a brother-in-law who gave him $700 to $800 to invest in land. It was while locating the land for this purchase that he met the committee of the Geneseo colony and became involved in their venture.[38]

Thus it happened that a Lane Rebel joined forces with a community from the Burned-over District in New York and became a leader among pioneers on the frontier of Illinois. Immediately after his land purchases were complete, Allan went to the state capital at Vandalia to have Henry County separated from the jurisdiction of Knox County, and when the new county was organized he served as clerk in the first election and was chosen for the position of county clerk.[39] In addition to many such civic roles, he was made president of the Henry County Temperance Society on Independence Day, 1838.[40] He did not, however, become a leader among the abolitionists in Illinois. Though he remained loyal to the antislavery principles he had affirmed at Lane, he had by 1836 become doubtful about the measures of abolitionists in dealing with slaveholders, even those who like his own parents were sensitive to the moral issues involved.[41]

A much more militant abolitionist role was played by the older brother William. After the Lane rebellion he and others continued their teaching among the Negroes of Cincinnati; [42] he was one of the leaders who organized an impromptu seminary in a suburb and as a member of its "faculty" helped his fellow Rebels carry on the study of theology and biblical

Carrolton as Presbyterian minister in Nov., 1835 (Norton, *History of the Presbyterian Church in Illinois,* I, 219–20).

[38] Allan, "Autobiography," Bradley MSS.

[39] Colby, "Historic Spots in Henry County," *Journal of the Illinois State Historical Society,* XXVIII (1936), 179–87.

[40] Peoria *Register and Northwestern Gazetteer,* Oct. 20, 1838. See this same paper, July 21, 1838, for an article by Allan on the quality of land in Henry County. Allan was the first postmaster of Geneseo, a major of militia, and a speculator for the site of the county seat.

[41] Allan, "Autobiography," Bradley MSS; Wm. T. Allan to Weld, Aug. 9, 1836, *Weld Letters,* I, 325. The father of the Allan brothers attempted to free his slaves in his will, but since that was forbidden by Alabama law, they were brought to Illinois and set free. One of them came to Geneseo and lived until his death with James.

[42] S. Wells to Weld, Dec. 15, 1835, *Weld Letters,* I, 178.

literature.[43] He joined the migration to Oberlin, realizing that so far as his native South was concerned he had crossed "the Rubicon" by going to an institution of such "concentrated" abolitionism as that headed by "that arch-heretic Finney." [44] During the autumn of 1835 he and several classmates received intensive tutelage from Weld for service as agents of the American Anti-Slavery Society, and from December to May he and his colleagues labored to convert Ohio to abolitionism.[45]

After returning to Oberlin to complete their theological training, Allan and his friends were torn between Professor Finney's urging that they "evangelize" as preachers and Weld's pleading that they labor as agents at "abolitionizing." [46] Allan decided to do the latter when he learned that a mob in Cincinnati had destroyed the *Philanthropist* press. Writing for himself and several of his classmates, Allan declared to Weld:

My mind has settled down upon the conclusion that it is *my* duty to plead *directly* the cause of the poor and needy. . . . My brethren are in bonds, not only the blacks, but the abolitionists. Dangers are thickening about them and troubles are coming like a whirlwind. I have helped to raise the storm. Shall I now avoid its fury by going into a less dangerous field? God forbid. No, my brother, come life, come death, our stand must be maintained. Onward, then, ye friends of man: Whither ye go, I will go and *where ye die will I die,* and *there* will I be buried.[47]

After Commencement in September, Allan served in the "Seventy," recruits for which he helped to screen in Oberlin.[48] He lectured in Ohio, New York City, western New York, and in Michigan.[49] Often he was likely to be treated as he was at Mt. Gilead, Ohio, where a mob tried to break up the meeting in the Presbyterian church with squibs of powder and by playing musical instruments; the ruffians tossed eggshells filled

[43] Weed to Weld, Jan. 8, 1835, *ibid.,* I, 189.

[44] William T. Allan to Weld, Jan. 8, 1835, *ibid.,* I, 189–90.

[45] Weld to Birney, Dec. 19, 1835, *ibid.,* I, 283–86; Weld to Birney, Jan. 5, 1836, *Birney Letters,* I, 292–93.

[46] Streeter to Weld, July 20, 1836, *Weld Letters,* I, 315–17.

[47] Allan to Weld, Aug. 9, 1836, *ibid.,* I, 323–25.

[48] *Ibid.;* Streeter to Weld, Aug. 9, 1836, *ibid.,* I, 328–29; James A. Thome to Weld, Sept. 9, 1836, *ibid.,* I, 339–42.

[49] Fletcher, *History of Oberlin,* I, 243.

with tar as he walked away after the lecture and threw an "earthern jar with filth" against the door of the house where they thought Allan was staying overnight.[50] It is understandable that when he returned in June of 1837 for a class reunion,[51] he found Oberlin a "haven of rest for a little season" after "the tossings and tumults and distractions" of his anti-slavery agency.[52]

William Allan dreamed for a while of going to Tibet as a foreign missionary, but this was changed to a plan for a team of three missionaries to go beyond the Rocky Mountains to the Indians of the Columbia Valley. His colleagues were Theodore Clark, a cousin of Weld's,[53] and Charles Stewart Renshaw, an "Oneida," a Lane Rebel, a theological student at Oberlin, and a member of the "Seventy" who was a particularly close friend of Allan's. These zealots intended to travel on their own, with the backing of no missionary agency, expecting to maintain themselves, though hoping that if need be "friends of the Redeemer" would help them. The three men got together with Weld in New York City, where on April 5, 1838, Renshaw was married to a graduate of the Ladies' Course at Oberlin. Next day the three would-be missionaries and the new bride set out for the Far West, traveling as fast as possible in order to get to Missouri before the spring caravan of fur traders got away. Allan and his companions went as far as the Platte River but did not catch up with the "mountain men," and since no other guides were available the scheme had to be given up.[54]

Allan and Renshaw then came back as far as Illinois, where in June the latter became pastor of the Congregational church in Quincy and remained until sometime in the summer of 1839.[55] Allan went to his relatives, the family of the Reverend

[50] Barton, *Joseph Edwin Roy*, pp. 23–24.
[51] H. Lyman to Weld, June 3, 1837, *Weld Letters*, I, 392–94.
[52] Allan to Weld, June 3, 1837, *ibid.*, I, 394–95.   [53] *Ibid.*, I, 26, note.
[54] Weld to Thome, April 5, 1838, *ibid.*, I, 620–22; Renshaw and Weld to Gerrit Smith, Aug. 6, 1839, *ibid.*, I, 780–81; Asbury, *Reminiscences of Quincy*, p. 121; Emery, ed., *A Memorial*, p. 29.
[55] Weld, ed., *American Slavery as It Is*, pp. 41, 70; Renshaw and Weld to Smith, Aug. 6, 1839, *Weld Letters*, I, 780–81.

Hugh Barr at Carrolton, Illinois.[56] By October, 1838, he was living in the next county, Macoupin, and was so far involved in the anti-slavery affairs of the state as to attend the first anniversary of the Illinois Anti-Slavery Society, in Fulton County, where he renewed his friendship not only with Renshaw but also with those other "Oneidas," Lane Rebels, and apostles of the "Seventy," John J. Miter and Hiram Foote.[57] Here he also encountered the leading abolitionists from west-central Illinois —from Galesbury, Quincy, Princeton, and Putnam County, who mainly conducted the affairs of the Illinois society for the next few years.

During the winter of 1838–39, William T. Allan made a substantial contribution to what was probably the most powerful anti-slavery book published before *Uncle Tom's Cabin.* This was a publication of the American Anti-Slavery Society edited by Weld under the title *American Slavery as It Is: Testimony of a Thousand Witnesses.* For this compilation Allan sent stories of cruelty to slaves, some of which he reported from his own knowledge, some of which had been related to him by his brother James, and some of which he learned from the family and friends of his aunt and uncle at Carrolton.[58] In the spring of 1839, William Allan was one of the greatly reduced number of agents appointed by the national anti-slavery society,[59] and in 1840 he was appointed general agent and lecturer for the Illinois Anti-Slavery Society, a position that he held until that organization petered out in 1845. His labors for that society will be described later. He resided during these years first in Sangamon County, at Chatham [60] and Springfield,[61] and later in Peoria. As early as 1841 his father had written from Alabama suggesting that William settle on one of the

[56] Weld, ed., *American Slavery as It Is,* p. 46.

[57] "Minutes of the Illinois Anti-Slavery Society," Oct. 1, 1838, MSS, Chicago Historical Society.

[58] Weld, ed., *American Slavery as It Is,* pp. 45–47, 61, 180.

[59] H. B. Stanton to Birney, June 10, 1839, *Birney Letters,* I, 489–91.

[60] Thome to Weld, June 20, 1840, *Weld Letters,* I, 843–45.

[61] Mrs. William T. Allan was addressed at Springfield by her sister Charlotte Bailey on Sept. 24, 1840 (Bradley MSS).

former's quarter sections near Geneseo,[62] and it was at that place, after more than a decade of wandering as a student, abolitionist agitator, and preacher, that William T. Allan settled down in 1844.[63]

The Lane Rebels possessed an extraordinary group feeling that derived from common educational experiences, from friendships that polarized with particular intensity toward Weld, and from those adventures as abolitionist agitators that gave them the *esprit de corps* of veterans of a dangerous campaign. Likely it was this feeling that explains the settlement of a third Lane Rebel at Geneseo. John Tappan Pierce was a nephew of the famous Tappan brothers of New York City whose wealth and leadership did so much to launch and to propel the ark of benevolence with its cargo of Lane and of Oberlin and of anti-slavery organizations. Pierce was born in a Massachusetts manse, graduated from Harvard, started in theology at Princeton, and would perhaps have gone on to a conventional ministerial career had he not gone to Lane in 1833. Though he held out longer than most against the infectious radicalism of his schoolmates, he was nevertheless converted by Weld to the doctrine of immediate emancipation, became an officer in the Lane anti-slavery society,[64] joined the rebellion against the seminary's authorities, exulted to Weld that "we are a reckless set and will take no *wholesome advice,* even from our best friends," [65] and migrated to Oberlin, from which he was graduated in the fall of 1836 in the same class as William T. Allan. He was one of the "Seventy," and like

[62] Bradley MSS.

[63] Chapman, *Portrait and Biographical Album of Henry County,* pp. 326–27. He must have made direct contact with Geneseo at least by the fall of 1841 because he reported collections there for the Illinois Anti-Slavery Society (*Western Citizen,* Sept., 1841). Very likely he visited there already in the summer of 1840, for he attended the meeting of the Illinois Anti-Slavery Society at Princeton in the next county. In December of 1844 he was invited to preach during the absence of the original pastor of the Geneseo colony, Jairus Willcox, who went to Chicago to take care of the Seaman's Bethel ("Minutes of the First Orthodox Church in Geneseo," MS; Roy, *Memorial Addresses,* p. 11).

[64] *Weld Letters,* I, 155, note.

[65] John T. Pierce to Weld, Dec. 15, 1834, *ibid.,* I, 183–84.

most of the others in that corps of abolitionist workers he still had to find a permanent career when the year of their great crusade was over. From 1839 to 1842 he taught and conducted schools in Jacksonville and Griggsville, Illinois, and thereafter in Henderson, Kentucky, and Arcadia, Missouri. In the last state he is reputed to have founded the first Congregational church. Agitation of the slavery question led to his banishment from Missouri in 1850, when he joined his former schoolmates at Geneseo and made it his permanent home.[66]

The Geneseo and Galesburg colonies paralleled each other almost exactly in their religious and educational objectives as well as in the time and place of settlement, and they had very close relations during the pioneer years. During the first year of settlement Knoxville was the county seat of both villages, and during the first winter the Geneseo colonists went south to buy corn among the Hoosiers at Henderson Grove,[67] where the Galesburg settlers lived at that time in a temporary "Log City" while their permanent frame houses were being built out on the prairie. A physician who had been one of the sub-scribers and founders of Galesburg[68] very shortly became the physician in Geneseo instead,[69] and the churches of both colonies shared the Geneseo music master, who directed choirs and conducted singing schools in both places and eventually moved to Galesburg.[70] His Geneseo and Galesburg choirs supplied the music for the annual meeting of the Illinois Anti-Slavery Society in 1841.[71]

The Lane Rebels associated with Galesburg were naturally

[66] Biographies of John T. Pierce may be found in an obituary in the Bradley MSS and in Chapman, *Portrait and Biographical Album of Henry County.* Pierce's Jacksonville school was associated with, though not a part of, Illinois College.

[67] Roy, *Memorial Addresses,* p. 7.

[68] Bailey, *Knox College,* p. 80. The earliest business records of the college demonstrate the initial connection of Dr. Enos Pomroy with the Galesburg colony. He is listed among the Galesburg men signing the call for the anti-slavery convention that met in Alton in October, 1837.

[69] Taylor, "A History of the First Congregational Church, Geneseo, Illinois," *Journal of the Illinois State Historical Society,* XX (1927), 112–27.

[70] *Semi-Centennial Celebration, First Church of Galesburg,* pp. 73, 79.

[71] "Minutes of the Illinois Anti-Slavery Society," June 9–11, 1841, MSS, Chicago Historical Society.

interested in the town of their classmates at Geneseo. One of these, John J. Miter, at the request of the Knox Presbytery, visited and kept in close touch with the settlement and reported to the American Home Missionary Society in 1839 that though they were poor the colonists were thoroughly imbued with the great principles of "practical goodness," which in the religious language of that day meant that they supported the benevolent, reforming causes.[72] When the Knox Presbytery was organized at Galesburg in November, 1838, Jairus Wilcox and the Geneseo church participated, and even after that church had been transferred to the Galena Presbytery, Jason Chapin, principal of the Geneseo Academy, remained in the Knox Presbytery.[73] Lucius Parker, another Lane Rebel belonging to the larger, richer, and more aggressive Galesburg colony, became a trustee of the Geneseo Academy.[74]

THE LYNDON AND LISBON COLONIES

Another colony closely associated both with Galesburg and, in the early years, with Geneseo was Lyndon, settled just north of Henry County, on the north bank of the Rock River. The original nucleus of Lyndon comprised three families that came together from New York state in 1835. To these were added thirty-seven other men by 1839, almost all with families, who came mostly from New York but also from Massachusetts, Connecticut, Pennsylvania, and Ohio. The largest single ingredient in the population of the early settlement came, significantly, from Oneida County, New York.[75] One of these "Oneidas" was Brainerd Orton, who had been steward of Oneida Institute while Gale was head of that school and who

[72] John J. Miter to Charles Hall, Feb. 4, 1839, A.H.M.S. Papers, Hammond Library, Chicago Theological Seminary. See also Sweet, ed., *The Congregationalists*, p. 284, note.
[73] "Records of the Presbytery of Knox," (MSS, Knox College Library), p. 3; [New School] *Minutes of the General Assembly of the Presbyterian Church, 1843*, pp. 61, 262; *ibid.*, 1846, pp. 113–14.
[74] *Rights of Congregationalists in Knox College*, p. 56.
[75] Bent, *History of Whiteside County, Illinois*, pp. 265–99; Way, *Rock River Valley*, p. 653. The heterogeneity of its early settlers might argue against its being regarded as a colony; that it was so regarded by contemporaries is evident from Sweet, ed., *The Congregationalists*, p. 282, note.

was briefly associated with the Galesburg colony before he settled in Lyndon.[76] Lyndon soon sprouted with revival and reform, as would be expected from a community with roots in the New York religious enthusiasms,[77] and bloomed with temperance and anti-slavery societies, with an academy and a Congregational church.[78] "The power of God came down and the prairies seemed to bud and blossom as the rose," according to President Jonathan Blanchard of Knox College, who helped conduct a religious revival in 1849 at Lyndon, where his brother, Reverend William Blanchard, had become the pastor in 1846.[79]

The mutual interests and similar origins of the Lyndon and Galesburg colonies are reflected in the fact that during the period before the Civil War the contingent of students at Knox College from Lyndon was larger than from any other town except Galesburg itself. A study of the geographical distribution of students coming to all the departments of Knox College (college, preparatory school, and academy) shows that Whiteside County, in which Lyndon is located, despite its greater distance from Galesburg, was often more within the educational sphere of the Galesburg colony than counties closer or even immediately adjacent to Knox County.

Even more striking in such a geographical study is the very large number of students coming to the academy, preparatory department, and collegiate classes of Knox College from Kendall County, which, though near Lake Michigan, sent more students downstate to Galesburg than any other county north

[76] With Matthew Chambers of the Galesburg colony he was a member of a church committee that corresponded with Charles Hall, April 30, 1838, from Knoxville (A.H.M.S. Papers). He is also listed next to Gale in the list of those from Galesburg who signed the call for the Alton convention that organized the Illinois Anti-Slavery Society, Oct., 1837. Gale refers to him as the steward of Oneida Institute in his autobiography.

[77] Way, *Rock River Valley*, p. 653.

[78] Barton, *Joseph Edwin Roy*, pp. 23–24; Roy, *Memorial of the One Hundredth Birthday of John Roy*, pp. 32–33. The academy languished, but the church almost immediately had a pastor, who already in 1839 anticipated that he would need no further subsidy from the A.H.M.S. (*Thirteenth Annual Report of the American Home Missionary Society*, 1839, p. 28.).

[79] Jonathan Blanchard to Samuel Williston, Galena, Illinois, Feb. 22, 1849 (transcript of Williston letters received from G. R. Carpenter of New York City).

of Galesburg. In Kendall County this interest in Knox College was particularly strong in the town of Lisbon. This community, significantly, was settled by a colony from Oneida County, New York,[80] particularly from the town of Vernon.[81] A leader in this colony was the Reverend Calvin Bushnell, whom Gale refers to in his autobiography as a "fellow immigrant to Illinois." [82] Gale, on one occasion, had assisted Bushnell for two weeks in conducting a revival in Vernon, and that community had followed the lead of its pastor in contributing money and building materials to help Gale establish Oneida Institute in Whitesboro, New York.[83] In 1840 the Lisbon colony was joined by the professor of classics from Oneida Institute, Innes Grant, but he departed in 1842 to rejoin his former associates at Galesburg, where he became professor of ancient languages in Knox College.[84] The Lisbon colony settled on land bought in 1835 and 1836 in Lisbon and Big Grove townships. Since 1834 there had been a Congregational church in Big Grove Township and Bushnell became the pastor of this congregation, which was the mother church for Congregationalism in Ottawa, Aurora, Newark, and Lisbon, all of which took a lead in the resurgence of Congregationalism and were identified with the reform "causes" of the day. This concern with reform was especially a characteristic of the Lisbon church that was founded in 1838.[85]

[80] Hicks, *History of Kendall County, Illinois*, pp. 140–41, 146, 164–65, 184–86. From the names of early settlers and church members and their land entries, it has been possible to reconstruct the original group of settlers and the locale of their settlement; Bateman and Selby, eds., *Kendall County*, I, 657, 664–706.

[81] Jones, *Annals and Recollections of Oneida County*, pp. 645–46.

[82] G. W. Gale, "Autobiography," p. 92.

[83] *Second Report of the Trustees of Oneida Institute of Science and Industry, Whitesboro, March 20, 1830.*

[84] Clipping Scrapbook, Galesburg Public Library.

[85] Bateman and Selby, eds., *Kendall County*, pp. 751–826, 931–32; Sweet, ed., *The Congregationalists*, pp. 165, 175. No particular educational project other than a local school was associated with the Lisbon colony, but in the fifties, when Fowler's Institute was established in Big Grove Township at Newark, the leadership for it came from Knox College (Bateman and Selby, eds., *Kendall County*, p. 815).

COLONIES ASSOCIATED WITH NAHUM GOULD

Another minister from the Burned-over District of New York who was associated with town planning on the Illinois frontier was the Reverend Nahum Gould. Following his seminary training, Gould had gone from New England to Oneida County, when it was still the focus of the Great Revival, and was sent by the Utica domestic missionary society to the next county south, Chenango, where in 1827 he became a fully ordained minister of Congregational and Presbyterian churches. During the next seven years his churches were warmed by many revivals, some of them fired directly by Jedediah Burchard.[86] In May of 1834 Gould was commissioned as missionary to Illinois by the American Home Missionary Society with the explanation that "a colony have chosen him for their pastor and have emigrated to Illinois." [87]

In identifying this colony the historian is confused by the circumstance that within three years Gould was involved not with one but with three groups that projected new towns and churches—the Hampshire colony, the settlement of Granville, and the Rockwell colony. For Gould stationed himself in an area of Illinois which at that time was a veritable crossroads both for settlers and for missionaries. His first location was made on the east side of the Illinois River, near the northern border of Putnam County, and across the river from present-day Bureau County.[88] Here, at Bailey's Grove (or Bailey's Point), Gould lived for a time with his brother-in-law, Deacon John Leonard,[89] who was a member of the Hampshire colony [90] that had been formed at Northampton, Massachusetts,

---

[86] Gould, "Diary," MSS, Hammond Library, Chicago Theological Seminary, pp. 1–27.

[87] *Eighth Annual Report of the American Home Missionary Society*, 1834, p. 34.

[88] Bureau County was set off from Putnam County in 1837, with Princeton as county seat. Marshall County was set off from the southern part of Putnam County in 1839.

[89] Gould, "Diary," p. 45; Elmer Baldwin, *LaSalle County*, p. 377.

[90] Elmer Baldwin, *LaSalle County*, pp. 291–92, 374.

in 1831. This colony had selected lands across the river in Bureau County, but the Black Hawk Indian troubles frightened settlers from that locale and the colonists remained east of the river at Bailey's Grove until a treaty with the Indians had been concluded.[91] Most of these colonists eventually settled in Bureau County, but Leonard remained in LaSalle County until 1849 when he and his family moved to Galesburg.[92]

Shortly after Gould's arrival at Bailey's Grove he received a request to preach from a church at Union Grove in Putnam County; his commission from the American Home Missionary Society for the next three years encompassed the new charge. Because of the importance of the Putnam County settlements in the anti-slavery movement, Gould's association with the Union Grove congregation is particularly significant. As he found it in the summer of 1834, its members were mainly of Southern origin, with only a few New Englanders.[93] Many of the former comprised an "Old School" party in the church that was fearful of the heterodoxy inherent in benevolent activities and in union with Congregationalists, and that was opposed to the "excitements" of revivals. Despite their protests Gould initiated a "protracted meeting," which led into a successful religious revival. Gould also promoted benevolent enterprises such as had come to be invariably associated with evangelistic religion in the Burned-over District. Among the members of this church Gould found several, including some of the Southerners, who were already very radical on the anti-slavery question, more so than Gould himself up to that time; Gould was soon enrolled with them in abolitionist ranks. Before the first year of his pastorate at Union Grove had run out, Gould's aggressive leadership on evangelistic, New School principles brought about a division of the congregation into two

[91] Matson, *Reminiscences of Bureau County, Illinois*, pp. 261–64.

[92] Elmer Baldwin, *LaSalle County*, pp. 291–92; Chapman, *History of Knox County*, pp. 688–89.

[93] Gould, "Diary"; American Home Missionary Society: *Ninth Annual Report*, p. 27; *Tenth Annual Report*, p. 30; *Eleventh Annual Report*, p. 27.

churches, an Old School and a New School, and in the latter Gould was formally installed as pastor.[94]

Soon after arriving in Illinois and while serving the Union Grove church, Gould started the town of Granville in Putnam County. The town was surveyed in April, 1836, and during that same spring ground was broken for a college which was central in the plans of the new community.[95] The village was later marked by its support of radical reform measures. According to a tradition that existed within the lifetime of the founders of Granville, George W. Gale came to Granville on a "prospecting tour," saw in the site the very resources of prairie, timber, and soil that he desired for his college-colony, and suggested to Gould that the two educational enterprises be combined. Gould, according to the story, rejected the proposal, and Gale went on to establish his college successfully in the Military Tract.[96] This account is in error in stating that Gale himself was on the spot in Granville at the time alleged, but the proposition to merge the two educational schemes is entirely plausible and fits in with what is known about explorations for the Galesburg site. Gould's ministry in New York, as noted above, lay within the Oneida sphere of influence; it is extremely likely that Gould and Gale were acquainted and certain that Gould would be familiar with Gale's educational experiment at Oneida Institute. Both the first and the second exploring committees of the Galesburg colony made their most extended investigations in the general vicinity of Granville, and the second committee specifically expressed disappointment

---

[94] Reports of the Union Grove church at this time may be found in the Gould diary and in letters of Gould to A. Peters, Sept. 16 and Dec. 5, 1834, and June 10, 1835 (A.H.M.S. Papers); also in Flavel Bascom, "Autobiography," in Sweet, ed., *The Congregationalists*, pp. 244–48, 268–69.

[95] Ellsworth, *Records of the Olden Time*, pp. 277, 280–81, 284–85; Ford, *History of Putnam and Marshall Counties*, pp. 91–93. The "college" became the Granville Academy, which was set in operation in December, 1837, and lasted till 1859. Its first teacher was Otis Fisher, its second a sister of Owen Lovejoy. In 1842 Fisher left to become superintendent of the short-lived "Judson College" that was founded on a site between Magnolia and Granville at the border between LaSalle and Putnam counties, where a promoter expected to establish the Yankee town of Mt. Palatine (Ellsworth, *Records of the Olden Time*, p. 259).

[96] Ellsworth, *Records of the Olden Time*, p. 385; Burt, *Past and Present of Marshall and Putnam Counties, Illinois*, pp. 95–96.

that suitable tracts in that area had already been taken up.[97] It is not unlikely that at some stage in the rather protracted search for the site of Galesburg, a merger with Gould's enterprise may have been suggested.

The land fever must really have infected Gould, for instead of settling down in Granville, he soon committed himself to the chief promoter or agent of the Rockwell colony, who promised $250 toward his support and a town lot if Gould would become pastor of that colony.[98] The agent and Gould were living on the new site by the fall of 1837 and were joined by a colony from Norwich, Connecticut, in 1838.[99] The settlement was badly stricken with sickness and the survivers scattered; the town never recovered, partly, no doubt, because the terminal site of the Illinois-Michigan Canal was placed at La-Salle, at which point the chief town development in that immediate locale occurred.[100]

The Hampshire colony, with a fragment of which Gould was associated on his arrival in Illinois, had meanwhile started the town of Princeton, which became the seat of the new county of Bureau on the west side of the Illinois River. During the delay in occupying their lands the original company had scattered and the church that they had organized back East with eighteen members reorganized in Illinois with only six communicants. Though the colony as such did not have the success its planners had anticipated, it did become the nucleus of a considerable "Yankee" community. By 1836 an academy

[97] Report on Knox College, 1861, pp. 11–14.

[98] Gould to Milton Badger, Sept. 10, 1837 (A.H.M.S. Papers). Gould reported to the A.H.M.S. that it was a very "respectable company" which put a clause into the title to town lots forbidding traffic in "ardent spirits."

[99] It was a town of eight houses in the summer of 1838 (Peoria Register and Northwestern Gazetteer, July 21, 1838).

[100] Elmer Baldwin, LaSalle County, p. 375. Gould was later pastor at Troy Grove when Prudence Crandall Philio founded an academy there for young women. Prudence Crandall created a stir in Canterbury, Connecticut, during the early thirties by accepting a Negro student in her girls' school. In retort to criticism she opened a fine arts school in Connecticut for Negro girls who came from large cities in the East. Her action was endorsed by Samuel J. May, William L. Garrison, and Arthur Tappan, who financed her in the long and bitter litigation resulting from her action (Tisler, "Prudence Crandall, Abolitionist," Journal of the Illinois State Historical Society, XXXIII [1940], 203–6).

was operating in Princeton with several of the pioneer Presbyterian and Congregational ministers of the Illinois frontier on
its board of trustees.[101] This school did not, however, become
more than locally significant, and a considerable number of
Bureau County youths went to the preparatory departments of
Knox College. Princeton ranked after Lyndon and Lisbon
colonies as a focal point from which college students went to
Galesburg.

COLONIZATION AS A MODE OF SETTLEMENT
AND AS A MEANS OF SOCIAL REFORM

The considerable number of colonies already discussed does
not nearly exhaust the instances that could be cited as examples
of this kind of settlement on the Illinois frontier during the
1830s. They appeared especially in the area between the Illinois
and Mississippi rivers and a particular concentration of them
occurred in Henry County, where in addition to Geneseo
four other "Yankee" colonies were projected between the
years 1835 and 1837. Two of these were purely speculative
enterprises, and though both of them induced five to ten
families to settle on their lands, no substantial community
began and they soon lost their original identity.[102] The two
other colonies, which were more successful, presented religious
and educational purposes and proposed to reserve land which
as it was sold was to support a manual labor school.[103] These

[101] Alton *Observer*, Sept. 29, 1836.

[102] The New York colony was organized in 1835–36 in New York City by a
land prospector to settle Morristown. Only about one fifth of the original
members of the association came west in 1836 and 1837 and they remained scattered over ten miles of prairie. The La Grange colony followed the pattern of
the New York colony. There is no evidence of religious or educational motives
in the migration. A seminary was planned, but like a proposed sugar beet company, never materialized. Twenty thousand acres were involved in the former
and 18,000 acres in the latter project, which charged its colonists twice what
they could have gotten land for elsewhere. Kett, *Henry County, Illinois, Its
Taxpayers and Voters*, p. 136; Colby, "Historic Spots in Henry County," *Journal
of the Illinois State Historical Society*, XXVIII (1936), 171–72.

[103] Alton *Observer*, March 30, 1837, quoting a communication from the *Connecticut Observer*; Kett, *Henry County, Illinois, Its Taxpayers and Voters*, pp.
116–17.

colonies were Andover and Wethersfield, both of which were due primarily to the promotion of a Presbyterian clergyman, the Reverend Ithmar Pillsbury, who had been a missionary to seamen in New York City and later a preacher in several churches in the East.[104] In 1834 he came to Illinois and observed the quality of the land available in the northern end of the Military Tract; [105] upon his return to the East he organized the New York Association, which entered a claim to a tract of more than 14,000 acres. During that same summer the New York Association actually began the settlement of Andover, but its development was retarded because the land was held up at too high prices; the college once talked about was never founded, and instead of worshiping in a fine church, the Presbyterians for twenty years continued generally to meet in Pillsbury's house.[106]

In the autumn of 1835, when Pillsbury returned from the location of and the purchase of land for Andover, he became involved with still another colonial enterprise to promote free education and religion in the Mississippi Valley. This project developed into the Connecticut Association, formed at a meeting in the Congregational church in Wethersfield, Connecticut. It received the backing of thirteen clergymen, other than Pillsbury, and interested stockholders from Maine to New York, some wealthy, others prominent in religious affairs. Again, early in 1836, Pillsbury went back to Henry County with a committee to buy land and to lay out the town of Wethersfield, Illinois. Settlement began in 1837, but of the sixty members of the association in the East only four came personally to assist in starting a town. It fell far short of being the instrument for

[104] A biographical portrait of his son Ira begins with a sketch of the father in Perry, *Knox County*, II, 520. *Minutes of the General Assembly of the Presbyterian Church, 1835*, p. 462.

[105] Colby, "Historic Spots in Henry County," *Journal of the Illinois State Historical Society*, XXVIII (1936), 167.

[106] Kett, *Henry County, Illinois, Its Taxpayers and Voters*, pp. 524–27. At the urging of the New York Association four Swedish families settled here in 1847 and became the vanguard of a migration that made Andover more and more a Swedish settlement.

saving the West that its potent religious sponsorship had augured.[107]

These Henry County ventures further exemplify the mingling of religious and educational purposes with worldy speculative motives that characterized so many of the towns projected at this time. R. Carlyle Buley, in his monumental study of the Old Northwest, declares that "the scramble for land which reached its height in 1836–37 was probably not again duplicated in our history, except for mining rushes, until the Florida boom of the 1920's." [108] "Speculative mania of 1836–37" is the phrase that recurs frequently in the sentences of a reminiscing old settler.[109]

By 1833 the frontier, which until this time had been moving up the state of Illinois from the South, had passed beyond Springfield and Jacksonville in the middle latitudes of the state. Here was a kind of cultural borderland where the pioneers from Kentucky, Tennessee, southern Indiana, Missouri, and southern Illinois met the new migration of settlers from New England and the Middle States. Hitherto, the Southerners or "Hoosiers," as they were often called, had claimed Illinois mainly for themselves, but their proprietorship was now challenged by the "Yankees." In the counties along the middle stretch of the Illinois River, the Hoosiers still clung mainly to the timbered lands found along the streams or in an occasional "grove," but the Yankees and New Yorkers edged out onto the small prairies and then settled upon the larger grasslands. The inland counties of the Military Tract, which had been only very thinly settled up to 1830,[110] now filled rapidly.

The mingling of the so-called Hoosier and Yankee settlers was accompanied with appreciable irritation. While the Yankee was often part farmer and part townsman in his heritage, the Hoosier was frequently half-farmer, half-hunter in his habits;

[107] *Ibid.*, pp. 119, 137–41, 517.   [108] Buley, *The Old Northwest*, II, 54.
[109] Ford, *History of Putnam and Marshall Counties*, p. 88. Statistical description of the land speculation in the Military Tract may be found in Carlson, *The Illinois Military Tract*, pp. 52–58.
[110] Buley, *The Old Northwest*, II, 54, 80, 107–8.

the one was more schooled in the formal learning and mechanical techniques of the older seaboard communities from which he was at most one generation removed; the other was better versed in the lore of pioneering in the timber during several moves from the mountain valleys, from the Cumberland Gap, from western Pennsylvania or Tennessee or Kentucky, from southern Illinois or southern Indiana. That the contrasts in culture were often trivial made them no less distinguishable: differences of dress and domestic economy, peculiarities of speech, odd manners. Though both might share a Calvinist theology, the Yankee was less likely a Baptist and more often a Presbyterian, and the Hoosier likely to lack, to disdain, and even to dislike the formal education of the Yankee seminary graduate. Stereotypes readily caricatured the Yankee as a tight-fisted outlander, greedy, stingy, snobbish, sober, aggressive, and the Hoosier as an openhanded, shiftless, ignorant, pleasure-seeking, backwoods ne'er-do-well.

Among the Yankee traits that provoked criticism was the greater frequency with which the Yankees migrated collectively in groups rather than separately as families or individuals. The older population in Illinois suspected that their motive for group migration was to form exclusive settlements that would retain peculiar "Yankee notions" rather than to acquire the tastes and habits of the people among whom they settled. Egotistical preservation of their distinctions as Yankees would keep them from learning what pioneers needed to learn in the new country; instead they would, rather arrogantly, want to reform the mode of life of their neighbors.[111]

The author of this study has discovered twenty-eight so-called colonies from the Eastern states that settled the Illinois frontier between 1830 and 1838.[112] Eighteen of these were under way from 1835 to 1837. In ten instances available data indicate that most of the colonists came from New York; in eight cases apparently they came from one of the New England States. One colony was from Ohio, one from Maryland, one from New

[111] *Ibid.*, II, 104–7.   [112] See Appendix.

Jersey. In six cases, including some cited above, the advertising and the selling of shares or subscriptions were apparently centered in the cities of New York and Providence.

A typical colony had a nucleus of at least six to ten families related to each other by kinship or by life in the same Eastern neighborhood. Usually some of these families traveled together in a "company," either departing from the same neighborhood or meeting at some agreed-upon place such as Albany, New York, before setting out for the West. Almost always an "agent," or an exploring committee, or one of the neighbors had previously been to the frontier and selected a site for settlement, and usually the land had been purchased before the migration occurred. In all but six of the colonies whose history was examined, a town was part of the colony plan, though this town was not always laid out before the settlers arrived. Speculation or the simple desire for good land to farm seems to have been the strongest motive for migration in all but a very few instances. The advance of education was alleged as one of the objects in six of the colonies, but only two actually accomplished this objective immediately, one founding a college, the other an academy. Several of the colonies eventually established an academy or a "college," but this institution was part of the later development of the town, being initiated after the community was founded and not when it was originated in the East.[113] A clergyman was the leader (or one of the leaders) of at least eight of the colonies studied, but this does not appear to have ensured that the motives of town planning were necessarily less materialistic than would otherwise have been the case.[114]

[113] The academy of the Hampshire colony at Princeton is an example. The Maryland colony that settled on the present site of Mt. Morris started a college very soon after settlement, but this seems to have become a community project after the colony had arrived in Illinois (Way, *Rock River Valley*, pp. 588–89; Peoria *Register and Northwestern Gazetteer*, April 21, 1838).

[114] The Delavan colony was promoted by and named for Edward Cornelius Delavan, noted early temperance advocate and a person of importance in the benevolent system. But the project of Delavan does not seem to have been anything other than an investment enterprise by the New York merchant and landowner. Delavan did not settle in the town, nor did he apparently intend to (*Delavan, 1837–1937: A Chronicle of 100 Years*).

Though several colonies were deeply concerned with religious and moral affairs, the ideal of "saving" the West was clearly the central purpose in the founding of only three of them; these were the Kishwaukee, Geneseo, and Galesburg projects, all of which stemmed directly or indirectly from the Burned-over District of New York and shared a common heritage in the Great Revival. Ministers were prominent in the leadership of these three settlements, each of which was committed to an educational institution on the manual labor plan. Of the three, Galesburg was the largest and made the most elaborate preparations for the continuity of church and school as well as for the immediate availability of such services as milling, merchandising, and medicine. It was homogeneous in the origins and religious composition of its settlers, and rather better provided with capital than most of the other colonies. Though the community planned to profit from an appreciation of land values, in which some of its members did very well for themselves, speculation was for the settlement as a whole clearly subordinate to the educational project that had been the real occasion for the planning of a new town. Furthermore, it had from the first, through its religious and educational institutions, important connections with several of the other "Yankee" colonies that extended its influence beyond its own immediate locality. To appreciate these relationships it is necessary to sketch certain of the religious patterns being formed in Illinois at this time.

RELIGIOUS ASSOCIATIONS OF THE YANKEE SETTLEMENT

The colonies that came from New York and New England were likely to have Congregational and Presbyterian churches organized under the Plan of Union, an interdenominational treaty made to deal with the needs of new churches on an advancing frontier. Under the Plan, churches might maintain denominational connections with either or both of the two sects, while their ministers might belong both to a presbytery and a Congregational association. The recently founded American Home Missionary Society that served both denominations was already operating with sufficient vigor by the early thirties

so as to subsidize several Illinois ministers of both denominations, thus assisting the colonies in their infancy to support a
minister. Through the A.H.M.S. these churches were directly
geared into the machinery of the benevolent system and its
several reform movements.

Just as the decade of the thirties began, the available supply
of Congregational and Presbyterian ministers in Illinois was
augmented by the colonization in Illinois of a corps of young
preachers from the East known as the Yale Band. It is extremely
significant, in view of the comparable contemporaneous developments at Oneida Institute, that this remarkable Band
originated as a group of seminarians at Yale—students who
pledged themselves to go as a body to the West to preach and
to promote education. Following the suggestion of an agent
of the A.H.M.S. in Illinois, they undertook to establish a
manual labor college in Jacksonville that became Illinois
College.[115]

The thirteen members of the Yale Band arrived in Illinois
between 1829 and 1833. Illinois College began instruction in
January, 1830, with nine students under the tutelage of one of
the Yale men, Julian Sturtevant. Members of the Band still
remaining in the East chose as president of the college Edward
Beecher, whose father was also presently to go West as the first
president of Lane Seminary. Though Illinois College required
much use of the energies of several of the Yale Band for a few
years in teaching and money raising, it provided the permanent
vocation of only one of them, Sturtevant. Two members were
soon engaged in other Illinois educational ventures: Romulus
Barnes promoted the short-lived college at Canton in 1836; [116]
Theron Baldwin founded Monticello Female Seminary in
1835 and served as its principal until 1843, when he became
secretary of the Society for the Promotion of Collegiate

[115] Rammelkamp, *Illinois College*, pp. 16–39; *Illinois Monthly Magazine*, I
(Dec., 1830), 111–12.
[116] Established in 1836 on land donated by the Reverend Romulus Barnes and
Nathan Jones. Receipts of sales from lots in the "Barnes and Jones Addition"
were to be used to supply operating expenses for the school (Eversole, "Canton
College," *Journal of the Illinois State Historical Society*, XXXIV [1941], 334–43).

and Theological Education at the West, a national organization which the members of the Yale Band had been most active in forming. All of the Yale Band were occasionally, and most of them were constantly, active as preaching missionaries on the Illinois frontier. Some of them must be identified for their roles in subsequent events described in this narrative. Asa Turner became pastor of the important church at Quincy and then moved across the Mississippi River intó the new Iowa country, acting as generalissimo for the American Home Missionary Society and receiving into his cohorts a so-called Iowa Band, similar to the Yale Band but coming from Andover. Albert Hale, William Kirby, and Flavel Bascom served as agents for the A.H.M.S. in Illinois. Lucien Farnam was associated through his wife with a colony at Hadley, near Lockport,[117] and also became the first pastor of the Hampshire colony church at Princeton.[118] Bascom was the first pastor of the Tremont colony [119] and eventually became pastor of the first church of the Galesburg colony.

Under the influence of these men, Congregationalism, which up to that time had been submerged in Presbyterianism, was revived. In some instances this revival was due to the availability of the Yale men to serve as Congregational ministers when a colony with definite Congregational antecedents arrived on the Illinois frontier. In other cases it was due to their protection of Congregational principles that might otherwise be submerged in a Plan of Union church.[120] Because Congregationalism was more "liberal," or radical, than its Presbyterian confederate, the emergence of the former strengthened movements such as abolitionism. Though members of the Yale Band were not abolitionists until after they came to Illinois, most of them did join that anti-slavery crusade when it ap-

[117] Mary H. Porter, *Eliza Chappell Porter*, p. 120.
[118] Kett, *The Voters and Taxpayers of Bureau County, Illinois*, p. 28.
[119] Flavel Bascom to A. Peters, Aug. 6, 1835, A.H.M.S. Papers. Bascom calls Tremont "a flourishing town, founded by an eastern colony of sixty families within the last year."
[120] The early history of Congregationalism in Illinois and the activities of the Yale Band are discussed in Spinka, ed., *History of Illinois Congregational and Christian Churches*, chapters 2 and 3.

peared in this area, and some of them were leaders in it, notably Lucien Farnam, Romulus Barnes, Asa Turner, William Kirby, and Flavel Bascom.

It is evident that the colonies from New England and New York on the Illinois frontier during the middle thirties did not settle in isolation from one another, but that they maintained or quickly established lines of religious and social communication through the American Home Missionary Society and the Yale Band and the mutual interests of their preacher leaders. At least five of the colonies came from the Burned-over District of New York and four of these stemmed from the Oneida locale, which was the very fountainhead of the Great Revival. Six of the Lane Rebels were associated with the founding or early history of the colonies. Among the colonies on the frontier the embers of the Great Revival burst into blaze most fiercely in Galesburg and Knox College, which assumed a primacy in religious affairs, in educational activities, and in reform agitation comparable to the leadership of Lane and Oberlin in Ohio.

PART THREE

Early Agitation

❧ VIII ❧

Beginnings of Abolitionism in Illinois

The clanking chains of more than two million of our countrymen
proclaim to the world that the principles to which our venerable
fathers pledged their dearest interests are trifled with, when
their language on the subject is by many of our countrymen
declared to be merely a flourish of rhetoric, and never designed
to apply to all men; when the sacred principles of liberty are
fast fading from the minds of multitudes, when the freedom of
debate is stifled in the halls of legislation; when ecclesiastical
courts inflict their highest censure upon those who plead for im-
partial liberty and who remonstrate against the enslaving by
their brethren of those whom Christ has made free, when our
temples dedicated to freedom are maliciously burnt down, in
spite of constitutional guarantees, and the rulers of the land are
winking at their enormities; when the press that dares to plead for
the oppressed is broken and cast into the street, and the blood
of those who gave voice to the press mingled on the ground with
its scattered types, with the entire impunity of the assassins;
when pious men and ministers of the gospel rebuke the sin at
the hazard of personal abuse or of life; at such a time it is proper
to wake up the spirit of our fathers to reassert the principles of
liberty, and with trumpet lung proclaim them through the land
till every tyrant trembles upon his seat, and every minion in his
train flies terror stricken at the sound, and the walls and ramparts
of slavery like those of Jericho fall to the ground.[1]

ON INDEPENDENCE DAY of 1837 the Galesburg colony
formed an anti-slavery society that was an auxiliary to the
American Anti-Slavery Society and also resolved to raise $100

[1] From a Fourth of July speech made by George Washington Gale to the
Anti-Slavery Society in Farmington, Illinois, in 1838; Peoria *Register and Northwestern Gazetteer,* July 14, 1838.

during the year for the abolitionist cause.[2] After the establishment of a church and the chartering of a college, this was the
first organization set up by the frontier village. In addition,
sometime before the next aniversary of the national society
the colony also organized a "juvenile" anti-slavery society,
thus faithfully reproducing the institutions of the Oneida
sector of the Burned-over District, where such juvenile auxiliaries had originated.[3] In April of 1839 still another "Youth's
Anti-Slavery Society" was formed.[4] No other community in
Illinois was so quickly and so thoroughly girded for the abolitionist crusade. The arrival of the colony was immediately
reflected at the Knoxville post office in a swelling of subscriptions to the *Observer* edited by Elijah P. Lovejoy.[5] And when
the first press of that paper was destroyed by a mob at Alton,
these Galesburg subscribers met to express approbation of
Lovejoy's principles and to send him fifty dollars to help reestab-
lish his publication.[6]

Occupation of their prairie purchase by the Galesburg colony
occurred at the very time that mob violence flared up along
the Ohio–Mississippi River boundaries. One of the Galesburg
families had fled before a mob from Palmyra, Missouri; others
had passed in fear through Cincinnati during the public hostility that culminated in the destruction of the offices of the
Philanthropist. Abolitionism was not only denounced by men
who believed that slavery was the best, as well as the biblical,

[2] Jerusha Loomis Farnham, "Diary," in Calkins, ed., *Log City Days*, p. 40.
Anti-slavery prayer meetings had preceded this organization.
[3] *Fifth Annual Reports of the American Anti-Slavery Society* lists the societies
and the dates of their organization. The earliest juvenile society was that of
Utica, New York. Of three listed for 1834, one was from Whitesboro, New York.
The Galesburg juvenile society is the only one listed for Illinois.
[4] "Minutes of the Galesburg Youth's Anti-Slavery Society," April 4, 1839, MSS,
Knox College Library. According to the *Genius of Universal Emancipation*, June
28, 1839, p. 19, this Galesburg Youth's Anti-Slavery Society resolved against
the use of the products of slave labor.
[5] Alton *Observer*, Dec. 22, 1836, and March 16, 1837. There is a letter in the
Observer for April 13, 1837, from Nehemiah West of Galesburg.
[6] *Ibid.*, March 15, 1838 (now published in Cincinnati since the destruction of
the fourth press at Alton). The relation of the Galesburg subscribers to the
publication of the *Observer* is discussed in a communication from Galesburg
dated Jan. 29, 1838.

condition of the sons of Ham, but was also derided by men of good will who disliked slavery. Until the middle thirties, even in the South, criticism of slavery and suggestions for its removal had been generally tolerated and many Southerners might be described as anti-slavery to some degree, but profits provided by the success of Whitney's cotton gin and expanding cotton markets were removing earlier doubts about slavery. Garrison's diatribes and the denunciatory tactics of the zealots that came out of the Great Revival evoked a stormy counterattack both in the North and in the South. Instead of proposing mitigation of the condition of the slaves, or their gradual liberation, or their removal through colonization, the abolitionists demanded immediate emancipation. Though this might be interpreted by some abolitionists to mean "immediate emancipation gradually accomplished," it nevertheless required without postponement steps that seemed recklessly to threaten the property of an entire section and proposed rashly to raise up a race that was generally regarded as naturally inferior. On the political plane abolitionists imperiled the Federal Union itself; at the religious level they proscribed slaveholding brethren and their defenders as sinners no less than murderers and adulterers and asked the churches to discipline them accordingly.

The importation of this radical brand of anti-slavery feeling into Illinois in the middle thirties inevitably provoked a riotous response. Illinois extended nearly as far south as Tennessee and as late as 1830 the settled parts of the state lay no farther north than Missouri or Virginia. Though the members of Congress from the South had fully acquiesced in the provisions of the Northwest Ordinance that slavery should be kept out of any part of the territory north of the Ohio River, many of the Southern immigrants to the Illinois country desired to revoke the restriction and had been partially successful in modifying the ban on slavery. In the legal guise of indentured servants, slaves were imported and sold, and though the constitution adopted when the state came into the Union limited indentures to one year, little attention might be paid to the time limit or to the

rule that the arrangement was optional with the Negroes.[7]
Free Negroes could not of themselves settle in Illinois without
certificates of their freedom; their civil rights were limited,
and they were inadequately protected against kidnapers who
might "recapture" them and transport and sell them in the
South. A movement to make Illinois truly a slave state had
been stimulated by the admission of neighboring Missouri on
that basis, had been encouraged by Southern politicians who
argued that since Illinois was a sovereign state it was no longer
restrained by the Northwest Ordinance, and had been aggravated by hard times in the early twenties. This pro-slavery
aggression reached its furthest advance in 1824 when the
legislature submitted to the people a proposal for a convention
that might revise the constitution.[8]

At this distance of time it appears hardly plausible that the
proponents of slavery for Illinois argued that it would be
humane for the slaves as well as profitable for the whites if
the constitution allowed slavery. A historian who sketched the
labyrinth of sophistry in the campaign of 1824 admits that he
was seized by a "savage desire" to present to posterity the following sentence from a pro-slavery gazette as a "caricature" of
the argument:

Other strong inducements I have for the introduction of slavery
into this state are, that in the sickly season, the sick could have more
attention paid them—the community would flourish, our state
would be more republican, and more populous—the condition of
the slaves much ameliorated, and the several churches of Christ
would be considerably enlarged.[9]

Voters with anti-slavery sentiments in Illinois during the
territorial period had remonstrated against the intrusion of
slavery, and they now rallied to defeat the convention in 1824.

[7] For persistence of this practice as late as 1845 and 1846 see Allen, "Slavery
and Negro Servitude in Pope County, Illinois," *Journal of the Illinois State
Historical Society*, XLII (1949), 411–23.
[8] Studies of the slavery question in Illinois previous to 1824 may be found
in Dillon, "The Anti-Slavery Movement in Illinois: 1809–1844" (Doctoral dissertation, University of Michigan, 1951), chapters 1–4; Harris, *Negro Servitude
in Illinois*, chapters 1–5; Pease, *The Frontier State*, chapter 4.
[9] Pease, *The Frontier State*, p. 86.

But their success was only in part a victory of high moral principles over hypocrisy and inhumanity. Those opposed to slavery were, like those favoring it, mostly of Southern extraction; a few of the former had, it is true, left the South on the noble mission of emancipating their slaves, but more of them had departed to escape for themselves from a slave economy and a planter-dominated society. They did not want an expanding slavocracy to follow them, but had no particular aversion to slavery if it stayed south of the Ohio. Indeed many of them were anti-slavery not out of principle but out of prejudice, for they disliked Negroes intensely, did not want them in Illinois, believed their servile condition in the South was a natural one, opposed their general emancipation because that would result in their migration outside that section, and agreed that those Negroes not in bondage should be allowed only the restricted status of freed slaves amongst free men.[10]

Certain of the leaders of the anti-slavery party in 1824 did, however, speak for freedom in terms of justice, humanity, and Christianity quite as noble as those uttered a decade later by abolitionists. Had this anti-slavery group at this time remained intact and joined the national crusade that was about to be aroused by the Great Revival, then abolitionism in Illinois would have been in the van—an indigenous growth rather than a transplantation from the East. But after the excitement of the convention contest died down the local societies in Illinois disappeared and the leadership was dispersed.[11] The Friends of Humanity, a tiny Baptist sect that had migrated from Kentucky and that had been distinguished by its condemnation of

[10] Barnhart, "The Southern Influence in the Formation of Illinois," *Journal of the Illinois State Historical Society*, XXXII (1939), 358–78; Eastman, "History of the Anti-Slavery Agitation, and the Growth of the Liberty and Republican Parties in the State of Illinois," in Blanchard, *Discovery and Conquests of the Northwest with the History of Chicago*, pp. 655–77; Dillon, "The Anti-Slavery Movement in Illinois," pp. 131 ff.

[11] Dillon, "The Anti-Slavery Movement in Illinois," chapter 4. Governor Edward Cole, a Virginia-born aristocrat in the best Jeffersonian tradition and friend of the Quakers of Pennsylvania, was frustrated in further political efforts and left the state in 1832. Morris Birkbeck, the English liberal of Quaker parentage, who as Jonathan Freeman had written brilliantly against the convention, was drowned in 1825.

slavery,[12] became more concerned in the late twenties with temperance and the coming of the millennium, repudiated its earlier rule of no fellowship with those who believed in slavery, and was unsympathetic with the abolitionists of the thirties.[13] Baptist and Methodist clergymen who had fought the admission of slavery into Illinois in 1824 were thereafter content with the colonization scheme, which satisfied both the dislike of slavery and the distaste for Negroes, of whom it was believed that they were incapable of appreciating and enjoying the blessings of freedom while remaining in the United States.[14] Even the colonization movement in Illinois lagged in the early thirties, was torpid in the middle thirties, and became by the end of that decade a collection of conservatives opposed to abolition.[15]

The firmest continuity between the convention contest of 1824 and abolitionist agitation of the middle thirties was maintained by a group of settlers who migrated northward from Bond County to Putnam County. The latter was then a large political unit enclosing the land through which the Illinois River veers sharply to a more southerly course and was located just below the point where that river receives tributaries that rise at the rim of the basin of Lake Michigan. At this strategic site there had developed by the early thirties a nest of settlements somewhat in advance of the continuous frontier line pushing up the river. Migrants to central Illinois from the north by way of the lake came upon these settlements first, after they had crossed the unoccupied tracts of northeastern Illinois. Here also began the shortest overland route from the Illinois River to the valley of the Rock River in northwestern Illinois. The forerunners of the migration from Bond County to Putnam County appeared in 1826 and the first families settled there in

[12] An early account of the Friends of Humanity is given by John Mason Peck in his "Brief View of the Baptist Interest in Each of the United States," *American Quarterly Register* (1842), pp. 42–58. An account of the sect is given by Sweet, ed., *The Baptists*, pp. 82–89.

[13] Sweet, ed., *The Baptists*, pp. 98–101.

[14] Dillon, "The Anti-Slavery Movement in Illinois," pp. 70–71, 131–36, 143–48, 150.

[15] *Ibid.*, pp. 141–51.

1827.[16] By the middle thirties most of the outspoken anti-slavery men of the former county had removed to such towns in the newer location as Hennepin, the county seat, Florid, Magnolia, and Union Grove.[17] These were people of Southern Presbyterian extraction who, previous to living in Bond County, had resided in southern Ohio. By the late thirties they received a permanent anti-slavery leader of the same antecedents in the person of the Reverend James H. Dickey, but meanwhile from other sources they received other accessions of strength and other leaders. Vermont-born Hooper Warren, who edited the chief anti-slavery journal in Madison County during the contest of 1824, but who had weakened his influence by moving to Springfield and then shortly again to Galena, came to Hennepin in 1831 and took office in the new Putnam County; in time he was to establish an anti-slavery paper here.[18] The missionaries of the Yale Band often passed through these settlements on their tours, and they served the church at Union Grove. The more radical anti-slavery principles of some of the settlers impressed these missionaries,[19] who were already predisposed to such convictions by their New School theology and through relations with the benevolent system of the East. At its beginning the Hampshire colony, which eventually founded Princeton fifteen miles west of Union Grove, was closely associated with these settlements in Putnam County. In 1834 the Reverend Nahum Gould arrived from the Burned-over Dis-

[16] Account of the settlement by James W. Willis in Peoria *Register and Northwestern Gazetteer*, Sept. 8, 1838.

[17] Dillon, "The Anti-Slavery Movement in Illinois," pp. 180–84. In 1835 the Reverend Henry Palmer (Campbellite denomination) settled in Marshall, then a part of Putnam County. He was originally from North Carolina and later from Wilson County, Tennessee. "His convictions became aroused on the subject of slavery, and he determined not to rear his family under the influence of the 'peculiar institution.' Collecting a colony of Tennesseans of similar views, he emigrated to this state, and settled in Edwards County, while Illinois was still a territory. . . . In 1818, he moved to Indiana." Upon his return to Illinois in 1835 he settled "with a numerous family on Half-Moon Prairie" in Marshall County and preached there till 1859 (Ford, *History of Putnam and Marshall Counties*, p. 155).

[18] Ellsworth, *Records of the Olden Time*, pp. 385–87; Ford, *History of Putnam and Marshall Counties*, p. 36.

[19] Flavel Bascom, "Autobiography," in Sweet, ed., *The Congregationalists*, pp. 244–48.

trict, became pastor of the Union Grove church, introduced a revivalistic kind of ministry, provoked a withdrawal of the Old School partisans, led in the founding of the town of Granville, and was otherwise concerned with town planting in this area. Gould, by his own admission, was a colonizationist when he arrived, but soon was associated with his parishoners in their abolitionism.[20] Quaker additions to this concentration of anti-slavery pioneers began to appear in Putnam County in 1833 and continued to arrive until 1840. Among these were kin of the noted anti-slavery journalist, Benjamin Lundy, who himself settled there in September, 1838.[21] As previously noted, the purchasing committee of the colony that founded Galesburg sought for land in this part of the state, and according to a Putnam County tradition attempted to merge their college project with the Granville enterprise promoted by Gould.

A Putnam County Anti-Slavery Society was the first local abolitionist body in Illinois listed by the American Anti-Slavery Society; this was in 1835. The year following there were still only two societies in the state that had come to the attention of the national organization, the one for Putnam County and another at Union Grove, with George B. Willis (one of the Bond County migrants) and Nahum Gould (the revivalist preacher from New York) as the secretaries.[22] During the next two years eleven other societies were noted, including two from Galesburg, and it was evident that the roots of abolitionism were spreading in Illinois. The complete machinery for reform, according to the blueprints of the benevolent system, required a state organization; this was supplied late in 1837 by the organization of a state anti-slavery society at Upper Alton, in Madison County.

A Madison County man, Thomas Lippincott, was the anti-slavery leader in Illinois whose career most closely linked the earlier campaign to keep slavery out of Illinois with the later

[20] Gould, "Diary," entries for June to Aug., 1836.
[21] Ellsworth, *Records of the Olden Time*, pp. 213–24, 238; Gamaliel Bailey to Birney, Cincinnati, Aug. 28, 1838, *Birney Letters*, I, 468.
[22] American Anti-Slavery Society: *Second Annual Report*, 1835; *Third Annual Report*, 1836.

abolitionist crusade.[23] His life had been shaped by most of the forces that entered into the national anti-slavery movement.[24] He was one of the leaders among the men of Madison and Bond counties who fought the convention in 1824, at which time he contributed for that purpose to Hooper Warren's *Spectator*. As a pioneer Presbyterian clergyman he was associated with the establishment of the first presbyteries and synods of that denomination in Illinois, and he was also one of the original promoters of Illinois College, an enterprise that brought him into close contact with members of the Yale Band. And he was a close friend of the Reverend Elijah P. Lovejoy.

Lovejoy had first come to St. Louis in 1827, where he was converted during a religious revival in 1832, had returned to Princeton for theological training, and had become a Presbyterian clergyman.[25] He received a commission for the St. Louis area in November, 1833, from the American Home Missionary Society, which helped to support him throughout most of his residence in Missouri.[26] His most important work was the editing of the *Observer*, a weekly newspaper that was definitely not a political but a religious journal, serving as a Presbyterian organ and presenting vigorously the benevolent and reforming causes that were precious to the New School and their Congregational associates. Though Lovejoy was not at first an abolitionist, he gave that "ism" a hearing and under the impact of hot hostility in St. Louis hardened to the most radical temper on the slavery issue. In June of 1836 he announced that the *Observer* would be removed from St. Louis to Alton, Illinois,

[23] A brief sketch of Lippincott may be found in Norton, *History of the Presbyterian Church in Illinois*, I, 147–52.

[24] He had been born of Quaker parents in Salem, New Jersey, reared to young manhood in Philadelphia, experienced a religious conversion in Sullivan County, New York, migrated to Illinois in 1817, and eventually settled in Edwardsville, Madison County. As elder of the Presbyterian church in Edwardsville he frequently conducted public worship in the absence of a regular minister, and in 1828 was licensed by the Presbytery of Missouri, which then included the whole of Illinois in its jurisdiction.

[25] Joseph C. and Owen Lovejoy, *Memoir of the Rev. Elijah P. Lovejoy*, pp. 33–66.

[26] American Home Missionary Society: *Eighth Annual Report*, 1834; *Ninth Annual Report*, 1835; *Tenth Annual Report*, 1836.

where it would enjoy equally good facilities for circulation and probably would get better support.[27]

While being removed the press of the *Observer* was destroyed on the wharf at Alton by a mob, the first of four presses so eliminated during the next sixteen months by Lovejoy's enemies. He thus became in Illinois not only the spokesman but the very symbol of the anti-slavery cause and of the principle of a free press. It was to him that anti-slavery men looked for leadership in initiating a state anti-slavery convention.

The extension of organized abolitionism into Illinois, as previously in New York and Ohio, was primarily a religious movement, in which the slavery issue was actually complicated by ecclesiastical politics and by its association with other "benevolent operations" such as the temperance cause [28] and even anti-Catholic agitation.[29] By the summer of 1837 anti-slavery agitation had been heightened by the increasing number of abolitionist settlers in the state, by the organization of local abolitionist societies, and by the spirited controversy on the Texas question. Furthermore, Presbyterians and Congregationalists were excited by the quarrel that broke out in the General Assembly of the Presbyterian Church in May, 1837.[30] The prevalence in the New School party of the more rabid anti-slavery doctrines had been a factor provoking the Old School to expel from the denomination the New School synods of the Burned-over District in New York and of the Western Reserve in Ohio, where the Great Revival and its benevolent causes had been largely cradled. In Illinois the preliminary discussions over the advisability of a state anti-slavery convention occurred in Presbyterian circles, and most

[27] Joseph C. and Owen Lovejoy, *Memoir of the Rev. Elijah P. Lovejoy*, p. 179.

[28] Beecher, *Narrative of Riots at Alton*, pp. 30–31; "Temperance," Peoria *Register and Northwestern Gazetteer*, April 21, 1838.

[29] Lovejoy campaigned vehemently against Catholicism in the *Observer* while in St. Louis. In his crucial editorials on Judge Lawless the slavery and Catholic issues are inextricably mingled (Joseph C. and Owen Lovejoy, *Memoir of the Rev. Elijah P. Lovejoy*, pp. 174–78 and chapter 7). Saving the West from Catholicism was a motive for Lyman Beecher's removal to Cincinnati and presumably is what Gale referred to in his prospectus for the Galesburg colony as "those who are no less the enemies of civil liberty, than of a pure gospel."

[30] Beecher, *Narrative of Riots at Alton*, p. 20.

of the leaders in this action were, like Lovejoy and Lippincott, clergymen affiliated with that denomination.

Lovejoy's call for a convention of those supporting immediate abolition of slavery was undersigned by two hundred and forty-five persons from seventeen communities in ten counties of the state.[31] Over half of these signatures were from three communities: sixty-one from Quincy, thirty-two from Jacksonville, and forty from Galesburg. This list, as well as the roster of delegates attending the convention at Alton, does not accurately catalogue the abolitionist forces in Illinois,[32] for the issue at that time was, in the minds of many men, including Edward Beecher, primarily that of free inquiry and only secondarily that of abolitionism. The geographical location of Alton near the southern edge of Yankee settlement in Illinois affected the attendance; Putnam County was to be much more important in the work of the Illinois Anti-Slavery Society than was apparent at the very outset; none of the Galesburgers who signed the call attended the convention, which was to be expected from a community still in the very first stages of town planting. Neither Alton nor Jacksonville were to be so prominent in the later stages as they were in the beginning, and Illinois College, far from following the early lead of its president, Edward Beecher, was a disappointment to abolitionists.[33]

The events surrounding the organization of the Illinois Anti-Slavery Society, October 26–28, 1837, made it painfully clear that Alton could hardly be its headquarters. The meeting of the convention called by Lovejoy was preceded by three months

[31] Muelder, "Printer's Error in Call for Antislavery Convention," *Journal of the Illinois State Historical Society*, XLVII (1954), 321–22.

[32] To facilitate analysis of the personnel in the Illinois Anti-Slavery Society the author prepared an index of all the persons mentioned in the minutes of the society from 1837 to 1845. Listed with each person were the anniversaries attended, offices held, committees served, and other forms of participation. Generalizations made regarding the role of persons or of communities in the business of the society are based on this index.

[33] Of the ten members of the Yale Band then in Illinois, eight participated in the launching of organized abolitionism either at the convention of October, 1837, or by attendance at the first anniversary meeting a year later at Farmington. The two members of the Band absent from these activities were also those most closely identified with Illinois College—Julian Sturtevant and Theron Baldwin. The former was Beecher's successor as president.

of bitter resentment which time and again came just short of actual personal assault upon Lovejoy. From across the river Altonians were goaded by Missouri warnings that

The good people of Illinois must either put a stop to the efforts of these fanatics, or expel them from their community. If this is not done, the travel of emigrants through their state, and the trade of the slaveholding states, and particularly Missouri, must stop. . . . We would not desire to see this done at the expense of public order or legal restraint; but there is a moral indignation which the virtuous portion of a community may exert, which is sufficient to crush this faction and forever disgrace its fanatic instigators.[34]

Twice, once in August and again late in September, mobs destroyed the presses of the *Observer* for the second and third times. It was even as a fourth press was awaited by the persistent editor that the delegates gathered for the convention.[35] When they convened in the Presbyterian church on October 26 in Upper Alton, their deliberations were thwarted for two days by a hostile crowd that by the ruse of desiring free discussion got control of the meeting and then effected its adjournment immediately after voting anti-abolition resolutions. In order to be rid of these "lewd fellows of the baser sort, sons of Belial," the proper delegates met in a private home and there founded the Illinois Anti-Slavery Society.[36]

Lovejoy was elected corresponding secretary of the new organization, the most important office in a society of this kind, especially while it was in the process of enlisting support. His tenure in this office was short-lived, however, for ten days later, while defending the newly arrived press of the *Observer* against another Alton mob, Lovejoy was shot and killed.

[34] *Missouri Republican*, Aug. 17, 1837, quoted in Joseph C. and Owen Lovejoy, *Memoir of the Rev. Elijah P. Lovejoy*, pp. 230–31.

[35] The events of July through October, 1837, are related in detail in Joseph C. and Owen Lovejoy, *Memoir of the Rev. Elijah P. Lovejoy*, chapters 12–15.

[36] *Ibid.*, pp. 266–67; Alton *Observer Extra*, "Proceedings of the Illinois Anti-Slavery Convention Held at Upper Alton on the 26th, 27th and 28th, October, 1837" (Alton, 1838).

❧ IX ❧

Leadership in the Illinois Anti-Slavery Society

> Let man serve law for man;
> Live for friendship, live for love,
> For truth's and harmony's behoof;
> The state may follow how it can,
> As Olympus follows Jove.
>   EMERSON, "Ode to Channing"

THE LEADING ROLE at the first annual meeting of the Illinois Anti-Slavery Society was played by the large delegation from Galesburg. Originally this anniversary was scheduled to be held at Peoria, immediately following the session of the Presbyterian Synod of Illinois.[1] Such an anti-slavery assembly would have been extremely unpopular in the river town, as was dramatically demonstrated four years later when an abolitionist meeting was violently suppressed. But in October, 1838, the issue was avoided, for Peoria was prostrate with a sickness that had infected the river valley since midsummer.[2] Despite the fever, and the fear of it, the synod managed to get through its business, which included the consummation in Illinois of the Old School-New School schism,[3] but the meeting place of the state anti-slavery society was changed to Farmington, which offered a site away from the fever-infested bottoms, up on the higher land to which many people had been taking refuge

[1] It is significant that this close following of the sessions of the synod and of a state anti-slavery convention had also occurred in 1837, though one met in Springfield and the other in Alton.

[2] Peoria *Register and Northwestern Gazetteer*, Aug. 18 and Sept. 15, 1838; Jeremiah Porter, "Journal," Oct., 1838, MS, Chicago Historical Society.

[3] Peoria *Register and Northwestern Gazetteer*, Sept. 29, 1838.

much of the season. This move brought the sessions of the state society near the border of Knox County, and Galesburg had already established close connections with Farmington for religious and reforming causes.

The change to Farmington was made at the urging of the Reverend Jeremiah Porter, who had moved there from Peoria late in 1837. Porter had participated in the organization of the Illinois Anti-Slavery Society at Alton.[4] Both he and his wife were zealots of the kind that made particularly good promoters of the benevolent system. The two had met while the former was a missionary and the latter a mission-teacher among the fur trading posts and garrisons on the straits of the upper Great Lakes, after which they labored together in the frontier village of Chicago.[5] In June of 1835 they were married at Rochester, New York, which was the home of the bride, Eliza Chappell. This was the locality where she had undergone protracted, nearly violent, emotional religious experiences that reached their climax at the time of Finney's evangelism in the Rochester area. At that time Eliza Chappell had worked closely with the evangelist Jedediah Burchard and had developed a close friendship with the Burchard family that was continued through correspondence after she had come to central Illinois.[6] Miss Chappell's teaching mission on the upper lakes had become one of the objects of benevolence for the Burned-over District; in fact, there had existed for a time at Utica, New York, a "Chappell Infant School Society" which sent out and supported several teachers. In promotion of this project she had gone to the very fountainhead of the benevolent system, New York City itself, where in 1832 she was often in the Finney home.[7] Her husband, Jeremiah Porter, had studied at Williams College and Andover Seminary and had taught school for two years in Troy, New York, during the period of the Great Revival, after which

[4] *Proceedings of the Illinois Anti-Slavery Convention Held at Upper Alton on the 26th, 27th, and 28th, October, 1837.*

[5] Porter was pastor of the First Presbyterian Church; his wife, the first public school teacher in Chicago, taught her classes for a year in that church.

[6] Porter, "Journal," entries for 1836.

[7] The best source on Eliza Chappell Porter is Mary H. Porter, *Eliza Chappell Porter*. The incidents mentioned above are discussed in the first 120 pages.

he had completed his theological training at Princeton.[8] He was a fervent believer in the revivalistic preaching that had come out of the Burned-over District and was keenly interested in the emotional expressions that accompanied such activities.[9]

Following their marriage the Porters returned to Illinois, where in 1836 Porter became pastor of the recently organized New School Presbyterian church in Peoria.[10] Soon after their arrival they made contact with members of the Galesburg colony, which included cousins of Mrs. Porter. A particularly warm friendship, based in part on mutual acquaintances in New York, developed with the family of "Father" Waters; one of the Waters girls came from Galesburg to Peoria in 1837 and became a schoolteacher, and "Father" Waters was a frequent colleague of Porter in the conducting of "protracted meetings" at the communities that lay within the Peoria orbit.[11] Porter, on one extended visit to Galesburg, had helped to conduct a rousing revival in the colony. Immediately after his return from the Alton convention that organized the Illinois Anti-Slavery Society, Porter, who was on commission from the American Home Missionary Society, moved from Peoria to Farmington. Here he actively promoted the abolitionist cause, within a year bringing thirty-five members into a local anti-slavery society. Twenty-two of these were enrolled on the Fourth of July of 1838, when Gale came with C. W. Gilbert from Galesburg to be the main speaker at a festival devoted to the twin objects of temperance and abolition.[12]

About one hundred members attended the state anti-slavery meeting held in Farmington, October 1, 1838; Porter believed

[8] Best sources on the life of Jeremiah Porter are his own "Journal," MS in the Chicago Historical Society, and the memoir on his wife written by their daughter, cited above.

[9] This is evident from numerous entries in his "Journal."

[10] The church was organized in December, 1834, by Flavel Bascom and Romulus Barnes, members of the Yale Band (Bascom to Peters, Jan. 10, 1835, A.H.M.S. Papers.)

[11] Porter, "Journal," numerous entries for 1836–39. The fact that Eliza Chappell Porter was a cousin of L. Chappell of the Galesburg colony is mentioned in the entry for Feb. 25, 1839.

[12] Porter, "Journal," July 5, 1838; Peoria Register and Northwestern Gazetteer, July 14, 1838. An extract from Gale's speech stands at the head of the preceding chapter of this study.

that it was "the largest number ever present at a meeting of
any society in the State." [13] Twenty-two of the men present
were Presbyterian ministers. The largest single delegation was
from Galesburg, twenty-four persons, about one fourth of the
total number. The citizens of Farmington entertained their
visitors gratuituously, the Porters themselves taking in ten
guests, among them Gale, "Father" Waters and two of his
daughters, Edward Beecher, and Benjamin Lundy.[14] The presence of Lundy, who had joined his family in Putnam County
only a few weeks previously,[15] meant that one of the greatest
anti-slavery veterans of the nation was at hand to share his experience with such seasoned campaigners as the Galesburg leaders and the four Lane Rebels, Hiram Foote, John J. Miter,
William T. Allan, and C. S. Renshaw, three of whom had been
students of Gale at Oneida Institute and all of whom had served
as anti-slavery agents under Weld's tutelage. Though these
latter four were novices in the state of Illinois, also present
were four members of the Yale Band who among themselves
had covered much of the length of the state in missionary tours
for several years. It is interesting to note that educational projects were represented by three of the principal participants at
the meeting, for in addition to Beecher from Illinois College
and Gale from the recently chartered Knox College, Dr. David
Nelson was also present. Since the spring of 1836, when a mob
had driven him out of Missouri, where he had been president
of Marion College, Nelson had founded a manual labor school
near Quincy, Illinois, called the Mission Institute. It was an
impressive group with which to carry on the work that had
been so violently interrupted by an Alton mob.

Though the martyrdom of Lovejoy had undoubtedly sancti-
fied the abolition cause, it had set back the actual work of anti-
slavery promotion in the state, for not only had the *Observer*

[13] Porter, "Journal," Oct., 1838. The MS minutes of this meeting are in the
Chicago Historical Society. They were also published by the *Genius of Universal Emancipation*, March 25, 1839.

[14] Porter, "Journal," Oct., 1838.

[15] "Benjamin Lundy arrived here last Friday, and will perhaps leave on next
Saturday. He is bound for Illinois." Gamaliel Bailey to Birney, Cincinnati,
Aug. 28, 1838, *Birney Letters*, I, 468.

come to an end but Lovejoy's leadership as corresponding secretary and member of the executive committee of the state society had also been lost. That position had been filled by the pastor of the Alton Presbyterian Church, Frederick W. Graves, but not very aggressively performed,[16] and except for the publication and circulation of the proceedings of the Alton convention little or nothing was done. At the Farmington anniversary a committee headed by Gale was appointed to provide a monument to Lovejoy, and another committee, also headed by Gale, was charged with solving the need for an anti-slavery press, a matter in which the Galesburg settlement had been especially interested.[17] That Gale was also chairman of the committee to raise funds was typical of the dominant role of the Galesburgers in the Farmington sessions, for Gale along with Porter made one of the two "set" speeches, "Father" Waters was chairman of the committee to prepare the business of the meeting, and other important committee assignments fell to Nehemiah West and to John J. Miter, Gale's protégé from Knoxville.[18]

Probably the most important decision at Farmington was the vote, as recommended by Gale's committee, to support Lundy in his revival of the *Genius of Universal Emancipation,* which he had previously published under a variety of adverse and hostile circumstances in Ohio, Tennessee, Maryland, the District of Columbia, and Pennsylvania.[19] This new Illinois paper was dated from Hennepin, in Putnam County, but it was printed at Lowell in adjacent LaSalle County, on Hooper Warren's press. Evidently it was intended that the direction of the

[16] Executive Committee Report, "Minutes of the Illinois Anti-Slavery Society," Oct. 1, 1838.

[17] At a meeting in January, 1838, the citizens of Galesburg adopted resolutions stating that they would be willing to aid in continuing a paper in Illinois conducted on the same principles as those followed by Lovejoy, just as they had previously donated to replace one of the destroyed presses of the *Observer.* They declared, however, that the new paper should not be located in Alton, for it was "not worthy of a paper consecrated to liberty." This communication was printed in the *Observer* of March 15, 1838, while the paper was temporarily and briefly issued in Cincinnati.

[18] "Minutes of the Illinois Anti-Slavery Society," 1838.

[19] Landon, "Benjamin Lundy in Illinois," *Journal of the Illinois State Historical Society,* XXX (1940), 55–67.

Illinois Anti-Slavery Society should be located, for a time at least, in Putnam County, where Lundy lived with his kinsfolk, for the Farmington meeting chose the working officers of the state society from that vicinity. The corresponding secretary, who was to function as general agent, and the recording secretary were both from Putnam County, and the treasurer was Hooper Warren. Furthermore, five of the eleven members of the "Board of Managers" were from Putnam County and five were from Princeton in the bordering county of Bureau.[20]

Misfortune, however, continued to hold back the state society under the Putnam County leadership, and according to the executive committee itself, progress was disappointing.[21] Much had been expected of the *Genius of Universal Emancipation* as an organ of the society, but the project became involved in the "booming" of the town of Lowell in LaSalle County, the promoters of which dreamed of exploiting the water power of the Vermillion River. They desired the location of a press in their settlement, and inducements of financial help, including town lots, were given to Lundy if he would move from Hennepin in Putnam County. Lundy constructed two small buildings, one for a home and the other for a printing press,[22] but only a dozen issues of the paper appeared before Lundy died on August 22, 1839, and publication ceased with the number for September 8, 1839.[23] The Reverend James H. Dickey, corresponding secretary of the state organization, a post that carried with it the position of "general agent," made a tour for the Putnam County society of several places in the northeastern counties, but was very coldly received and found that use of churches and schools for anti-slavery lectures was generally denied to him.[24] A financial agent appointed in December, 1838, resigned after two or three weeks because of sickness; two other men declined to serve, and a request made to

[20] "Minutes of the Illinois Anti-Slavery Society," 1838.

[21] Executive Committee Report, "Minutes of the Illinois Anti-Slavery Society," 1839.

[22] Kett, *Past and Present of LaSalle County, Illinois*, p. 289; Hoffman, *History of LaSalle County*, p. 116.

[23] F. W. Scott, *Newspapers and Periodicals of Illinois*, p. 197.

[24] Harris, *Negro Servitude in Illinois*, p. 131.

the national society to send an agent brought no response. When the year 1839 was about half over, the Reverend Chauncey Cook, recording secretary of the state society, agreed to serve for three months on an agency to lecture, raise funds, and promote the organization of local auxiliaries. Though Cook was a relative newcomer to the state, he was probably not a total stranger to many of the recent settlers who, like himself, had come from the Burned-over District. He had been a minister at Adams, New York, shortly before Gale preached there,[25] and had served in western New York as a Congregational-Presbyterian missionary during the years of the Great Revival, especially in the Rochester vicinity, where he had witnessed particular evangelistic success at the time Finney campaigned in that part of the state.[26] During the late spring and early summer of 1839 Cook traveled through the counties bordering the Illinois River as far south as Tazewell, plus the Rock River Valley, and visited the inland counties of Knox, Fulton, and Sangamon, making more than threescore lectures in more than forty towns. Cook reported that ten or a dozen local societies were organized under his influence, but most of his visits were to communities where there were already active anti-slavery organizations. Cook's agency manifested the most vigor that had yet been shown in the state society, but it was not self-supporting, since in all his travels for the society he collected only $107.44, with additional pledges of sixty dollars more.[27]

In general Cook had found it rather easy to get a favorable hearing, though there were a half-dozen exceptions even in the northern counties, but downstate, where there were numerous "Hoosier" settlers, his "lecture" was likely to be more than

[25] G. W. Gale, "Autobiography."

[26] American Home Missionary Society: *Second Annual Report*, 1828, p. 19; *Third Annual Report*, 1829, p. 20; *Fourth Annual Report*, 1830, p. 18; *Sixth Annual Report*, 1832, p. 19. That Cook was delegate from the Cayuga Presbytery to the General Assembly of 1836 fixes his presence in western New York as late as the spring of that year (*Minutes of the General Assembly, 1836*), p. 235.

[27] Descriptions of Cook's agency are found in the Executive Committee Report in the "Minutes" for 1839. Harris, *Negro Servitude in Illinois*, chapter 9, summarizes Cook's own reports as printed in the *Genius of Universal Emancipation*. The latter, however, omits items included in the report of the executive committee.

a routine speaking assignment. At Knoxville, in the church of John J. Miter, the opposition, led by one of the local saloon habitués, first tried to keep him from speaking by a noisy occupation of the building, and that failing, they withdrew, provided themselves with ripe eggs, many of which were contributed by a woman who broke up the nests of her setting hens, and pelted the platform. Cook, though corpulent and past middle age, did a better job of dodging than the younger Miter.[28]

Of three new county societies organized during this year, one owed its origin to Cook's efforts, but two resulted from the initiative of the Galesburg colony itself. One of these was the Knox County society, formed during the winter at Knoxville; William Holyoke drove over from Galesburg to act as chairman, and Matthew Chambers, grocer of the colony temporarily located in Knoxville, was elected president.[29] More eventful was the trip made to Monmouth, seat of Warren County, on January 2, 1839, by Gale and Miter to address an anti-slavery convention called for the purpose of organizing a society. Considerable opposition was encountered from very "respectable gentlemen" and the arguments lasted from late in the morning until late in the afternoon without the object of the convention being accomplished. While the meeting was adjourned over the supper hour, "the friends of the slave, in order to facilitate the business of the day, and prevent any attempt to forestall the formation of a society," met in the office of Dr. George H. Wright, a former neighbor of Gale's in Whitesboro, New York, a member of the Knox College board of trustees, and the only citizen of Warren County who had signed Lovejoy's call for a state anti-slavery convention in 1837. In Wright's office a Warren County Anti-Slavery Society was organized.[30]

Gale was described as "the great champion of abolitionism in Illinois" [31] by one of his opponents in the long debate at Mon-

[28] Chambers, "Reminiscences of Early Days," paper read to the Knox County Historical Society, MS, Knox College Library; *Genius of Universal Emancipation*, June 28, 1839, p. 17.
[29] Chapman, *History of Knox County*, p. 405.
[30] Peoria *Register and Northwestern Gazetteer*, Jan. 19, 1839; *Genius of Universal Emancipation*, March 8, 1839.
[31] Peoria *Register and Northwestern Gazetteer*, Jan. 19, 1839.

mouth, and though this may have been merely forensic hyper-
bole, Gale had done much to earn such a reputation and to de-
serve both the rewards and the penalties that went with it. It
was about this time that he went to Farmington for an anti-
slavery lecture, and despite previous hospitality to such visitors,
a mob broke up the meeting, Gale was rotten-egged, and the
mane and tail of his fine riding mare were closely shaved.[32] In
May of 1839 Gale represented Illinois at the annual meeting of
the American Anti-Slavery Society. Though the national society,
through its appointment of a vice-president and of "managers"
for Illinois,[33] had recognized that state since 1837, Gale was the
only Illinoian ever to appear in the deliberations of the national
body,[34] and in 1839, out of 435 delegates, he was one of only
three from the area west of Pennsylvania. For Gale this meeting
was a time of reunion with the delegates from New York, including the Tappan brothers, Beriah Green, who was his successor at Oneida Institute, former ministerial colleagues from
the Oneida Presbytery such as John Cross, and close friends
such as John Frost and H. H. Kellogg, the president-elect of
Knox College who was serving as agent of the school in the
East.

Gale witnessed at this anniversary the internal convulsion
that reduced to virtual impotence one of the great reform bodies
that had grown out of the Great Revival. More and more William Lloyd Garrison had been of doubtful value to the cause of
emancipation, because of the essential anarchy in his repudia-

[32] "E. P. Williams Tells Interesting Incidents of Early Life of the City," Galesburg *Evening Mail*, Oct. 5, 1923, in Scrapbook No. 2, Galesburg Public Library.
[33] Gale and James M. Buchanan were appointed managers for Illinois three
times, in 1837, 1838, and 1839. William Stewart, Asa Turner, G. Kimball,
F. W. Graves, Edward Beecher, Benjamin Lundy, Owen Lovejoy, and James H.
Dickey were appointed managers for Illinois either one or two of the three
years. David Nelson, who was a manager for Missouri in 1836, was vice-president
for Illinois in 1837 and 1838.
[34] F. W. Graves was listed for Illinois along with Gale, but elsewhere in the
minutes he is listed under New York City (*Sixth Annual Report of the American
Anti-Slavery Society*, 1839, pp. 46–47). Graves had ceased his pastorate in Alton,
Illinois, in November, 1838, and early in April, 1839, was dismissed to the Third
Presbytery of New York. He was therefore no longer a resident of Illinois at the
time of the anniversary of the American Anti-Slavery Society in May, 1839
(Norton, *History of the Presbyterian Church in Illinois*, I, 219).

tion of all institutions, secular and sacred, in any way associated with slavery—government, political parties, that covenant with hell the Constitution, and the churches. He had antagonized most of the clergy and alienated many from the cause. In May of 1839 he came to New York intent upon seizing control of the national society from the Tappans and their allies in the benevolent system. In this maneuver he was opposed by the overwhelming majority of the large New York delegation, but he nevertheless succeeded, partly because of the loose procedure which made it possible for a large number of women from New England, who supported Garrison, to vote.[35] Particularly critical debates occurred about the right of women to have a full voice in affairs of the anti-slavery society (which Garrison favored) and about the issue of political action—whether or not abolitionists should use the ballot to further the cause (which Garrison opposed). On both of these matters Gale voted on the side of the greater number of the New York delegation, who were opposed to Garrison. He also signed the minority protest against the voting privileges accorded women, in which it was made clear that the issue was not simply the abstract principle of women's rights, on which some of the New Yorkers were quite as liberal as Garrison, but also the practical consideration that the abolitionist cause would be injured if it were confused with the feminist controversy.[36]

In September of 1839 Gale, his son William Selden, and three others from Knox County went to the second anniversary of the Illinois Anti-Slavery Society in Quincy. In this town, which had a population of mixed origins and was located directly across the Mississippi River from the slave soil of Missouri, there was considerable opposition to abolitionism, but according to an observer from Jacksonville, it was better off than many towns which had elements in its citizenry friendly to slavery, because it also possessed "a band of resolute, patriotic men who from a very early period defended the right of free speech," some of

[35] Barnes, *Anti-Slavery Impulse*, pp. 93, 159–76.
[36] *Sixth Annual Report of the American Anti-Slavery Society*, 1839, pp. 29–44. Gale served on the finance committee of this meeting.

them abolitionists but some of them "simply good men and good citizens." [37] The test of toleration for abolitionists in Quincy had taken place dramatically late one night in May of 1836 when Dr. David Nelson arrived there wet and muddy from head to foot after having crossed the river and waded the flooded bottoms in flight from a mob of Missourians who had driven him from Palmyra and Marion College.[38] Some people in Quincy wanted to deny Nelson and his family the refuge of Quincy, but he had influential supporters there, including the pastor of the Congregational Church, Asa Turner, a member of the Yale Band who had met Nelson at a camp meeting in Missouri, had become his friend, and under Nelson's influence had developed into a strong anti-slavery protagonist. The members of Turner's church rallied behind their pastor to prevent persecution of Nelson,[39] and the following month resolute supporters of free discussion thwarted plans to break up an anti-slavery meeting by getting the most likely mob leader out of town and by driving from the church the rioters that did start to stone the meeting by sallying against them with hickory clubs.[40]

Turner had already followed the frontier into Iowa to become the pathfinder there for the American Home Missionary Society, for Congregationalism, and for abolitionism, and though he was back in Quincy to attend the Illinois anti-slavery meeting there in September of 1839, the leading abolitionist in Quincy at this time was Dr. Nelson. Within two months of his flight from Missouri, Nelson had built a double log-cabin a short distance outside of Quincy and had started another school, known as the Mission Institute, to train needy young men for religious work. This school fully applied the rules for simplicity and the discipline in self-reliance that had been set by Gale when he launched the manual labor movement a decade earlier

[37] Sturtevant, *Autobiography*, p. 226.
[38] *Fourth Annual Report of the American Anti-Slavery Society,* 1837, p. 79; *Birney Letters,* I, 328, 332, 490; Merkel, "Abolition Aspects of Missouri's Anti-Slavery Controversy, 1819–1865," *Missouri Historical Review*, XLIV, 242–46.
[39] Magoun, *Asa Turner*, pp. 147–59.
[40] Asbury, *Reminiscences of Quincy*, pp. 64–68.

at Oneida Institute. At the outset Nelson's students were expected to fell their own oak trees and to build the lodges in which they lived; by the spring of 1837 a half-dozen of these dwellings, each planned to house three or four men, had been completed. Students did their own washing and their own cooking (which was simple enough, for they lived on bread, mush, and molasses at an expense of thirty-seven and a half cents a week),[41] though on Sundays Quincy church people often asked them to dinner.[42]

In 1838 Nelson was reenforced by the arrival of the Reverend Moses Hunter, who formed "Mission Institute No. 2." Hunter, who stemmed from the Burned-over District, had contemplated a similar educational venture himself; when he heard of Nelson's plan of training missionaries, he came to Quincy to examine the enterprise and stayed to supplement the work Nelson was doing.[43] Hunter was among the more eccentric of the admirers of Finney, under whose influence he came during the period of the Great Revival while a missionary in Allegheny County, New York.[44] Hunter called the location of his branch of the Mission Institute "Theopolis," and walked about in this City of God in imitation of Christ in a sort of seamless robe.[45] It is not surprising that Mission Institute, like its prototype Oneida Institute, trained some reckless zealots for the anti-

[41] Alton *Observer,* May 4, 1837; details of student life are also given in the *Observer* for June 22 and June 29, 1837.

[42] Selby, "Recollections of a Little Girl in the Forties with Apologies for a Somewhat Lengthy Sequel," *Journal of the Illinois State Historical Society,* XVI (April, 1923), 157–83; Richardson, "Dr. David Nelson and His Times," *ibid.,* XIII (Jan., 1921), 433–63. One of the Galesburg colonists, John Kendall, studied for the ministry at Mission Institute (*Semi-Centennial Celebration, First Church of Galesburg,* p. 11).

[43] *A Memorial of the Congregational Ministers and Churches of the Illinois Association on Completing a Quarter Century of Its History* (Quincy, Illinois, 1863), p. 29, note.

[44] American Home Missionary Society: *Second Annual Report,* 1828, p. 27; *Third Annual Report,* 1829, p. 28; *Fourth Annual Report,* 1830, p. 24. Moses Hunter to Finney, June 7, 128, Finney Papers, Oberlin. In this letter Hunter asked Finney for a team of revivalists to come to Allegheny County to meet the great need there.

[45] Asbury, *Reminiscences of Quincy,* pp. 71–74. An obituary of Hunter is in the *Western Citizen,* Oct. 21. 1841.

slavery cause. So long as the Quincy school lasted, the Galesburg colony had a faithful ally in the cause of reform.

Hunter and Nelson, with Gale and Miter from Knox County, and Chauncey Cook from Putnam County as chairman, comprised the committee to prepare the business for the Quincy anniversary of the Illinois Anti-Slavery Society. Cook, who had been serving as the society's agent, was the only delegate present from Putnam County, despite the fact that the officers and the direction of the society had been concentrated in that locality the preceding year. That Cook, Gale, and Miter made the three addresses set for the convention suggests the degree to which the recent settlers in Illinois from the Burned-over District in general and from the Galesburg colony in particular were taking over the work of the society.[46] Evident disappointment over the operations of the past year was expressed in the executive committee report, and it was decided that a special committee consisting of one delegate from each county represented be appointed to report both on the location of the next executive committee and on the establishment of an anti-slavery newspaper in the state. This special committee reported that the executive committee should be situated at Galesburg, a selection which was voted by the convention. The same committee recommended also that the state anti-slavery paper should be published in Galesburg, and stipulated that it be the same size as the *Anti-Slavery Lecturer* issued from Utica, New York. This specific assignment of the paper to the colony from the Burned-over District was not, however, fixed by the delegates in Quincy, who voted instead that the matter should be referred to the new executive committee and that meanwhile the *Philanthropist* of Cincinnati, Ohio, should be the organ for Illinois.[47]

In accordance with the decision of the delegates to center the

[46] The Adams County delegation, which was host to this annual meeting, was the largest present, being thirty-nine in number. Next in size were the LaSalle and Knox county delegations, with five each. The roster showed a total of seventy delegates. Gale served on the nominating committee with Nelson (chairman) and Owen Lovejoy. Thomas Simmons of Galesburg was on the committee concerning a state newspaper.

[47] "Minutes of the Illinois Anti-Slavery Society," 1839.

direction of the society in Galesburg, those offices that the year before had been assigned to Putnam County men now went to Knox County; Gale became recording secretary, Miter became corresponding secretary, and Matthew Chambers became treasurer. This shift in the directorate of the society was also evident in the appearance on the board of managers of Augustin Smith and John C. Ward from the Lyndon and Geneseo colonies, which in their origin and settlement so closely paralleled the Galesburg colony.

The same Galesburg officers were retained in office at the annual meeting held in Princeton in 1840, which in addition elected Hiram Marsh of Galesburg as one of its vice-presidents and chose a board of managers in which the Galesburg colony had a majority.[48] Abolitionists throughout the state were impressed with the zeal with which apparently the entire town was devoted to the anti-slavery cause. They heard, and possibly saw themselves, that here was a community that celebrated not only the Fourth of July as an anti-slavery festival but also the anniversary of the emancipation of the slaves in the West Indies, and that on such occasions the village could provide its own band and its own junior and senior choirs and, if need be, its own orators of the day. The crowds, swollen by visitors from as far away as Peoria, and estimated on one occasion as numbering more than a thousand and on another as between two and three thousand, assembled for abolitionist jubilees about a liberty pole or under an immense bower built from boughs hauled into the prairie village from the grove to the north. For one such anti-slavery celebration twenty-eight wagons averaging eight persons each drove from Galesburg ten miles southwest to Cherry Grove; of conspicuous note in the procession was the fact that Negroes rode "promiscuously" with the others and that they freely enjoyed the exercises along with their white companions.[49]

[48] *Ibid.*, 1840.

[49] Descriptions of these assemblies in Galesburg are given by H. H. Kellogg in the *Western Citizen*, Sept. 2, 1842, and in British and Foreign Anti-Slavery Society, *Proceedings of the General Anti-Slavery Convention, London, 1843*, p. 266; by Mary Brown Davis in the *Western Citizen*, July 25, 1844; by E. S. Wilcox

When in June of 1841 the five-year-old town of Galesburg was itself host to the state society, the visitors noted how successfully the colony had matured, how the farms seemed no longer new, how the village had an air of "urbanity," how unusual was the quality of the music presented by its choirs, assisted by the one from the Geneseo colony. But most of all they noted its educational establishments and how their officers and teachers were "not afraid of losing custom by an open avowal of their anti-slavery principles and acting in accordance with them." Such institutions, they resolved, deserved their support.[50] The anniversary of 1841 must have had much of the spirit of a "reunion" for men from the Burned-over District, for in addition to the Galesburg delegation of sixty-one, there were six delegates from the Geneseo colony, and from their several locations had come Hiram and Horatio Foote, Chauncey Cook, John Cross, and others. Except for Owen Lovejoy and Romulus Barnes, the discussions and committee work were done almost entirely by these former New Yorkers.[51]

The period when leadership was concentrated in Galesburg was one of marked increase of activity by the Illinois Anti-Slavery Society. In addition to the regular anniversaries at Princeton in 1840 and Galesburg in 1841, interim conventions were held at Canton in December, 1839, at Joliet in February, 1840,[52] and at Lowell in February, 1841.[53] Two experienced veterans from the eastern campaigns directed by Weld were brought into service for Illinois—John Cross in 1839 and William T. Allan in 1840, both former members of the "Seventy." [54] And in 1840, as abolitionism entered into national party politics for the first time, Galesburgers had considerable weight in shifting much of the momentum of the evangelistic movement in Illinois to political action for the Liberty Party.

in "Reminiscences of Galesburg," Scrapbook No. 6, Galesburg Public Library; and in *Western Citizen*, Aug. 3, 1843.

[50] References to Knox College and Galesburg in *Genius of Liberty*, June 19, 1841, and Jan. 8, 1842, and in the *Western Citizen*, Sept. 2 and 23, 1842.

[51] "Minutes of the Illinois Anti-Slavery Society," 1841.

[52] Executive Committee Report, *ibid.*, 1840.

[53] *Genius of Liberty*, Feb. 6, 27, 1841.

[54] The agency of Cook was continued for six months in 1839.

Cross arrived in Illinois late in the fall of 1839 as an agent for the American Anti-Slavery Society, but that organization was so weakened by internal dissension that it had to instruct its agents to depend entirely upon local collections for traveling expenses and salary. Even this source of livelihood might be denied to them, for out of organizational tensions had resulted a ban on agents operating in any state without the consent of that state's society. In the East such permission had been refused, thereby hastening the decline of the national society.[55] But when Cross arrived in Illinois, he was cheerfully accepted by the executive committee and furnished with a certificate that recommended him to anti-slavery supporters in the state.[56] The readiness with which he was received likely resulted in part from the fact that he came from the same section of New York whence the Galesburg colony originated and that he had been a colleague in the Oneida Presbytery both of Gale and of Miter, officers of the Illinois society. As previously noted, Cross settled his family in Knox County within the Galesburg sphere of influence, and Galesburg people contributed generously to sustain his agency.[57] Though he gave abolitionism a fresh impulse, how successfully he raised funds elsewhere is not evident, and he may have had to put his family on short rations. However, he continued at least two years as an itinerant lecturer in many

[55] Barnes, *Anti-Slavery Impulse*, chapter 16; Birney to Arnold Buffum, Nov. 8, 1839, *Birney Letters*, I, 502–3. By the middle of 1840 there were two national societies, neither with much vigor: the American Anti-Slavery Society, now controlled by Garrison, and a new "American and Foreign Anti-Slavery Society" recently set up by the New York leaders of the benevolent system. The business committee of the Illinois Anti-Slavery Society at the anniversary in Princeton, July, 1840, reported a resolution repealing the auxiliary relation of the Illinois society to the American Anti-Slavery Society and making it instead auxiliary to the American and Foreign Anti-Slavery Society. Miter was chairman of the committee making this recommendation. The state society went along with the recommendation so far as to repeal the alliance with the society now controlled by the Garrisonians, but rejected the new connection with the American and Foreign Anti-Slavery Society, declaring that they were "unwilling to express an opinion as to the claims of the two societies" ("Minutes of the Illinois Anti-Slavery Society," 1840).

[56] Executive Committee Report, "Minutes of the Illinois Anti-Slavery Society," 1840.

[57] "Minutes of the Illinois Anti-Slavery Society," 1842, reports a collection from Galesburg of $93.30, apparently made in 1841.

parts of Illinois, into the fall of 1842.[58] He assumed a leading
role in the affairs of the state society and was particularly aggressive in the promotion of the Liberty Party. The recklessness
with which he worked on the Underground Railroad earned
him the title of "Superintendent" and involved him, along
with other members of the Galesburg colony, in the litigation
over Andrew Borders's slaves. Late in the spring of 1843 he
moved from Knox County to a preaching charge in Bureau
County, but a dozen years later he was back in Galesburg assisting in the leadership of another important anti-slavery venture.

For at least a year while Cross was still traveling the state on
his anti-slavery agency Illinois was also toured by William T.
Allan. The circumstances which led to his settlement in the
state, where a brother of his who was also a Lane Rebel had
helped to settle the Geneseo colony, have already been described. William T. Allan attended the first anniversary of the
Illinois Anti-Slavery Society in Farmington, a year later acted as
secretary pro tem of the society at the Quincy annual meeting,
and participated in the convention of 1840 at Princeton. He
must therefore have been well known to the Galesburg abolitionists, who at this time largely directed the affairs of the state
society; [59] in fact, he had been at Lane and at Oberlin and in the
notorious Seventy with Miter, who was a member of the executive committee at this time. Shortly after the Princeton meeting
in July, 1840, the executive committee tendered him a commission as agent for the state society, in fulfillment of which he began his duties in September of that year.[60] He remained the
agent of the state society until that body was fading out of
existence.

[58] *Genius of Liberty*, Jan. 16, April 10, May 15, July 7, 1841, reports him respectively in Union Grove, Chicago, Farmington, Quincy. He spent the winter
of 1841–42 back in New York (*ibid.*, Nov. 6, 1841, and Feb. 12, 1842).

[59] Not only was the executive committee still located at Galesburg, but the
Princeton anniversary had also set up a Committee on Agencies of which Gale
was chairman and of which C. W. Gilbert of Galesburg and Nahum Gould, who
stemmed from the same part of New York, were the other members ("Minutes
of the Illinois Anti-Slavery Society," 1840).

[60] *Ibid.*, 1841.

During the first year of his agency Allan traversed the section of the state from which the main support of abolitionism was drawn, from Madison County, across from St. Louis, to Winnebago County on the boundary line with the Wisconsin Territory, dividing his itinerary into three tours, the first during the fall and early winter of 1840 in counties south and west of his pastorate in Chatham, Sangamon County, the second in the Military Tract during the winter and early spring of 1841, and the third up the Rock River Valley after the annual meeting at Galesburg in June of the latter year. On the first of these tours he discovered that popular prejudice still reacted violently against the presence of white fanatics who befriended the cause of the Negroes, quite as much as had formerly been the case when the Lane trustees had moved to expel him from the seminary, and his former neighbors in Alabama had talked of cutting his throat, and rioters in Ohio had pelted him with black tar. Around Alton and north from there to Jacksonville mobs demonstrated against him, at Manchester, Jerseyville, Lemons Settlement, and Lower Alton.[61] Even in the Congregational church of Jacksonville someone threw a black rag-baby at his head,[62] and in his own home county the threat of mobs closed the churches of Springfield to him, for, as Allan noted, there was "little leaven" in the capital city of the state.[63] But in the Military Tract he was better received; he talked in a good many places and sometimes had large audiences. In Galesburg he delivered a week-long lecture series,[64] and it was this community and Knox County that gave him the largest contributions.[65]

During the second year of his agency, early in 1842, Allan moved to Peoria, which was nearer the heart of the area that

[61] Allan, Greenfield, Illinois, Dec. 7, 1840, to the *Genius of Liberty*, Jan. 30, 1841.

[62] Heinl, "Jacksonville and Morgan County, an Historical Review," *Journal of the Illinois State Historical Society*, XVIII (1925), 5–38.

[63] Allan, Groveland, Illinois, May 27, 1841, to the *Genius of Liberty*, June 5, 1841.

[64] *Genius of Liberty*, April 24, 1841.

[65] Allan's agency for this year is discussed in the executive committee report of the state society for 1841 and in communications to the *Genius of Liberty*, particularly in the issue of Oct. 2, 1841, which reports his collections.

had been supporting the state society. Here he became the minister of a small New School Presbyterian church that contained the nucleus of what little abolitionism there was in the town. At first there was unrest about his radicalism, but that died down as Allan won respect for having more "ideas than one," and late in the year a series of abolition lectures by him was well attended and courteously listened to. Where there had been only two avowed abolitionists three years before, there were now twenty to thirty "most respectable citizens" apparently enlisted in the cause.[66] But a smoldering hostility blazed forth in February, 1843, when a meeting was called to organize a Peoria anti-slavery society. A mass meeting in the courthouse concentrated its animosity on Allan, affirming that the people of Peoria might have regarded the public organization of an abolition society "with contempt and indifference," for only an insignificant number of persons were concerned in it, but now "an active and latterly arrived agent of a foreign society was at the head of the attempt," from which it was "apparent that the puny infant was destined, by the aid of foreign nurses and tutelage, to become a giant, whose strength would bid defiance to all efforts to resist his treasonable objects." "Such forced products," the Peorians resolved, were not wanted; in Allan they saw "a disturber of the public peace, and one whose business is agitation." [67]

The rioters who gathered at the anti-slavery meeting and prevented Allan from organizing a Peoria abolition society threatened to complete their work by tearing down the meetinghouse, but the "better class" in the mob restrained the "rabble" from that excess.[68] The disturbance might have remained merely another of those disorderly demonstrations that were common in Allan's experience had not those "foreign nurses" of a "foreign society," especially those in Galesburg, exploited the Peoria riot to the advantage of the anti-slavery cause. Within three weeks Peoria's violation of the rights of free assembly and free

[66] *Western Citizen,* Feb. 9, 1843.
[67] These events, with copious extracts from contemporary documents, are set forth in detail in McCulloch, *History of Peoria County,* II, 138–42.
[68] Ballance, *The History of Peoria,* pp. 104–10.

speech was the main theme of a special anti-slavery convention at Farmington, about midway between Peoria and Galesburg. Several towns in that part of the Military Tract were represented, but by far the largest number came from Galesburg, which sent a delegation of forty-two, including a choir and the two most articulate participants in the discussions, Gale and the president of Knox College, Hiram H. Kellogg. Peoria had thirteen of its citizens there including Allen, who of course was very active in the meeting, and Samuel H. Davis, a Whig newspaper man, whose recruitment to the anti-slavery cause as a result of the Peoria riot was probably the most important immediate outcome.[69] Though the effort to stigmatize Peoria as a pro-slavery Gomorrah alongside the Sodom where Lovejoy had been martyred was hardly plausible, the episode did prove to be a turning point for abolitionism in Peoria, and was followed by much close collaboration between the persecuted minority in the river town and the radicals of the college-colony. This included the initiation of a state female anti-slavery society, in the early activities of which Allan's wife had a prominent share. Not until his labors as an agent were over did Allan leave Peoria to settle in the much more congenial Geneseo colony.[70]

[69] *Western Citizen*, March 23, 1843.

[70] On March 30, 1843, he lectured for two evenings at Dover to a meeting of "friends of the slave in Bureau County," where resolutions were adopted about the Peoria riot praising Allan and the "little band of faithful ones, who adhere to him in persecution." The next month he lectured two evenings to S. G. Wright's church at Rochester, Stark County. Early in June he stood with Gale on the affirmative side of a debate about abolitionist principles held at Cherry Grove in Knox County, and later that month he gave a series of lectures just preceding the annual meeting of the state society in Chicago, at which he was one of two delegates from Peoria. Still later that same month he attended the semi-annual meeting of the Wisconsin Anti-Slavery Society and lectured there. By July 4 he was back in Galesburg assisting Gale and "Father" Waters in that colony's anti-slavery celebration. He gave a course of lectures early in October at Bloomington despite a mob-threat, and by the 24th of that same month had traveled to Rockford to play what appears from the minutes to have been the leading role in the semi-annual meeting of the Illinois Anti-Slavery Society that transformed that organization into a machine for the Liberty Party. In April of 1844 he was far south in the state lecturing in Randolph, Perry, and Jackson counties. At the annual meeting of the state society in Jacksonville, on May 29, 1844, he was one of three delegates from Peoria. He presented a bill for services and the society acknowledged a debt of $230.46. A committee was appointed to raise the money for this obligation and "to further sustain him in the field," but

Though the Farmington convention illustrated the continuing abolitionist zeal of the Galesburg colony, by that time the central direction of abolitionism had shifted to Chicago. This change was particularly associated with the development of an anti-slavery press, the serious lack of which had been recognized at the time the excutive committee was located at Galesburg in 1839. In December, 1840, the LaSalle County Anti-Slavery Society had undertaken the publication of the *Genius of Liberty* at Lowell in that county, resuming the use of the press on which Lundy had briefly printed his *Genius of Universal Emancipation* until his death in the summer of 1838. At the Galesburg anniversary of the state society in June, 1841, which was well attended by LaSalle County men, including Zebina Eastman, Lundy's former assistant and now editor of the *Genius of Liberty*, the press committee, of which Gale was chairman, recommended that the state society take over the LaSalle County paper, and this recommendation was accepted by the delegates.[71]

This development was reflected in the election of state officers in 1841, for the posts of corresponding secretary, recording secretary, and treasurer, which had been given to Knox County men two years previously when the society voted to locate the executive committee in Galesburg, now went to Putnam County men.[72] Furthermore, in setting up the organization in June, 1841, the board of managers, on which Knox County had a majority, now was composed almost entirely of men from LaSalle, Putnam, and Bureau counties, the area immediately around Lowell.[73]

This placing of the abolitionist directorate was, however, only

the society was already in decline. That the Allans still lived in Peoria as late as August 8, 1844, is evident from a letter by Mrs. Allan to the *Western Citizen,* issue of Sept. 5, 1855, but by the end of that year they had settled in Geneseo (*Western Citizen,* April 20 to Oct. 19, 1843, April 25, 1844; "Minutes of the Illinois Anti-Slavery Society," 1843 and 1844; Wright, "Journal," April 13, 1843; Pierce, *A History of Chicago,* I, 245).

[71] "Minutes of the Illinois Anti-Slavery Society," 1841.

[72] Two of these Putnam County men, James H. Dickey and Hooper Warren, had each held one of these offices during a previous year, at the time that the *Emancipator* had been dated in Hennepin and printed in Lowell about twelve miles away.

[73] "Minutes of the Illinois Anti-Slavery Society," 1841.

transitional, for already in February, 1842, steps were being taken to establish an anti-slavery paper in Chicago; in April the *Genius of Liberty* ceased publication; three months later Zebina Eastman, its editor, had run off the first number of the new *Western Citizen* of Chicago, and that paper now became the anti-slavery organ for the state.[74] Meanwhile in 1842 the state society held its anniversary in Chicago for the first time, and a large number of the delegates appeared from counties in the northeastern part of the state that had not been represented at previous annual meetings.[75] The choice of officers at this convention showed the trend toward Chicago, and it was there that the anniversary of 1843 also was held.

Though Galesburg and Knox County delegates attended these Chicago meetings and Gale and President Kellogg had active parts in the deliberations,[76] it is apparent from the proceedings that the primacy held by the Galesburg colony in the state society ever since the first anniversary at Farmington had passed to the booming city at the tip of Lake Michigan. By this time, however, the abolitionist crusade had begun to change from what was essentially religious evangelism aroused by preachers to party politics that was more the province of laymen. The Illinois Anti-Slavery Society, which at the outset was the device of the former, had by 1843 probably fulfilled its function, for the general propagation of anti-slavery principles was by 1844 vigorously performed by the Liberty Party, and there were other ways by which the particular religious aspects of the abolitionist doctrine could be emphasized.

But even as Chicago men assumed the leadership, Knox College remained at front center of the abolitionist stage because of the singular role in which President Kellogg was cast in the spring of 1843 through his appointment by the executive com-

[74] Harris, *Negro Servitude in Illinois,* pp. 134–42.

[75] "Minutes of the Illinois Anti-Slavery Society," May 26, 27, 28, 1842.

[76] Ten men appeared at the anniversary of 1842 from Knox County, headed by President Kellogg, who served on the business and press committees, was very active in the sessions of the convention, and was elected one of six vice-presidents. Four Knox County delegates attended the anniversary of 1843, including Gale, who was chairman of the committee to prepare the business of the convention, was active in its discussions, and was chosen one of five vice-presidents (*ibid.,* 1842 and 1843).

mittee as the delegate from the Illinois Anti-Slavery Society to the World Anti-Slavery Convention in London.[77] There were those in Illinois who thought that whatever money there was to pay Kellogg's expenses might be better spent in Illinois to support an agent and to distribute tracts,[78] though the action of the executive committee could not be considered arbitrary, since in 1839 the state society had voted to send a delegate to the World Anti-Slavery Convention in London in 1840, at which time no one had gone.[79] Nor was the connection between the abolitionism of the Mississippi Valley and that on the Thames so farfetched as would appear to the uninformed or the superficial observer, for in both places the main force of the anti-slavery impulse came from evangelical religious circles, and the development of the abolition movement in the United States had been directly affected by men and events from the British Isles.[80] In fact a favorite theme for discussion at anti-slavery meetings in Illinois at which Gale was a speaker was the emancipation of slaves in the British West Indies,[81] in which American abolitionists found proof for the feasibility of their principles.

In 1840 delegates from Oberlin had combined attendance at the World Anti-Slavery Convention with a fund-raising campaign in which their college was presented to the reformers and philanthropists of Great Britain as the particular training school of anti-slavery workers. They succeeded in bringing back to the Ohio college the amazing sum of $30,000.[82] Since the origins, methods, and purposes of Knox so exactly paralleled those of Oberlin, it is not surprising that as early as November, 1841, the Knox College trustees should have contemplated that President Kellogg might also solicit funds in Europe.[83] In January, 1843, Kellogg wrote to Gerrit Smith of his intention to

[77] Western Citizen, March 30, 1843.   [78] Ibid., April 20, 1843.
[79] "Minutes of the Illinois Anti-Slavery Society," 1839.
[80] Barnes, Anti-Slavery Impulse, pp. 29–32, 47–48, 53, 56, 142–43, 171.
[81] Peoria Register and Northwestern Gazetteer, July 14, Sept. 1, 1838, Aug. 5, 1842. On such occasions Gale was armed with a book, Horace Kimball and James A. Thome, Six Months Tour of the West Indies in the Year 1837, from which he read extracts.
[82] Fletcher, History of Oberlin, I, 457–69.
[83] Knox College, "Trustees' Minutes," MSS.

go to the World Anti-Slavery Convention,[84] and Gale suggested to the tricounty anti-slavery convention of March 8 and
9, 1843, that Illinois send a delegate to that assembly.[85] Within
less than a week the financial needs of Knox College had become tragically urgent as a result of the burning of the newly
finished college building,[86] and before the end of the month
the executive committee of the state anti-slavery society had
appointed Kellogg to the London convention. At the annual
meeting of the society in Chicago in June, 1843, a special
committee was appointed to receive donations for Kellogg's
expenses.[87] He was by then already on his way.

Kellogg's mission to Britain was followed in detail by Illinois
readers for over a year. The *Western Citizen,* immediately after
his appointment, announced as a special attraction for new
subscribers that the president of Knox College would favor it
with his correspondence while on his travels,[88] and beginning
in April, 1843, and lasting until June of the following year it
published thirty-eight of his letters, averaging one and a half
to two columns in length, and almost always given the leading
place on the first page. Traveling to the East via the Illinois,
Mississippi, and Ohio rivers, Kellogg embarked at Peoria about
the middle of April, taking with him some pamphlets entitled
"Free Discussion Suppressed in Peoria" which were given to
him by the author, Samuel H. Davis, and which Kellogg
planned to distribute en route. At Alton he visited the spot
where the Illinois martyr, Lovejoy, had fallen.[89] On the upper
Ohio and beyond he had as his traveling companion another of
the delegates to England, Jonathan Blanchard, now the pastor
of the Cincinnati church that had been at the center of the
Lane Rebellion. On the boat Kellogg and Blanchard baited an
Old School Presbyterian preacher who was carrying a slave
with him.[90] Kellogg himself attended the New School Presbyterian General Assembly in Philadelphia, where he led the

[84] Kellogg to Smith, Jan. 11, 1843, Gerrit Smith Papers.
[85] *Western Citizen,* March 23, 1843.   [86] *Ibid.*
[87] "Minutes of the Illinois Anti-Slavery Society," June 7, 1843.
[88] *Western Citizen,* April 20, 1843.
[89] *Ibid.,* May 18, 1843.   [90] *Ibid.,* July 6, 1843.

fight for a more advanced stand on slavery by that denomination. While in that city he attended public worship with a Negro congregation.[91] He sailed on the *Great Western*.

Probably no other delegate traveled so far to attend the London convention of anti-slavery workers. Kellogg identified himself to the assembly as a "thousand miles nearer the setting sun" than the delegate from Massachusetts, which was perhaps as accurate a geographical reference to the American interior as his English auditors could quickly comprehend.[92] Though he was sick one day of the session and hardly able to attend the next,[93] he took an active part in the deliberations, avoiding the loquaciousness which marred the behavior of at least two of the thirteen Americans present.[94] He served on the committee which considered the questions involved in the *Creole* case and the problem of Negro fugitives to Canada,[95] and also was a member of the committee to which was referred the papers on American slavery.[96] By assignment he had the duty of delivering one of the longer formal addresses to the convention, his subject being: "United States—Prejudice against Color." [97] In this discourse, which he presented in a very scholarly manner, he cited at some length the absence of a color line at Knox College.[98]

It was another year before Kellogg was back in Illinois, for he remained in Britain until the following May.[99] The length of his stay is explained by his effort to raise money for Knox College from the reform-minded British philanthropists. Before leaving Galesburg he had written to James G. Birney, who had been to England at the preceding world convention, for a letter "to promote . . . my intercourse with individuals and

[91] *Ibid.*, July 20, 1843.
[92] British and Foreign Anti-Slavery Society, *Proceedings of the General Anti-Slavery Convention*, London, 1843, pp. 25–26.
[93] *Western Citizen*, Aug. 3, 1843.
[94] Charles Stuart to Weld, Bathwickhill-Bath, England, July 10, 1843, *Weld Letters*, II, 978–79: "Leavitt, Phelps, Kellogg, Pennington and L. Tappan did justice to their country, Blanchard and Howells *would* speak too much."
[95] British and Foreign Anti-Slavery Society, *Proceedings of the General Anti-Slavery Convention*, London, *1843*, p. 45.
[96] *Ibid.*, p. 198.   [97] *Ibid.*, pp. 265–74.   [98] *Ibid.*, p. 266.
[99] *Western Citizen*, June 6, June 27, 1844.

general society" in order to secure assistance for the school.[100]
In England he issued a circular appeal "To Christian Philan-
thropists in Great Britain and Ireland" in which he said of
Knox:

It is not exclusive in its privileges. This is true with respect to persons of different complexions. Colored youth will be welcomed and
treated with equal kindness and attention with others.[101]

This appeal for help was endorsed by three of the other American delegates, Joshua Leavitt, Amos A. Phelps, and Jonathan
Blanchard.[102]

During his British travels Kellogg visited notables, not only
in the anti-slavery movement but also in allied humanitarian
enterprises such as prison reform. He addressed the Birming-
ham Anti-Slavery Society, to which he traveled in company
with Leavitt and the Reverend J. W. Pennington, an American
Negro; he spoke in London to the annual meeting of the
British and Foreign Anti-Slavery Society and received the com-
pliments of the great Irish orator Daniel O'Connell for speaking "with so much intelligence and good sense, so much
moderation and firmness, in condemnation of slavery in his
own country." [103] He visited Cambridge University, attended
the Congregational Union of England and Wales at Leeds and
the General Assembly of the Free Church at Glasgow, and
served actively as a member of a committee to bring about a
World Temperance Convention. Like a true disciple of the
Great Revival, he was sensitive to all schemes for the world's
renovation, attended one of the famous meetings held by
Cobden and Bright, was deeply interested in the anti-corn-law
movement then stirring England, and devoted much of his
writing to the *Western Citizen* to the free-trade principles, of
which he was, or became, a strong advocate.[104] The British
connections which Kellogg made during his travels were not
entirely broken by his return to the United States, for in 1846

---

[100] Kellogg to Birney, April 5, 1843, *Birney Letters*, I, 228–30.
[101] *Report on Knox College, 1861*, p. 27.
[102] *Ibid.*, p. 121.   [103] *Western Citizen*, July 18, 1844.
[104] Kellogg's letters to the *Western Citizen*, 1843–44.

the *Western Citizen* printed at length an anti-slavery address he had received from British clergy and laymen.[105]

Kellogg's correspondence was particularly commended by the Illinois Anti-Slavery Society in its sixth anniversary meeting in Chicago, in June, 1843.[106] There were present four delegates from Galesburg, Gale serving as chairman of the committee to prepare the business of the convention and being elected a vice-president.[107] In 1844, after two years in a row in Chicago, the annual meeting was held in Jacksonville. Gale was again one of the vice-presidents, and the Reverend Levi Spencer, one of the first anti-slavery preachers trained and sent out by the Galesburg colony, was appointed secretary.[108] But the session was poorly attended, partly because of bad roads, and possibly also because the meeting place was too far south of the heart of the abolitionist population in the state. It became apparent, however, that the impulse which had set the state society going was either dying out or directing its force in other directions. The Illinois Anti-Slavery Society had only two more years of nominal existence; by 1846 the chief topic of the annual meeting was the society's debts, and no new officers were elected.[109]

This did not signify that the state organization had been a failure; rather it indicated that it fulfilled its function of sustaining an unpopular cause until its principles had become widely enough adopted to make abolition a persistent civil and eccleciastical issue. There was now a vigorous anti-slavery paper in the state, the *Western Citizen,* and a few others were also soon to appear. Most important of all, the state society had committed itself to political action, and by 1844 that was being effectively carried on by the Liberty Party, to which many of the abolitionists who once had borne the burdens of the Illinois Anti-Slavery Society now contributed their strength. The transition from one type of activity to the other is well exemplified by the Galesburg colony.

[105] He also received an address from "The Friends of Peace of New Castle upon Tyne . . . to the Inhabitants of Illinois and Neighboring States of North America" in 1846 (*Western Citizen,* Sept. 22, 1846).

[106] *Ibid.*, June 5, 1843.

[107] "Minutes of the Illinois Anti-Slavery Society," 1843.

[108] *Ibid.*, 1844.   [109] *Western Citizen,* June 10, 1846.

❧ X ❧

Launching the Liberty Party

We seek no selfish end. The preservation of our own liberty; the
rescuing of the right of petition and freedom of speech from the
dust; the restoration of the north to its relative importance in
our national affairs; the deliverance of the enslaved; the eleva-
tion of the colored man to the enjoyment of his long lost rights;
the deliverance of our country from the inconsistency and guilt
of slavery; these are our objects; and are there any objects before
the mind of any political party so important as these? [1]

POLITICAL PARTIES DURING THE FORTIES began
to feel the strain of abolitionism as churches and schools had
felt it during the preceding decade. Among the many signs of
growing political tension on the issue of slavery was the appearance of new political parties; first the Liberty Party, and by
the end of the forties, the Free Soil Party. The Galesburg
colony had much to do with the starting of this political activity
in Illinois. By 1850, as the president of Knox College looked
over his board of trustees, he could see the man who had
presided over the first Liberty Party convention in the state
and still another who had been chairman of the second convention of that party in Illinois. Both in 1840 and in 1844
a Knox College trustee had been candidate for presidential
elector on the Liberty ticket, and in 1848 the president of the
college had himself been one of the electors listed by the
Free Soil Party. Six Knox board members at one time or an-

[1] "Address" prepared for the Knox County Liberty Party Convention, April 23,
1842, by a committee consisting of George W. Gale, Ozias Marsh, and Nehemiah
West (Peoria *Register and Northwestern Gazetteer,* June 17, 1842).

other had held the following places in the Liberty Party: two vice-presidencies of state conventions, in 1842 and 1846; a candidate for Congress; two candidates for the state senate; five presidencies, vice-presidencies, or secretaryships of district and county party organizations. From the faculty had come a candidate for the Illinois General Assembly. Nor did this include other prominent preachers and laymen from the colony who had achieved leading roles in the Liberty Party. What makes this catalogue of party chores most significant is that they were all performed by men from a single village which in 1850 had not yet reached the number of 900 souls, counting women and children as well as voters.

The starting of a separate anti-slavery political organization in Galesburg and elsewhere required some rethinking on the nature of the abolitionist crusade, for it was at first distinctly a religious and not a political movement, a campaign for converts rather than a canvass for candidates, and to the end of the thirties its proponents believed it should remain a religious activity. Abolitionists did conduct powerful petition programs, and the "gagging" of anti-slavery petitions by Congress became one of the critical issues of the day. Abolitionists also had questioned and discriminated among office seekers; but the first proposals that abolitionists should nominate their own candidates and form a third party found support only from a scattering of anti-slavery men, the most conspicuous being certain radicals in the Burned-over District. Garrison, of course, denounced any degree of political involvement, but the idea of a third party was also reproved by the New York committee, publicly condemned by Lewis Tappan, and rather generally regarded as "monstrous." [2] When certain heedless abolitionists persisted in the third-party "folly" during the presidential contest of 1840, not one abolitionist in ten followed them; as a result they made a ridiculously poor showing, polling less than seven thousand votes throughout the nation. [3]

Sixteen years later the stone rejected by the builders had

[2] Barnes, *Anti-Slavery Impulse*, pp. 147–48, 164, 176–77, 181.
[3] Theodore C. Smith, *Liberty and Free Soil Parties*, p. 47.

become the cornerstone of the temple. In the Republican Party of 1856 were many leaders who had served their political apprenticeship in the Liberty Party.[4] For example, in Illinois one of the Republican congressmen elected in 1856 had been one of the abhorred abolitionists in 1840, a preacher dabbling in politics and brother of the Lovejoy who was murdered defending an anti-slavery press.

The genesis of the Liberty Party occurred while the abolitionist organization in Illinois was largely under the direction of the leaders of the Galesburg colony, and a great deal of interest therefore attached to their attitude toward anti-slavery politics. The earliest clue is found in Gale's vote at the anniversary of the American Anti-Slavery Society in May of 1839, when the delegates debated a resolution that it was a duty to employ the "political franchise" to promote the abolition of slavery, and divided eighty-four in favor and seventy-seven against this opinion. The New York delegation overwhelmingly took the former and the Massachusetts delegates, led by Garrison, took the latter position. Gale, the sole delegate from Illinois, voted the same as his former New York associates, among whom were two other Oneida County men who were soon to be in Knox County, Illinois; one of these was Hiram H. Kellogg, president-elect of Knox College; the other was the Reverend John Cross.[5] In September following the New York discussion of this issue, Gale was a leader in the annual meeting of the Illinois Anti-Slavery Society at Quincy at which it was resolved that abolitionists should carry their principles to the polls. It was this meeting that located the executive committee of the society in Galesburg and made Gale one of the officers.

The propositions adopted at New York in May and at Quincy in September of 1839 did not specifically countenance the formation of an independent political party. But by July of 1840, when the Illinois abolitionists met in Princeton for their next state anniversary, they faced this specific issue rather than

[4] *Ibid.*, pp. 1–2.
[5] *Sixth Annual Report of the American Anti-Slavery Society*, 1839, pp. 42–44.

the general question, for despite the discouragement of the mass of the anti-slavery men, certain zealots in the East, following the initiative of leaders in the Burned-over District, had formed the Liberty Party.[6] They presented James G. Birney and Thomas Earle for the presidency and vice-presidency of the United States and thus compelled the anti-slavery men of Illinois to choose or reject candidates of undoubted anti-slavery principles. The business committee of the Princeton meeting presented a resolution declaring that it was the "imperative duty" of anti-slavery men to withhold their votes from pro-slavery men and specifically stating that the Democratic and Whig candidates for president and vice-president "equally forfeited all claims to the support of those men who adhere to the doctrine of inalienable rights." [7] Though this resolution did not commit its proponents to the new third party, it left little other choice than to vote for Birney and Earle unless the voter abstained from participation in the presidential poll. The committee reporting this resolution consisted of five members, three of whom were former Oneida County men who were part of or closely associated with the Galesburg colony: Miter, John Cross, and William Selden Gale, son of the leader of the colony. The other two were Owen Lovejoy of Princeton and the Reverend Roswell Grosvenor of Sangamon County, who had been a prominent person in the state society since its formation.

The proposition that abolitionists should deny their votes to the presidential candidates of either major party was defended by most of the leading persons at the Princeton anniversary, by the elder Gale, by Cross, who had been serving as agent of the national society in Illinois, by Lovejoy, by Chauncey Cook, who served for a short term as agent of the state society, by Dr. David Nelson, and by two members of the Yale Band, Farnam and Barnes. The only delegate of comparable standing in the state society who argued for the negative was Miter. This indicated, however, that the Knox County delegation,

[6] Theodore C. Smith, *Liberty and Free Soil Parties*, pp. 36–38.
[7] "Minutes of the Illinois Anti-Slavery Society," 1840.

as well as the convention generally, was divided on the issue.[8] Among the delegates, about 100 in number, three opinions existed, some contending earnestly for an anti-slavery ticket headed by Birney, some opposing this action but declaring that abolitionists should vote for neither of the major party candidates, and others, the greatest number, desiring that the convention should adopt no position but should allow each man to decide for himself.[9] The debate extended throughout an entire day. The original proposition was not adopted, despite its prominent supporters; instead a milder substitute offered by Miter was accepted. This motion simply stated that the abolition of slavery should be regarded as the paramount political question before the nation, but that it was "inexpedient to recommend any definite mode as to the manner" in which anti-slavery men should use their influence in behalf of the slave. However, immediately after this resolution was carried, one of the proponents of the stronger resolution moved for the indefinite postponement of the matter, and it was with formal avoidance of the question that the discussion ended.[10]

Failure to commit the state society to the Liberty Party did not deter a little band of fifteen Liberty proponents [11] from getting their candidates into the field. Before they left Princeton, the day following the adjournment of the state society, they convened and set up the first anti-slavery electoral ticket in the Northwest.[12] A clue regarding the leadership of the little group that thus inaugurated the Liberty Party in Illinois is found in the fact that their presiding officer was William Holyoke of the Galesburg colony. He had been acquainted with Birney in Cincinnati even before the latter had moved there from Danville, Kentucky,[13] and they both were members of

[8] *Ibid.*   [9] Peoria *Register and Northwestern Gazetteer,* July 10, 1840.
[10] "Minutes of the Illinois Anti-Slavery Society," 1840. The records of this meeting are in the handwriting of Gale, recording secretary of the society, and the report of the debate must be regarded as his. The discussion and decision of the Illinois society closely parallels that occurring in the Ohio state society in May, 1840 (Theodore C. Smith, *Liberty and Free Soil Parties,* pp. 39–40).
[11] Peoria *Register and Northwestern Gazetteer,* July 17, 1840.
[12] Theodore C. Smith, *Liberty and Free Soil Parties,* pp. 42–43.
[13] Weld addressed letters on Aug. 18 and 19, 1835, to Birney in Cincinnati in care of "W. Holyoke" (*Birney Letters,* I, 238–40).

that Sixth Presbyterian Church which was then particularly the focus of the radicals in Cincinnati. The Reverend David D. Nelson of Quincy was secretary of the Princeton group, and a committee of five was appointed to nominate electors. This committee included three men who had come from the Burned-over District of New York: John Cross and Chauncey Cook, who had both served as anti-slavery agents in Illinois, and Innis Grant, who had recently settled in the Lisbon colony but was shortly to rejoin his former associates from Oneida Institute by becoming a member of the Knox College faculty. The fourth member of the committee was N. P. Barnard, like Grant from Kendall County, and the fifth man was William Lewis of Putnam County.[14]

While nominating Birney and Earle, the Princeton convention revealed an ominous insight into the consequences of their principles, for their platform declared that in supporting candidates pledged to end slavery, they wanted to accomplish abolition "by law at sacrifice of time and money but not blood." Interesting but less prescient was the resolution that the seat of the national government should be moved to some place northwest of the Ohio River.[15]

In the balloting at the presidential election the voice of Liberty was faint indeed, for only 160 votes were cast for Birney and Earle in the entire state.[16] The campaign had been most raucous, especially on the part of the Whigs, who made strenuous efforts to win the West by portraying Harrison as the particular friend of the pioneer. Much hullabaloo was made over the danger that Liberty men, by robbing the Whigs, would in effect elect Van Buren. From Illinois it was reported: "Many who when times were perilous, when Lovejoy fell, re-

[14] Peoria *Register and Northwestern Gazetteer*, July 17, 1840. The presidential electors on the Liberty ticket in Illinois in 1840 were Holyoke, Erastus Benton of Adams County, Ripley E. Adams of Will County, William Lewis of Putnam County, and Eli Wilson of Peoria County. All of these men had been active in the state society.

[15] *Ibid.*

[16] These were scattered in twenty-two counties, Adams leading with forty-two, Will ranking next with sixteen, while Putnam, Bureau, and Knox followed with thirteen each (Pease, *Illinois Election Returns*, pp. 117–19).

mained unshaken by the threats and howlings of mob fury, were borne headlong by the shout of 'Tip and Tyler.' Prominent members and officers of the State Society, and men in the garb of the Christian ministry even, voted for Harrison." [17] The division of opinion in Galesburg was probably typical of anti-slavery men; Horatio Foote, the spellbinding evangelist who was pastor of the colony church, supported the Liberty candidates in a stirring speech, but he was opposed by Hiram Marsh, one of the young preachers then teaching in the academy, who was a vice-president of the state anti-slavery society. Only a baker's dozen voted for the ticket on which their neighbor Holyoke was a presidential elector, and local tradition does not include Gale among these resolute few.[18] Those who were presently ashamed that they had not done likewise might find some comfort in the fact that only in Putnam County had there been a stronger Liberty vote relative to the total number of ballots cast.

Even if the voters of Galesburg had unanimously supported the Liberty ticket in November of 1840 it would not have dented the armor of the old-line parties, for Galesburg was still only a small frontier village, and in fact remained a small college town until the mid-fifties when the railroad arrived. The importance of the vote in Knox and Putnam counties lay not in the quantity of voters [19] but in the quality of leadership. The attitude of the leaders of the college-colony carried weight in abolitionist circles, as became evident in the early issues of the *Genius of Liberty*. The establishment of this paper at Lowell, the month following the presidential election, overcame what had probably been the chief weakness of the Liberty Party in the campaign, the lack of a partisan press. Early the next February, Miter, as corresponding secretary and member of the executive committee which was still centered at Gales-

[17] Theodore C. Smith, *Liberty and Free Soil Parties,* pp. 45–46.

[18] Chapman, *History of Knox County,* p. 406.

[19] The most populous counties of the state were Morgan, Sangamon, Adams, and Madison, each of which had over 14,000 residents, which was twice that of Knox County. Quincy in Adams County was the largest town in the Military Tract, and its 2,319 residents were several times more than the population of Galesburg.

burg, placed in the *Genius of Liberty* a call for a special meeting of the state society.[20] The chief topic of this gathering, which was presided over by James H. Dickey, leader of the Putnam County anti-slavery men, was political action by abolitionists. After a protracted discussion it was agreed by the majority that abolitionists should not vote for pro-slavery men, and if need be should nominate their own candidates. The most active and aggressive proponent of this opinion seems, from the proceedings, to have been John Cross.[21] In the same issue of the *Genius of Liberty* that reported these doings Cross also supplied an article revealing his particular concern with the political stand of the Galesburg colony. Cross described in detail and with evident pleasure the prospering of the colony and of its school and he lauded its anti-slavery principles, but he also regretted that it had failed to produce more than a dozen anti-slavery votes at the recent election. An editorial in this same issue of the *Genius*, referring to Cross's comments, both blunted and pointed up Cross's complaint by assuring the readers that the Galesburg abolitionists who had voted Whig in 1840 could not be blamed for the "improprieties and fooleries" of the hard cider and log-cabin arguments. And this was followed in the very next issue by the printing of a letter which Gale had given to Miter to carry to the Lowell meeting. Gale regretted that he had not had the time to do more for the anti-slavery cause but endorsed the idea of political action. He expressed the opinion that it was now clearer to abolitionists that they must use the ballot to put anti-slavery men into office and questioned whether the major parties had such men.[22]

The expectation that the Galesburg colony would sustain the third-party movement more fully was fulfilled at the first opportunity the following summer. This was in the contest for a congressman in the third district, which included all the northwestern third of the state and most of the area in which the state anti-slavery society had been operating. At seven

[20] *Genius of Liberty*, Feb. 6, 1841.　　　[21] *Ibid.*, Feb. 27, 1841.
[22] *Ibid.*, March 6, 1841. Gale was definitely a Liberty Party man in the campaign of 1842 (Peoria *Register and Northwestern Gazetteer*, June 17, 1842).

o'clock in the morning on June 11, the day after the state society had completed its annual meeting in Galesburg, some
of the delegates who had been attending that anniversary met
to nominate a Liberty candidate. Nehemiah West of the Galesburg colony was president of this convention and Levi Spencer,
also of that colony, was the secretary.[23] Frederick Collins of
Adams County, the most populous in the Military Tract, was
chosen as the nominee.

The result of this second Liberty campaign in the state, the
only one by this party during 1841, was very encouraging to
abolitionists, for the 492 ballots cast for Collins were more
than thrice those given to Birney the preceding November and
were sufficient to be a balance of power in this congressional
district, where the Whigs and Democrats were very closely
matched. It encouraged an awakened interest in the northern
part of the state, where the third party would have the best
chance to make a successful bid for office.[24]

Knox County gave Collins four times more Liberty votes
than it had given Birney, and of its fifty-seven votes practically
all must have come from Galesburg.[25] This amounted to nearly
5 percent of the county vote, being equaled in that proportion
only by Bureau County (where anti-slavery leadership was
centered in the Hampshire colony church), and being exceeded
only by Henry County (where the abolitionist leadership lay
in the Geneseo colony) and by Putnam County, which cast a
remarkable 26 percent of its vote for Collins.[26] These other
counties lay farther north in the state, as was reflected in the
smaller Democratic poll. Galesburg, more than these other anti-
slavery communities, was surrounded by a numerous "Hoosier"
population who hated "that abolition village" and some of
whom actually made threats to burn it.[27] Those few in Knox

---

[23] *Genius of Liberty*, June 19, 1841. Hiram Marsh, who had been strong for
Harrison in the colony the preceding fall, now served on the nominating committee, along with Cross, and three men from Fulton, Marshall, and Putnam
counties.

[24] Harris, *Negro Servitude in Illinois*, p. 148.

[25] Local election returns are not available, but this is a reasonable opinion
on the basis of later Knox County votes, which are known in greater detail.

[26] Pease, *Illinois Election Returns*, pp. 122–25.

[27] "Reminiscences," Scrapbook No. 2, Galesburg Public Library, p. 26.

County outside of Galesburg who wanted to vote an anti-slavery ticket found it advisable to go to Galesburg, if possible, to do so. At the town of Henderson, just north of the college-colony, one of the judges of the election shook his fist in the faces of the abolitionists and declared that they could not vote for their candidates in that place.[28]

Really effective state-wide organization for the Liberty Party was first accomplished at a convention held in Chicago in May, 1842. The drift of leadership toward the lake counties was apparent in the proceedings, for men of Cook County (where only one Liberty vote had been cast in 1840) were very prominent.[29] When the Illinois Anti-Slavery Society held its annual meeting that year in Chicago, only three delegates opposed committing the organization to political action and the nominating of anti-slavery candidates.[30] This was a substantial shift from the political neutrality assumed at Princeton two years previously. During the summer eleven counties, including Knox, held Liberty conventions.[31] The chairman and secretary of the Knox County convention, William Holyoke and Eli Farnham respectively, were both from Galesburg. Holyoke addressed the assembly, pointing out the inconsistency between the practice of slaveholding and the principles set forth in the Declaration of Independence, and asserting that this inconsistency between professed principles and practice made the nation a laughing-stock before the world. He called attention to laws in Illinois that discriminated against free Negroes. The older political parties could not be looked to as a source of relief for the slave, both having courted the favor of the slaveholders. A small company of two hundred and fifty thousand of the latter class had dominated the country for years and determined all points of national policy. Freemen who would take the work in their hands and assert their rights must rally around the ban-

---

[28] Chapman, *History of Knox County*, pp. 404–5.

[29] Harris, *Negro Servitude in Illinois*, pp. 146, 148.

[30] Peoria *Register and Northwestern Gazetteer*, June 24, 1842. A Knox County delegation of ten, headed by Kellogg, was present at this anniversary. Kellogg was very active in its sessions ("Minutes of the Illinois Anti-Slavery Society," 1842).

[31] Harris, *Negro Servitude in Illinois*, p. 150.

ner of the Liberty Party. Resolutions adopted by the convention declared it the duty of all Christians regardless of sect to band together against slavery, lauded John Quincy Adams as the defender of the right of petition against slaveholders, denounced the censure of Congressman Joshua R. Giddings as a trampling by the slave interests on liberty and the Constitution, and asserted that freemen were obliged to rebuke and resent "this spirit in Congress." [32]

A manifestation of the increased Liberty Party activity was the nominating for the first time in Illinois of candidates for offices in the state government. Matthew Chambers of the Galesburg colony ran for the Illinois senate in the election of August, 1842, and received eighty-seven votes, all from Knox County.[33] This was the largest Liberty vote polled in any county in the state for this office. That county also gave ninety-four votes for the Liberty candidate for the lower house in the state legislature, a number exceeded only by Adams County. In the vote for governor Knox County was exceeded in Liberty votes only by Adams County and in the percent of that vote by Putnam and Bureau counties.[34]

Reapportionment increased the Illinois congressional districts in 1843 to seven, four of which had Liberty candidates that year. Galesburg was now in the sixth district, which extended two or three counties deep from the Wisconsin line along the Mississippi River to its westernmost bulge about halfway down the length of the state. Matthew Chambers of the Galesburg colony was the candidate. Of the sixteen counties involved, both Ogle and Winnebago gave him more votes than his own, which was indicative of the rising Liberty tide in the northern part of the state, as well as of the increasing population of that area. In this and the two other congressional elections of the middle forties it was the district comprising the northeast counties that had the largest number of Liberty votes, the sixth district always running a poor second.[35] This

[32] Peoria *Register and Northwestern Gazetteer*, June 17, 1842.
[33] This does not include the one vote each for William Holyoke and H. H. Kellogg.
[34] Pease, *Illinois Election Returns*, pp. 126–28, 349–79.   [35] *Ibid.*, pp. 135–59.

shift northward and particularly toward the northeast coincided with the previously noted growth of Chicago's importance in other abolitionist activities. In October, 1843, a semi-annual meeting of the state anti-slavery society at Rockford virtually transformed that body into an arm of the Liberty Party.[36] Leaders of the latter set out to replace the local anti-slavery societies by Liberty Associations, and Galesburg men fell in with this change of tactics.[37]

How extensively the Galesburg settlers were now persuaded of the necessity of voting their anti-slavery principles was revealed in letters from President Kellogg to both Gerrit Smith and James Birney in 1843; he boasted that "our precinct casts more votes for Liberty than both the other parties united." [38] The old-line Whigs particularly were disturbed because this large Liberty majority "had all of the talk their own way." The Whigs tried to reorganize so as to save the remnants of their party in the village. Democrats, of course, were hardly to be looked for in this community.[39]

The president of the state Liberty convention early in 1844 was John Cross. At that time he was enjoying wide notoriety because he and a number of Galesburg abolitionists, including Gale, were under indictment in Knox County for harboring fugitive slaves, and the affair was receiving much publicity.

[36] "Minutes of the Illinois Anti-Slavery Society," Oct. 24, 1843.

[37] According to Harris (*Negro Servitude in Illinois*, pp. 152–53), the first of these, organized in Chicago in Oct., 1843, served as a model for the rest. Members agreed not to vote for anyone not committed to anti-slavery principles. One of the fourteen organizations formed on this basis during the next three years was in Galesburg. It was probably formed late in 1843, Nehemiah West acting as chairman of the meeting and Eli Farnham as secretary. Matthew Chambers and Leonard Chappell were elected president and secretary respectively. The other signers of the pledge at this time were John Waters, A. S. Bergen, S. Williams, Innes Grant, A. Neely, S. Tompkins, F. Leonard, R. C. Dunn, G. A. Marsh, R. Paine, and A. V. Pennoyer (Mary Allen West, "How Galesburg Grew," MS dated May 23, 1873, in Galesburg Public Library).

[38] Kellogg to Birney, April 5, 1843, *Birney Letters*, II, 729–30. "In this town where about 120 votes are polled only 13 votes were cast for Birney two years ago. At our last August election we gave for the Liberty candidates 68 votes, being more than were cast for the candidates of both the other parties" (Kellogg to Gerrit Smith, Jan. 10, 1843, Gerrit Smith Papers).

[39] William Selden Gale, "Autobiography" (MS, Knox College Library); Churchill, "Galesburg History," *Republican Register*, July 29, 1876.

One of the Galesburg men involved in the litigation, A. S. Bergen, was chairman of the Liberty convention of the sixth congressional district, at Lyndon, where he also served with Sherman Williams of Galesburg on the nominating committee. John Cross was selected as the congressional candidate.[40] Innes Grant, professor of ancient languages at Knox College, was appointed as the corresponding member for Knox County on the central committee. He was probably also the candidate for representative in the General Assembly.[41] And when the congressional and legislative poll of August was followed in November by a presidential election, Nehemiah West of Galesburg was one of the nine Liberty electoral college candidates. Only Cook, Kane, Will, and Dupage counties in the extreme northeast corner of the state exceeded the Knox County Liberty vote in numbers.[42]

In 1845 and 1846 the arrival of two new officers in the Galesburg colony supplied new leadership for the Liberty Party. One was a son-in-law of William Holyoke, the Reverend Lucius H. Parker, who served for a time as pastor of the colony church; the other was the Reverend Jonathan Blanchard, who came early in 1846 to assume his responsibilities as second president of Knox College. Both of these men, like other clerical colleagues of New School Presbyterian and Congregational connections, acted contrary to the widely prevailing taboo against men of the cloth participating in politics. Blanchard almost immediately followed up his Cincinnati activities in anti-slavery politics by involving himself in the affairs of the Liberty Party in Illinois.[43] In fact within a few weeks of his arrival he issued a vigorous apology for his or any other clergyman's doing so. He conceded that the pulpit should never be

[40] *Western Citizen,* June 6, 1844.

[41] Pease, *Illinois Election Returns,* p. 391, lists a James Grant as a candidate with no affiliation. Innes Grant, however, was also known as James Grant, according to account books of G. W. Gale and also the diary of O. H. Browning. The Edward Hollister listed as a third candidate in the district shared with Mercer County very likely was the man of the same name who was pastor at that time of the colony church.

[42] *Ibid.,* pp. 149–51.

[43] On Feb. 21, 1846, he spoke at a Liberty convention in the Galesburg vicinity (*Western Citizen,* March 11, 1846).

partisan in its position on "mere political questions as of
boundaries, banks, and tariffs" lest the preacher behind the
desk become an "unwelcome messenger," but he declared that
because slavery threatened the very foundations of free government, action against it was a religious no less than a civil
duty. This opinion was part of his endorsement of the call
for another Liberty convention for the sixth congressional district, a call which the *Western Citizen* used as a leading article.[44]
That spring he addressed for two hours a Liberty meeting at
Knoxville at which Gale and Parker also spoke. How much
Knox County Liberty politics was still mostly Galesburg in
content is further suggested by the fact that at this meeting
Silvanus Ferris and Eli Farnham were two of four vice-presidents, that A. S. Bergen acted as secretary, and that Nehemiah
West was nominated for the state senate.[45] Other Galesburg
campaign activities, beyond the county, may also be noted in
this contest of 1846, for Parker was prominent in the state
convention held at Princeton, being elected a vice-president
and serving on the nomination and business committees. Blanchard and Parker made the leading addresses and Parker served
on the business committee of a large campaign meeting in
Farmington.[46]

The number of counties with Liberty men receiving votes
for the lower house in 1846 expanded to twenty-six. The total
Liberty votes had risen beyond 5,000 in five congressional districts. Though a small fraction of the 80,000 total in those
areas, this number represented a potential nuisance to politicians of the major parties, a fact which must have added zest
to the zeal actuating anti-slavery men. This had been particularly true in the districts to which Galesburg belonged, for
two of the last four congressional elections had been lost to one
of the old-line parties by a margin less than the ballots going
to the anti-slavery candidate. In Knox County itself that had
been true of three of the last four congressional elections.

By 1848 the political scene had been much altered by the

[44] *Ibid.*, May 26, 1846.   [45] *Ibid.*, April 22, 1846.
[46] *Ibid.*, June 3 and July 27, 1846.

internal dissensions that appeared in the major parties, particularly over the question of slavery in the territories conquered from Mexico. Many Whigs and Democrats who could not stomach abolitionism were nevertheless offended by the prospect that the territory with slavery would be extended. At the same time leaders in the Liberty Party had come to realize that only by political alliances could a third-party movement achieve success in the elections. In 1848 a great concourse of "Barnburners," Free Soil Democrats, "Conscience Whigs," Land Reformers, and Liberty Party men met in Buffalo and organized the more inclusive Free Soil Party, with a platform in which the Liberty Party men had to be content with slavery planks milder than those they previously preferred and in which that issue was shared with other measures, notably that of free land for settlers.[47] The political phase of the anti-slavery crusade was thereby broadened, but it lost some of the toughness of its moral intensity.[48] One of the nine delegates who went to Buffalo for the Liberty Party of Illinois was the Reverend Lucius Parker of Galesburg. And it was fitting recognition of the share that the college town had in forcing the slavery issue that one of the nine Free Soil electoral college nominees in Illinois was President Blanchard.

As the stream of anti-slavery politics increased in volume in the fifties the waters of Liberty that had risen in Putnam and Knox counties joined and were lost in the Republican flood. Of the preacher leaders who had first spread the seeds of abolitionism and then cultivated the seedling of Liberty, only one, Owen Lovejoy, of Princeton, received for himself the fruits of prominent political office. And he by that time had come to dislike "rash, violent, ranting, denunciatory" abolitionist preachers and wished that "they would learn to be a little more prudent, use a little more oil and not so much of

[47] Theodore C. Smith, *Liberty and Free Soil Parties*, chapters 8 and 9.
[48] Already in 1846 Blanchard wrote to Salmon P. Chase: "The rancor of hatred which is now directed against Anti-Slavery men I find *mainly* respects their determination to *vote* against slavery. The conflict for the principle seems well nigh given up. Is it so?" (Blanchard to S. P. Chase, Cincinnati, Sept. 12, 1846, Chase Papers, Library of Congress).

the fire and hammer." [49] Such prudence had not, in the years when abolitionism first came to Illinois, been the primary trait of the preachers Lippincott and Gale, nor of Dickey, Miter, Cross, or Allan, nor of Lovejoy the Martyr.

[49] Theodore C. Smith, *Liberty and Free Soil Parties,* p. 96.

❧ XI ❧

The Family of a Female Reformer and the Freedoms of Speech and Press

Called to face a cold wind while I ride twenty-miles to plead the cause of the oppressed. A crowded house listened over two hours while I spoke of the condition of the *slave,* the *nature* of the *system,* and our *duty.* Praise the Lord for any who will receive the truth.[1]

DURING THE LATE FORTIES the abolitionists in Galesburg found themselves more and more frequently associated with a family of pioneer printers who lived in Peoria. By the end of the decade this Davis family moved to Galesburg, where a son had already attended Knox College, and brought to the colony a skill in journalism which greatly enhanced the influence of the community. What most distinguished this family was the strong character of the mother, Mary Brown Davis. She exemplified the feminist tendency often manifest in both the temperance and the abolitionist movements, a tendency sometimes encouraging but often encumbering or embarrassing to the male enthusiasm for those causes. The female branch of the anti-slavery movement in Galesburg was developed in collaboration with Mrs. Davis while she still lived in Peoria. This chapter of the story opens in that location.

When a mob in Peoria prevented William T. Allan from forming a local anti-slavery society, the *Western Citizen* noted,

[1] Diary of Levi Spencer, Nov. 13, 1843, quoted in Blanchard, *Memoir of Rev. Levi Spencer,* pp. 91–92; Spencer, a member of the Galesburg colony, was a preacher, missionary, and anti-slavery agitator in Canton, Bloomington, and Peoria.

somewhat sarcastically, that the only "active labourers" there
were "non-resistants" and "females." [2] The slur was not intended for the "females," for the *Western Citizen* had already
opened its columns frequently to a Peoria woman who wrote
very good anti-slavery copy; rather the editor wished to drive
home the truth that in Peoria women conducted the anti-
slavery crusade more aggressively than men. These women were
members of the Main Street Presbyterian Church that had received as its pastor in November of 1835 the Reverend Jeremiah Porter, who had brought with him his bride from the
Burned-over District. Eliza Chappell Porter, as previously
noted, had been an aggressive worker and leader in revivalistic
and reforming activities and was well known to the top leaders
in the benevolent system. Full-time pursuit of a benevolent
vocation was interrupted at this period of her life by the new
duties of keeping house and rearing children,[3] but it is extremely likely that the militancy of the ladies of the Peoria
church reflects an influence by Mrs. Porter when she was their
pastor's wife.

In Porter the town of Peoria had a strong anti-slavery leader
at an early stage of the abolitionist movement in Illinois. Possibly if Porter had remained in the river town a more active
anti-slavery group would have developed, but a Peorian reported that as late as 1839 there were only two avowed abolitionists,[4] and one of these was the woman making this ob-

[2] *Western Citizen*, Feb. 23, 1843.

[3] Her later career in several benevolent enterprises, notably the Sanitary
Commission, is set forth in Mary H. Porter, *Eliza Chappell Porter.*

[4] *Western Citizen*, Feb. 9, 1843. When Lovejoy issued his call for a convention
in Alton, it was signed by Porter and eighteen other men from Peoria County.
But these were evidently not all very resolute anti-slavery men, for only one of
the signers went with Porter to Alton, and only one other ever again appeared
in the proceedings of the state anti-slavery society; none of the others again is
noted in the archives of Illinois abolitionism. The first anniversary of that
society was held in Farmington, to which Porter had moved, but though it was
just across the county line only three men from Peoria were present. Only one
attended the anniversary at Quincy in 1839, and no one from Peoria was at Princeton in 1840 or Galesburg in 1841, though that was only fifty miles away. The first
record of an anti-slavery society in Peoria County is not in the town of Peoria
but of a Harkness Grove Anti-Slavery Society in the western part of the county
toward Farmington. The existence of such a society was revealed when it placed
a call in the Peoria *Register* of February 18, 1842, for the formation of a county

servation. According to Porter there were in the Main Street Church two especially "devoted sisters," Mrs. Pettingil and Mrs. Davis.[5] Lucy Pettingil's husband, Moses, was a merchant who was so much the mainstay of the little church that it was often called "Pettingil's Church." He was a New Hampshire Yankee who taught school a while and then entered the mercantile business in Rochester, New York, in which vicinity he was living at the time that Finney fanned the flames of the Great Revival in that part of the Burned-over District.[6] He was an anti-slavery man but was not active in the cause until the middle forties.[7]

The other "devoted sister" was Mary Brown Davis, who arrived in Peoria in 1837 with four sons to join her oldest son and her husband, Samuel, who in the spring had started to publish the Peoria *Register*. The Davis family came from Virginia; they were not the most likely converts to abolitionism, for the father still owned two slaves [8] and the mother had been born on a plantation where her father at one time owned forty-five to fifty slaves, one of whom had been Mary Brown's mammy.[9] Mutual interest in writing brought Mary Brown and Samuel Davis together in Alexandria, Virginia, where Mary was living with slaveholding relatives and where Samuel had found employment as a printer, following an apprenticeship in New Jersey and a period of travel with his trade in New York. After their marriage the Davises joined with J. B. Patterson in the publishing of the Winchester (Virginia) *Republican* until 1832, when the Pattersons went west to settle at Oquawka, Illinois, a town on the Mississippi that served as a river port for the northern part of the Military Tract to which the frontier

society at a meeting to be held at the schoolhouse near Charles Kellogg in township 8 north, 6 east, on February 22 (Peoria *Register and Northwestern Gazetteer*, Feb. 18, 1842).

[5] Porter, "Journal," Sept., 1839.

[6] McCulloch, *History of Peoria County*, II, 463.

[7] He signed the call for the convention of 1837 at Alton, but does not appear in the affairs of the state society until after the Peoria riot of 1843.

[8] Peoria *Register and Northwestern Gazetteer*, Dec. 16, 1837.

[9] Jeanne Humphreys (DeNovo), "Mary Brown Davis, Journalist, Feminist, and Social Reformer," MS, Knox College Library, an honors paper based primarily on Mary Brown Davis's extensive correspondence to the Oquawka *Spectator*.

was then advancing. After the Pattersons left Winchester, the Davises published the Wheeling (Virginia) *Gazette* until 1835, when Samuel and the oldest son went to southwestern Wisconsin where they planned a pioneer press in Cassville. They were soon disappointed in this speculation and returned with their press down the Mississippi River as far as Oquawka. During the winter of 1836–37 they hauled their printing equipment across the Military Tract to Peoria,[10] which had a location on the Illinois River corresponding approximately to that of Oquawka on the Mississippi. Here Davis began publication of the Peoria *Register*. This was truly a family venture, for the mother helped with the editing and even the ten-year-old son helped with the printing.[11]

As a good Presbyterian and one active in the temperance cause, Samuel Davis shared some common ground with most of the zealots who preached abolition in Illinois.[12] And when the *Observer*, which had been the printed organ for the Presbyterians of Illinois, was forcibly discontinued by an Alton mob, the clerk of the Illinois Synod sent Davis its proceedings for publication, expecting that the Peoria *Register* would serve more or less as a substitute. This, however, surprised Davis,[13] for the policy of the *Register* was one of impartiality in religious matters and neutrality in politics. He was most decidedly not an abolitionist. At the time of Lovejoy's murder his was one of only three newspapers in the state to rebuke the crime, but he did so strictly on the principles of law and order and of a free press, making it plain that he opposed abolitionism:

We may be the only slave owner connected with the press of this state—owning as we do two slaves in Virginia—and yet we hesitated not to lift our feeble voice against the outrages the moment we

[10] Rufus Miles, "The Early Days," Galesburg *Republican Register*, April 21, 1888.

[11] Peoria *Register and Northwestern Gazetteer*, Sept. 22, 1838.

[12] If the Galesburg colonists knew that he was a Mason, the one appointed to be master of the first lodge of Peoria, that would have counted against him, for anti-masonry was one of the "isms" indigenous to the Burned-over District, and at this time many if not most of the Galesburg settlers were opposed to secret fraternities. Davis was elected secretary of the Peoria Temperance Society (*ibid.*, March 10, 1838).

[13] *Ibid.*, Dec. 9, 1837.

heard them. We did so as an American citizen, who values the preservation of the laws as equal in importance to the preservation of life; we did so as a slave owner, anxious for the preservation of property, because we saw in the act that the cause of abolition would receive an impetus not to be checked without a dissolution of the union.[14]

In February, 1840, the establishment of a Democratic paper in Peoria justified Davis in departing from his political neutrality, and the *Register* then staunchly supported Harrison and Tyler and remained strongly Whig as long as Davis controlled it down to the fall of 1842. As a good Whig he opposed the Liberty Party, arguing that the abolitionists were injuring their own moral cause by running local political tickets that would only help the Democrats elect their men.[15]

Both as a neutral and later as a Whig, however, Davis faithfully adhered to his obligations as a just dispenser of the news for the Peoria area, comprising many communities inland from the river where no press had yet been set up. The activities of the anti-slavery societies, both state and local, were news, and he reported them, withal making it clear that he was not to be imposed upon.[16] The abolitionizing efforts of the Galesburg colony and of its leaders beyond Knox County were frequently, fairly, and fully reported, as was other news about the colony and its educational institutions.[17] His relations with Knox County started at least as early as September, 1839, when Davis met Gale in Miter's church in Knoxville, at a Knox County cattle show for which Gale distributed the premiums and Davis made a speech.[18]

While Samuel Davis was still only courteous to abolitionism, his wife had fully committed herself to that cause and aided its agitation in about the only public way permitted to women. To her public she was known most of her life as "M.B.D.," the author of tales, essays and letters, travel and autobiographical sketches, and of news correspondence from Peoria, later from

[14] *Ibid.*, Dec. 16, 1837.   [15] *Ibid.*, July 17, 1840; July 29, 1842.
[16] *Ibid.*, Sept. 8, 1838.
[17] *Ibid.*, July 4 and Sept. 1, 1838; Jan. 19, 1839; July 17 and Aug. 14, 1840; June 17 and Aug. 5, 1842.
[18] *Ibid.*, Sept. 7 and Sept. 21, 1839.

Galesburg, and eventually from Chicago—the writer of rather sentimental and highly moral journalism in which she carried the torch for abolition of slavery, for temperance, prison reform, poor relief, and women's rights. Even before Samuel died she seems to have done little housekeeping; after his death she made her living by her pen and by labors such as missions among the poor, and for nearly a year she was a police matron in Chicago.[19] Though most of the career summarized in the foregoing sentence occurred after she left Peoria, it does indicate the unusual personality of the woman who began to agitate against slavery late in the thirties.

Mary Brown Davis's first pieces of anti-slavery journalism appeared in 1839 in the short-lived *Genius of Universal Emancipation* that Lundy published in the last months of his life in Illinois. These articles, signed "M.B.D. of Peoria," were entitled "The Cause of the Oppressed" and "Cruelty of Slavery." [20] Lundy was assisted in publishing the *Genius* by Zebina Eastman, who for a short time in 1839 worked for the Davises on the *Register* and then at the advice of Mr. Davis went up the river to Lowell to help the Quaker reformer.[21] Three years later Eastman became editor of the *Western Citizen,* established at Chicago to serve continuously as the organ of abolitionism in Illinois. "M.B.D." appeared early in the new paper; in the third issue, August 12, 1842, she told how despite her childhood she had become anti-slavery in her convictions; three weeks later she continued to draw upon autobiographical sources in an article entitled "Early Impressions of Slavery." From then on her literary attacks on the "peculiar institution" appeared at least twice a month, a steady contribution made easier after September, 1849, when her husband sold the *Register.*[22] During the first five years of the *Western Citizen,* this faithful woman from Peoria supplied at least sixty articles, and all but one of

[19] Humphreys, "Mary Brown Davis."
[20] *Genius of Universal Emancipation,* June 28 and July 26, 1839.
[21] *A Memorial of Zebina Eastman by His Family* (n.p., 188?), p. 7.
[22] Peoria *Register and Northwestern Gazetteer,* Sept. 23, 1842. He retired "to a farm in the suburbs of Peoria" (Chicago *Democrat,* Oct. 5, 1842), but continued to edit the *Register* for the new proprietors until the following February.

these was on some phase of slavery, a subject on which she reenforced her direct evidence during a visit to her mother in
Virginia in 1846. While on this visit her utterances against
slavery provoked the suggestion that she should make her stay
"as short as possible." [23]

Early in 1842 the little frame church on Main Street where
the Davises and Pettingils worshiped received as its preacher
one of the most notorious abolitionists in the state, the Reverend William T. Allan, who for over a year had been serving
as the agent for the Illinois Anti-Slavery Society. Allan at first
was greeted in Peoria with a hue and cry, but that seemed to
die down, and the day after Christmas Mrs. Davis wrote confidently to the *Western Citizen* that abolitionism was making
headway "in this destitute vineyard," and that probably twenty
to thirty of the "most respectable" people in the town were now
earnestly dedicated to the unpopular cause.[24] But "M.B.D."
had spoken too soon, for the next issue of the anti-slavery paper
related how the Peoria mob had risen to prevent the organization of a local anti-slavery society, which they said would be
used as a "wooden horse for the introduction among us of
runaway slaves, free negroe loafers, practical amalgamation,
treason, disunion, and other evils." [25]

The riot made an abolitionist out of Samuel Davis. Though
he had not attended the meetings of either the protagonists or
the antagonists of abolition, he was deeply stirred when informed of what happened and particularly disturbed when he
learned that Whigs as well as Democrats had forcibly suppressed
freedom of speech and assembly. Particularly offensive to him
were resolutions adopted by the mobocrats asking the proprietors of papers and presses in Peoria not to publish notices
of anti-slavery meetings, nor their proceedings, nor communications advocating their doctrines, and threatening that if any
paper or press refused this demand patronage would be with-

[23] *Western Citizen*, June 30, 1846.   [24] *Ibid.*, Feb. 9, 1843.
[25] Peoria *Democratic Press*, Feb. 15, 1843. Contemporary documents from this
episode are extensively quoted in McCulloch, *History of Peoria County*, II,
138–42.

drawn from it.[26] Davis informed the owners of the *Register*
that he would strongly denounce the action of the mob, and
when they refused him the columns of the paper he immediately withdrew as its editor, in which capacity he had
continued after selling the *Register* to them.[27] The very day
after the disorders he sent a communication to the *Western
Citizen* describing the Peoria disturbances, denouncing the
suppression of free speech, expressing his sympathy for abolition, and indicating his faith in its ultimate triumph.[28] The
anti-slavery crusade had gained an important recruit, for
though "M.B.D." thought that the standing of the Davises had
declined in the community and that they had lost friends [29]
by their notoriety on the anti-slavery issue, other evidence indicates the continuing respect for, if not the popularity of, Samuel
Davis in the town.[30]

Peoria was the leading town and commercial outlet for many
communities in the Military Tract. The assault upon the cause
of emancipation in that place was both a challenge and an opportunity for the Galesburg colony, which was only fifty miles
distant, and a call went out for a special convention in behalf
of free discussion.[31] Three weeks after the riot the Galesburg
leaders brought a company of forty-two abolitionists, including
the colony choir, to Farmington, halfway toward Peoria, for
an anti-slavery convention, at which the violation of free speech,
free assembly, and free press in Peoria was the principal theme
of discussion. In this gathering from the three counties of
Peoria, Fulton, and Knox the largest delegation was that from
Galesburg and the most prominent persons in the proceedings
were Gale, President Kellogg of Knox College, and Levi Spencer, a member of the colony who was now preaching in Fulton

[26] Peoria *Democratic Press*, Feb. 15, 1843.
[27] Peoria *Register and Northwestern Gazetteer*, Feb. 17, 1843; McCulloch,
History of Peoria County, II, 141–42.
[28] *Western Citizen*, Feb. 23, 1843.   [29] *Ibid.*, Aug. 31, 1843.
[30] His leadership in numerous organizations, religious, educational, agricultural,
temperance, and promotional, is evident from the files of the Peoria *Democratic
Press* during the next two years; see the issues for Sept. 25 and Oct. 9, 1844;
July 2, Sept. 17, and Sept. 24, 1845; April 1 and April 8, 1846.
[31] Peoria *Register and Northwestern Gazetteer*, March 3, 1843.

County. There were thirteen Peoria men present, including the Reverend William Allan, Samuel Davis, and Moses Pettingil. Allan and Davis were, next to the Galesburgers, most evident in the discussion, the latter reading a paper on "Free Discussion Suppressed in Peoria" which in pamphlet form became a propaganda piece for the Illinois abolitionists.[32]

These events mark a growth in strength for the anti-slavery cause in Peoria, a development fostered by continuing intervention from the Galesburg zealots and accompanied by closer attraction of the Davis family to Galesburg. In May, when President Kellogg went to Peoria to take a steamboat on which to start his journey to the World Anti-Slavery Convention in London, he paused to preach in the church where the mob had prevented the organization of an anti-slavery society, using the text: "Fear not, for they that be with us are more than they that be with them." [33] He picked up copies of the Davis pamphlet, "Free Discussion Suppressed in Peoria," to distribute along the Illinois, Mississippi, and Ohio rivers. A few weeks later "M.B.D." visited Galesburg and provided for the *Western Citizen* a laudatory portrayal of that community with its anti-slavery character.[34] And a year later the Davis family spent nearly a week in the same place on the occasion of one of those great anti-slavery festivals that were held on Independence Day. Samuel Davis made one of the speeches and his son Southwick was also on the program.[35]

Meanwhile on July 27, 1843, the women of Peoria had done what the men failed to do by forming an abolitionist organization. Mrs. Davis, who was evidently the moving spirit in this action, was elected secretary and Mrs. Pettingil became directress of a Female Anti-Slavery Society.[36] The circumstance that several local female societies were formed in Illinois about this time suggests some concerted action from a central impulse, but whence it came is not apparent. A society had been formed at Jerseyville the preceding April, and one was founded at Galesburg the following September, by which time there was

[32] *Western Citizen*, March 23, 1843.   [33] *Ibid.*, May 18, 1843.
[34] *Ibid.*, June 22, 1843.   [35] *Ibid.*, July 25, 1844.   [36] *Ibid.*, Aug. 17, 1843.

also one in Putnam County.[37] The wife of President Kellogg was president of the Galesburg society.

The female societies of Peoria and Galesburg now took the lead in a movement for a state organization of their sex. The call for a convention to meet May 23, 1844, at Peoria to form the Illinois Female Anti-Slavery Society was written by Mrs. Davis and issued from the Peoria organization over the signatures of Lucy Pettingil, Mary Davis, Irene B. Allan (wife of the Peoria pastor), and five other Peoria women. At the convention, which was attended by forty-five women, Mrs. Kellogg of Galesburg acted as president and Mrs. Davis as secretary, and these two women with Mrs. Pettingil and Mrs. Nehemiah Losey, wife of a Knox College professor, were the most active persons in the proceedings.[38]

The special project that this new state organization undertook was the education of Negro children "at Galesburg or any other place where opportunity may offer." [39] This probably reflected the influence of the Galesburg society, which already had taken "measures for the support of a colored young gentle man and lady in a course of education that will fit them for teachers." [40] It is not surprising that Irene B. Allan was especially interested in this project, not only because of her husband's professional role as anti-slavery agent, but also because she had been a student at Oberlin where special point was made of obliterating the color line. In July following the formation of the state female society she announced in the *Western Citizen:* "The Galesburg school is open for the education of colored youth, and we wish to get a number of youth of both sexes under the influences of that institution as soon as may be." [41] The next month Mrs. Allan was author of a long letter in the *Western Citizen* addressed from Peoria to the managers of the

[37] The Jerseyville society was described by Mrs. Irene B. Allan in a letter dated April 22, 1844, but which gives the exact date of founding as April 20, 1843. The founding of the Galesburg society is dated as of September 1, 1843, in a letter from Mrs. Kellogg in the *Western Citizen*, May 16, 1844. Reference to a Putnam County Female Anti-Slavery Society is made in the *Western Citizen*, Sept. 7, 1843.

[38] *Ibid.*, April 25, May 23, June 20, 1844. [39] *Ibid.*, June 20, 1844.
[40] *Ibid.*, May 16, 1844. [41] *Ibid.*, Aug. 8, 1844.

Illinois Female Anti-Slavery Society and devoted to the objective of entering Negro students in the Galesburg school that
fall.[42] How much actually came of this particular enterprise is
not known. There is record of the fact that in June, 1846, two
applications from Galesburg to educate Negro children were
actually on hand but could not be filled because there were no
funds in the state female society; [43] and in September of that
year Mrs. Davis told a free Negro she met in Virginia that he
could educate his fourteen-year-old son at Knox College.[44]

Annual meetings of the Illinois Female Anti-Slavery Society
were held at Alton in 1845 and at Princeton in 1846, though
at this last meeting only the "Galesburg or Knox" and the
Putnam County organizations were represented,[45] and another
state meeting was held later in the year in June at the Chicago
Tabernacle. One of the four vice-presidents elected at this
last meeting was Mrs. Kellogg of Galesburg, whose husband
had now stepped down from the presidency of Knox College
to the pastorate of the colony church.[46] Still another meeting
was held that same year in Granville, Putnam County, in conjunction with a Christian Anti-Slavery Convention.[47]

At a special Female Anti-Slavery Society meeting held in
Farmington, July 8, 1847, Mrs. Mary Davis was selected
moderator, and Mrs. Mary A. Blanchard, wife of the new president of Knox College, was chosen secretary.[48] As Mrs. Blanchard
reported to the *Western Citizen,* the body of women assembled
at Farmington undertook to bring about a mammoth state-

---

[42] *Ibid.,* Sept. 5, 1844.   [43] *Ibid.,* June 10, 1846.

[44] *Ibid.,* Sept. 29, 1846. In a contribution to the *Western Citizen,* Dec. 14, 1847,
Mrs. Davis told how well Negroes were treated in Galesburg, contrasting it in
that respect with Peoria. She wrote of six sisters who had purchased a lot and
built a neat home and barn in Galesburg. She made particular point of the fact
that they owned a pew in the colony church and were educated.

[45] *Ibid.,* June 10, 1846.   [46] *Ibid.,* Aug. 11, 1846.

[47] *Ibid.,* Sept. 29, Nov. 14, 1846. The last meeting of the Female State Anti-
Slavery Society to which the author has found reference was held in Chicago,
March 14, 1848 (*ibid.,* March 21, 1848).

[48] *Ibid.,* March 21, 1848. Mrs. Blanchard, previous to her coming to Galesburg,
had been actively engaged in female anti-slavery activities in Cincinnati, particularly the promotion of education for the free Negro population (Fischer, *Blessed
Memories,* pp. 34–50).

wide petition by women against the "black code" of the state.[49]
It is significant that several weeks later Mrs. Davis was moved
to defend this action against those who regarded women's interference in political affairs as improper. She announced, furthermore, that the Davis's Job Printing Company in Peoria had
run off copies of the petition, and that these could be secured
there by those interested.[50] In fact, it appears that Mrs. Davis
was the chief proponent of this project, Mrs. Blanchard being
the chief assistant.[51] When finally presented, the petition despite
all their efforts had only five to six hundred signatures. The
small number may be indicative not only of the feebleness of
opinion on this matter but also of the unpopularity of something tainted with feminism. That the latter was a factor is
strongly suggested in Mrs. Davis's last article on the petition
in the *Western Citizen,* for she concluded by asking whether
with all the other current reform movements (anti-slavery,
land, reform, temperance, etc.) there could "not be some reform with regard to the rights of woman." She referred particularly to laws unfavorable to married women and to the father's
exclusive legal rights to children.[52]

Meanwhile men of abolitionist sentiments in Peoria had
stirred to action. Early in 1844 they finally formed a local anti-
slavery society, and when the state society met at Jacksonville
in May, the Reverend William Allan did not have to go alone.[53]
Davis was active in the state convention of the Liberty Party at
Princeton the same month,[54] and several Peorians tried to persuade him to be the Liberty candidate for governor; [55] Moses
Pettingil did run for state senator on that ticket.[56] This was
done furthermore in the face of continuing, violent hostility of
Peorians to abolitionism. Even in the Main Street Presbyterian
Church, which had previously sheltered that cause, the board
of trustees were unsympathetic, for Mary Brown Davis wrote

[49] *Western Citizen,* Aug. 3, 1847.   [50] *Ibid.,* Aug. 24, 1847.
[51] *Ibid.,* Nov. 28, 1848.   [52] *Ibid.,* Feb. 27, 1849.
[53] He was accompanied by Moses Pettingil and William Nurse; "Minutes of the
Illinois Anti-Slavery Society," May 29, 1829.
[54] *Western Citizen,* June 3, 1846.   [55] *Ibid.,* April 8, 1846.
[56] Peoria *Democratic Press,* Aug. 12, 1846.

to the *Western Citizen* that new members had been added to keep the building from being used by abolitionists, the particular occasion for this being an invitation that had been issued to the new president of Knox College, Jonathan Blanchard, to deliver a series of lectures on "American Slavery." [57] Blanchard's first communication to the *Western Citizen* after arriving in Illinois was to endorse an anti-slavery mass meeting to be held in that unfriendly territory.[58] On May 6 the abolitionists met in a room over the store of Moses Pettingil—"Liberty Hall" they called it—since no church auditorium was opened to them. Blanchard spoke in the afternoon, and the noted abolitionist orator, Ichabod Codding, was scheduled to speak in the evening, but a mob violently broke up the evening meeting.[59] The mob also attacked the house where Nehemiah West of Galesburg was staying with the Reverend Levi Spencer, his brother-in-law, a former member of the colony who was now an anti-slavery preacher in Bloomington; Spencer was seriously injured.[60]

The abolitionists again acted to hold up Peoria to public condemnation. The morning after the mob's action President Blanchard presented to the anti-slavery meeting a strong "Protest," and this the *Western Citizen* spread in its most prominent columns. Samuel Davis related the violation of constitutional rights before the state convention of the Liberty Party.[61] Finally a few weeks later the mobsters in Peoria went too far by a brutal assault on Davis. While Davis was sitting in front of a store next to his home, a fellow citizen came to berate him for a certain objectionable article in the *Western Citizen* mistakenly ascribed to Davis. His accuser started to beat him, and pushed him against a window and tried to gouge out his eyes. The printer was no longer a young man—he had fought in the War of 1812—and was crippled with rheumatism, but a crowd that gathered merely looked on. A magistrate who tried to interfere was held back by a confederate of Davis's attacker, and

[57] *Western Citizen*, March 4, April 22, 1846.   [58] *Ibid.*, March 18, 1846.
[59] *Ibid.*, May 20, June 3, 1846.
[60] Bonham, *Fifty Years Recollections*, pp. 520–26.
[61] *Western Citizen*, June 3, 1846.

when Davis's son came to rescue his father he was hit on the head with a cane. Finally two citizens with more honorable characters came to help Davis and assisted him into his home. Both father and son were badly and bloodily battered.

Such a low-down attack could not be approved. Before the day was over one of the guilty men had been heavily fined; another had fled. A third man, who was very influential in the town, became alarmed over the rapid prosecution, and when Davis learned of this, he called upon him to make an agreement advantageous to abolitionists in the future. Davis promised that he would not push the charges for the assault if the guilty man, who had been one of the chief instigators of the riot of 1843, would promise that in the future the Liberty Party would meet no interference either from him or from the public at his instigation. It was also agreed that in the future the courthouse would be available for anti-slavery meetings.[62] Abolitionism had won a real triumph in Peoria. Davis, who a decade before had opposed abolitionism, was now one of its heroes; he served as president of the state Liberty Party convention in July, 1846, and was very prominent in the state Free Soil Party convention of the following month. Moses Pettingil was one of the nine delegates sent from the Illinois Liberty Party to the Buffalo convention at which the Liberty Party was joined to a national reform movement under the Free Soil standard.[63]

Late in 1848 the Main Street Church, which recently had changed its polity to Congregationalism, invited to its pastorate the Reverend Levi Spencer. He was no stranger to the trials of anti-slavery men in Peoria, for while a missionary preacher in Fulton County, residing in Canton, he had served as secretary of the Farmington convention that met to denounce the Peoria mob of 1843,[64] and in 1844 he had come by invitation to the meeting that organized an anti-slavery society in Peoria.[65] He was an officer in the Peoria mass meeting of 1846 and was

[62] *Ibid.*, July 7, 1846.
[64] *Ibid.*, March 16, 1843.
[63] *Ibid.*, July 11 and Sept. 5, 1848.
[65] *Ibid.*, March 14, 1844.

seriously injured by the rioters who attacked the abolitionists on that occasion.[66] Since early in 1844 he had been a minister in Bloomington and had served as the leading abolitionist agitator in McLean County [67] and the adjacent area, working as a lecturer, as a contributor to the columns of the *Western Citizen,* and as spokesman for the Liberty Party.[68] There too he had suffered from mob violence,[69] the worst instance being in June, 1846, in Bloomington at the hands of volunteers for the Mexican War who were stimulated by whiskey and angered by the denunciations of abolitionists against the war.[70] At eleven o'clock one night they paraded before Spencer's home. When Mrs. Spencer, who had also come to Illinois with the Galesburg colony, refused to open the door they broke the windows and departed, but left a guard to watch the house. An hour after midnight they were back in force to send brickbats hurtling into the house. The Spencer family hid in the corners until some friends came to their rescue, when they escaped by the back door. The house inside and out was smeared with rotten eggs and littered with broken window sashes, glass, and bricks.[71] Spencer was pastor of the "Abolitionist's Church" in Peoria from November, 1848, until his

[66] *Ibid.,* June 3, 1846; Bonham, *Fifty Years Recollections,* pp. 520–26.

[67] Erastus Mahan, "Friends of Liberty on the Mackinaw," *Transactions of the McLean County Historical Society,* I (1899), 396–404.

[68] Spencer was a delegate to the state anti-slavery society several times, the last time in May, 1844, when he was listed as from McLean County. On that occasion he was appointed secretary ("Minutes of the Illinois Anti-Slavery Society," 1844). His anti-slavery activities in McLean County are frequently mentioned in the *Western Citizen:* June 2, Aug. 22, 1844; Sept. 8 and 11, Dec. 6, 1845; Feb. 13 and 18, March 25, May 27, Nov. 3 and 14, Dec. 22, 1846; Nov. 2 and 9, 1847.

[69] In a letter dated June 8, 1844, he tells of a mob which six months previously had broken up the first attempt at an anti-slavery meeting in Bloomington (*Western Citizen,* June 12, 1844). Two years later he described a meeting at which Owen Lovejoy was to speak, which had to be held in a wagon shop because the members were denied the courthouse. A mob threw eggs at them, both before and after the meeting (*ibid.,* June 23, 1846).

[70] Prince, "The War with Mexico," *Transactions of the McLean County Historical Society,* I, 17–30.

[71] This episode is described in an entry from Spencer's diary quoted in Blanchard, *Memoir of Rev. Levi Spencer,* p. 96; in Prince, "The War with Mexico," *Transactions of the McLean County Historical Society,* I, 17–30; in *Western Citizen,* July 28, 1846.

death in April, 1853.[72] His untimely death was widely mourned and President Blanchard of Knox College immediately wrote a memoir celebrating the life of this anti-slavery hero, one of the first and best to come out of the Galesburg colony to labor for piety and reform. This book was distributed by the American Reform Tract and Book Society.[73]

By this time the Davis family had moved to the Galesburg colony, for Samuel died of cholera on June 19, 1849,[74] and the mother and three of the sons moved to the college town, with which they had had more and more to do during the past half-dozen years. One son, Southwick, had graduated from Knox College in June, 1846, at the first college commencement; another, James Scott, was a college student there in 1849; still another was in the Knox academy. The following pages will show how Southwick and James Scott faithfully followed the anti-slavery principles of their parents and used the journalistic training they had received at home, for Southwick was a pioneer newspaper publisher in Galesburg in 1849 and again in 1854.[75] Mrs. Davis continued in her new home the aggressive promotion of reforms. She organized female auxiliaries to the Sons of Temperance, when that moral fad was going strong.[76] She defended the dress reforms of the notorious Mrs. Bloomer, declaring in the Galesburg *News Letter* that she was in favor of

---

[72] *Semi-Centennial of the Organization of the First Congregational Church of Peoria. Held on Sunday and Monday, December 21 and 22, 1884,* pp. 36–37.

[73] Blanchard, *Memoirs of Rev. Levi Spencer.*

[74] Drown, *Drown's Record and Historical View of Peoria,* p. 139.

[75] Already before the family moved to Galesburg, Henry Kirk White Davis had been a partner in a newspaper business in Peoria. The uninsured printing building, belonging to the Davis estate, was destroyed by an explosion and fire that killed two persons in January, 1850. Among the materials lost was the press on which H. K. W. Davis and his partner had begun to publish a daily paper a month before. After an unsuccessful attempt to revive this project, this one of the Davis sons also left Peoria. In 1851 he established the *Illinois State Bulletin* in Bloomington, Illinois, but in 1853 he removed to Missouri where he became proprietor and editor of the Lexington *Union.* R. McKee Davis was at one time connected with the Onarga *Mercury,* Iroquois County, Illinois. James Scott Davis, as will be noted below, was for a time the Kentucky correspondent for the *Congregational Herald* (Peoria *Democratic Press,* Jan. 30, 1850; Drown, *Drown's Record and Historical View of Peoria,* pp. 121–22; Oquawka *Spectator,* July 6, 1851; Sept. 27, 1860; Sept. 3, 1863).

[76] Oquawka *Spectator,* July 10, 1850.

that costume,[77] and expressing satisfaction that in Galesburg there were women who did not fear to assume the Bloomer style of dress.[78] Her journalistic output increased with the beginning of her widowhood, for she became a regular contributor to one of the best pioneer periodicals of the Military Tract, the Oquawka *Spectator*, which had been established by the Pattersons, partners and close friends of the Davises back in Virginia. She was also a contributor to the Galesburg *Free Democrat* while her son was editor of it in 1854.

"M.B.D." was less partisan for the abolitionist cause by the middle fifties. She wrote from Chicago, to which she had moved by 1854: "I used to be a strong abolitionist myself, and still am so far as *right* and *truth* are concerned, but when *intrigue* and *self-promotion* are the ruling motives I say *away with it*." [79] It is evident that the schemings that attended the now mature political phase of the anti-slavery movement disgusted her. She still could attend a convention of Negroes in Chicago and compare them favorably with whites; [80] she denounced the violation of the Missouri Compromise and continued to deplore the Fugitive Slave Law of 1850, but she had no sympathy with those who would fly in the face of law and order. When *Uncle Tom's Cabin* appeared she pointed out that there were many St. Clairs as well as Legrees in the South. The dramatization of the horrors in the novel provoked her to comment that there were horrors aplenty in Chicago that would be useful for the same purpose.[81] It was the social problems of this city that absorbed more and more of her life and appeared ever more frequently in her writings. She became a social worker and a police matron in that raw, growing city,[82] and there she found new material for the reform agitation, which, like the earlier anti-slavery movement of the thirties, was still mainly moral and not yet political in character.

[77] *Ibid.*, June 25, 1851.   [78] *Ibid.*, July 9 and 22, 1851.
[79] *Ibid.*, Dec. 19, 1854.   [80] *Ibid.*, Oct. 19, 1853.   [81] *Ibid.*, June 14, 1854.
[82] See her contributions to the Oquawka *Spectator* during 1858 and 1859.

PART FOUR

Pressing the Issue

❧ XII ❧

Freedom's Highway through Galesburg

Thou shalt not deliver unto his master the servant which is escaped
from his master unto thee. He shall dwell with thee, even among
you, in that place which he shall choose, in one of the gates,
where it liketh him best: thou shalt not oppress him. Deuteron-
omy, XXIII:15–16.

In the providence of God several fugitive slaves, at different times,
had found their way into our neighborhood, and although the
laws of our state are exceedingly severe rendering one liable to a
fine of $500 who shall feed or harbor a colored man who does
not give undoubted evidence of his freedom, yet our brethren
felt that the statutes of Heaven were to be regarded before those
of men and did not hesitate to "feed the hungry." Dec. 27, 1842.
(From Samuel G. Wright, "Journal.")

"THE LITTLE NIGGER STEALING TOWN . . . a nest
of nigger thieves" is what Galesburg was called in Quincy,[1]
just on this side of the Mississippi River from the slave soil of
Missouri. Indeed runaways knew that Galesburg was the most
important point for them to reach after crossing the river; if
they got to that town they were reasonably safe, for Galesburg
was probably the principal Underground Railroad station in
Illinois.[2] This running of fugitives was the most dramatic

---

[1] Galesburg *Free Democrat*, Feb. 23, 1854; Nov. 27, 1856.

[2] Siebert, *Underground Railroad*, p. 97; Cooley, "Illinois and the Underground
Railroad to Canada," *Transactions of the Illinois State Historical Society*, 1917,
p. 83; Chapman, *History of Knox County*, p. 210. George Davis, active in the
railroad out of Galesburg, has these words put into his mouth by Clark E. Carr
in his partly historical, partly fictional, *The Illini:* "Galesburg is the most important station after leaving the Mississippi. If a fugitive can get to Galesburg,
he is reasonably safe. That place is known to colored people all through
Missouri as the first and most important point for them to reach; they know

phase of the anti-slavery movement. Otherwise respectable, cautious, and law-abiding citizens who were cast in the role of aiding fugitives were participants in mysterious hideaways, stealthy night-rides, feverish flights from pressing pursuers, narrow escapes, arrests, and contentious courtroom scenes. Such episodes made an incalculable addition to abolition propaganda, for hardly anyone could avoid being excited one way or the other by such theatrical activities. They occurred even before abolitionism was organized in Illinois, for Lovejoy's martyrdom was really the climax of a series of dramatic scenes opening late in 1835 with "abolition excitement" over the "abduction" of several Negroes from Missouri into Illinois—"by some persons," wrote Lovejoy to his brothers, "it is not certainly known who." [3]

Few contemporary records remain of this illicit traffic. Communication between the various stations depended upon the zeal or rashness of the operators and on their faith in each other rather than upon a hierarchy of officers. Though the trails of these humane lawbreakers ran most frequently through the same neighborhoods, they dared not touch exactly the same homesteads too frequently. Hence regular "routes" cannot be traced today, though it is possible to trace the general pattern of runaway transportation.

"Conductors" generally directed their "passengers" to the western and northern part of the state; and in this area the lines of escape chiefly converged on Galesburg. A map prepared by Wilbur H. Siebert for his general history of the Underground Railroad depicts five fugitives' routes entering the college town and the same number leaving on the way toward Chicago and other lake ports, whence the Negroes might find passage to Canada.[4] Though Galesburg was fifty miles away from the

that if they get there they will find friends who will hide them and help them" (pp. 67–68). Carr was in a position to know the facts about the Underground Railroad in this part of Illinois. The story that he uses to hang together the reminiscences and historical incidents comprising this work is that of a fugitive slave who escaped through Galesburg.

[3] Joseph C. and Owen Lovejoy, *Memoir of the Rev. Elijah P. Lovejoy*, pp. 155–57.

[4] Siebert, *Underground Railroad*, p. 135.

Mississippi and nearly a hundred miles away from the nearest
part of Missouri, it had the advantage of lying within short
rides from other communities with abolitionist families that
would readily carry the fleeing slaves farther to greater safety.
In Galesburg a fugitive was beyond the immediate reach of

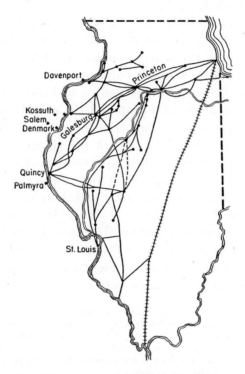

The Underground Railroad in Illinois

Redrawn from Wilbur H. Siebert, *The Underground Railroad from Slavery to
  Freedom* (New York, 1898).
Gaps in lines of route or broken lines indicate uncertainty regarding the exact
  direction by which fugitives were conducted.

pursuing masters. Right up to the Civil War, however, the
people of Galesburg could never be entirely sure that a Negro
might not be returned to slavery from their midst. Throughout
the autumn of 1859 there were repeated reports that kidnapers
were prowling in the vicinity to capture a Negro boy to return
him to servitude. To provide him with "free papers," the

woman who had brought him into the county from Kentucky executed an instrument of manumission and emancipation before witnesses, including a son of G. W. Gale. Even then suspicion of a plot against the boy persisted and the local paper warned that he would be "protected by this community" against "such fiendish designs." [5]

In the environs of Galesburg the operation of the railroad was dominated by the leaders of the college community. Gale, the founder; Kellogg, the first president; Blanchard, the second president of Knox Manual Labor College; and several of its trustees all helped in the harboring and transporting of the runaways.[6] The house of a pastor of the colony church was a "station" [7] and so was the cupola of the church building.[8] The homes of colonists near the edge of the village and the barns and hay-piles of settlers on nearby farms were also used as hide-outs.[9] Samuel Hitchcock, probably the most active of the "conductors," on one occasion got away with four passengers at one haul by laying them head by toe on the straw-covered wagon bed, covering them with chaff-filled sacks, and setting off toward the Chicago market as if with a load of grain.[10] Nor was such a large consignment of Liberty freight exceptional, for groups of two to five Negro fugitives were mentioned several times.[11]

[5] Galesburg *Free Democrat*, Sept. 7, Oct. 15, Dec. 10, 1859. The insecurity of a Negro in Illinois at this time is illustrated by the case, noted by the *Free Democrat* on Sept. 10, 1859, of a Negro, Geo. Bowlin, who in Carrolton was sold "to the highest bidder." His offense was a violation of a law prohibiting emigration of Negroes into the state. Bowlin was found guilty, fined $63, and, not being able to pay, sold to Felix Morton for six months.

[6] Names may be found in Chapman, *History of Knox County*, chapter 8; Siebert, *Underground Railroad*, appendix E, p. 405; George Churchill, Scrapbook No. 2, p. 62; Mars, "Recollection of Half a Century," Galesburg *Republican Register*, June 19, 1909; Leeson, *Documents and Biography Pertaining to the Settlement and Progress of Stark County, Illinois*, p. 124.

[7] Testimony to the writer of a descendant of the Reverend Lucius H. Parker.

[8] Cooley, "Illinois and the Underground Railroad to Canada," *Transactions of the Illinois State Historical Society*, 1917, p. 87.

[9] Scrapbook No. 2, Galesburg Public Library, p. 26; Carr, *The Illini*, p. 222.

[10] Mars, "Recollection of Half a Century," Galesburg *Republican Register*, June 19, 1909.

[11] Chapman, *History of Knox County*, pp. 209–11; Samuel G. Wright, "Journal," Jan. 5, 1847, and July 24, 1854; Peoria *Register and Northwestern Gazetteer*, Sept. 2, 1842. The Galesburg *Free Democrat*, for Dec. 3, 1859, reported that "Last

ROUTES TO GALESBURG

During the early years of the Galesburg colony most of the fugitives passing through its division of the Underground Railroad had started their escape by crossing the Mississippi River in the vicinity of Quincy. Most active in assisting, or even encouraging, these runaways were persons associated with the Mission Institute, a manual labor school founded outside Quincy in 1837 by Dr. David Nelson. Nelson's reputation helped to bridge the boundary between free and slave soil at this location, for he was the most hated of all the abolitionists that in 1836 were driven away from Marion College near Palmyra, Missouri, which was about twenty miles across and down the river and only a little way inside the state. In 1838 Nelson was joined in the operation of the Mission Institute by the Reverend Moses Hunter, a zealot from the Burned-over District, whose particular branch of the Institute, Theopolis, became known as "Station Number One" on the road from Quincy to Chicago.[12] Gale and other members of his colony made direct contact with both Nelson and Hunter at Quincy at the second annual meeting of the Illinois Anti-Slavery Society in 1839. It was about this time that the regular conducting of escaped slaves along the route from Quincy began.[13]

Widespread advertisement of this way to freedom resulted from the adventures of three men from the Mission Institute who were captured in July, 1841, on Missouri soil while encouraging slaves near Palmyra to escape in a skiff which the men had rowed to the Missouri side. Two of the men, George Thompson and James E. Burr, were ministerial students; the third, Alanson Work, was a man of forty who was living at the Institute for the sake of educating his children.[14] These three radicals were particularly close to Hunter, who was the first to

---

Monday night" ten Negroes belonging to seven persons from the vicinity of La Grange, Lewis County, Missouri, escaped by stealing a flatboat and crossing the Mississippi River.

[12] Merkel, "The Underground Railroad and the Missouri Borders, 1840–1860," *Missouri Historical Review*, XXXVII (1943), 275.

[13] *Ibid.*, pp. 272–73.   [14] Thompson, *Prison Life and Reflections*, p. 1.

visit them in jail, bringing them a lawyer and reading matter such as the *Book of Martyrs* and *Pilgrim's Progress*.[15]

The arrest, trial, and conviction of Thompson, Burr, and Work, for stealing slaves, and their sentence to twelve years in the penitentiary [16] were boisterously approved by most people on the slavery side of the river, but deeply resented by many on the free side. The severe punishment meted out to the Mission Institute men did not stop the escape of slaves, for in their "foolish zeal to excite public odium" against the captured abolitionists their persecutors spread abroad the news to slaves that liberty was within reach,[17] and even while waiting trial the prisoners learned from their captors that slaves were escaping faster than ever.[18] In September, 1842, reports from Quincy indicated that "a brisk business was doing" in helping fugitives across the river in that area,[19] and in June, 1843, two more Illinoians were apprehended in the vicinity of La Grange, Missouri, and jailed at Palmyra for enticing slaves to leave their masters.[20] President Kellogg of Knox College wrote to Gerrit Smith in January 10, 1843: "The slaveholders in Missouri admit that they erred greatly when they arrested and imprisoned Burr Thompson and Work—for this circumstance has served to spread among the slaves the knowledge of freedom's highway. Fugitives have multiplied ten-fold since this occurred—Several whom I here saw informed me that it was thro' these men that they rec'd their information." [21] During the very week that President Kellogg made this observation, one of the "conductors" at Quincy, Dr. Richard Eels, himself used this section

---

[15] *Ibid.*, pp. 24, 26, 35, 47, 56, and 57.

[16] *Ibid.*, pp. 75–95. Work was pardoned after serving a little over three and a half years, Burr after slightly more than four and a half years, Thompson after nearly five years (*ibid.*, p. 414).

[17] *Ibid.*, pp. 52, 55.

[18] *Ibid.*, p. 45. "Posters warning negro stealers that they would be mobbed if caught were conspicuously displayed," and the escape of slaves from owners in Marion and adjoining counties continued (Sosey, "Palmyra and Its Historical Environment," *Missouri Historical Review*, XXIII [1929], 366).

[19] Peoria *Register and Northwestern Gazetteer,* Sept. 2, 1842.

[20] *Ibid.*, June 17, 1843. An instance was reported of a Negro fugitive from Arkansas who crossed the river in this general area (*ibid.*, May 27, 1842).

[21] Kellogg to Smith, Jan. 10, 1843, Gerrit Smith Papers, Syracuse University Library.

of "freedom's highway" to evade prosecution. Samuel G. Wright, closely associated with the Galesburg settlement and leading abolitionist in the next county to the northeast, noted in his journal on January 9, 1843, that his horse was lamed in "conducting along Dr. Eels." It was feared that the governor of Illinois would hand Eels over to the state of Missouri, which wanted to prosecute him for grand larceny for assisting fugitive slaves.[22] About a month later, when it was apparent that the governor would not turn Eels over to Missouri justice, he came back by the same route [23] and was tried in the circuit court at Quincy; he got off with a fine of $400 at the hands of Judge Stephen A. Douglas for harboring and aiding fugitives.[24]

Slaveholders in Missouri became increasingly enraged "at the practice of their property taking to itself legs and running away." [25] Early in March of 1843 a band of about a dozen Missourians met in a store in Palmyra, crossed the river carrying turpentine and gunpowder, and burned the chapel of Mission Institute.[26] This blow to the school had been preceded in the autumn by the death of Hunter [27] and was followed by the death of Nelson the next year. The Mission Institute persisted under a new name for three more years and then died out.[28] Knox Manual Labor College was left as the only thoroughly abolitionist college in the state.

Along the more than one hundred miles from Quincy to Galesburg there were Yankee villages or neighborhoods that would help the escaping Negroes farther north and east through Hancock, McDonough, and Fulton counties.[29] Among the

[22] Samuel G. Wright, "Journal," Jan. 9, 1843.   [23] Ibid., Feb. 13, 1843.

[24] Scammon 4,498 (*Reports of Cases Argued and Determined in the Supreme Court of the State of Illinois,* by J. Young Scammon).

[25] *Western Citizen,* March 23, 1843.

[26] Ibid.; Sosey, "Palmyra and Its Historical Environment," *Missouri Historical Review,* XXIII (1929), 366.

[27] *American Quarterly Register,* XV (1843), 336.

[28] Richardson, "Dr. David Nelson and His Times," *Journal of the Illinois State Historical Society,* XIII (1921), 433–63.

[29] See the Siebert map. According to accounts from children of abolitionists in McDonough County, the route from Quincy ran to homes in Round Prairie in Hancock County; from there to abolitionists' homes in McDonough County at Industry, Chalmers, and Scotland Township. Thence it went to Fulton County at the home of Henry Dobbins, "from whence cargoes of negroes were dispatched

"stations" that have been remembered are those in Mendon, Round Prairie, Plymouth, Roseville,[30] Canton, and Farmington. These were without exception communities with New School or Congregational churches in them, belonging to the same religious and benevolent system as the Galesburg colony. The fact that runaways had started on this route, however, by no means put them beyond the clutch of the law. In the autumn of 1850 three fugitives crossed the river just below Quincy and were guided on their way toward freedom by abolitionists, but in the middle of the night at a bridge about sixty miles northeast of Quincy in McDonough County their pursuers caught up with them. After a fight the Negroes, having only a dirk knife and cudgels, were subdued and carried by their captors back to slave soil at Hannibal.[31]

Farther up the river from Quincy in the neighborhood of Burlington, Iowa, a route leading from the Missouri border through the southeastern corner of Iowa crossed the Mississippi to the relative safety of Galesburg. In this angle of Iowa the chief stations for the early operation of the anti-slavery underground were Salem and Denmark. The former was a Quaker community, settled in 1835, that served as the gateway for Friends who settled farther along on the Iowa frontier.[32] These Quaker communities not only gave sanctuary to Negroes fleeing from Missouri but carried them, if need be, as far east as Galesburg.[33]

Denmark was a Yankee colony with strong religious purposes planted with the establishment of an academy as one of its

to Galesburg, Princeton and on to Canada." From episodes related in these accounts it is evident that often the contact in Missouri that led to flight of a fugitive came from a Negro who was trying to bring his family out (Blazer, "The History of the Underground Railroad of McDonough County, Illinois," *Journal of the Illinois State Historical Society*, XV [1922], 579–91).

[30] Montgomery, "My First Illinois Ancestor," *Journal of the Illinois State Historical Society*, XVII (1925), 608–9.

[31] *Missouri Republican* (St. Louis), Nov. 2, 1850.

[32] Garretson, "Traveling on the Underground Railroad in Iowa," *Iowa Journal of History and Politics*, XXII (1924), 418–53.

[33] Testimony of George Davis in *Semi-Centennial Celebration, First Church of Galesburg*, p. 19; Chapman, *History of Knox County*, pp. 209–10.

objectives.[34] It was the cradle of Congregationalism in Iowa, for the Reverend Asa Turner, member of the Yale Band who already in 1834 had extended his ministry from Quincy into Iowa, had settled in 1838 at Denmark to become the pastor of the first Congregational church in that Territory. This was his charge for three decades and during the early years his outpost for missionary tours and headquarters for his agency in Iowa for the American Home Missionary Society. His prayers for help were answered in 1843 by the arrival at Denmark of the "Andover Band," whose role in Iowa was to be similar to that of the Yale Band in Illinois about a dozen years before. Seven members of the Andover Band entered Iowa by the same route that runaways later used, for on the last leg of their journey to meet Turner at Denmark they rested over a Sabbath in Galesburg.[35] These guests of the abolitionist colony must have heard a good deal about runaway slaves, for Gale and two of the leading laymen of the town were then under indictment for harboring fugitives and their trial had been set for the next month. The case had been one of the chief subjects of the anti-slavery press for over a year. The coordination of the labors of abolitionists in Iowa and in Illinois would be facilitated by their mutual membership in the same New School Presbyterian-Congregational benevolent system, and by the fact that Asa Turner, who introduced these young missionaries to their fields of labor, had been until 1840 an active participant in the affairs of the Illinois Anti-Slavery Society.[36] One of these Andover Band members became pastor of the church in Burlington early in 1844 and was active in the underground of that river town.[37]

[34] Hill, *Rev. William Salter*, p. 575.

[35] *Ibid.*, pp. 575–79; Jordan, *William Salter, Western Torchbearer*, pp. 31–39; Douglass, *The Pilgrims of Iowa*, pp. 51–63; Magoun, *Asa Turner.*

[36] In May, 1843, Aaron Street, of Salem, Iowa, wrote to the *Western Citizen* that he and friends wanted to organize an Iowa Territory Anti-Slavery Society. He invited fourteen persons from Illinois to come to the convention, including G. W. Gale, Mr. and Mrs. Samuel Davis, and Moses Pettingil (*Western Citizen*, May 18, 1843).

[37] Hill, *Rev. William Salter*, p. 640.

To stop escaping slaves and to check on strangers, Missourians resorted to patrolling the Des Moines River along this angle of the Iowa border. On one occasion a gang from Missouri descended upon Salem, the Quakers of which had neither the arms to defend themselves nor the willingness to use force, but a company of Yankees who had no such compunctions about violence came to their help from Denmark and dispersed the invaders.[38]

In November, 1848, the Reverend Lucius Parker, one of the operators of the Underground Railroad in Galesburg, was visited by the Reverend John Todd, a former schoolmate at Oberlin. Todd was one of the leaders of a colony from Oberlin that was settling on the Iowa frontier in the extreme southwest Missouri-Nebraska corner, a colony that was to develop into the college town of Tabor. At the time of his visit to Parker he was returning from the site of the enterprise to bring out his family. According to Todd's reminiscences the first passengers got aboard the Underground Railroad at Tabor in July, 1854.[39] Evidently these passengers were directed via Galesburg, for late that month Samuel G. Wright recorded in his journal that he received and carried on five fugitives who had escaped from their master as he was transporting them through Tabor.[40] That town soon became an important depot for antislavery men after companies of emigrants from Illinois to Kansas who were traveling across northern Missouri were turned back at the ferries of the Missouri River by armed pro-slavery men in 1856. Early in the summer of that year, therefore, Free Soil migrants to Kansas began to use a route lying north of the Missouri boundary, and Tabor became the western entrepôt at the farther end of this Iowa trail.[41]

There were, of course, other crossings of the Mississippi [42]

[38] Garretson, "Traveling on the Underground Railroad in Iowa," *Iowa Journal of History and Politics*, XXII (1924), 430–36.

[39] Todd, *Early Settlement and Growth of Western Iowa*, pp. 17–78, 134.

[40] Samuel G. Wright, "Journal," July 24, 1854.

[41] Todd, *Early Settlement and Growth of Western Iowa*, pp. 115–22; Richman, *John Brown among the Quakers*, p. 15.

[42] Merkel, "The Underground Railroad and the Missouri Borders," *Missouri Historical Review*, XXXVII (1943), 276–77, 282, 284.

along its many miles below Quincy, and in their northward flight fugitives from these sources might find their way through Galesburg. Indeed the most notorious group of runaways in the history of the town, those of the Borders case, showed that Negroes getting on the Underground Railroad far to the south in Cairo might arrive in Knox County. But from Alton and St. Louis and points south, the routes to Canada most likely lay east of the Illinois River.[43]

ROUTES FROM GALESBURG

Liberty was toward the Pole Star, for the escaped slave was not really beyond the reach of bondage until he touched the soil of Canada. Of this magic earth the nearest portion from Galesburg was the southwestern tip of Ontario, and directly or indirectly the trail of the fugitive led him there. Gale and the other migrants from Oneida County, New York, had a particular interest in that region, for one of Gale's former students at Oneida Institute had prepared a haven in Ontario to receive the self-emancipated slave. This was Hiram Wilson, of the notorious Oneida-Lane-Oberlin axis, who after graduation from Oberlin had in 1836 continued in Canada the benevolences among Negroes that the Lane Rebels had begun in Cincinnati. Wilson's enterprises for the benefit of the freedmen included a manual labor school.[44] In 1841, in one of the very early issues of the *Genius of Liberty,* he described to Illinois abolitionists how the fugitives were cared for;[45] in 1845 a Negro from Canada reported directly to the Congregationalists in Chicago on the situation of his race; and four years later Wilson himself gathered contributions in Illinois for the alms he gave to former slaves.[46] The wife of one of Wilson's former classmates at Lane and Oberlin, Mrs. William T. Allan, reported in 1844 that one of the female anti-slavery societies in Illinois was organized to make garments for the refugees in

[43] Siebert, *Underground Railroad,* see map.
[44] Fletcher, *History of Oberlin,* I, 55, 183, 246–47, 398.
[45] *Genius of Liberty,* Jan. 23, 1841.
[46] Cooley, "Illinois and the Underground Railroad," *Transactions of the Illinois State Historical Society,* 1917, pp. 90–95.

Canada,[47] and so fitting a charity must have been practiced by other women.

The first stage of "Freedom's Highway" from Galesburg to safety in Canada was usually the dozen miles to Ontario Township, located on the northern line of Knox County. Here other settlers from Oneida County, New York, had a community centering about the Camp School,[48] and "freight" addressed to Canada could be confidently entrusted to this neighborhood. Eventually, in 1855, Erastus Child, one of Hiram Wilson's assistants in the work among refugees in Canada, joined this Ontario Township settlement. He too came from Oneida County, where he had attended that training school for zealots, Oneida Institute.[49] From Ontario Township the runaways might be carried northward across the line into Henry County, to the Andover [50] and Geneseo [51] colonies, but the greater part of the traffic went northeast through Stark County and on into Princeton in Bureau County where a brother of the martyred Lovejoy was a notorious "slave stealer." [52]

About this division of the Underground Railroad in eastern Knox County and adjacent Stark County we have rather detailed knowledge from the journal kept by the Reverend Samuel Guild Wright, who had been persuaded by Gale to become a missionary in the settlements to the east and northeast of Galesburg. Wright collaborated closely with the preachers of the Galesburg colony, made frequent visits to the religious and educational activities of the town, and became a trustee of Knox College. He used his journal mainly to keep track of his missionary travels, of his sermons and their texts, of converts and backsliders, baptisms and burials, hot and cold

[47] Western Citizen, May 16, 1844.
[48] Perry, Knox County, I, 634–35; Chapman, History of Knox County, p. 211; Leeson, Documents and Biography Pertaining to the Settlement and Progress of Stark County, Illinois, p. 124.
[49] Chapman, History of Knox County, pp. 203, 662.
[50] Perry, Knox County, I, 665–66.
[51] Taylor, "A History of the First Congregational Church, Geneseo, Ill.," Journal of the Illinois State Historical Society, XX (1927), 112–27.
[52] Haberkorn, "Owen Lovejoy in Princeton, Illinois," Journal of the Illinois State Historical Society, XXXVI (1943), 284–314.

weather, contributions, mileage, and soul searchings, but over the years he also made entries such as the following:

Feb. 6, 1843. Friday another Fugitive from slavery came along which makes 21 that have been through this settlement on their way to Canada.

May 27, 1844. Last week Court set no complaint against nigger stealers.

Jan. 5, 1847. Arrived Home Friday eve. and learned that 2 fugitives had been along with only Christmas papers, and that Mr. *Gordon* & Smith fr. Farmington had pursued & got out a search warrant for stolen horses & two colored persons who were supposed to have stolen them. Neither horses or men were described except that one man called himself Major. They searched our premises in vain however for the birds had flown having got a wink from friends at Farmington that they were pursued. Several Constables & others pursued to Osceola but before they reached there, the fugitives were out of the county & we trust safe.

June 6, 1848. Friday carried a fugitive to Osceola & preached at ½ past four.

Sept. 18, 1854. Sab. preached 3 times & just after I got to sleep was awakened by the arrival of fugitive on the U.G.R.road—& I went & carried him to Mr. Winslows.[53]

The first entry quoted above contains a rare statistical record of the traffic in runaways. Wright was living at the time in the southwest corner of Stark County very near the Peoria and Knox County lines at a place locally designated as "Niggers Point." He had been residing in this settlement since late in 1841, though he had been preaching near that point at a place called Rochester since late in the summer of 1840. Thus he may mean either that during a period of thirty months, or that during only fifteen months, twenty-one fugitives had to his knowledge passed through the settlement, but in either case the indication is that a surprisingly steady stream of fugitives was going through this segment of the underground.

At Princeton a number of other "lines" came from the west near or through Geneseo, and thence some lines went in the

---

[53] Samuel G. Wright, "Journal." In the entries quoted above certain unusual abbreviations and shorthand symbols used by Wright have been filled out to facilitate reading.

general direction of Lowell,[54] where other runaways' trails came up the Illinois River from Putnam County and below.[55] Other lines went direct from Princeton to Chicago, toward which almost all the trails in Illinois converged.[56] "Conductors" at one particular point had no immediate knowledge exactly what route was improvised by friends of the escaped bondsmen farther along the way, though the meetings of laymen and preachers at presbyteries and Congregational associations and the gatherings of anti-slavery men in county and state organizations provided occasions for comparing notes about passengers.

AN ATTACK ON THE UNDERGROUND RAILROAD REPELLED

The most serious threat to the Underground Railroad occurred shortly after it was formed, in the early forties, the period of greatest litigation in Illinois on such issues as the treatment of fugitives, the security of free Negroes, and the indenture system that enslaved Negroes in Illinois.[57] The climax in the attempt to prosecute the lawbreaking operators of the runaway traffic in Illinois occurred in 1843 when Dr. Eels of Quincy and Julius Willard of Jacksonville were convicted and fined for assisting escaped slaves,[58] and when similar action was instituted against Owen Lovejoy at Princeton and against Samuel Guild Wright in Stark County.[59] But of all the cases

[54] Haberkorn, "Owen Lovejoy in Princeton, Illinois," *Journal of the Illinois State Historical Society*, XXXVI (1943), 292.

[55] In Tazewell County there was a "main depot" in Elm Grove Township at the home of Josiah Mathews, and in Morton Township Uriah H. Crosby had a station in his home. Next beyond Crosby's there was an agent, Mr. Kern, who lived above Washington. Kern would take the fugitives to the "Quaker settlement" (Chapman, *History of Tazewell County, Illinois*, pp. 318–19). Above Tazewell in Woodford County the "Morse brothers" received consignments of runaways and delivered all "packages" coming into their hands to William Lewis and other friends in the vicinity of Magnolia in Putnam County, whence they were forwarded through Lowell to Chicago. This route lay on the east side of the Illinois River.

[56] A detailed map showing stations in Kendall, Grundy, LaSalle and Livingstone counties accompanies an article by Mrs. Sarah E. R. Fitzwilliam, in Bateman and Selby, eds., *Kendall County*, p. 633.

[57] Harris, *Negro Servitude in Illinois*, p. 222.

[58] The Eels case and that of Willard, along with two cases rising from Borders's fugitives, were appealed and heard in the Supreme Court of Illinois, term of December, 1843 (Scammon 4, 341, 351, 461, 498).

[59] Samuel G. Wright, "Journal," May 30, Oct. 16, 1843.

occurring at this time the greatest and most protracted attention
was given to the case of Andrew Borders's slaves, with most of
the action centering in Knox County.[60] During a period of
nearly two years, six Negroes and thirteen others were involved
in one aspect or another of the litigation, in the course of which
not only the fugitives and the self-styled "Proprieter" of the
Underground Railroad but the master of the bondsmen and
his son were jailed at Knoxville. Ten members of the Galesburg
colony were involved in lawsuits concerning assistance given to
the runaways. Though no important points at law were won
by the abolitionists, they did score a triumph with public opinion, for excellent use was made of the situation by the friends
of the refugees to put their persecutors in a bad moral light and
even in a ridiculous position.

The bondage of Borders's Negroes bore down on the conscience of Illinois citizens with greater weight because it was
the use and abuse of Illinois indenture law that made it possible. One of the slaves, Sarah, had been brought to Illinois
from Kentucky in 1815 and had been indentured for forty
years. She had passed through the hands of three masters before Borders acquired her in 1825. She had a daughter, Hannah,
nineteen years old, whose case illustrated the misuse of the indenture rules, for though she had filled her term as servant,
Borders had continued her in servitude for over a year longer.
Another of the slaves was Susan or "Suky," a fine-looking
woman of about thirty, whom Borders had brought with him
from Georgia. Her indenture had only about a year longer to
run, but there was always the danger that her master would take
her to slave territory before she had secured her freedom and
sell her into irredeemable bondage. The same was to be feared
for Susan's three children, a boy of twelve and two very small
youngsters, about four and two years old.[61] Borders and his

[60] The files of the *Western Citizen* for 1842–43 quickly reveal the extended
publicity given to this series of incidents.

[61] This information about Borders's slaves has been put together from Scammon 4,341 ff., and 351 ff.; from "Report of a Committee appointed by the Knox
County Anti-Slavery Society to inquire into the facts in the case of the colored
women and children who were arrested and confined in the jail at Knoxville last
fall," *Western Citizen*, April 6, 1843; from a letter written by H. H. Kellogg,

"servants" lived in Randolph County, where the institution of slavery had existed continuously since the French colonists had introduced it at Kaskaskia.

Borders treated his Negroes so inhumanely and provided for them so poorly as to excite the sympathy of the whole neighborhood. The climax came when he cruelly beat the forty-year-old Sarah and badly wounded her arm. His lawyers later explained that "he was necessarily compelled . . . to use a little force, restraint, and beating" to compel Sarah to perform her duties and to remain in his service. But Sarah escaped the following night, was taken into a neighboring house and lodged, and then fled where it would be harder for her master to find her. Borders and some assistants went about blaming and bullying the neighborhood for secreting his property. But some of these people were not to be cowed; they entered suit in Sarah's name for assault and battery and for the wages for the time she had lived with Borders, and they formed a society, "Friends of Rational Liberty," to carry on the litigation. When Sarah's case came up in April, 1842, counsel on both sides agreed to try the general question whether slavery could constitutionally exist in Illinois. The chief issue was the effect of the Ordinance of 1787, since Sarah had been indentured before Illinois became a state. The court found in Borders's favor, but the case was appealed to the Supreme Court of Illinois.[62] Before it could decide about Sarah's freedom, her daughter Hannah, Susan, and Susan's three children had also run away.

The exodus of these five was prompted by the threat of a lashing for Susan at the hands of Mrs. Borders. A squabble between the children of the two mothers had led to the whipping of those of the bondswoman, and when Susan showed her resentment the mistress wanted Susan punished. Though Mr. Borders would not do this himself, on his wife's insistence he agreed to tie the Negroes so that she might herself do the

Nov. 29, 1842, to the *Western Citizen*, Dec. 23, 1842; and from Chapman, *History of Knox County*, pp. 204-5.

[62] *Western Citizen*, Oct. 28, 1842; Sarah, alias Sarah Borders, a woman of color v. Andrew Borders, Scammon 4,341; Matthew Chambers, plaintiff in error, v. People of the State of Illinois, defendants in error, Scammon 4,351.

lashing. But Susan learned of this plan, and that night she and her children and the girl Hannah fled to Cairo, where they got on the Underground Railroad.[63] How they traveled up the long axis of Illinois to the Military Tract is not recorded, except that somewhere along the line they acquired from a "respectable gentleman" well known in this area a paper certifying that they were born in the state. On September 5, 1842, they arrived in Farmington in the extreme northeast corner of Fulton County near both the Peoria and Knox County lines. Here they were picked up by Eli Wilson and his son, who belonged to a little group of abolitionists at Harkness Grove [64] in western Peoria County,[65] and were carried in broad daylight into Knox County to the home of the notorious anti-slavery agent, the Reverend John Cross. The Wilsons drove their passengers right past the home of a justice of the peace, Jacob Knightlinger, a neighbor of Cross, who had warned the abolitionist preacher against breaking the state laws about harboring runaways.[66]

This brazen delivery of so large a consignment of fugitives occurred at a time of mounting resentment among many people in the locality against the abolitionists and their illegal traffic. Exactly two weeks previously Samuel Wright, who lived just across the Stark County line, had recorded in his journal that many citizens had become highly prejudiced against him and his loyal church members because "we have formed lines for helping runaways, hence are as bad as horse thieves" [67] —a strong comparison, for horse stealing was the foulest of felonies on a farming frontier. "Now," as Wright described it a few months later, "of a sudden a storm which had been covertly gathering burst upon us . . . , we were watched night

---

[63] Chapman, *History of Knox County*, pp. 203–6; Susan was still living in Galesburg and was known to the author of the chapter on the Underground Railroad in this county history.

[64] At Harkness Grove the abolitionists had organized a local society when such a step was still not feasible in the town of Peoria, and in February, 1842, had called for the formation of a county society (Peoria *Register and Northwestern Gazetteer*, Feb. 18, 1842).

[65] *Ibid.*, Sept. 23, 1842.   [66] Chapman, *History of Knox County*, p. 214.

[67] Samuel G. Wright, "Journal," Aug. 22, 1842.

after night by *armed men* in order to detect us running away negroes." [68]

When the magistrate Knightlinger saw the transit of the five Negroes, he gathered seven or eight men and ran down the Wilsons; after a rough time he forced them to stop, only to discover that the wagon was empty. The officer's party then hurried to the Cross place and found the abolitionist gone, but discovered his wife boiling a suspiciously large pot of corn on the cob and potatoes in the skin. In a cornfield they found Susan and her children and Hannah, all of whom they took to the jail in Knoxville. [69]

But the day was not over. The reason Knightlinger had not found Cross at home was that he had gone south after some other Negroes. Fearful that his neighbor would also seize these from him, Cross resorted to a ruse that would taunt and distract the officious magistrate until the fugitives were out of his reach. Cross sent a confederate from Farmington to Knightlinger's home about midnight to spy on him while pretending to be the owner of some escaped slaves. While they were talking a wagon rumbled across the bridge nearby. When the scout betrayed his knowledge that this was Cross, Knightlinger realized that some trick was being played on him and ran to get a horse. The scout was off well ahead of him, rode to Cross, described the situation, and together they transferred their illicit freight to the wagon of Wilson, who had also come along. Cross then drove by Knightlinger's gate just as he and a helper rode out. The abolitionist put whip to his team and ran down the road with the officers after him yelling for people to stop the thief. After about a mile and a half Cross was stopped when both his horses were struck down with a pole. But Cross's wagon was empty, and Wilson had escaped across the Spoon

---

[68] Wright to Milton Badger, Dec. 22, 1842, A.H.M.S. Papers.

[69] Chapman, *History of Knox County*, p. 214; Peoria *Register and Northwestern Gazetteer*, Sept. 23, 1842; *Western Citizen*, Sept. 16, 1842; Sept. 23, 1842, a letter from Cross dated Sept. 10, 1842; Oct. 7, 1842, a letter from Kellogg dated Sept. 26, 1842; March 23, 1843, report of the Knox County committee dealing with the Borders case.

River with his passengers. Knightlinger had been outwitted.[70]

The bitter feelings that now flared up in the county were probably expressive not merely of differing convictions on slavery but also of cultural conflicts between the older Hoosier-Kentuckian pioneers, such as those at Knoxville, and the newer settlers of "Yankee" background. It was to be almost two years before the legal bickering resulting from this day's events had quieted down. The first round in the courts occurred the next day when the abolitionists brought Knightlinger and one of his confederates before another squire, Nehemiah West, the leading layman of the Galesburg colony, who fined his fellow magistrate $100 for his attack on Wilson. Knightlinger appealed to the circuit court.[71] To deal with such litigation and to secure the freedom of the women and children in the Knoxville jail, the Knox County Anti-Slavery Society set up a special committee consisting of Cross, Gale, and three others. President Kellogg of Knox College took it upon himself to keep the *Western Citizen* informed, and through it abolitionists throughout the nation.[72] In a letter to Birney, Kellogg declared that he and Gale had "covenanted" to meet the expenses of the fugitives, had retained the best lawyer they could, and had given him their note for fifty dollars.[73] In the spring of 1843, when several aspects of the Borders episode approached trial, Gale presented the work of the special committee to a convention of abolitionists from Fulton, Peoria, and Knox counties held at Farmington, and that assembly undertook to bear the expenses.[74]

The five Negro captives were kept in a closely guarded jail while the sheriff advertised and corresponded widely in an attempt to find their owner. A man came from Missouri in hopes that they were some of his departed property. Finally, Borders, after spending more than a month beating the corn-

[70] Chapman, *History of Knox County*, pp. 214–15; Peoria *Register and Northwestern Gazetteer*, Sept. 23, 1843; *Western Citizen*, Sept. 23, 1843.
[71] *Western Citizen*, Sept. 16, 1842.   [72] *Ibid.*, Sept. 26, Oct. 7, 1842.
[73] Kellogg to Birney, April 5, 1843, *Birney Letters*, II, 729.
[74] *Western Citizen*, March 23, 1843.

fields and thickets in Randolph County, learned that his servants were being held three hundred miles to the north.[75] He appeared late in September in Knox County and claimed them all but Hannah, who he admitted was free. The abolitionists insisted that he prove his rights to Susan and her children before the proper authorities, but this he could not do for he had no indenture papers for them. Having been denied the custody of the Negroes, he immediately returned to Randolph County without further argument.[76]

The abolitionists now sent to Borders's neighborhood for information, and a gentleman from that locality came north with documents declaring that Susan's children had never been registered as Borders's servants. The testimony of this witness also made it clear that Borders had abused the law by keeping Hannah in servitude for at least a year after she was free. But when this evidence was presented to the sheriff he questioned the authenticity and completeness of the documents and refused to release any of the prisoners, even Hannah, whom Borders himself had failed to claim. Came the time, however, when under the law the prisoners must be sold to pay their jail fees, and accordingly they were put up at public auction. In the crowd that assembled to witness this novel spectacle none was disposed to bid—though at last someone did offer fifty cents for the girl Hannah. The others had to be returned to the care and service of the sheriff, who after a few weeks allowed them on surety to go where they pleased. They were out of jail when the circuit court sat for the fall term and no action was taken to restore them to their master. The abolitionists believed that Borders would give himself no further trouble about them, an opinion confirmed by friends of the anti-slavery men in Randolph County. Hannah found employment in a neighboring town, and Susan worked in Knoxville, got a few furnishings together, and rented a house.[77]

The day after Susan had started living in her own home, Borders and his son unexpectedly appeared. Susan, who was

---

[75] Ibid., Oct. 28, 1842, and April 6, 1843.   [76] Ibid., April 6, 1843.
[77] Ibid.; Chapman, History of Knox County, p. 205.

doing the washing at the Presbyterian parsonage, was warned and secreted the two small children with friends. But the sheriff helped Borders to find these youngsters and hide them in a loft, and also to capture the twelve-year-old boy, who was working on a farm. All three of Susan's children were then jailed during the raw weather of late November in a log hut without stove or fireplace and warmed only by an open vessel on the floor, from which the smoke drifted out through holes in the walls. Borders assumed that having the youngsters he would soon attract the mother. She was, indeed, in a pitiful quandary, for if she went to her children to rejoin them in bondage it might be to no avail since it was possible that Borders would separate the children from her by sending them to the South and selling them there. Friends persuaded her to put herself beyond Borders's reach, and in order to get her to the safety of Galesburg they disguised her in the clothes of the Presbyterian minister's wife and veiled her and carried her off in the sleigh of Charles Gilbert, one of the most active of the abolitionists of the college town.[78]

That evening the abolitionists had Borders and his son served with a writ for trespass; the next morning when these two appeared before a justice of the peace in Galesburg they were also served with a writ for false imprisonment of Susan's children. On this latter charge they were found guilty and bound over in the sum of $500 to appear at the next session of the circuit court. The sheriff, who had acted as the Borderses' counsel, went their bail, and that day they were able to send the Negro children secretly to Randolph County. The next day the Borderses were again brought before the Galesburg magistrate for continuing the false imprisonment of the children. This time the defendants produced papers purporting to sustain Borders's claim to Susan's family, but they were carelessly and incompletely drawn up, as if with haste, and the court again found the Borderses guilty. Because they refused to enter into bonds of recognizance in the sum of $400 they were committed to the very jail in which they had kept the

---

[78] Chapman, *History of Knox County,* p. 205.

children. Their friend the sheriff did turn the key on the Borderses but saved them any long discomfort by getting others to join him in supplying bail again. After their release the father and son followed the recaptured children, who were on their way back to servitude.[79]

The emancipation of the Negroes now depended upon the action of the circuit court at the spring term. The temper of that tribunal, presided over by Stephen A. Douglas, had already been tested during the fall of 1842 when it acted on the appeal of Knightlinger and his confederates from the conviction for assault that had occurred in the court of Nehemiah West, justice of the peace in Galesburg. It turned out that the clerk of the circuit court had failed to subpoena the needed witnesses against Knightlinger and company, and that one of the men complained against was on the grand jury that would need to bring in the indictment. The Reverend John Cross, who was ready to testify against them, was even threatened with a perjury charge by members of that jury. So the case against Knightlinger and his friends was quashed.[80]

The suits against Borders came up in May. When the jurymen were sworn the anti-slavery protagonists saw at once that both the grand and the petit juries would be packed to do the "dirty work of the slave holder." Borders had brought from Randolph County a barrel of peach brandy for the sheriff and others "who loved a glass or more," and the fumes about the courthouse indicated its ample and free distribution. The men from that "moral old pest hole," Galesburg, would hardly be able to match such persuasion, for the college had written into all deeds of land to the colonists a proviso that if intoxicants were made or sold on the land it would revert to the college. Borders won in the cases against him.[81]

The juries then turned on Borders's persecutors in a flurry of indictments in which they "seemed determined to wreak the vengeance of the slave holder," not only on those concerned in the Borders cases but upon many other abolitionists avail-

[79] *Western Citizen*, Dec. 3, 1842.   [80] *Ibid.*, April 6, 1843.
[81] *Ibid.*, July 6, 1843. The phrase "moral old pest hole" is quoted about Galesburg in Sandburg, *Abraham Lincoln: The War Years*, II, 412–13.

able in the Galesburg colony. The grand jury indicted Cross, Gale, Nehemiah West, and Charles Gilbert for harboring fugitive slaves, and Borders gave surety that he would appear against them as a witness in the November term. The petit jury brought in a verdict of thirty dollars damages against the Galesburg magistrate who had tried Borders in the first instance, the grounds being that the justice of the peace had improperly detained Borders's papers from Saturday night to Monday morning. Spiteful suits were initiated in which it was apparent that the enemies of the colony were resolved to "indict every man who could be indicted under any pretence." One Galesburg man was charged with assault for beating his wife; and five others, the whole board of trustees of the common schools in Galesburg, were charged with misapplying funds. Significantly the school funds case was quashed at the next November term and the wife-beating case taken on a change of venue to Warren County, where nothing came of it.[82]

The indictments against Cross, Gale, West, and Gilbert for harboring Borders's slaves remained in the court somewhat longer. In November, 1843, the charges against West were dropped and Gilbert took a change of venue to Warren County, where there is no record that the case was prosecuted. Gale, however, failed to show up and a writ was issued against him returnable at the next term; but in June, 1844, still another writ had to be issued to prosecute, and Gale was discharged from the indictment.[83]

While Gale met the accusations against him with passive contempt, Cross used them to place his prosecutors in a most unpopular position. We know from the correspondence of the Reverend Samuel Wright that already in December of 1842 public sentiment was moving away from the anger expressed four months earlier against those who helped runaway slaves, for in his quartely report to the American Home Missionary Society he wrote: "Indeed many of our *then* bitter enemies

[82] *Western Citizen*, July 6, 1843; Knox County Circuit Court Records, Book I, June 14, 1841–May 16, 1849, MS; search of the Warren County Circuit Court records reveals no reference to the wife-beating case.
[83] Knox County Circuit Court Records, Book I.

would *now* succor a *needy fugitive themselves.*" [84] A year later
he was even stronger in this opinion, declaring that the prosecution of those who harbored fugitives injured the prosecutors:
"The reaction upon their heads was tremendous. A better move
for the cause of the oppressed probably could not have been
started. Many who before were full of prejudice are now enlightened and their confidence gained." [85] Cross cleverly aggravated and exploited this alteration of popular attitudes by
transforming his arrest and imprisonment into ridiculous and
outrageous escapades.

Cross made his arrest a joke on the officer who apprehended
him. About the time of his indictment in Knox County he had
moved to Bureau County, to the settlement of La Moille, which
was then in the limelight of social reform because of a project
to establish in the vicinity a community along the lines of
Fourier's communism.[86] In November of 1843 a writ for Cross's
arrest had to be directed by the Knox County court to the
sheriff of Bureau County, returnable at the next term in the
spring of 1844.[87] Consequently before he was brought to trial
Cross was free to serve as president of the state Liberty Party
convention early in the year 1844.[88] In April a deputy sheriff,
John Long, arrested him, but could find no one to transport
him to the authorities in Knox County. Cross, however, offered
to take his own team, carrying the deputy along, for Cross had
a preaching appointment at Osceola in Stark County the next
day, and that was on the way to Knoxville where Cross was to be
jailed.[89] Long at first did not want the preacher to fill the
appointment, explaining that the law did not allow him to let

[84] Wright to Milton Badger, Dec. 27, 1842, A.H.M.S. Papers.
[85] Wright to Milton Badger, Dec. 30, 1843, A.H.M.S. Papers.
[86] *Western Citizen,* April 6, 1843.
[87] Knox County Circuit Court Records, Book I; Chapman, *History of Knox County,* p. 212.
[88] *Western Citizen,* Feb. 1, 1844.
[89] This episode is described in detail both in Chapman's *History of Knox County,* pp. 212–13, and in somewhat different though greater detail in Matson, *Reminiscences of Bureau County,* pp. 367–70. It was evidently a story with considerable popularity in anti-slavery circles and no doubt lost nothing in the telling. It could have originated only with Cross, and fits with what is otherwise known about that anti-slavery agent's personality and with contemporary records of his arrest and trial.

his prisoner deliver abolition lectures. Indeed the officer had good reason to be cautious, for they were now in the pastoral precincts of the Reverend Samuel Wright, who had himself recently been under indictment for harboring runaway slaves [90] and was slated as a witness for Cross in the forthcoming trial.[91] Cross's friends at Osceola insisted that he be allowed to preach, intimating that there might be trouble if the deputy tried to take his prisoner away, and the officer finally consented. The sermon aroused much sympathy for the man going to trial.

When Cross had finished preaching, Long summoned a posse to assist him, but he found that they were all friends of Cross and more likely to do harm than good. The officer then offered to pay Cross for delivering himself peaceably to the jailor in Knox County, and after some bargaining they agreed on a fee of seven dollars and continued on their journey with the "prisoner" carrying the sheriff's deputy along. The latter was very uneasy and frequently asked Cross if he thought that his friends would get rough in the event that a rumored "rescue" was attempted. To this the preacher replied that he could not be responsible for what his friends would do, for they were very angry over his arrest, but that he wanted very much to earn the fee of seven dollars and would do what he could to avoid trouble. By the time the two men got to the Spoon River, Long was very nervous and excited, and when they saw two men in the road leading down through the timber, the deputy was sure that the rescue was to be attempted. Cross knew better but told the deputy to get down out of sight so that if the men were friends of the abolitionist they would see him traveling alone and not think him a prisoner. Accordingly the officer lay down in the bottom of the wagon and Cross covered him with a buffalo robe and some horse blankets. When he passed the men on the road Cross spoke to them and then whipped up his horses to pass on in great speed. A little later he pretended to speak again to some imaginary persons and whipped his team into a gallop to get by them; this he did

[90] Samuel G. Wright, "Journal," Sept. 14, 1842; June 24, 1844.
[91] Ibid., May 30, Oct. 16, 1843.

again and again. For about two miles over an extremely rough timber-bottom road the wagon rattled and creaked as it bounded over stumps and ragged ruts, while the sheriff's deputy under the blankets bounced more or less helplessly on the floor of the vehicle, bumping against the side of the box and cracking his head under the seat. Finally Cross halted his team and uncovered his victim and told him all danger was past. The officer, as Cross told it, arose, looked cautiously around him, examined his pistols, and said, "If they attacked me, I would have made a powerful resistance." [92]

After the provocation he had given the Knox County authorities, Cross could hardly expect any favors, and his imprisonment was everything that a propagandist might wish. He found the log jail "exceedingly filthy, and without bed, chair, table, stove or any other article of furniture" except his trunk. When four anti-slavery men called on him, only "Father" Waters of the Galesburg colony was admitted to his "den." Cross lost no time advising the anti-slavery press of his treatment by writing a letter to the *Western Citizen* that was full of clichés about his being torn from the bosom of his family and about being shut up like the vilest felon in the common prison. His situation did attract widespread attention, which Cross believed caused the sheriff to moderate his severity, allowing Cross visitors more freely and permitting them to bring him bed, table, chair, and refreshments, though as an offset to these privileges the jailor moved Cross to the "Inner Prison," which was "filthy without description, with just enough of light to make filth visible." He spent over two weeks in jail before he was released, apparently on the bail of Galesburg friends, though why this was not done sooner does not appear, unless avoiding imprisonment would have spoiled the effect.[93]

When his case came to trial Cross, to the judge's distress, insisted on being his own attorney. Borders, however, was not on hand, and lacking his evidence, the state's attorney wanted to

[92] Chapman, *History of Knox County*, pp. 212–13; Matson, *Reminiscences of Bureau County*, pp. 367–70.
[93] *Western Citizen*, May 9, 16, 23, July 18, 1844; Chapman, *History of Knox County*, p. 215.

continue the case to the next term. To thwart this move Cross offered to admit what they proposed to prove by the absent witness. This took the prosecutor by surprise, for he was not ready for trial, and he entered a *nolle prosequi,* thus depriving Cross of an opportunity for an anti-slavery lecture by way of an address to the jury.[94]

LIBERTY LINE.

NEW ARRANGEMENT---NIGHT AND DAY.

The improved and splendid Locomotives, Clarkson and Lundy, with their trains fitted up in the best style of accommodation for passengers, will run their regular trips during the present season, between the borders of the Patriarchal Dominion and Libertyville, Upper Canada. Gentlemen and Ladies, who may wish to improve their health or circumstances, by a northern tour, are respectfully invited to give us their patronage.

SEATS FREE, *irrespective of color.*

Necessary Clothing furnished gratuitously to such as have *"fallen among thieves."*

"Hide the outcasts—let the oppressed go free."—*Bible.*

☞For seats apply at any of the trap doors, or to the conductor of the train.

J. CROSS, *Proprietor.*

N. B. For the special benefit of Pro-Slavery Police Officers, an extra heavy wagon for Texas, will be furnished, whenever it may be necessary, in which they will be forwarded as dead freight, to the "Valley of Rascals," always at the risk of the owners.

☞Extra Overcoats provided for such of them as are afflicted with protracted *chilly-phobia.*

Underground Railroad Advertisement

From the *Western Citizen,* July 13, 1844

The abolitionists believed that they had inflicted a "mortifying defeat" upon the "slaveites." The *Western Citizen* celebrated the event by printing an illustrated card for "J. Cross, Proprietor" of the "Liberty Line," picturing the Underground Railroad and advertising its facilities. The series of legal attacks started against the Knox County abolitionists had failed utterly to frighten them, for on the very day that the state of Illinois abandoned its suit against Cross, two Negro passengers on the "Liberty Stage" passed right by the county courthouse in broad daylight with no attempt at concealment, and stopped almost opposite to it for nearly an hour before

[94] *Western Citizen,* July 18, 1844; Knox County Court Records, Book I; Chapman, *History of Knox County,* p. 213.

continuing northward. And as Cross exulted: "Not a dog, or puppy, from the tall lank Kentucky Ranger of Knox, to the fat, cowardly, wagon-puppy of Bureau, moved his tongue, except a *disappointed,* and *hungry mastiff,* of Stark, which was running at full cry on a coon track."[95] This may have been sheer bravado on this occasion, but before long such flagrant disregard of the law seems to have become common, as the following entries in Wright's journal show:

July 26, 1847. Sat. a black man from slavery came here & I carried him on the public highway by daylight, & in the middle of the day to the next station.

June 11, 1848. Tues. I brought a colored man fr. H. Rhodes to town, & he went on by day with a company from Osceola, & next day on in the stage to Princeton. All which shows that the railroad has risen nearly to the surface here.[96]

The Negroes involved in the Borders affair had less reason for elation. Sarah lost her appeal for freedom to the Illinois State Supreme Court;[97] Hannah, though acknowledged as free, got nowhere when she sued for wages earned in the time served beyond her bond;[98] the twelve-year-old son of Susan was killed in Borders's horse mill before the Borders litigation was completed;[99] and Susan, who settled in Galesburg for the rest of her days, never saw any of her children again.[100]

In addition to Susan, at least one other fugitive is known to have become a resident of Galesburg, and there may have been others, since it would appear that some of the runaways delayed for some time, working in the community before going further north.[101] A number of free Negroes also settled here.[102] A Negro had been one of the very first settlers in this community, for he had been hired by the party of colonists that came in the canal boat, and had remained in the colony and

[95] *Western Citizen,* July 18, 1844.

[96] Samuel G. Wright, "Journal"; some of the abbreviations used by Wright have been spelled out for the sake of clarity.

[97] Scammon 4,341.   [98] *Western Citizen,* July 6, 1843.

[99] *Ibid.,* April 24, 1844.   [100] Chapman, *History of Knox County,* p. 206.

[101] *Ibid.,* chapter 8.

[102] Lewis Carter, "The Negro Race," in Perry, ed., *Knox County,* I, 761–63.

joined the church.[103] Negroes were very well treated in Galesburg;[104] Mary Brown Davis emphasized this fact in an article published in the *Western Citizen* in 1847, in which she defended the thesis that Negroes did very well if treated properly. With the poor condition of the Negro inhabitants of Peoria she contrasted the happy situation of those in Galesburg, citing the example of six sisters who had purchased a lot, built their own neat home and a barn, owned a slip in the colony church, and had received a good "English education."[105] Sixteen Negroes lived in Galesburg in 1849;[106] during the fifties this number increased to eighty-nine.[107] They took an active part in promoting the cause of their people. In August, 1857, a Negro festival was held on the Gale premises in honor of the anniversary of emancipation in the West Indies, and Negroes from Quincy, Monmouth, Kewanee, Burlington, and from Coles and Edgar counties were present.[108] On the day of John Brown's execution, December 2, 1859, the Galesburg Negroes held a meeting in tribute to him, and Clark E. Carr, a young white Galesburg politician who was to go far with the new Republican Party, was among the speakers.[109]

Since the organization of the colony, free common school privileges had prevailed, open to Negro residents without regard to age.[110] The railroad, however, built in the middle fifties, brought in citizens who diluted the original "Yankee" nucleus of the community and who did not share its reforming ideals. Probably it was this new white population that caused trouble

[103] Earnest Elmo Calkins, "Pioneer Who's Who . . . Tentative Roster of the Original Settlers of Galesburg," *Official Program Galesburg–Knox College Centenary.*

[104] H. H. Kellogg in the British and Foreign Anti-Slavery Society, *Proceedings of the General Anti-Slavery Convention, London, 1843,* p. 266.

[105] *Western Citizen,* Dec. 14, 1847.   [106] Knoxville *Journal,* Oct. 1, 1850.

[107] *Statistics of the United States, Compiled from the Original Returns of the Ninth Census, June 1, 1870 . . . by Francis A. Walker, Superintendent of the Census* (Washington, 1872), p. 114; in 1860 there were 151 Negroes in the entire county. *Ibid.,* p. 24.

[108] Galesburg *Free Democrat,* Aug. 12, 1857, p. 2.

[109] Galesburg *Semi-Weekly Free Democrat,* Dec. 3, 1859.

[110] "E. P. Chambers Tells Interesting Incidents of the Early Life of the City," Galesburg *Evening Mail,* Oct. 5, 1923.

over mixed schools, when that problem was made acute by the flooding of the community with Negroes from Missouri and Kentucky during the Civil War.[111] Some of these were "contrabands" coming before the Emancipation Proclamation, though the greatest number came after that event.[112] One Stoke Williams, a mulatto barber, reputed to have a white wife, besieged the Board of Education demanding that the freedman regardless of age or sex should be promptly offered the school benefits that had always been open to Negroes in the town. Reputable members of the board were strongly of this same sentiment, and one of them expressed his feeling about the new white population that had troubled the colony since the railroad boom by remarking about the Negroes: "I think they would be better associates for our little children than the Irish and Dutch children now attending the schools." It was argued, however, that to crowd these new arrivals into the public schools would be unjust alike to blacks and whites. A suitable room with the daughter of Nehemiah West as their teacher [113] was supplied to all the emancipated Negroes regardless of age. At one time this school numbered more than one hundred of all ages, for many adults took advantage of the free education offered them. This action by the board was, nonetheless, an issue at the next supervisors' election, but the plan for a Negro school was sustained.

[111] The Galesburg Negro population increased over 700 percent (89 to 630) between 1860 and 1870 while the white population only approximately doubled (*Statistics of the U.S. . . . Ninth Census, June, 1870*, p. 114).

[112] Carter, "The Negro Race," in Perry, ed., *Knox County*, I, 763–65.

[113] "E. P. Chambers Tells Interesting Incidents of the Early Life of the City," Galesburg *Evening Mail*, Oct. 5, 1923; Bonham, *Fifty Years Recollections*, an article on "Mary Allen West," pp. 262–67.

❧ XIII ❧

The Coming of Jonathan Blanchard

An enlightened intellect with a corrupt heart is but a cold gas-light
over a sepulcher, revealing, but not warming the dead.[1]

IT WAS WARM and the windows of the academy building were open to a perfect spring Sunday morning. The members of the Galesburg colony congregation entered eagerly,
for they knew that the Reverend Jonathan Blanchard had arrived the night before and they were to hear one of the most
famous abolitionist preachers of the nation. Even more exciting was the knowledge that the colony leaders wanted this man
to become the new president of Knox College. There was some
delay. Then from without came the sound of people talking,
and through the window one could see the Reverend Mr. Gale
and Mrs. Gale approaching with a man of truly striking appearance, dressed in very genteel garb. Many of that congregation remembered the sight of him at this time because the
man they now saw for the first time began at this instant a
very lively chapter in their lives. They remembered the pleasure of their surprise as he removed his hat, proceeded to the
preacher's desk, and stood before them, a young man of medium
height but erect and with "but little of the student's stoop of
the shoulders," his raven-black hair just beginning to recede
from a high, full forehead that beetled over dark, flashing eyes
—truly a "lion-like looking man." [2] This was the Reverend
Jonathan Blanchard.

[1] Blanchard, *Sermons and Addresses*, pp. 116–17.
[2] A "Reminiscence" among the papers collected by Earnest Elmo Calkins, in
the Knox College Library.

Though the actual site of this college-colony from the Burned-over District was new to Blanchard, its spiritual climate was familiar, for he had followed Asa Mahan as pastor of that church in Cincinnati which had been an outpost of the Great Revival and the rallying point for the "Oneidas," former students of Gale, and other zealots whom Weld led to Lane Seminary. One of those Lane Rebels was now pastor of the Galesburg church. And in the congregation was William Holyoke, one of the founders of the Sixth Presbyterian Church in Cincinnati served by Mahan until the Rebels took him with them to the presidency of Oberlin. Holyoke had been one of Mahan's stalwart defenders and a Lane trustee who supported the Rebels. Though he joined the Galesburg colony in 1837, he was still in 1845 one of the three titleholders of the Cincinnati church building of which Blanchard was even then the pastor.

Blanchard was a Yankee from the Green Mountains who had been "converted" and fired to evangelical fervor for a perfect state of society about a year after the Great Revival was ignited in New York. He was graduated from Middlebury College in 1832 and then taught for two years in the Plattsburg academy. Like so many of the reformers of that generation he was inducted into the reform movement by lecturing on temperance, and while at Plattsburg he became an advocate of the immediate abolition of slavery. During the next two years, while a theological student at Andover, he began his public agitation for the abolitionist cause, though he risked his student pastorate by so doing, and was mobbed in Haddonsfield, New Jersey, at his very first public anti-slavery lecture.[3] At Andover he was uneasy because he believed the authorities too tolerant of slavery.[4] He looked westward toward Oberlin, and as that school emerged as the militant anti-slavery home of the Lane Rebels he tried, unsuccessfully, to join its faculty.[5]

[3] Jonathan Blanchard, "My Life Work," a brief autobiography read by Blanchard at the celebration of his eightieth birthday by the faculty, trustees, and students of Wheaton College, Jan. 19, 1891, MS, Knox College Library; also published in Blanchard, *Sermons and Addresses*.

[4] *National Cyclopedia of American Biography*, XXII, 447.

[5] Fletcher, *History of Oberlin*, I, 194.

In September of 1836 he was admitted, however, to that corps of anti-slavery agents, the "Seventy," recruited about the nucleus of the Lane Rebels.[6]

It was Blanchard's lot to discover the grapes of wrath in that place where seventeen years later men were treading out the vintage in the most famous campaign of the Civil War. Two of the other agents assigned by the American Anti-Slavery Society to Pennsylvania became ill and Blanchard bore the brunt of the agitation there.[7] Within the span of one month twenty-five of the thirty meetings he opened were interrupted by hostile auditors and many of them were broken up.[8] Once he was cornered in an inn on a town square by some two thousand men who swore they would "raze the house" unless the proprietor would give him up to the mob. But the landlord dispersed the angry gathering by a trick; by a back way he sent into the outskirts of the crowd a person who ran down the street crying, "Here he goes! Here he goes!"; and the whole crowd, pursuing him, ran off.[9] Yet "hosts" were converted to the unpopular cause.[10]

Early in 1837 he went to the capital of the state, at Harrisburg, to get up a state anti-slavery convention. He was hissed and in open daylight stoned as he walked in the streets, but here, in February, he made his most famous convert, Thaddeus Stevens, the leader of a faction of the Anti-Masonic Party, then badly split and frustrated. Blanchard presented abolition as a greater and more durable issue than anti-masonry and suggested to Stevens that he turn his Anti-Masons into abolitionists. As tangible evidence of his support for the new cause, Stevens gave Blanchard a roll of bills, forty dollars in all, saying, "Take that, & go down into Adams County and lecture, and if they Morganize you, we'll make a party out of it." The young agitator did get into trouble in that border county, for at Gettysburg a mass meeting resolved against all agitation of the slavery issue and made it plain that Blanchard should get

[6] E. Wright to Weld, Sept. 22, 1836, *Weld Letters*, I, 337.
[7] Weld to Angelina Grimké, Oct. 16, 1837, *ibid.*, I, 459–62.
[8] Wilson, *History of the Rise and Fall of the Slave Power in America*, I, 293.
[9] Blanchard and Rice, *Debate*, p. 271.   [10] *Weld Letters*, I, 337, note.

out. When Stevens heard of this action he came at once from Harrisburg, called another meeting, met the local leaders head-on, and effected a complete reversal of the suppression of free speech. Blanchard was actually invited to continue his labors. This assistance to his agency Blanchard described to the anniversary meeting of the American Anti-Slavery Society in May, and that body passed resolutions praising the Pennsylvania politician. Thus Stevens began the change from a defeated Anti-Masonic leader to a potential leader in a new crusade.[11]

Later in 1837 Blanchard went to Cincinnati, where he preached to two Negro churches, lectured to the Ladies' Anti-Slavery Society in the home of a sister of Salmon P. Chase, and completed his theological studies under Lyman Beecher at Lane, which by this time had dropped its offensive gag rules. In March, 1838, he began to preach to Mahan's former congregation in the Sixth Presbyterian Church, whose membership at this time included James G. Birney. Here he was ordained the following October and formally established in one of the key abolitionist posts of the nation.[12] Among the events soon testifying to his prominence in the reforming clique of the city was the attack, in September, 1839, by a mob comprised partly of Kentuckians on Blanchard's church, where Birney was lecturing at the time.[13] Recognition from the extremists on the other side came that same month when he spoke during the Oberlin commencement on a "Perfect State of Society," [14] the printing of which went through two editions. He was offered a professorship in the college, which he declined.[15]

Among the manifold functions Blanchard soon was performing for the abolitionist cause in the West,[16] the two that

[11] Current, *Old Thad Stevens*, pp. 34–35, 42–44; Woodley, *Great Leveler*, pp. 68–70; *Fourth Annual Report of the American Anti-Slavery Society*, 1837, p. 19.
[12] Blanchard, "My Life Work"; William Birney, *James G. Birney and His Times*, pp. 206, 241.
[13] Birney to Lewis Tappan, Sept. 12, 1839, *Birney Letters*, I, 498.
[14] Blanchard, *Sermons and Addresses*, p. 51. [15] *Ibid.*, p. 10.
[16] The confidence of the abolitionist leaders in Blanchard was evident in the suggestion in June, 1838, that he be sent to the Wayne, Indiana, convention in order that the attempt to form a state anti-slavery society proceed well (Gamaliel Bailey to Birney, June 28, 1838, *Birney Letters*, I, 461–64). Bailey also mentioned

were most important were essentially political in character, though one was civil and the other ecclesiastical. The latter comprised those activities by which he relentlessly forced slavery as an issue, disruptive and sectional in effect, upon ecclesiastical organizations. It was in this role that he eventually achieved national prominence. In October, 1841, he preached by appointment a sermon "On Slaveholding," in Mt. Pleasant, Ohio, before the New School Presbyterian Synod of Cincinnati. Slaveholding, he declared, necessarily corrupted and eventually destroyed all true religion in those churches where it was tolerated; it caused man to be regarded as a mere animal; the men who were guilty of it lost their notions of justice, and thus it brought about the death of virtue. The sermon was printed and circulated as a pamphlet.[17] In June, 1842, at a convention of western Congregational and Presbyterian ministers in Cincinnati, he tried unsuccessfully to get that body to pass a resolution instructing young ministers going to the slave states to form churches on anti-slavery principles.[18]

In 1842 he made an analysis regarding the relation of schools and churches to public questions in the form of a speech before the Literary and Moral Society of Ripley College, in Ohio. In view of his later career as a college president this utterance is deserving of special examination. He undertook in this discourse to answer the question, "What is the duty of men occupying posts of influence in Churches, Colleges, and Theological Seminaries:—on Questions of Reform, involving the Elements of Morals, which agitate and divide the public mind?" He asserted that the opinions and measures of religious denominations were largely determined by a comparatively few leading minds prominent in church offices, especially those connected with schools and benevolent agencies. Colleges, be-

---

him as one of the eight key men who ought to arrange the preliminaries for the annual convention of the Ohio Anti-Slavery Society for 1841, saying, "Mr. Blanchard, of course, must give an address" (Bailey to T. E. Thomas, Cincinnati, Jan. 11, 1841, in Alfred A. Thomas, ed., *Correspondence of Thomas Ebenezer Thomas*, pp. 31–32). William Birney informed his father in 1843 that Blanchard did not receive the prominent mention of his work that he deserved (Wm. Birney to J. G. Birney, Feb. 18, 1843, *Birney Letters*, II, 721).

[17] Blanchard, *Sermon on Slaveholding*.
[18] New York *Evangelist*, I (June 23, 1842), 196.

nevolent societies, and churches depended for endowments on wealthy men, who as propertied persons dreaded reforms which affected the institutions of private property. Blanchard cited banking connections in particular. In America, he declared, a "large part of the property is in a moral sense, tainted," meaning the capital invested in slaves. The propertied classes North and South "being one in interest, are often so in spirit." As a result of the connection of churches and colleges with these propertied interests, "the most formidable antagonism to every reform in this country is church opposition." The colleges of the country, placed as they were "between the corruptions of property on the one hand and church corruptions on the other," also have this "moral leprosy," the exceptions being "like individual stars in a night of clouds" which "only reveal the darkness of the firmament in which they are set." Blanchard struck hard and long against "non-committalism" for the sake of "peace" and "influence" and "worldly popularity." He announced: "We want a martyr-age of Colleges and Seminaries"; faculties "ought to lead their students, both by precept and example . . . into a zeal for reformation." [19]

This bold and direct statement of the responsibility of schools and churches in the abolition crusade was published as a pamphlet in Cincinnati, and reprinted widely in newspapers and circulated as a tract in several states. Illinois anti-slavery men were able to read it in the *Western Citizen,* which used it as the leading article for two of its issues in March, 1843,[20] and also published it as the second number of *Liberty Tree.*[21] And this is the utterance by Blanchard that Gale printed in 1845 along with his *Brief History of Knox College* upon the occasion of Blanchard's election to the presidency.

Blanchard only partly understood why he so frequently was the center of controversy. "It seems," he wrote to a friend on the Oberlin faculty, "to be a standing affliction of mine to perceive clearly what is right and with too much softness of nature to stand up for it. . . . I feel much of the time like a

[19] Blanchard, *Public Men and Public Institutions,* republished with Gale's *Brief History of Knox College* (Cincinnati, 1845).
[20] *Western Citizen,* March 9 and 16, 1843.   [21] *Liberty Tree,* Vol. I, No. 2.

person without a skin in the midst of thorns."[22] Actually Blanchard's dogmatism did not derive so much from confidence of his own righteousness as from fear that inner uncertainty be mistaken for cowardice. The tempest that whirled about him over the third-party issue in 1840 exemplifies these traits of his personality.

The disturbance of old political party lines by the abolition agitation involved Blanchard shortly after he became pastor of the Sixth Presbyterian Church. Gamaliel Bailey, editor of the *Philanthropist* in Cincinnati, had been rather rough on the Whigs, and antagonized those important pillars of this church, the Melendys. It was Blanchard's influence that kept them from withdrawing their support from the *Philanthropist* and from using their influence to deprive it of subscribers.[23] Before the spring of 1840 the minority of abolitionists in New York favoring independent nominations found hardly any encouragement in Ohio. Until the middle of April, at least, Bailey agreed with Blanchard that the Liberty Party ticket of Birney and Earle was a mistake in policy, likely to split and injure the cause, and that especially in Ohio, abolitionism would best be served by the election of the Whig candidate, William H. Harrison.[24] At first Blanchard revealed only in private conversation that he would vote for Harrison and Tyler, but at the state anti-slavery convention at Massilon he was "surprised" and "embarrassed" by the accusation that he was "ashamed openly to avow what in secret I was willing to do." Thus provoked, Blanchard published in the *Philanthropist* a letter expounding his determination to vote for the Whig candidates.

This announcement, to Blanchard's surprise, ran a veritable gauntlet of public opinion, receiving comment both in papers opposed to abolition as well as in those favoring it.[25] The most stinging of these comments came in a public letter issued in the *Friend of Man* in which Gerrit Smith denounced Blanchard

[22] Blanchard to Cowles, Cincinnati, Aug. 4, 1840, MS, Oberlin College Library.
[23] G. Bailey to Birney, Oct. 28, 1838, *Birney Letters*, I, 475.
[24] Blanchard to Gerrit Smith, Sept. 14, 1840 (Smith Papers, Syracuse University Library); Bailey to Birney, Feb. 21, March 3, April 18, 1840, *Birney Letters*, I, 531-32, 535-38, 556-58.
[25] Blanchard to Gerrit Smith, Aug. 5, 1840, Smith Papers.

and an Ohio colleague for their "sin" in supporting Harrison, for their "political party delusion" and "unprincipledness," and referred to them as "sham abolitionists." Smith wrote to Weld that his rebuke of Blanchard was "severe but not too much so," [26] but this was not the opinion of others; Finney, who was favorable to the third-party idea, wrote to Smith that he approved of the sentiments of the letter to Blanchard but regretted its spirit. "My precious Brother," wrote Finney to Smith, "you will not take it amiss if I touch upon your elbow and say 'guard your spirit' when your feelings are greatly tried and when you take your pen to reprove or rebuke a brother? Your rebuke was merited by B. Blanchard in my apprehension but I almost feared as I read that Br. Smith's spirit has a little caustic." [27] Bailey, though now himself on Smith's side, wrote the latter that he did not adequately appreciate the peculiar political situation of abolitionists in Ohio in his denunciation and that Blanchard "should be dealt with kindly—he will 'go right,' I doubt not." [28]

In a strong but kindly reply, that was "by no means to be published," Blanchard explained to Smith the dilemma of a man who wished both to be right and to vote—a situation which has been the quandary of the "independent" many times since:

I am equally clear that your ground principle is a wrong one— viz—that it is a sin to vote for a slaveholder, because he is a slaveholder. As a general rule I would not vote for a slaveholder or duellist; yet if Clay had emancipated his slaves and declared for abolition I would have voted for him, though he had not published his repentance for partaking in duels. God requires the rulers to be just—perfectly just—yet seeing that perfect men are somewhat scarce, he requires me to obtain the best ruler I possibly can. Either Van Buren or Harrison is as certain of being elected as if one was now in the chair—My vote, if I vote for Harrison, goes to keep one I consider most dangerous, out. If I vote for Birney, it takes one vote less to elect V. Buren. If both were now in the chair, and it was re-

[26] Gerrit Smith to Weld, July 11, 1840, *Weld Letters,* II, 849–50.
[27] Finney to Smith, July 22, 1840, Smith Papers.
[28] Bailey to Smith, July 21, 1840, Smith Papers.

ferred to me, should I sin against God in putting the one I considered the worst one, out? [29]

From letters written during the summer of 1840 we get a picture of a man of principle trying to find the path of righteousness in the pattern of party politics—of an anti-slavery Whig by fits and starts moving to the Liberty Party. To his friends in Oberlin Blanchard had written, the day before he replied to Smith, "The providence of God is fast leading to the establishment of an Abolition political party, and I do not wish to throw any obstacle in the way." [30] Bailey informed Smith that Blanchard was already "mourning not a little his unfortunate letter" supporting Harrison, and though unwilling to cooperate with the promoters of a third party in Ohio, yet was vindicating their course to the members of his church.[31] At mid-September Blanchard wrote Smith that he would "not yet join the third political party," but that he found himself nearly as much on Bailey's side in Ohio as on that of his critics. As Harrison "crouched to slavery" during the campaign, Blanchard authorized Bailey to tell his readers that he would not then write a letter favoring Harrison as he had in the spring. "I will stand still till I can see something better to do. My private vote I shall give on the day of election according to my conscience." [32]

A year later Blanchard had definitely, though not yet certainly, moved into the Liberty Party ranks by signing the call for a county convention; and on the day it met he wrote Smith of his action. Looking forward already to the campaign of 1844, Blanchard remarked, "From all that I can see I shall vote for Birney and Morris if candidates at the next election. Yet if Seward, or a like man was the Whig or Democrat I should not." [33] A little over six months later Blanchard was himself fully involved in a maneuver to extend the third party by

[29] Blanchard to Gerrit Smith, Aug. 5, 1840, Smith Papers.
[30] Blanchard to Cowles, Aug. 4, 1840, MS, Oberlin College Library.
[31] Bailey to Smith, July 21, 1840, Smith Papers.
[32] Blanchard to Smith, Sept. 14, 1840, Smith Papers.
[33] Blanchard to Smith, Sept. 11, 1841, Smith Papers.

bringing his friend Thaddeus Stevens into the movement. Admiration for and loyalty to that Pennsylvania politician had been a source of Blanchard's aversion to the Liberty Party ticket in 1840, for Birney's running mate, Thomas Earle of Pennsylvania, had been utterly unacceptable to both Stevens and Blanchard. While doing his stint as anti-slavery agent in that state during the thirties Blanchard had heard Earle express egalitarian views which included not only justice for the slave but opposition to "all exclusive privileges and monopolies, grounded on learning, birth, property or color," [34] and during a ride in the stage from Philadelphia to Harrisburg listened while Earle had "talked incessantly" for the annual election of judges. Such sentiments were much too radical, even for Blanchard. Furthermore, Earle was then Stevens's "bitter and uniform foe," and during those hectic days when Blanchard had been stoned almost as often as he crossed the street in Harrisburg, Earle gave him no help, whereas Stevens had been a tower of strength in a time of trouble. [35]

In April of 1842, Blanchard, writing his "first line" for the Liberty Party, undertook by letter to introduce his Cincinnati friend, Salmon P. Chase, to Stevens. Blanchard explained that one of his reasons for writing was to tell about the men who had recently organized a state Liberty Party in Ohio. He emphasized especially the merits of Chase, setting forth his abilities as a jurist, as well as his political plans and movements. Another objective of the letter was to ask Stevens, even though Blanchard was not yet sure whether his correspondent would come into the Liberty Party, to speak at a meeting that Chase and others were planning to hold in Cincinnati. Finally, Blanchard revealed, "Another thing I want is that you should help Chase displace the name of Birney and substitute that of Seward or J. Q. Adams as Anti-Slavery Candidate for Presidency; and that in a way will prevent a break between Eastern and Western Abolitionists." [36]

Blanchard's letter accompanied one that Chase had also

[34] Joshua Leavitt to Birney, May 19, 1840, *Birney Letters*, I, 574.
[35] Blanchard to Smith, Sept. 14, 1840, Smith Papers.
[36] Blanchard to Thaddeus Stevens, April 9, 1842, MS, Library of Congress.

written to Stevens regretting that they were strangers to one another. Chase sent along a pamphlet containing an address to the people of Ohio issued by the state convention of the Liberty Party held at Columbus the preceding December. He described the party as growing stronger, as having a gubernatorial candidate, and as having no general expectation of winning the present campaign but anticipating victory two years hence. He argued for making anti-slavery a political as well as a moral issue. The special purpose of the letter was to draw Stevens's attention to the movements of the party, to get him to express his views on it, and to ask him to "bring the old Anti-Masonic Party of Pennsylvania on to the Liberty Platform." He talked of candidates who might be nominated instead of Birney—possibly Governor Seward of New York or Judge McLean of Ohio. Stevens's opinion was asked.[37]

Stevens answered both letters by writing to Blanchard and requesting that he show the letter to Chase. He agreed with their objective entirely but was not in full agreement "as to the means most likely to accomplish it." His own belief was that it was still best to decline to organize a distinct political party. He favored General Winfield Scott as a possible candidate in the anti-slavery direction.[38]

Though the object of this correspondence was not immediately achieved, it is not the less significant; bringing together these two men who were to have so much influence in national politics was an important historical incident.[39] Hereafter it is clear that Blanchard was reconciled to the policy of a third party, even when the Whigs ran a candidate popular with abolitionists and friendly to Negroes.[40]

In 1843 Blanchard went to London as delegate to the world anti-slavery convention from the Ohio State Anti-Slavery Society and from the Ladies Education Society of Ohio.[41] It was at this time that his career became linked with the affairs of

[37] S. P. Chase to Thaddeus Stevens, April 8, 1842, MS, Library of Congress.
[38] Stevens to Blanchard, May 24, 1842, MS, Library of Congress.
[39] Current, *Old Thad Stevens*, pp. 76–77; Woodley, *Great Leveler*, pp. 141–42.
[40] Remarks by Blanchard in British and Foreign Anti-Slavery Society, *Proceedings of the General Anti-Slavery Convention, London, 1843*, p. 237.
[41] *Ibid.*, p. 342.

Knox College, for its president, Hiram H. Kellogg, became
his traveling companion. Kellogg was also going to England
to serve as the delegate from the Illinois Anti-Slavery Society
and to raise money for his school.

At the world convention in London, Blanchard took a very
prominent part. He was one of the two Americans elected
vice-presidents of that body, and on the first day of the session spoke briefly to express for the American delegation their
sense of the kindness and confidence manifested by the convention in that election.[42] He was appointed to a number of
committees and spoke at greater or lesser length on a number
of subjects; in fact, one of the American delegates complained
that he spoke too much.[43] Among his activities was the presentation of the report from the Committee on American Papers,
in which committee he served with Kellogg. His speech on
American Presbyterianism was his longest parliamentary effort,
a significant fact in view of his later labors for ecclesiastical
sectionalism. The New School and Old School Presbyterian
schism of 1838, he maintained, had been caused by the slavery
issue, and he boasted that the western presbyteries of the New
School, with which he was connected, were even then discon-
tented with the stand of their own General Assembly on
slavery.[44]

While in London Blanchard endorsed President Kellogg's
published appeal to British philanthropists for funds to sustain Knox College. Shortly after the return of Kellogg to
Galesburg in the summer of 1844 he wrote to Blanchard asking
him to serve as an agent for Knox College for a year or more,
and proposed that he pick Blanchard up on the way East in
November, spend two months with him in that field, and then
leave the agency to Blanchard.[45] The college was desperately
in need of funds, and Kellogg's financial solicitation in England had been disappointing. In February, 1845, the board of

[42] *Ibid.*, pp. 7 and 9.
[43] Charles Stuart to Weld, Bathwick-Bath, England, July 10, 1843, *Weld Letters*, I, 978–79.
[44] British and Foreign Anti-Slavery Society, *Proceedings of the General Anti-Slavery Convention, London, 1843*, pp. 92–95, 198, 275.
[45] Kellogg to Blanchard, Aug. 22, 1844, *Report on Knox College, 1861*, p. 33.

trustees very respectfully but unanimously expressed the opinion that Kellogg ought to be asked to resign.[46] Then in April Blanchard appeared in Galesburg, "providentially" but "unexpectedly." [47] He had been invited to the presidency of the Mission Institute at Quincy, and he was asked to come to Galesburg by some of the leaders there, including Kellogg.[48] Blanchard in any event wanted to come to Galesburg to see William Holyoke of the colony, for he was one of the three original founders and titleholders of the anti-slavery church which Blanchard was serving in Cincinnati. The other two titleholders had agreed to quitclaim their interests in the property in order that the congregation would have more interest in paying off a debt which had accumulated, and Blanchard wanted Holyoke to give up his legal rights in the church.[49]

Kellogg resigned in May, 1845, suggesting Blanchard as his successor.[50] Gale wrote to the latter arguing that two institutions such as Mission Institute and Knox, so similar in their stand on the "liberal" isues of the day, ought to get together, the implication being that Blanchard should give up his consideration of the other school and come to Knox.[51] The board of trustees resolved unanimously on June 21 that it was desirable that Blanchard become president, and appointed a committee to communicate this fact to him.[52] He was appointed president on July 23 and severed his connection with the Sixth Presbyterian Church in October, the understanding being that he was to be in the East on an agency for the college in the fall and to take up his duties in Galesburg the following February.[53] His vigorous and uncompromising anti-slavery

[46] Knox College, "Trustees' Records, Transcript," Part A, p. 84; "Statement by Blanchard," Rights of Congregationalists in Knox College, Appendix Q, p. 76.
[47] Gale to J. P. Williston, Galesburg, June 24, 1845, Report on Knox College, 1861, p. 38.
[48] Nehemiah Losey, to Blanchard, Galesburg, May 20, 1845, ibid., p. 36.
[49] Samuel Greenleaf Holyoke, "A Historical Sketch," Galesburg Republican Register, July 7, 1911.
[50] "Trustees' Records, Transcript," Part A, p. 84. Following his resignation Kellogg served as pastor of the colony church. In July of 1847 he returned to Clinton, New York (Western Citizen, July 3, 1847), where he reopened the female seminary of which he had formerly been head (ibid., Oct. 10, 1847).
[51] Gale to Blanchard, June 5, 1845, Report on Knox College, 1861, p. 37.
[52] "Trustees' Records, Transcript," Part A, p. 86.   [53] Ibid., pp. 89–90.

principles were fully appreciated and accepted by Gale,[54] and
Kellogg hoped that Blanchard's connections in the East might
secure assistance for the college which the former president
believed was being refused in conservative circles because
of the radical anti-slavery reputation of the school. Blanchard's
conviction that schools and churches should actively agitate
against slavery was definitely and publicly associated with the
future of Knox College when his address on "Public Men and
Public Institutions," described above, was republished in 1845
in a pamphlet together with a brief history and description of
Knox College and of the colony written by Gale.[55]

The establishment of Blanchard in the presidency of Knox
College was accompanied by the appointment of persons with
Blanchard connections to other administrative posts in the institution. His brother Cyrus came along from Cincinnati to
become Principal of the Preparatory Department;[56] a brother-
in-law, Joseph Avery Bent, became Principal of the Academy;[57]
and a niece of the Melendys of Cincinnati became Preceptress
of the Female Department.[58]

Blanchard's reputation as an anti-slavery agitator was reem-
phasized just as he was taking up his new academic responsibilities. In October, 1845, at Cincinnati he participated in a great
debate with one of the foremost leaders of the Old School
Presbyterian denomination, the Reverend Nathan L. Rice, nationally notorious for his performances in the great public
debates of that era. The basic issue in the debate was whether
slaveholding was a sin. The debate attracted much attention
and the published record of it went through many editions.[59]

[54] Gale to John Payson Williston, June 24, 1845, and Feb. 21, 1846, *Report on Knox College, 1861*, pp. 38 and 40.
[55] Gale, *A Brief History of Knox College.*
[56] Knox College business records, "Blotter B," Nov. 10 and Dec. 17, 1846, Jan. 22, 1847.
[57] George Brent, who attended Knox College during the years after 1846, was also a brother-in-law of Blanchard and lived in Galesburg with the Blanchard family.
[58] Mary E. Melendy came from Jacksonville where her father was a very active abolitionist (Eames, ed., *Historic Morgan County and Classic Jacksonville*, pp. 72, 142–49); Luella Wright, *Peter Melendy*, p. 17 and p. 303, note.
[59] *Weld Letters*, I, 337, note.

Such in fact was the notoriety of it that Mrs. Blanchard, on her way to Galesburg with her children, was afraid as she got off the boat at Cape Girardeau to rest over the Sabbath, lest pro-slavery people identify them through the names on their baggage as the family of the man who had taken the unpopular side in the recently published contest.[60]

A writer in the Cincinnati *Herald* commented on the fact that Blanchard closed his career in the city as he opened it, in debate.[61] He probably did not appreciate how excellent a commentary that was on the man's life when viewed from the perspective of the twentieth century. One whose fate it was to be a victim of Blanchard's moral and intellectual pugnacity made this striking commentary on him:

It is his nature to wage war. We find him at his favorite occupation in all the positions of life in which he has ever been placed,— the Church, the State, and Educational Institutions, forming no exception. Uniting talent and education with his disposition to fight the institutions of the world as he found them when born into it, he is a man to be watched by the safer part of the community, and the avenues of influential positions, in which much harm can be done by evil disposed persons, should be well-guarded against him.[62]

However, another critic, who had exactly the same reason to complain of Blanchard's ideas [63] and yet admired his courage, commented on the "mild and gentlemanly manner" of his attacks and his "moral sublimity." [64] It was true that those social reflexes which cause a man to flinch from fulfilling convictions if the consequences are unpleasant seem never to have developed far in him. A moral principle once comprehended must be relentlessly pursued and a deviation from right ruthlessly revealed. Though he would be a leader in the cause of temperance,[65] yet he would not tolerate the Sons of Temperance because they were a secret society.[66] Lest Puritan abhor-

[60] Fischer, *Blessed Memories*, p. 55.   [61] *Western Citizen*, Oct. 23, 1845.

[62] Knoxville *Republican*, Nov. 30, 1859.

[63] Blanchard's hostility to secret societies.

[64] Oquawka *Spectator*, Sept. 4, 1850.

[65] He was one of the three main speakers at the State Maine Alliance in Springfield, Illinois, Feb. 22, 1854, and was chairman of the committee reporting a resolution of political tactics (*ibid.*, March 9, 1854).

[66] Blanchard, *Secret Societies*.

rence for even the semblance of Romanism relax and Christmas Day be observed, he gave orders that classes be held on that day as well as on others.[67] He was once heard in a conversation to say of some suggestion, "Why I would as soon cut a pack of cards." [68] He warned Knox students against attending "theatres, horse races, Methodist meetings and other places of amusement"; [69] and denounced a locally projected "National Horse Show and Equestrian Fair" because it must be to Galesburg as the "bear garden to Paris, the cock-pit to New Orleans, or gladitorial shows to ancient Rome." [70] In his inaugural address at Knox College he depicted slavery as containing "all the worst principles of European despotism and Asiatic caste," and concluded with an impassioned plea for moral courage, declaring "an enlightened intellect with a corrupt heart is but a cold gas-light over a sepulcher, revealing, but not warming the dead." [71]

The setting that this vigorous actor had chosen was still simple and small in scale, for Galesburg was in 1846 a village of only 130 families [72] in which President Blanchard milked his two cows and fed his hogs before college exercises each school morning.[73] It seemed inappropriately pretentious when Blanchard wore academic regalia at the first college commencement exercises in June of that year. But he never dropped his broader national associations by his removal to a frontier community, for that same fall found him on a protracted tour to the East, during which he visited, among others, Thaddeus Stevens. On this itinerary he heard Webster speak in Faneuil Hall and described his "cold, cautious, calculating and measured allusions to slavery"—which Blanchard compared to "Saul after the spirit of God had departed from him.[74] Com-

[67] Galesburg *Weeks Review*, March 17, 1906.

[68] "Dr. T. R. Willard Gives Glimpses into the Past," Galesburg *Evening Mail*, Oct. 5, 1923.

[69] "Our City Was Discussed," Galesburg *Daily Mail*, Jan. 30, 1895.

[70] Galesburg *Free Democrat*, Nov. 1, 1855.

[71] Blanchard, *Sermons and Addresses*, pp. 110–11, 116–17.

[72] *Western Citizen*, Feb. 18, 1846.

[73] Blanchard to Samuel Williston, April 29 ,1849, Williston Letters, Transcript, Knox College Library.

[74] *Western Citizen*, Dec. 8, 1846.

munications such as the one with these comments were frequently sent by Blanchard to the *Western Citizen,* in which speeches by Blanchard were often the leading article. After his first appearance in Chicago following his inauguration at Knox, that anti-slavery paper remarked:

We cannot forbear adding in conclusion that Mr. Blanchard is an honor to the institution over which he has been called to preside, as well as to the State in which he has lately taken up his residence.[75]

[75] *Ibid.,* July 28, 1846.

❧ XIV ❧

Abolitionism in Education: Loss and Profit

Now on the men of wealth the college depends for its endowments,
the society for patrons, and the denomination for its popularity.
And, as the givers of money always influence the receivers; while
the politics of the country will be controlled by the voters, whether
rich or poor, the wealth of the nation will always give character to
its literary and religious institutions.

There would be no harm in this, were it not the experience of mankind, that the wealthiest portion of the church is not usually the
purest. From its very nature, *property* dreads a disturbance; even
though caused by wholesome and necessary reform.[1]

WHILE GALE'S FOLLOWERS were preparing, in the
spring of 1836, for their journey to the Illinois frontier, the
editor of the leading magazine in the West, in Cincinnati,
expressed his satisfaction that Gale's first educational foundation, Oneida Institute, would likely be purified by the New
York legislature, just as Lane and other institutions had been
purged of abolitionism, and that but one school, Oberlin,
remained "in which murder and robbery are openly inculcated
as Christian virtues." [2] There had indeed been a concerted and
general suppression of abolitionism in academic circles; professors had been gagged or removed from faculties, students
disciplined.[3] In an appeal to English philanthropists in 1839
Weld summarized the situation for Negroes in American collegiate institutions as follows:

[1] Blanchard, *Public Men and Public Institutions.*
[2] James Hall, "Colleges," *Western Monthly Magazine,* April, 1836, pp. 220–26.
[3] Barnes, *Anti-Slavery Impulse,* p. 228 and note; Fletcher, *History of Oberlin,*
I, 183–85, 237–38.

With the noble exception of the Oneida Institute in the state of New York, which has stood erect in the midst of persecutions, pre-eminently true to the slave, mighty in its *free* testimony, and terrible to the oppressor, Oberlin is the only Institution in the United States in which the black and colored student finds a *home* where he is fully and joyfully recognized as "a man and a brother." A few other Institutions do not *refuse* colored students, but though they are admitted to membership, they are subject to humiliating associations.[4]

It was in these unseasonable years that the founder of Oneida Institute and his colony carried their subversive seeds from the Burned-over District to the frontier and planted a college which, like Oberlin, was distinguished among the species by its abolitionist fruit. Several colleges were founded in Illinois during the thirties and were chartered by a reluctant legislature particularly fearful of denominational institutions promoted by Yankees with anti-slavery opinions, institutions with preachers who meddled in politics and inveigled "pious young men and females into an ignorant and blind support of the schemes of plunder and treason of the abolitionists—which have their origin in the lust of money." [5] Of these first colleges in the state, some were by antecedents, clientele, or location conditioned to repudiate abolitionism. The board of trustees of McKendree, two years after Lovejoy's murder, required that persons expressing abolitionist sentiments leave the college.[6] Shurtleff also was "gagged" on slavery discussion.[7] Originally three col-

---

[4] *Weld Letters,* II, 742.

[5] James Hall, "Colleges," *Western Monthly Magazine,* April, 1836, pp. 220–26; also from the *Western Monthly Magazine* see "Editorial Remarks," Jan., 1836, pp. 1–10, and "Editorial," June, 1836, pp. 369–74. A mutual antagonism is reflected in this reminiscence by President Blanchard: "The first college charter had to be smuggled through the legislature by legislative engineering. They [the colleges] were unpopular with that class of preachers who, at that day, boasted their inspiration direct from Heaven, and despised all 'collige larnt men.' They were unpopular with those emigrants from slave States whom the slave system had sunk below the negroes, and crept out from under its mill-stones into this state and Indiana, hating the Yankee, hating God and hating man, and all human institutions but the Democratic party, colleges included" (Chicago *Tribune,* Nov. 7, 1866).

[6] Hildner, "Colleges in Illinois One Hundred Years Ago," *Papers in Illinois History, 1942,* Illinois State Historical Society, p. 30.

[7] *Western Citizen,* April 27, 1843.

leges founded in the west-central part of the state gave promise of being academic strongholds for anti-slavery opinions; these were the Mission Institute at Quincy, Illinois College at Jacksonville, and Knox College. The first of these was truly an abolitionists' outpost until the middle forties,[8] but the death of its leaders, Nelson and Hunter, by 1844, weakened it. Blanchard, having the choice of heading either Knox or Mission Institute in 1845, chose the former, and the latter soon faded out of existence.

As the abolitionist movement slowly gained impetus in Illinois during the middle thirties it seemed for a time that Illinois College might serve as the educational center for the crusade. President Edward Beecher befriended Lovejoy and helped to guard his press and participated prominently in the convention establishing the Illinois Anti-Slavery Society. Most of the Yale Band, who had helped to found Illinois College, also were active in the formative sessions of that abolitionist body. But this promise of radical support for the unpopular cause was not fulfilled.[9] The trustees and most of the faculty feared to offend patrons; students from the South gave some pro-slavery tone to campus life; and Jacksonville society and wealth reflected a strong Southern element.[10] Aggressive leadership of the Beecher quality might have hazarded the fortunes of the college for the abolitionist principle, but in 1842 Edward Beecher went East on a protracted fund-raising tour, taking his family with him, and he never returned; [11] he received a letter telling him he was no longer needed.[12] His successor,

---

[8] A summary of American colleges made in 1843 found only seventeen, excepting Catholic schools, that were willing to accept Negroes on the same terms as whites; only seven of these were outside New England. Two of the latter were in Illinois—Knox College and Mission Institute (Amos A. Phelps, "Influence of Slavery upon Religion and Education," in British and Foreign Anti-Slavery Society, *Proceedings of the General Anti-Slavery Convention, London, 1843*, pp. 84–87); *Western Citizen*, March 23, 1843.

[9] *Western Citizen*, Feb. 23, 1843; Rammelkamp, "The Reverberations of the Slavery Conflict in a Pioneer College," *Mississippi Valley Historical Review*, XIV (March, 1928), 447–61.

[10] Carriel, *Jonathan Baldwin Turner*, p. 60; *Western Citizen*, Oct. 23, 1845; July 14, 1846.

[11] Rammelkamp, *Illinois College*, pp. 40–93.

[12] Carriel, *Jonathan Baldwin Turner*, p. 60.

Julien Sturtevant, a member of the Yale Band, believed that the Lovejoy episode and Beecher's connection with the beginnings of abolitionism in Illinois were obstacles to the development of the college. He regarded the abolitionist agitation as "impractical declamation" which tended "to irritate rather than to convince men." [13] The only really outspoken abolitionist on the faculty was increasingly uneasy under such cautious college leadership. This was Jonathan Baldwin Turner, one of the great men of Illinois in the mid-nineteenth century whose truly independent spirit and soaring intellect were not to be confined within conventional institutions and their authorities. He was harassed for his indifference to orthodox theological doctrines, and this indifference, along with his anti-slavery opinions, made his relations with the college very unpleasant. In April of 1847 he wrote a remarkable letter to Gerrit Smith suggesting the organization of an "Anti-Hierarchical Society" to be formed along the pattern familiar in other reforming bodies of the benevolent system. This Turner proposed quite earnestly, for if Smith would finance the venture, Turner was ready to dedicate himself to battle both in church and state against the "hierarchies" which imperiled liberty and caused slavery.[14] Though this project was not added to Smith's progeny of causes, Turner resigned from the Illinois faculty—and most of his colleagues heaved a sigh of relief.[15] About the same time the only other abolitionist on the faculty also left Illinois College.[16]

Because of the mutual denominational associations of Illinois and Knox colleges, the rather timid stand of the former contrasted all the more sharply with the militant abolitionism of the latter. Partly the difference derived from the more northern and somewhat less dangerous location of Galesburg and by the circumstance that the town was coeval with the college.

[13] Sturtevant, *Autobiography*, pp. 217–26; Rammelkamp, *Illinois College,* pp. 102–17.

[14] J. B. Turner to Gerrit Smith, April 23, 1847, Smith Papers, Syracuse University Library.

[15] Carriel, *Jonathan Baldwin Turner*, p. 62.

[16] Rammelkamp, *Illinois College,* p. 152.

Nevertheless it is significant that of the men originally associated with Illinois College, Edward Beecher returned to Illinois in the mid-fifties to a Galesburg pastorate and that the member of the Yale Band who most staunchly stood in abolitionist ranks, Flavel Bascom, became a trustee of Knox in 1845 and pastor of the colony church in 1849. Conversely, those of the Yale Band who were most cautious about abolitionism in education remained closest to Illinois College. During the middle forties the leaders at Knox believed that these connections of the Jacksonville school were an important advantage in financial matters. The difference between the aggressive Blanchard and the moderate Sturtevant was exemplified by a debate in the General Association of Congregational Churches of Illinois in 1854. President Blanchard had presented a report with regard to slavery in the church, but a "deep laid scheme" was made to squelch it. One great objection was to Blanchard's statement that American slavery was the "greatest obstacle to the spread of the Kingdom of God." This President Sturtevant pronounced an "untruth." [17] Samuel Guild Wright, who witnessed this discussion, noted in his journal that "there was an appearance of rivalry between the Pres. of Knox, & Ill. Colleges. The conservatism of Sturtevant is not pleased with the constant efforts of Blanchard at reform movements." [18]

A reading of the *Genius of Liberty* and the *Western Citizen* leaves no doubt that Knox College was regarded by Illinois abolitionists as the outstanding anti-slavery school in the state. Considerable space was frequently given to communications from its faculty, to descriptions of its affairs and development, and to its association with anti-slavery activities.[19] During the

[17] Galesburg *Free Democrat*, June 1, 1854.

[18] Samuel G. Wright, "Journal," May 23, 1854. Three years previously Blanchard had directly accused Sturtevant in the *Western Citizen* of obstructing the anti-slavery movement in one of its ecclesiastical phases (*Western Citizen*, June 17, 1851).

[19] For example: in the *Genius of Liberty*, Feb. 27, June 19, 1841, and Jan. 8, 1842; in the *Western Citizen*, Sept. 23, 1842; March 9, 14, 23, 1843; Aug. 29, 1844; July 15, Sept. 18, 1845; Feb. 18, July 3, 1846; July 21, 1849. These are not nearly all the references to Knox College or its personnel; for example, the long series of letters by Kellogg while on his trip to England have not been mentioned, as well as some of the following annotations.

early forties the attention thus given to Knox was unique, and was accompanied by special editorial endorsement.[20] In June, 1841, the editor of the state anti-slavery paper especially called attention to the open avowal by Knox of anti-slavery principles without regard to losing patronage; and the state anti-slavery society passed a resolution pledging a preference to such schools.[21] As the college was about to open in September, 1842, the *Western Citizen* advised plainly, "Place your sons and daughters in this institution." [22] More conservative institutions might shy from publicity in such a journal; Knox College invited it.[23] A leading article in this paper on September 18, 1849, was devoted to a description of Galesburg and of Knox College and its faculty. The anti-slavery character of the school was emphasized:

Indeed so thoroughly anti-slavery have they been that on this account they incurred the hatred of the surrounding country, were called by every low epithet in the pro-slavery vocabulary, and insulted in every way which pro-slavery ingenuity could devise.[24]

Looking back at the controversy a generation after the Emancipation Proclamation, President Sturtevant of Illinois College concluded, "I went too far against slavery to win the favor of its advocates, and not far enough to gain the approbation of its assailants." [25] Knox College, on the other hand, profited in the long run from its steadfast adherence to the cause, though in the early years the financing of the school was an uphill affair. The original scheme to finance the college had been based on endowing it with lands that were expected to rise in value above the minimum government sale price. Parallel with this community venture were several private projects that also presumed early prosperity for that segment of the frontier. Two of these special enterprises, large-scale cheese manufacture and wool production, were plain enough, though optimistic of a market, but in the realm of fancy were the plan to process sugar

[20] *Western Citizen*, Sept. 23, 1842; Aug. 15, 1844; July 20, 1847.
[21] *Genius of Liberty*, June 19, 1841.   [22] *Western Citizen*, Sept. 2, 1842.
[23] See, for example, the request to copy a notice in the *Knox Intelligencer* (Oquawka *Spectator*, March 17, 1848).
[24] *Western Citizen*, Sept. 18, 1849.   [25] Sturtevant, *Autobiography*, p. 223.

from corn stalks and the planting of 1,000 mulberry trees for silkworms.[26] When the panic of 1837 and the subsequent depression frustrated such expectations the college leaders looked for funds to the East, and they did so with a frank avowal and even exploitation of the school's radical anti-slavery reputation. The reform-minded philanthropists of the East, who had underwritten the anti-slavery movement, who had favored Oneida Institute, who had rescued the Lane Rebels, and who had taken Oberlin under their wings, ought to be induced to help finance the college by appeals, not to a popular, but to a distinguishing, characteristic—abolitionism.

The financial needs of Knox College became tragically urgent on March 14, 1843, when the recently completed college building burned.[27] This disaster probably hastened a plan, contemplated since 1841,[28] that President Kellogg should go to Europe to raise money among philanthropists friendly to the anti-slavery cause. In 1840 two agents from Oberlin had been astonishingly successful on such a mission, bringing back $30,000 after presenting to the groups of reformers in England the role of Oberlin in the abolitionist crusade.[29] The common origins, identical aspirations, and mutual friends of the two colleges made it extremely likely that the Knox leaders were well informed about the progress of the Oberlin enterprise, and it is probable that they followed its example in this particular.[30]

[26] The Peoria *Register and Northwestern Gazetteer* on April 15, 1842, in its leading editorial reported that Galesburg "has the most flourishing college, not excepting Jacksonville," in the state and that Galesburg excelled every other part of the state in cheese making, and that for the wool-growing business President Kellogg of Knox College had gone to Kentucky with several Galesburg citizens to purchase 1,000 sheep. This article also reports the corn sugar project. The silk-mulberry business is reported in the same paper on July 28 and September 29, 1838.

[27] *Western Citizen*, March 23, 1843.

[28] Knox College, "Trustees' Minutes," Nov. 23, 1841.

[29] Fletcher, *History of Oberlin*, Vol. I, chapter 29.

[30] Among the many features that Knox and Oberlin had in common was the scheme to profit by development of a silk industry (Fletcher, *History of Oberlin*, I, 454; Knox College, "Trustees' Minutes," July 5, 1843). Gale had visited Oberlin in 1835 and had been well impressed with its operations, reporting to the Galesburg colony that he got "some useful hints" (*Report on Knox College, 1861*, pp. 11–12). Next to its abolitionism the most distinguishing feature of Oberlin was, perhaps, its coeducation of women with men. All the indications are

The Oberlin agents had gone in 1840 as delegates to the World Anti-Slavery Convention in London, and President Kellogg planned to go in the same capacity in 1843. In January of that year he wrote Gerrit Smith that he thought "somewhat" of attending the world convention the following June, and expressed the hope that by tutoring two or three youths on a "traveling tour" he might be able to finance his stay abroad for as long as a year.[31] In April, after the burning of the Knox College building, Kellogg made definite preparations for such a trip by writing to James G. Birney, who had been to the world convention of 1840, for an endorsement.[32] The executive committee of the Illinois Anti-Slavery Society appointed him the Illinois delegate to the world convention, and at its annual anniversary that society appointed a committee to raise funds to help defray his traveling expenses.

Like the Oberlin agents three years previously, Kellogg was reenforced in his approach to English reformers by the recommendations of leading American abolitionists. The two American delegates who were honored by vice-presidencies in the London assembly, Joshua Leavitt and Jonathan Blanchard, both endorsed his appeal for benefaction to Knox College.[33]

---

that Knox also planned from the beginning a strong emphasis on women's collegiate education. This is apparent in Gale's *Circular and Plan* and also in the circumstance that President Kellogg had developed some reputation as principal of a female seminary. The *Western Citizen*, Sept. 23, 1842, particularly recommended Knox College for women. It was probably intended that the first building, after general college use, would be the female "seminary," and it was called the "Seminary." Its burning and the desperate straits of the college prevented immediate fulfillment of this scheme. Offering of collegiate education to some women seems to have begun in 1847 ("A Record of the Preparatory and Female Collegiate Department of Knox College," MS, pp. 1–4).

[31] Kellogg to Gerrit Smith, Jan. 10, 1843, Smith Papers.

[32] In this letter Kellogg gave the following succinct summary of the college finances: "We are not only in debt but we are limited in our resources, having only $25,000 permanently invested at 7% of interest, and as much in unsold land besides our large college farm of 720 acres" (Kellogg to Birney, April 3, 1843, *Birney Letters*, II, 729).

[33] Amos A. Phelps, a delegate from the Massachusetts Abolitionist Society, also endorsed the appeal "To Christian Philanthropists in Great Britain and Ireland" which said of Knox: "It is not exclusive in its privileges. This is true with respect to persons of different complexions. Colored youth will be welcomed and treated with equal kindness and attention with others" (*Report on Knox College, 1861*, p. 27).

Kellogg seems to have contacted pretty much the same persons and places touched by the Oberlin men; in fact for three weeks he was a guest in the home of one of the major contributors to Oberlin.[34] He was in England about a year. The results were, however, very disappointing, for he collected only $900 and some gifts of books,[35] which in view of the embarrassed circumstances of the college was seriously inadequate. Kellogg offered to relinquish his claim for salary and expenses during the year he was abroad. Though the trustees' minutes vaguely record Kellogg's report about "the influence of certain causes" that kept him from obtaining "remedial aid to the full extent that was desired," the implication is clear that Kellogg had failed as a money raiser.[36]

But on a recent tour Gale himself had done no better. While Kellogg was in England, Gale was in the East during the winter of 1843–44 trying to secure funds. After traveling expenses were deducted his labors netted the college only about $180;[37] he found his task difficult in all the principal cities to which he went, for in all of them he had been preceded by representatives of a new benevolent agency, the Society for the Promotion of Collegiate and Theological Education at the West.[38] The impetus for this new organization had come from New School Presbyterian and Congregational ministers in Illinois and Ohio, and particularly from men closely associated with Illinois College. Its leading promoter was Theron Baldwin, a member of the Yale Band who had been very active in the affairs of Illinois College and then had become principal of Monticello Female Seminary in Illinois. In June of 1842, while on his way East to raise money, he attended

[34] The Oberlin campaign in England is discussed by Fletcher, *History of Oberlin*, I, 457–69; Kellogg's travels in England were described in regular letters to the *Western Citizen*, June, 1843, to June, 1844.

[35] Knox College, Business Records, "Blotter B," entry for Feb. 19, 1845.

[36] Knox College, "Trustees' Minutes," July 13, 1844.

[37] Most of the gross collections had come from towns in the Burned-over District of New York whence the Galesburg colony had come. A trip to New England had grossed him less than $100, nearly half of which came from two individuals, Samuel Lawrence of Lowell and Amos Lawrence of Boston, Mass. (Dunn, "List of Donors to Knox College," I, 1836–1895, mimeographed MS).

[38] Gale to the Reverend Mark Tucker, Jan. 27, 1844, Simon Gratz MSS, Historical Society of Pennsylvania.

a convention of about a hundred New School Presbyterians and Congregationalists in Cincinnati that met to discuss the religious situation in the West, which had been somewhat unsettled by the Presbyterian schism of 1838. One of the actions of this gathering had been specifically to recommend five colleges—Lane, Western Reserve, Wabash, Marietta, and Illinois—and to express concern over the decreasing aid these schools received in the East. It occurred to Baldwin, after he resumed his journey to the seaboard, that one organization could coordinate the interests of all these schools and eliminate the humiliating annual begging in the East of independent college agents whose several efforts overlapped and conflicted with each other. In a stagecoach in Connecticut Baldwin met Edward Beecher, who was making the rounds for Illinois College, and discovered that he had the same idea. On the way West in the fall of 1842 Baldwin presented the plan to Lyman Beecher and they arranged for a meeting at the latter's home of representatives from the colleges that had been recommended by the convention of the previous spring. This gathering resulted in the organization of the Society for the Promotion of Collegiate and Theological Education at the West, which in the course of time came to be known for the sake of brevity as the "Western College Society." Baldwin became the executive secretary. The first meeting of the society was held in June, 1843, in New York City.[39] Significantly, of the five schools admitted to the advantages of this financial agency only Lane was mentioned in a list of American colleges presented to the World Anti-Slavery Convention as being anti-slavery by abolitionist standards, and even Lane's place on such a list was still doubtful, though it was true that the gag rules which had repelled the Lane Rebels were now revoked. Of the four other schools, Marietta, Western Reserve, Wabash, and Illinois, none was on the abolitionists' list, while Oberlin, Mission Institute, and Knox,[40]

[39] Theron Baldwin, "Historical Sketch of the Society," *Proceedings at the Quarter Century Anniversary of the Society for the Promotion of Collegiate and Theological Education at the West, Marietta, Ohio, November 7–10, 1868*, pp. 38–111.

[40] British and Foreign Anti-Slavery Society, *Proceedings of the General Anti-Slavery Convention, London, 1843*, pp. 84–87.

which were not to be favored by the new money-raising body,[41] were listed.

Gale's experience during the winter of 1843–44 had demonstrated the disadvantage of an agent for an individual college who followed in the wake of the concentrated raising of pledges by representatives of the Western College Society, and the Knox College board of trustees immediately voted to instruct either Gale or Kellogg to apply to that society for aid.[42] This application forced the society to consider whether it was designed to limit its assistance only to the five colleges already in the plan or to broaden its benevolence. In December of 1844 the board of the society voted in favor of the principle of not limiting patronage to those originally favored, but by that time the application of Knox was rejected on the more particular grounds that "the interests of education in the State of Illinois would not . . . justify . . . extending aid to more than one College in that state." It was suggested, however, that the society would discuss the possibility of aid at Knox to an institution of less than college standing, which amounted to saying that while Illinois College continued to develop, Knox College should be reduced to a preparatory school.[43]

The leaders of Knox College found such degrading terms unacceptable and believed that the reasons given by the society for declining aid to a college at Galesburg were the "ostensible" and not the real reasons. President Kellogg was convinced that the directors of the society acted "under influence of anti-abolition feelings" and declared that one of the directors who opposed the application of Knox said to him privately, "I tell you what—if you will only consent to keep the slavery question out of the [New School Presbyterian] Assembly, it will make a great

[41] The convention in Cincinnati in June, 1842, that had marked these five schools for a vote of confidence had merely "referred to the Institution called 'Center College,' at Blendon, Ohio [also called Central College, established in 1841; New York *Evangelist*, July 21, 1842], and one at Galesburgh, Illinois, called Knox Manual Labor College, both of which (say they) we hope will advance the cause of sound learning and piety" (*ibid.*, June 27, 1842).

[42] Knox College, "Trustees' Records," March 1, 1844.

[43] *Eighteenth Annual Report of the Society for the Promotion of Collegiate and Theological Education at the West*, 1861, p. 13; Nehemiah Losey to J. P. Williston, Dec. 13, 1844, *Report on Knox College, 1861*, p. 34.

difference." [44] Gale informed a certain friend of the college, "I am not sorry, never have been, that the college society did not receive us. 'It is better to trust in the Lord, than to put confidence in princes' and better to be free, than to be trammeled with time serving systems." [45] About the time that Blanchard took up his duties as the president of Knox, Gale informed him, "In regard to the College Society, I am not (and that is the feeling of the trustees) desirous of a connection with them; at least we would take no special pains for a connection of that kind. The friends of Anti-Slavery and Reform generally will the sooner confide in us, if we stand by ourselves." [46]

The failure of Gale and Kellogg to find substantial help for Knox College at this time had one shining exception—a patron who befriended the college for the very abolitionism which rendered it generally unpopular. This was J. P. Williston of Northampton, Massachusetts, the well-to-do son of a Congregational minister and brother of Samuel Williston, founder of an exceedingly prosperous business manufacturing buttons and other notions. His first knowledge of the college came from A. S. Bergen, one of the citizens of Galesburg who along with Gale and others had been indicted in 1843 for harboring the runaway Negroes of Andrew Borders. Bergen had called upon J. P. Williston as an anti-slavery man who might give substantial assistance in the Borders suit. Not long afterward Gale had also called upon him to ask for assistance to the college. Williston was impressed by Gale's being an active and zealous anti-slavery man and gave him a contribution. The next summer Williston came West to visit Galesburg and was there on the day in July, 1844, that the colony welcomed Kellogg back from his financially disappointing tour of England. By the end of the summer Williston sent Bergen $300 more for the college, and during the succeeding months also shipped about $200 worth of badly

[44] *Report on Knox College, 1861*, pp. 35, 61. Kellogg was one of the chief agitators at the General Assembly of 1843.

[45] Gale to J. P. Williston, June 24, 1845, *ibid.*, p. 38.

[46] Gale to Blanchard, Oct. 17, 1845, *ibid.*, pp. 39–40; Gale contrasted the "ostensible" reason for refusal of aid with the unstated reason, "our Anti-Slavery character," in a letter, Gale to Blanchard, Aug. 4, 1846, *ibid.*, pp. 40–41.

needed books that he collected from secondhand supplies in Eastern colleges. The following January the college received $450 from him, and by June his total contributions in cash amounted to $1,154. How critical the financial needs of the school were is evident from the business records, where the notation receipt of funds from Williston is immediately followed by entries showing salary disbursements to faculty. The amounts of his gifts were substantial for an institution with a faculty of only seven members at a time when the "female" in charge of the Preparatory Department got only $250 in salary for a year, a male instructor $300, and a professor $600.[47] Williston's help had come to the college at the time of its most serious need and of discouraging disappointments. His contributions were to continue until the college was on a sound financial basis, for he had singled out Knox and Oberlin as the chief recipients of his charity because he saw that they "were likely to lose assistance because of their advocacy of practical Christianity." [48]

It was during this time that Blanchard became president of the college, with the expectation that his reputation would appeal to abolitionists and to the Congregationalists of New England, who on this as some other issues were generally more advanced than their New School Presbyterian brethren. The confidence in the college of J. P. Williston was greatly strengthened by Blanchard's high reputation among anti-slavery men. The new president soon opened correspondence with him,[49] and, when the opportunity offered, visited the Williston family in the East. Blanchard and J. P. Williston became very good friends; the former named one of his sons Williston and Blanchard's eldest daughter spent the winter of 1855–56 at the J. P.

[47] By 1854 top salary for a professor had gone up to $750.
[48] Details of Williston's first connections with the college and his early gifts are revealed in J. P. Williston to Southwick Davis, July 27, 1857, Galesburg *Free Democrat*, Aug. 6, 1857; Gale to Williston, Aug. 30, 1844, *Report on Knox College, 1861*, p. 34; Gale to Williston, June 24, 1845, *ibid.*, p. 38; Gale to Blanchard, June 25, 1845, *ibid.*, p. 39; E. P. Chambers, "Reminiscences of Early Days," a paper read to the Knox County Historical Society, Papers of the Society; Knox College, Business Records, "Blotter B," entries for Jan. 20, and Sept. 23, 1845.
[49] Williston to Blanchard, July 27, 1857, Galesburg *Free Democrat*, Aug. 6, 1857.

Williston home in Northampton, Massachusetts.[50] As long as Blanchard remained at Knox Williston was a regular benefactor. It is not possible from the business records themselves to make an accurate estimate of the total amount, but it would appear that from 1848 to the end of 1857 he sent Blanchard an average of $400 a year, usually in separate payments of $100 each, and possibly these went to pay the president's salary.[51] In addition, between 1852 and 1858 there are over eighty entries in the records for students' tuition and fees that were charged to Williston. The treasurer's and trustees' records also show an entry for $1,000 donated in 1851 for building purposes and the offer of a gift in 1853 of $1,500.[52] One of two buildings constructed between 1843 and 1846 was named Williston Hall. In 1860 it was estimated by a friend of the college that Williston's aggregate gifts to Knox amounted to $8,000, exclusive of the $2,000 more which had been expended for needy students.[53]

Samuel, the very wealthy brother of J. P. Williston, was also a donor to Knox College, though for much smaller amounts, and these mainly in the form of consignments of buttons or other goods.[54] The amounts he gave to this Western college were mere crumbs from his philanthropy, which included large benefactions to Amherst and Mt. Holyoke and the founding of Williston Academy.[55] But through this member of the Williston family

[50] Fischer, *Blessed Memories,* pp. 112–13.

[51] In a report to the Western College Society for 1852 Blanchard stated, "I have received some volunteer aid for my support from different persons, of which I have, as they have directed, credited the College $500" (*Ninth Annual Report of the Society for the Promotion of Collegiate and Theological Education at the West,* 1852).

[52] "Blotter" Book A, B, and C of Knox College business records; Dunn, "List of Donors to Knox College"; Knox College, "Trustees' Minutes," June 22, 1853; *Report on Knox College, 1861,* p. 45.

[53] Bailey, *Knox College, by Whom Founded and Endowed,* p. 42.

[54] College business records show only an entry for dry goods amounting to $50, dated Feb. 12, 1852. The Blanchard-Williston correspondence, however, mentions on September 28, 1848, a consignment of $100 already received and a shipment of buttons about to come. A letter of May 7, 1849, mentions receipt in Galesburg of "an order of $50 for goods on your New York correspondent." The fact that these two items are not mentioned reflects the incompleteness of the college business records.

[55] Frederick T. Persons, "Samuel Williston," *Dictionary of American Biography,* XX, 309–10.

Blanchard had an important connection with the benevolent system in the East, for Samuel Williston was a corporate member of the American Board of Commissioners for Foreign Missions, before which Blanchard carried his contest to purify missions of any association with slavery. The college president corresponded frequently with him about the ecclesiastical tactics to be employed in this campaign[56] and had his traveling expenses to the East paid by Williston.

The direct donations of the Willistons to Knox College had special significance because the regular channel for such contributions in the New School and Congregational system was the Western College Society, to which as a matter of fact the Willistons made occasional though modest contributions during the same years that they aided Knox.[57] As noted previously, this society in 1844 refused to make Knox one of its beneficiaries, but a year later, when the request was renewed, it did agree to send a committee West to investigate the school in Galesburg. It was originally expected that this committee would arrive in June, 1846,[58] at the time of the college commencement, an affair which Blanchard had initiated during the first year of his presidency. When the two Eastern clergymen acting as the committee did visit Galesburg in August, Gale was not encouraged to expect that the society might come to the assistance of the college. He was particularly disturbed because the visitors inquired about the anti-slavery principles of the college and the community. In a letter to Blanchard the day after the investigators departed, Gale predicted that aid would be refused for the "ostensible and professed reason" that "two institutions so near as this and Jacksonville ought not to be sustained in the West," but this reason, he asserted, some of the directors would use to

[56] Blanchard to Samuel Williston, Northampton, Mass., Oct., 1846; Galesburg, Ill., Dec. 2, 1847; Feb. 17, 1848; Boston, Sept. 14, 1848; Manchester, Conn., Sept. 28, 1848; Galesburg, Ill., Dec. 9, 1848; Galena, Ill., Feb. 22, 1849; Galesburg, Ill., April 29 and May 7, 1849. These are transcripts in the Knox College Library received from G. R. Carpenter, New York City.

[57] Annual reports of the society mention gifts from five to a hundred dollars from one or both of the Williston brothers for 1847, 1848, 1853, 1854, and 1856.

[58] Knox College, "Trustees' Records," July 11, 1845; Jan. 24, 1846; July 1, 1846.

cover their real reason for denying Knox, namely "our anti-slavery character," which some opposed and which others feared would hurt the society if it helped a school with the reputation of Knox.[59] For that reason Gale advised Blanchard to go to the meeting of the society himself to present the case of the college.

At the time that the investigators of the Western College Society were in Galesburg, Blanchard was attending a convention of Western Congregationalists in Michigan City, Indiana, preparing a maneuver that would outflank the society in the chief source of its financial strength, in New England. Such a move seemed to him especially urgent when he learned that Theron Baldwin, secretary of the society, had by letters urged the location of a college at Davenport, Iowa, only about forty miles distant from Galesburg. Blanchard's plan was to exploit the circumstances that most of the funds given to Western colleges came from Congregationalists, that Congregationalists were more strongly anti-slavery than their New School Presbyterian colleagues in the benevolent system, and that Congregationalists were increasingly self-conscious about the development of their own denomination,with the result that in the East they were beginning to be uneasy because funds that they contributed to the mutual benevolent agencies were being used to promote the Presbyterian form of church government.[60]

For Blanchard's purpose the Michigan City convention was made to order. It was the first exclusively Congregational convention for the Northwest and had been initiated by men who had come to the conclusion that the Plan of Union had been unfairly used by the Presbyterians to their own denominational advantage, by men who resented the derogatory attitude of their Presbyterian colleagues toward Congregationalism.[61] This Western Congregational convention was attended by forty-eight ministers and laymen, nine of whom came from Canada, New York, and New England, twelve from Ohio, Indiana, Wis-

---

[59] Gale to Blanchard, Aug. 4, 1846, *Report on Knox College, 1861*, pp. 40–41.
[60] From a report to the Knox board of trustees in 1847, cited in *Report on Knox College, 1861*, pp. 33–34.
[61] *Minutes of the Western Congregational Convention*, pp. 3–5.

consin, and Iowa, and the bulk of whom, twenty-seven in all,
came from Michigan and Illinois.[62] In the roster of the convention Blanchard's name headed the list of the dozen men who
had answered the call from Illinois, and though most of these
Illinoians were probably as yet new acquaintances of Blanchard,
one of them, the Reverend James B. Walker, was already well
known to the college president as a man of his own stamp, for
Walker had lived in Cincinnati from 1840 to 1842 while he
published the *Watchman of the Valley,* a religious paper of decidedly radical anti-slavery principles tainted with some of the
deviations of Oberlin theology. Walker had just started a new
paper at Chicago called the *Herald of the Prairies.*[63] Blanchard
was distinguished early in the convention by election to one of
the two vice-presidencies and was assigned the chairmanship of
one of the eight committees, that dealing with a topic of special
interest to him, the relation of the American Home Missionary
Society to Congregational churches in the West.[64] It augured
well for Blanchard's ambitions for Knox College at the convention that the man chosen president of the convention was the
Reverend John J. Miter.

As anticipated by its originators, the chief topics for discussion
at the convention had to do with the reaffirmation of Congregationalism and reclamation of the ground it had lost in the West
by cooperation with the Presbyterians under the Plan of Union.
Blanchard's committee on the American Home Missionary Society endorsed this particular agency that was shared by the two
denominations, but emphasized an issue that was helping to
widen the rift between them. That issue was the relation of the
society to churches with slaveholding members,[65] one of the
several anti-slavery agitations that made Congregationalists in
the West increasingly aware of their sectarian difference from
Presbyterians.

Early in the sessions of this convention, before any of the reg-

[62] *Ibid.,* pp. 7–8.
[63] Robert Hastings Nichols, "James B. Walker," *Dictionary of American Biography,* XIX, 347.
[64] *Minutes of the Western Congregational Convention,* p. 9.
[65] *Ibid.,* p. 11.

ular committee reports had been presented, Blanchard addressed these Western Congregationalists on the "claims of Knox College," and he introduced a resolution on that subject. Two days later the topic came up for discussion and the convention took formal note of the circumstance that Blanchard was soliciting aid to erect two buildings for Knox College, indicated its "confidence in the character and standing of the College," and stated the belief that its growth would "promote the religious education so much needed among us." [66] No other educational institution was referred to in this manner, or so far as the formal record of the proceedings shows was even mentioned, though one of the other Illinois delegates was a Yale Band member who had helped to found Illinois College and had remained one of its leading supporters.[67] And to make sure of the specific object of this signal endorsement of Knox College, it was commended "to the benevolent regards of the Society for Collegiate and Theological Education at the West." [68]

Blanchard was thus well girded when he appeared two months later before the Western College Society to present the cause of Knox College. Meanwhile the investigating committee of that organization made its report on the locale, history, finances, and educational character of Knox College. That the anti-slavery issue had been a source of concern in the society's consideration of that institution is plainly evident in its report, for it had found that the "town of Galesburg, the College, and indeed that whole section of the country are marked with strong anti-slavery principles." But the report went on to say that the committee had conferred with the "gentlemen" of the college and that these had declared "that they were not peculiar nor ultra in their views on this subject, nor did they intend the College should be." [69] Gale, who was present at the time of the committee's visit, no doubt was one of these gentlemen; Blanchard, who was absent, could not have given such gentlemanly assurance. The report of the committee was as a whole favor-

[66] *Ibid.*, pp. 10, 23, 38.   [67] Rev. William Kirby of Jacksonville, Illinois.
[68] *Third Annual Report of the Society for the Promotion of Collegiate and Theological Education at the West*, 1846, p. 3.
[69] *Ibid.*, pp. 35–36.

able and might in any event have persuaded the officers of the
society to give Knox College some subsidy. But Blanchard was
at hand and made it quite clear that if Knox was again rejected
by the society he would take his special endorsement from the
Western Congregationalists to the Eastern Congregationalists
despite the decision of the society. And one of the most important members of the society's board strongly agreed that Knox
College must be added to the institutions assisted in order to
prevent this "appeal to the rising spirit of Congregationalism
in the East." [70] The society voted a donation of $2,000 to Knox
College.

More than local interest in Blanchard's success is revealed
by a news item appearing later that fall in the *Western Citizen,* which spoke of his success in "advocating the claims" of
Knox and mentioned this appropriation from the Western College Society along with the "private" donations of J. P. Williston.[71] But much as Blanchard deserved congratulations, he
was not satisfied with the extent of his success with the society.
Of its initial grant it was able to pay only $549,[72] and later ap-
propriations were below what the society saw fit to grant other
Western colleges. Blanchard persistently complained to the
Willistons that there was "no just reason" why the society
should not place Knox "on an equality with other western institutions," [73] and hinted that the discrimination was due to
the anti-slavery stand of Knox.[74] That the college in Galesburg
did rank low in the benevolence of the society's directors was
evident in the plan adopted by the society in 1848 for distrib-
uting its funds. After expenses were taken out, receipts were
to be disbursed to colleges according to the ratio of numbers in
this scale: [75]

[70] Blanchard's report to the Knox College board of trustees in 1847, *Report on
Knox College, 1861,* pp. 33–34.
[71] *Western Citizen,* Dec. 1, 1846.
[72] Blanchard to S. Williston, Dec. 2, 1847, Williston Letters.
[73] Blanchard to S. Williston, Feb. 17, 1848, Williston Letters.
[74] Blanchard to S. Williston, May 7, 1849, Williston Letters.
[75] Receipts of the society for this year were $12,339.38. Wittenberg College was
to get an "absolute" appropriation of $600 (*Fifth Annual Report of the Society
for the Promotion of Collegiate and Theological Education at the West,* 1848, pp.
18–19). Blanchard wrote to S. Williston, May 7, 1849, that the college society had

Western Reserve	60
Marietta	45
Wabash	40
Illinois	40
Lane	20
Knox	20

Apparently one of the explanations given for slighting Knox was that the other schools were more deeply in debt, but this Blanchard declared was unfair, for the other institutions had constructed buildings while Knox suffered from delay in erection of its main building.[76] Another difference of opinion between the Knox officers and the society's directors was over the scholarship privileges possessed by families who had originally subscribed to and taken land in the college-colony enterprise. Not unnaturally one of the concerns of the investigators of the society in 1846 had been to determine that the scheme to finance the college by a rise in land values was not primarily a speculative private promotion. They had reported "after the most minute inquiry" that Knox College "was founded in good faith, and not for pecuniary gain," but that the scholarships granted to the first colonists stood as a "charge upon the institution." [77] The first grant by the society had been for one year on condition that the scholarship rights be converted into a "charitable fund." Though this condition was not met, grants were annually renewed, while the society continued to protest failure to make the stipulated change and the college authorities continued to argue for the propriety of the outstanding scholarships. During the year 1848-49 these were partially reduced, to the amount of $1,232.[78] Over the ten years from 1846

---

sent, in all for "this year," $440. This would appear to be about one half of the annual gift the college would receive under this system.

[76] Blanchard to S. Williston, Feb. 17, 1848, Williston Papers.

[77] *Third Annual Report of the Society for the Promotion of Collegiate and Theological Education at the West*, 1846, pp. 35-36.

[78] Society for the Promotion of Collegiate and Theological Education at the West: *Third Annual Report*, 1846, p. 40; *Fourth Annual Report*, 1847, p. 19; *Fifth Annual Report*, 1848, pp. 18-19; *Sixth Annual Report*, 1849, p. 25; *Seventh Annual Report*, 1850, p. 26; Knox College, "Trustees' Minutes," Feb. 6 and 16. 1848.

to 1856 the college received a total of $5,864 from the society,[79] in yearly subsidies ranging from $450 to $750.

Of the schools dependent upon the Western College Society, Knox College was the first able to relinquish its claim for support. At the annual meeting of the society in 1855 it was reported that Knox no longer needed or expected an appropriation. The achievement of this financial security, the report of the society explained, was due to the "economy and sagacity" with which Knox had been managed and to ownership of lands that made it "one of the best endowed institutions of the country." [80] Mainly this prosperity had been earned by Blanchard, who had found funds to run the school so that its lands could be retained until they brought a good price.[81] During the lean years he had kept at the job of raising money wherever he could; it might be from a friend and anti-slavery man such as Salmon Chase of Cincinnati, though the amount was only twenty-five dollars; [82] or it might be from Philo Carpenter of Chicago, who in 1851 gave $100 [83] to a school which like himself came west with the enthusiasms of the Great Revival of the Burned-over District and remained loyal to reforming causes; [84] it might be from "friends" in Connecticut who in 1848 gave $300; [85] or it might be from donors whom he touched at the series of revival meetings he conducted in 1849 in the settlements north and west from Galesburg as far as Iowa City, Iowa.[86] The greatest single gain occurred in 1853 from a donor who wished to benefit the youth "who must at no distant day, take part in the great and never-ceasing struggle between right and wrong, between Freedom and Slavery, Liberty and Tyranny." [87]

[79] Sixteenth Annual Report of the Society for the Promotion of Collegiate and Theological Education at the West, 1859, p. 55.

[80] Twelfth Annual Report of the Society for the Promotion of Collegiate and Theological Education at the West, 1855, p. 23.

[81] Chapman, History of Knox County, p. 654.

[82] Blanchard to Chase, June 30, 1849; see also reference to a Chase subscription in Blanchard to Chase, Sept. 12, 1846 (Chase Collection, Library of Congress).

[83] Knox College, "Trustees' Minutes," June 25, 1851.

[84] Roy, Pilgrim Letters, pp. 143–45.

[85] Blanchard to S. Williston, Sept. 28, 1848, Williston Letters.

[86] Blanchard to S. Williston, Feb. 22 and May 7, 1849, Williston Letters.

[87] Charles Phelps to Blanchard, May 28, 1853, Report on Knox College, 1861, p. 45.

This gift from Charles Phelps of Cincinnati proved that fidelity to principles had been the best policy, for it comprised eighteen quarter sections of land of an estimated value of $30,000, which according to Phelps's stipulation was to endow professorships "for the equal benefit of males and females, to be educated in Christian Principles of Humanity, Anti-Slavery, Literature, Science and Morality, based on the Attributes of God." [88] *Humanity, anti-slavery, science,* and *morality* were italicized by Blanchard when he reported this gift to the Western College Society,[89] to whom Knox no longer need be beholden.

[88] Phelps to Blanchard, March 8, 1853, *ibid.,* p. 45.
[89] *Tenth Annual Report of the Society for the Promotion of Collegiate and Theological Education at the West,* 1853, p. 25.

❧ XV ❧

Ecclesiastical Sectionalism

The General Assembly was one of the most impressive as well as powerful bodies in the world. On its floor were some of the ablest, wisest, most enterprising, and influential men from almost every state in the Union. In its relation to educational, charitable, and missionary enterprises, in the appellate jurisdiction of hundreds of local churches, it swayed a power rivaling, if not really surpassing, that of Congress. . . . What power could suffice, then, to shatter the mighty edifice from turret to foundation, opening in the midst a chasm as by earthquake? [1]

EXCITED BY REPORTS that abolitionists were holding a convention in the Pennsylvania Hall for Free Discussion,[2] that the notorious Garrison and several shameless females were speakers, that whites and blacks "promiscuously" composed the audience, and that some of them promenaded in an "ostentatious amalgamation of color," a Philadelphia mob on the evening of May 17, 1838, burned to the ground the "temple of Freedom" that the abolitionists only two weeks past had dedicated to "free discussion" and "equal rights." The mayor pled, the sheriff intervened, the police protested, but all were helpless before a mob reported to number twenty-five to thirty thousand, while the firemen deliberately refrained from extinguishing the blaze which the rioters had started.[3]

Earlier that same day in the same city at another auditorium happened an event less violent but more lasting in its effects. A "great ecclesiastical earthquake" occurred, for the moderator

---

[1] Charles Beecher, ed., *Autobiography of Lyman Beecher*, II, 423–24.
[2] Weld to S. Webb and Wm. H. Scott, Jan. 3, 1838, *Weld Letters*, I, 511.
[3] *Niles' National Register*, May 26, 1838.

of the General Assembly of the Presbyterian Church refused to enroll or to recognize delegates from the New School synods in the Burned-over District of New York or the Western Reserve of Ohio; and amidst cries of order and hissing the New School elected their own moderator and, while the Old School looked on aghast at the confusion, marched down the aisle to the street and over to another church. Here they organized a "constitutional" Presbyterian Church of the United States of America.[4]

This denominational schism was more momentous to the anti-slavery movement than the riotous destruction of a building. Until 1838 a unity of Congregational and Presbyterian institutions was the taproot of that spreading tree of benevolence and reform of which abolitionism was but one branch.[5] Nearly half a century previously, the General Assembly of the Presbyterian Church had made agreements with the several associations of New England Congregationalists for the exchange of "standing committees of correspondence," the members of which might participate in each other's organizations. In 1801 a Plan of Union provided for even closer coordination in the West, by allowing churches with either form of church government to have pastors of either sect and by permitting "mixed" congregations to have a "standing committee" instead of a proper Presbyterian "church session" of elders as the governing body. Deputies from such "mixed" congregations might participate in the tribunals of Presbyterianism even up to the General Assembly itself. In the Burned-over District of New York began a most thorough mingling of elements from both denominations, and as the Plan of Union operated farther west the pioneer churches formed hundreds of capillary conjunctions between the two denominations.

Missionary activities also became interdenominational. The Presbyterians shared in the American Board of Commissioners for Foreign Missions, which had been Congregational in origin.

[4] Charles Beecher, ed., *Autobiography of Lyman Beecher*, II, 429–31.

[5] The summary of Congregational and Presbyterian church relations that follows is based on Hermann R. Muelder, "Jacksonian Democracy in Church Organization" (Doctoral dissertation, University of Minnesota, 1933), pp. 198–208.

Later, in 1826, delegates from Congregational and Presbyterian churches organized the American Home Missionary Society as their common agency in domestic missions. As still another mutual benevolent body, the American Education Society, developed, it appeared as if the two denominations might be making a "United Church in New England and the North." [6] And as other nondenominational societies for reform came into being (temperance, manual labor in education, and abolition of slavery) these too benefited from this denominational integration, intertwining at the top through overlapping directorates with Presbyterian-Congregational leadership, and diffusing locally through the ministers and churches of the widespread Congregational-Presbyterian communion. This unity made it possible for an itinerant reformer, such as Weld, to presume on Presbyterian parsonages and pulpits for hospitality and for a hearing as far south as Alabama and as far west as Missouri. It was this integration that made the General Assembly of the Presbyterian Church a strategic place for Weld to lobby for the cause of immediate emancipation. [7]

THE PRESBYTERIAN SCHISM OF 1838 AND THE SLAVERY ISSUE

One of the Beechers, looking back at this ecclesiastical structure in the years before 1838, described it in the glowing words that stand at the head of this chapter, and asked: "What power should suffice, then, to shatter the mighty edifice?" Some of the schismatic energy had been let off by controversy over the "New Haven speculations," which Old School partisans regarded as heretical. But their opponents charged that the conservatives rang this alarm bell of doctrinal heresy mainly to keep control of the denomination, for many of the New School did not so much embrace the novel theology as defend the principle of tolerance. The most clear-cut lines of cleavage were not creedal but governmental. The Old School complained that Presbyterian polity was corrupted by popular and egalitarian devices of Congregationalism under the Plan of

[6] Atkins and Fagley, *History of American Congregationalism*, pp. 147–48.
[7] Weld to E. Wright, June 6, 1835, *Weld Letters*, I, 224–25, and p. 222, note.

Union, and that the discipline of the denomination was weakened against deviations of doctrine as well as against "vulgar" practices such as the "New Measures" originating in the Great Revival. The Old School differed with the New over the use of "voluntary" societies such as the A.H.M.S. and the American Education Society, which the Old School regarded as the "offspring of Congregationalism." The New School, on the other hand, wished to continue close coordination with Congregationalists, cherished the Plan of Union, defended "voluntary associations," and tolerated or preferred any resulting irregularities in preaching and polity.[8]

In that Jacksonian era of widespread modifications in church government, each session of the General Assembly witnessed the sparring between the two ecclesiastical parties. The New School checked any important reactionary moves until 1835, when the conservatives marshaled their following in a convention held a week previous to the sessions of the General Assembly and commanded a majority sufficient to initiate many of their measures.[9] This shift in power toward the Old School was due to a factor that was not clearly uttered in the formal debates: the South "got scared about abolition." [10] The doctrine that slavery was a sin, propounded with all the evangelical zeal of the Great Revival, the proposal of certain radical synods in the North that slaveholders be treated as sinners, and the lobbying of Weld himself at the assembly of 1835 greatly disturbed or antagonized both the Northern conservatives and the Southern moderates. According to Lyman Beecher, the South had generally stood neutral, opposing extremes either way on the controversial matters dividing the two parties, but now it finally took the Old School side.[11]

[8] Muelder, "Jacksonian Democracy in Church Organization," pp. 197–228.
[9] Ibid., pp. 252–53.
[10] Charles Beecher, ed., Autobiography of Lyman Beecher, II, 428.
[11] Ibid., pp. 428–29. "It is generally admitted that the Presbyterian church in the United States was split on the slavery question. Of forty-one presbyteries located in the slave states, who sent commissioners to the General Assembly in 1837, only three sent commissioners to the New School Assembly in 1840" (A statement by Jonathan Blanchard, in British and Foreign Anti-Slavery Society, Proceedings of the General Anti-Slavery Convention, London, 1843, pp. 94–95).

The Old School was temporarily checked in 1836 by the tardy but timely arrival of delegates from Illinois and Missouri who helped the New School invalidate most of the conservative enactments of 1835, but by 1837 the Old School was not to be stopped. The conservative delegates of the North, together with embittered or frightened delegates from the South, resorted, under Southern leadership, to "drastic surgery." [12] The Plan of Union was abrogated. The synods of the Burned-over District of New York and the Western Reserve of Ohio were forthrightly expelled from the General Assembly, for these were the tribunals most mixed with Congregationalism, most affected by the evangelistic work of Finney's followers and imitators, and most infected with abolitionism. When the moderator announced the vote to cut off these New School bodies, an Old School partisan standing in the lobby swung his hat and gave three cheers. And finally, the General Assembly voted that the "voluntary" societies were to cease operations in the denomination and their functions were to be conducted by sectarian boards.[13]

New School leaders prepared for another show of strength in 1838; they went to Philadelphia ready to dispute the "unconstitutional" and "oppressive" actions of 1837 and to insist that the delegates from the "exscinded" synods be seated. When they failed in this, they withdrew to organize a separate General Assembly comprising not only the representatives from the expelled bodies but also New School supporters from many other presbyteries. By 1840 the existing Presbyterian synods and presbyteries of the nation had either aligned themselves with one General Assembly or the other or had divided into majorities and minorities that did so. At that time the New School had about 100,000 communicants, being dominant in the Burned-over District, in the Western Reserve, and generally in the Northwest,[14] and also retaining a significant number of

---

[12] Staiger, "Abolitionism and the Presbyterian Schism of 1837–1838," *Mississippi Valley Historical Review*, XXXVI (1949), 391–444.

[13] Muelder, "Jacksonian Democracy in Church Organization," pp. 259–60.

[14] *Ibid.*, pp. 262–64.

adherents south of the Ohio River. This last was an important circumstance, for it meant that the slavery issue would persist even in the New School's General Assembly and in its missionary activities. This further agitation, in which the Galesburg colony was extremely active, would further shatter that unity which prevailed when the benevolent system was in its prime.

THE STATUS OF THE GALESBURG COLONY
IN DENOMINATIONAL POLITICS

The purging of the New School by the Old approached its climax during the same years that most of the "Yankee" colonies were settling in Illinois from the Burned-over District of New York and from New England. Among these communities, Galesburg assumed by far the most important status in religious matters; in fact it was in ecclesiastical politics that the colony from Oneida County probably exerted its widest influence. The Galesburg church was never a small congregation [15] dependent upon missionary subsidies, and at the time of the schism of 1838, though only a year old, its congregation was already the second largest in the Schuyler Presbytery, which then included most of the Military Tract in Illinois as well as the pioneer churches on the western bank of the Mississippi River in what was still called Wisconsin (Iowa) Territory.[16] By 1840 Galesburg had the third largest New School church in the state; during most of the forties it was exceeded in size only by the First Presbyterian Church of Chicago,[17] where the Reverend Flavel Bascom was pastor. And when Bascom left this pastorate in 1849 to become minister of the Galesburg church it was the largest New School congregation in the state.[18] During the early fifties, under Bascom's

[15] *Minutes of the General Assembly of the Presbyterian Church*, 1837, p. 594.

[16] [Old School] *Minutes of the General Assembly of the Presbyterian Church, 1838*, pp. 22–23.

[17] [New School] *Minutes of the General Assembly of the Presbyterian Church, 1840*, pp. 58–59; *ibid.*, 1843, pp. 60–61; *ibid.*, 1846, pp. 110–13. There were ninety-nine New School Presbyterian churches in Illinois in 1846.

[18] *Western Citizen*, Dec. 25, 1849; *An Account of the Fiftieth Anniversary of the*

ministry, this mother church was delivered of both Presbyterian and Congregational daughters, yet it still ranked in 1856 as the largest Illinois church of the Congregational connection,[19] to which it had completely changed by that time. In 1860 this was only one of the thirteen Congregational churches in Knox County, which exceeded all others in the state in the number of churches of that denomination and exceeded all other counties except Cook in the total of Congregational church property values.[20]

Leadership in Presbyterian circles was achieved by the ministers, laymen, and teachers of the Galesburg church almost as soon as it was organized. In August, immediately following the establishment of a separate New School General Assembly, "Father" Waters exerted himself to make as amicable as possible the division of the Schuyler Presbytery, in which ten Old School members withdrew while the eighteen who remained continued as a New School presbytery for which Gale acted as moderator.[21] In September the New School Synod of Illinois set off from the Schuyler Presbytery a new body, the Presbytery of Knox, comprising most of the northern half of the Military Tract. The synod ordered that the new presbytery be constituted the next month at Galesburg with Waters as moderator.[22] In the affairs of this frontier presbytery the Galesburg ministers and laymen, together with their protégés in the missionary churches of the area, were dominant. Until the General Assembly of 1846 the delegates sent from this body were all men identified with Galesburg.[23] As the northern settlement of Illinois advanced and it became expedient for the synod of Illinois to be divided, it was Gale whom the

Organization of the First Presbyterian Church, Chicago, Illinois, p. 31. In May, 1850, there was still "but one principal 'meeting house' for the whole town," but "the edifice" in which they worshipped was "very large" and a visitor reported that on a Sabbath "there were between six and eight hundred persons composing the audience" (Burlington *Hawk-eye*, May 16, 1850).

[19] Spinka, *History of Illinois Congregational Churches*, p. 101.
[20] *United States Census*, 1860.
[21] Jeremiah Porter, "Journal," MS, Aug., 1838; [Old School] *Minutes of the General Assembly of the Presbyterian Church, 1839*, pp. 145, 242.
[22] "Records of the Presbytery of Knox." MSS Knox College Library, pp. 1–3.
[23] *Ibid., passim.*

General Assembly appointed to preside temporarily in the new Peoria Synod comprising the northern half of the state.[24] Four times before the Civil War the pastors of the Galesburg church and presidents of Knox College were moderators of this synod.[25]

As more of the Congregationalists formed religious associations of their own, alongside the tribunals of their New School allies, the Galesburg leadership was also in the fore. In 1845 the Lane Rebel Lucius H. Parker, a Congregationalist, in accordance with Plan of Union principles became pastor of the Galesburg Presbyterian church.[26] Parker participated in the convention that in June, 1844, organized a General Congregational Association for Illinois,[27] and the following October he and "Father" Waters and Levi Spencer of the Galesburg colonists shared in the founding of the Central Association of Congregationalists,[28] a lesser body, though extending across the middle of the state from the Mississippi to the Wabash.[29] Parker earned the title of "father" of the Central Association (which by 1856 was the largest in the state), for he was the "moving force in the organization, not only of the association, but also of many churches themselves within it." [30] Though his pastorate in Galesburg was brief, he continued to reside there and from that location to supply destitute churches [31] and to found many new ones.[32] It is indicative of the conjunction of the Galesburg colony with this Congregational expansion that the same Eastern philanthropist, J. P. Williston, who during this time came to the aid of Knox College, also

[24] [New School] *Minutes of the General Assembly of the Presbyterian Church, 1843*, p. 11.

[25] "Records of the Peoria Synod," MSS, Knox College Library, *passim*.

[26] Gale, *Articles of Faith and Covenant*, p. 19.

[27] Spinka, *History of Illinois Congregational Churches*, p. 92.

[28] Lathrop Taylor, "History of the Central Association," in Illinois Society of Church History, Congregational, *Historical Statement and Papers*, pp. 91–96.

[29] Spinka, *History of Illinois Congregational Churches*, p. 101.

[30] Lathrop Taylor, "History of the Central Association," in Illinois Society of Church History, Congregational, *Historical Statement and Papers*, p. 92.

[31] Gale to J. P. Williston, May 16, 1846, *Report on Knox College, 1861*, p. 40.

[32] Roy, "Fifty Years of Home Missions," *In Commemoration of the Fiftieth Anniversary of the General Congregational Association of Illinois*, p. 17.

gave $3,000 to the Central Association for aid to feeble churches.[33]

GALESBURG COLONY AND ANTI-SLAVERY AGITATION
IN THE NEW SCHOOL

As these new ecclesiastical channels were opened they circulated a warm stream of abolitionism, such as the Old School had tried to constrict by the exscinding acts of 1837. The Galesburg church exemplified thoroughly how to enforce an anti-slavery discipline, for opposition to slavery was a condition of joining the church; even a new wife of Gale himself had to bear an inquiry into her convictions on that issue. Anti-slavery activities were recommended as benevolent enterprises and part of the congregational funds was given to them.[34]

The meeting in Galesburg that organized the Knox Presbytery occurred on the first anniversary "of the death by the hands of cruel murderers" of Elijah P. Lovejoy, "one of the most beloved and distinguished members of our synod." As an appropriate recognition of the day,[35] the new presbytery as its first action reaffirmed and wrote into its minutes a condemnation of slavery that had been adopted by the General Assembly back in 1818, before the denomination had become afflicted with an "Old School." The presbytery further asserted that if the time ever came when "our church" would "do or say anything that would imply that slavery is not a violation of the law of God" it "would be a flagrant dereliction from duty." After underlining this moral declaration that had rested in the denominational records for twenty years, the new presbytery called for action by the denominational government by resolving "that the church ought to purify itself from this long continued and enormous evil." It was this proposal, urged by a number of like-minded presbyteries in the North, but as yet

[33] Lathrop Taylor, "History of the Central Association," in Illinois Society of Church History, Congregational, *Historical Statement and Papers*, pp. 91–96.
[34] "Records of the First Presbyterian Church" (Galesburg, Ill.), MSS, Knox College Library, Book A, p. 11; Book B, pp. 75–76, 93, 126; Flavel Bascom, *Historical Discourse: Commemorative of the Settlement of Galesburg*, pp. 21–23; George Churchill in the Galesburg *Register Mail*, March 5, 1887.
[35] Peoria *Register and Northwestern Gazetteer*, Feb. 2, 1839.

too extreme for others in that section, and utterly offensive to the remaining New School communicants in the South, that continued to agitate the New School Presbyterians for the next twenty years and that eventually shattered that part of the benevolent system and the union with Congregationalists that the New School had salvaged from the scission of 1837–38. In this disruptive argument the Galesburg church immediately became notorious; indeed Gale went to the General Assembly the following spring with instructions to present the views of the Knox Presbytery on this issue, which it was underlined had been "unanimously" adopted.[36]

In September of 1839 Gale reported to the presbytery on the "doings" of the General Assembly, which he had attended with C. W. Gilbert of Galesburg and eight other representatives from Illinois presbyteries.[37] To Gale's constituency the "doings" were disappointing, for the assembly had referred the entire subject of slavery back to the inferior judicatories of the denomination for such action as in their judgment was "most judicious and best adapted to remove the evil." This evasion of general legislation that would purify the church of slavery was not satisfactory to presbyteries such as the one centered about Galesburg. Accordingly it immediately appointed "Father" Waters, Gale, and Miter to a committee to draft a memorial to the General Assembly of 1840 asking for the excommunication of all slaveholders.[38] Miter carried this petition of the Knox Presbytery to the General Assembly, but that legislature again evaded action by voting to postpone "indefinitely" action on the resolutions regarding slavery. Miter was one of the ten delegates who had their names entered upon the minutes as "dissenting" from this vote, the only representative from Illinois to do so.[39] As if to add insult to injury this General Assembly (near the close of its session and after "a number of

[36] "Records of the Presbytery of Knox," pp. 4–8, 12–13.
[37] [New School] *Minutes of the General Assembly of the Presbyterian Church, 1839*, p. 6.
[38] "Records of the Presbytery of Knox," pp. 25, 34.
[39] Of the eight presbyteries from Illinois, only three were represented at this Assembly ([New School] *Minutes of the General Assembly of the Presbyterian Church, 1840*, pp. 5, 17–18).

firm friends of the slave" had departed,[40] especially delegates
from the West) [41] took the reactionary step of rebuking those
presbyteries which had cast out slaveholders from their fellowship and of requesting them to rescind the rules under which
they excluded slaveholders from their pulpits and communion.

The General Assembly might as well have advised the abolitionist presbyteries "to vote that asses were horses," as Blanchard
of the Cincinnati Presbytery expressed it.[42] Immediately after
Miter reported to the Knox Presbytery, in October, 1840, Gale,
Miter, and John Kendall, a ministerial student from the Galesburg colony, were appointed a committee to report on what
action the presbytery should take.[43] Over Gale's signature, the
committee presented a verbally violent, strongly punctuated
document that condemned the General Assembly for treating
with "little regard, the sentiments and feelings" of a large
portion of the presbyteries and complained "that the *OP-
PRESSOR* of his fellow men, the *Slaveholder,* found much
more sympathy and favour on the floor of the assembly, than
the advocates of Liberty and Right," an observation that was
"humiliating and painful" to make.

The request of the General Assembly that presbyteries
rescind any rules against fellowship with slaveholders was
answered by the Knox Presbytery in a forceful statement of the
obligation to retain the very rules that the assembly had found
objectionable. The presbytery reaffirmed its excommunication of slaveholders and flaunted its insubordination by asking
for publication of its sentiments in the *Philanthropist,* leading
abolitionist journal of the West.

The presbytery will neither receive to this body any Slaveholder
though ordained to preach the Gospel nor license any to preach
the Gospel while guilty of this Sin, nor will they admit to their pulpits men of this character, and they enjoin it upon all their church
sessions to receive no such persons to their communion, and if any
such are found in their churches, to take up a course of discipline
with them, as they would if chargeable with other crimes.

We will cooperate with any other presbytery or presbyteries in

---

[40] "Records of the Presbytery of Knox," Oct. 16, 1840, pp. 44–45.
[41] Blanchard in British and Foreign Anti-Slavery Society, *Proceedings of the
General Anti-Slavery Convention, London, 1843,* pp. 94–95.
[42] *Ibid.*　　　　[43] "Records of the Presbytery of Knox," Oct. 12, 1840, p. 39.

any constitutional and Christian measures for purging this sin from the Presbyterian Church to which we belong.[44]

These provocative resolutions were carried to the next General Assembly by President Kellogg of Knox College,[45] which meant that for the third time in a row the spokesman for the Knox Presbytery was a clergyman originally from the Oneida focus of the Burned-over District. Kellogg participated very prominently in the assembly arguments over the slavery problem; in fact it was he who made the substitute motion about which most of the debate revolved.[46] Kellogg took the position that an original motion, prepared by the assembly's own committee, concealed the number of memorials on slavery, gave an equivocal answer to the question as to how the assembly stood, and avoided on a constitutional technicality its obligation to pronounce on a moral issue. The motion Kellogg presented instead would have the assembly forthrightly declare slavery against the law of God, a sin, and would have the highest body in Presbyterianism urge its synods and presbyteries to treat slavery like all "other sins of great magnitude." [47] After discussion extending over parts of three days, Kellogg's motion was defeated in favor of action which merely confirmed the acts of the two preceding assemblies, which had committed the slavery "business" exclusively to the lower judicatories of the church.[48] Thirty-three delegates, one third of the total number, voted against these evasive resolutions, presumably because they favored the stronger statement that Kellogg proposed. Twenty-two of these negative votes came from only four of the nineteen synods; the rest were scattered, not more than two from a synod. These four radical anti-slavery synods were from Illinois and from Genesee, Geneva, and Utica in the Burned-over District.[49]

Bitterly it was noted in the Knox Presbytery that the Gen-

[44] Gale sent the resolutions to the *Genius of Liberty*, Feb. 6, 1841.

[45] "Records of the Presbytery of Knox," pp. 44–48.

[46] [New School] *Minutes of the General Assembly of the Presbyterian Church, 1843*, pp. 15–18.

[47] *Western Citizen*, June 22, 1843.

[48] [New School] *Minutes of the General Assembly of the Presbyterian Church, 1843*, pp. 17–19.

[49] *Ibid.*, pp. 3–6, 19.

eral Assembly "passed resolutions condemning *dancing*, as an immorality deserving church censure, but . . . after much discussion . . . resolved that it was not for the edification of the Church for the Assembly to take action on the subject of slavery." The committee reporting on the proceedings of the assembly pointedly raised the question "whether it is not the duty of this Presbytery to renounce all connection with the General Assembly of the Presbyterian Church, until they shall lift up their voice in solemn rebuke against the sin of slavery." It appeared that the slavery issue had brought the Knox Presbytery to the breaking point.[50]

By the time that the General Assembly met again in 1846, the disruptive effects of the slavery controversy among Presbyterians were already clearly apparent, not only among themselves but in their union with Congregationalists in the West. The Galesburg leadership in this agitation moved on to even greater notoriety in that year with the arrival of Jonathan Blanchard as second president of Knox College, and in this arena of ecclesiastical politics the Galesburg group remained foremost until the Civil War. Their leadership in the more secular aspects of abolitionism in Illinois had by this time passed from the college village to the booming town of Chicago. Even there, however, the agitation was rooted in religious soil, for the seed of abolitionism first sprouted in the First Presbyterian (New School) Church, while Flavel Bascom was serving as pastor. And the affinity of both of these abolitionist centers for each other (one civil and journalistic, the other religious and educational) was evident in Bascom's being elected a trustee of Knox College early in 1845 [51] and his becoming pastor of the Galesburg church in 1849.[52]

The restlessness of New School Presbyterians in Illinois was

[50] "Records of the Presbytery of Knox," pp. 133–34.

[51] Knox College, "Trustees' Minutes," March 11, 1845.

[52] Bascom, "Autobiography," in Sweet, *The Congregationalists*, pp. 269–73; Pierce, *A History of Chicago*, I, 243–44; Eastman, "History of the Anti-Slavery Agitation, and the Growth of the Liberty and Republican Parties in the State of Illinois," in Blanchard, *Discovery and Conquests of the Northwest with the History of Chicago*, pp. 661–65; "Minutes of the Illinois Anti-Slavery Society," MSS, 1842 and 1843.

aggravated by the more forthright stand of the Congregational associations with which many of them maintained a dual affiliation. The embarrassing position of New School abolitionists was plainly evident at the meetings of the Illinois Anti-Slavery Society in October, 1843, at Rockford, and in May, 1844, at Jacksonville, where the delegates debated the proposition: "That it is the duty of all abolitionists to come out from the Episcopalian, Baptist, Methodist, and Presbyterian churches on the ground that those denominations are fully committed to the system of slavery." [53] Though finally rejected, this resolution had clearly implied that of the major denominations only the Congregationalist was not tainted with slavery. It was indeed true that Congregationalism, because of geographical and historical factors, had no membership in the slaveholding states to encumber or discourage radical treatment of the evil. Furthermore, under Congregational polity all such matters were locally determined and there was no national tribunal whose legislative acts were binding on the lesser bodies, defining their general obligations to communicants either south or north of the Mason-Dixon line. While the Presbyterians, if they were true to the principles of their church government, had to wait "until the great wheel of the General Assembly should come round in its revolution," the Congregationalists with their system of autonomous local churches and "minor associations, conferences, and conventions could act at once without waiting." [54] Thus while many New School Presbyterians were still chagrined by the action of their General Assembly of 1843, Congregationalists in Illinois organized, on their own volition, a state association which so far as its members were concerned could pronounce as it pleased on the slavery question. This it did by providing that the association "ought to receive no minister to its fellowship who does not rank slaveholding with other heinous sins"; and this became part of the bylaws of the association the following year.[55]

[53] "Minutes of the Illinois Anti-Slavery Society," Oct. 23 and 24, 1843, and May, 1844.
[54] Barton, *Joseph Edwin Roy*, pp. 18–19.
[55] "Historical Papers of the General Congregational Association of Illinois,"

Accentuation of the slavery issue greatly accelerated the self-assertion of Congregationalism. Until the 1830s the general attitude among Congregationalists had been that under the Plan of Union it was better to leave the West to the Presbyterians, who had a general denominational organization able to follow an advancing frontier. The Western churches generally took the Presbyterian form of government; Congregational settlers accommodated themselves to that polity; Congregational ministers, though trained in Congregational seminaries and supported by the A.H.M.S., were generally willing to join presbyteries. In fact it was not till the thirties that there were local Congregational associations for minister and church to join.[56] The increasing self-assertion of Congregationalism by the mid-forties is exemplified by developments in the Galesburg church. Originally, in 1837, it had been wholly Presbyterian in polity, for most of the projectors of the colony were Presbyterians, though in the highly modified sense of those from the Burned-over District. Though Gale used his influence against those who preferred the Congregational mode, he declared that he himself cared little for anything in the Presbyterian system above the presbyteries. He argued that the church had better agree to the name Presbyterian because it was "in better odor" in the East and would help bring aid to the college. The Congregationalists were persuaded that the preference of the other sect should be heeded because it had taken the lead in forming the colony. Nothing can be uncovered concerning the denominational issue in the local church until the middle forties, when it appeared that dissension delayed completion of the church building. The Congregationalists asserted that in view of their large representation in the church, the polity should be modified somewhat in their favor. It is very likely, though there is no direct evidence, that the issue of church polity was aggravated by the disappointment among Presbyterians over the failure of the General Assembly to take

In Commemoration of the Fiftieth Anniversary of the General Congregational Association of Illinois, pp. 105–6.

[56] Atkins and Fagley, *History of American Congregationalism*, pp. 144–48, 153–56, 192–93; Spinka, *History of Illinois Congregational Churches*, chapter 2.

a strong stand on the slavery issue. Finally a compromise was arranged in 1845 along the lines suggested by the Plan of Union. The internal organization became both Congregational and Presbyterian and dual denominational connections were established.[57]

Gale seems to have expected the church to operate peacefully under the compromise, and certainly he had had as yet no great abhorrence of Congregational influences, for he urged the coming of Blanchard as president of Knox College. The latter, though pastor of a Presbyterian church in Cincinnati, had expressed his intention of affiliating with the Congregationalists if he came to Illinois. In fact Gale expected the new president to use his influence with Congregationalists in the East for the sake of the college, and hoped he would be able to "unite the Presbyterians and Congregationalists in this part of the state." [58]

Events in Cincinnati occurring between the time Blanchard was elected to the Knox presidency and his arrival in Galesburg presented him as the spokesman in the West for the excommunication of all slaveholders. A prominent Old School Presbyterian minister of Cincinnati, Nathan Lewis Rice, had been the author of a series of resolutions adopted by the Old School General Assembly. *The Watchman of the Valley*, edited by James B. Walker, and another abolitionist paper of that Western metropolis had attacked Rice's resolutions so violently that he replied in a series of lectures, which were published. These lectures provoked a group of men of the city, including William Birney, Gamaliel Bailey, and Salmon P. Chase, to challenge Rice to a debate, and when the latter accepted they persuaded Blanchard to be their champion. The question was: "Is slaveholding in itself sinful, and the relation between master and slave a sinful relation?" [59]

The debate was held during the first week of October in the Tabernacle, the largest room in the city, before crowded audiences. That some of the crowd occasionally withdrew after

[57] Muelder, "Congregationalists and Presbyterians in the Early History of the Galesburg Churches," *Papers in Illinois History and Transactions for the Year 1937*, pp. 60–62.

[58] *Ibid.,* pp. 63–64.   [59] Blanchard and Rice, *Debate*, pp. ii, iii, 337.

their favorite had finished speaking is understandable, for the argument consisted of thirty-two speeches extending over the afternoon and evening of four days for a total speaking time of twenty-four hours. Publication of this forensic contest had been planned from the outset; two expert reporters were on hand to take it down, and during the winter the debate, duly revised by both speakers, was issued in a volume of nearly five hundred pages. It was widely circulated and frequently exploited for ammunition in the abolitionists' campaigns of the next fifteen years.[60]

The debate between Blanchard and Rice measured the extremity of the former's radicalism, for Rice could hardly by ordinary standards be described as pro-slavery; he frankly recognized the evils associated with the institution of slavery—the cruelty, the illiteracy, and the violation of marriage vows; he believed it should be removed by colonization and gradual emancipation; and he deplored the radical abolitionism advocated by men such as Blanchard because, so Rice charged, it only hardened the lot of the Negroes in the South and hindered their eventual freedom.[61] But to men of Blanchard's party no Christian could maintain any ecclesiastical relation that implied approbation of slavery or any church connection in which silence meant assent to slavery.[62] In practice this meant that Southern slaveholding ministers coming North should not be admitted to pulpits and that Northern ministers should not be formally granted letters if they desired to transfer to presbyteries with slaveholding members; indeed, Southern ecclesiastical bodies should not be recognized.[63] A Northern theological seminary should not have men on its board of trustees who came from Southern presbyteries; [64] missionaries operating in the South must not establish mission churches containing slaveholders; even a Southern minister who freed his slaves might

[60] Ibid., pp. iii, 220, 291, 311.   [61] Ibid., pp. 30-35.
[62] Western Citizen, Nov. 3, 1846.
[63] Actions by the Presbytery of Cincinnati described by Blanchard, in British and Foreign Anti-Slavery Society, Proceedings of the General Anti-Slavery Convention, London, 1843, pp. 94-95.
[64] Galesburg Free Democrat, Feb. 16, 1854.

still be objectionable if he was not soundly anti-slavery in his public utterances.[65]

BLANCHARD AND THE "DISFELLOWSHIP" OF SLAVEHOLDERS

Blanchard realized that for a body such as the Old School Presbyterians "to make slave-holding a bar to communion would be to dissolve itselfe." [66] During the year of Blanchard's election to the Knox presidency and his debate with Rice, both the Methodist and Baptist denominations divided over slavery, but by the stringent tests that he would apply the cleansing was not complete, even in the New School and Congregational bodies with which Blanchard was connected. For the next fifteen years the agitation for "disfellowship" was his main extracurricular activity. This movement had many interrelated ramifications. Occasionally it drew men of diverse sects together in conventions of anti-slavery Christians, which was as near as the crusade came to concerted national or regional activity. Much more persistent was the excitement in particular denominations over the separation of benevolent bodies from slavery connections, an issue for which Blanchard became the chief spokesman from the West. Related to this was the continuing argument for rejecting of pro-slavery men from the New School Presbyterian communion—in the course of which Blanchard came to be labeled the chief enemy of Presbyterianism in the Northwest. And finally, the slavery question was a factor in the closer drawing together of Congregationalists, in their rejection of union with the Presbyterians, and in the convening of the first national Congregational convention, which particular event Blanchard did much to bring about. Each of these four aspects of the general movement will be described in turn.

The occasional conventions of anti-slavery Christians were sporadic and loosely connected events, not part of a well-integrated system such as that which existed until 1840 when Garrisonism split the American Anti-Slavery Society. Its suc-

[65] Blanchard and Rice, *Debate*, p. 252.
[66] Goodell, *Slavery and Anti-Slavery*, p. 156.

cessor, the American and Foreign Anti-Slavery Society, which the Tappans had established, never operated so vigorously, though it did continue the emphasis on the churchly aspects of abolitionism and called for disfellowship of slaveholders. An effort to vitalize the organization was made in 1852, when an "Address to the Anti-Slavery Christians of the United States" was issued. It is significant that of the forty-two men endorsing this "Address," twenty-nine came from New England, New York, and New Jersey, three from Pennsylvania, four from Ohio, and only two from Illinois; these two were Flavel Bascom of the Galesburg church and Blanchard of Knox College. Other signers of particular interest to the Galesburg community were J. P. Williston of Massachusetts, the philanthropic patron of the college, and John G. Fee, whose anti-slavery mission in Kentucky was presently to become a special concern to members of the college community.[67] Except that the American and Foreign Anti-Slavery Society sometimes offered a medium for broadcasting their views it does not, however, seem to have had any direct relation to the several Christian anti-slavery conventions that had been held in the West during the preceding half-dozen years.

One of Blanchard's first public pronouncements after coming to Galesburg was to endorse at length in the *Western Citizen* a call for an anti-slavery convention in Peoria, in which there was a strong accent on the disfellowshiping of pro-slavery men.[68] Later that year, in October, a Christian Anti-Slavery Convention met in Putnam County, at Granville, and issued an "Address to the Christians of Illinois on the Subject of Slavery." The chairman of the committee to prepare this "Address" was Hiram H. Kellogg, former president of Knox and now pastor of the colony church. The convention called on all Christians to sever any connections through religious bodies with slavery.[69] Four years later the faithful of Illinois were again called to a Christian Anti-Slavery Convention for Northern Illinois at Ottawa. This call was addressed to "all those Christians of what-

[67] *An Address to the Anti-Slavery Christians of the United States* (New York, May, 1852).
[68] *Western Citizen*, March 18, 1846.   [69] *Ibid.*, Nov. 3, 1846.

ever denomination who believe in *non-fellowship* as the only proper position toward slaveholders" and stated that the purpose of the gathering was to devise "some plan by which future cooperation may be secured." [70] Apparently a permanent constitution was adopted at this meeting; six months later the "First Semi-Annual Meeting" of the Anti-Slavery Convention of Illinois met at Granville, in Putnam County,[71] but it is not apparent that this led to the renewal of a state organization such as existed during the late thirties and early forties.

This attempt to establish a continuing organization in Illinois to promote severance of religious ties with slavery probably reflected or was suggested by a "Christian Anti-Slavery Convention" at Cincinnati in April of 1850 that had been called early in the year by a committee of fifteen including twelve clergymen of eight different denominations.[72] One hundred and fifty delegates attended from most of the Middle and Northwestern states.[73] To this gathering "Blanchard and others" sent a letter attacking the American Home Missionary Society and the American Board of Commissioners for Foreign Missions for failure to take steps that would eliminate slaveholders from their benevolent operations.[74] On the motion of J. G. Fee the delegates pledged to separate themselves from all churches, ecclesiastical bodies, and missionary associations that were not fully divorced from slaveholding, unless their churches would "speedily separate themselves from all support of, or fellowship with, slaveholding." The convention appointed a committee of eleven including Blanchard, Lewis Tappan, and John G. Fee to "hold under general consideration the general subject of Christian action against slavery and to call another convention." [75]

[70] *Ibid.*, May 7, 1850; *Tenth Annual Report of the American and Foreign Anti-Slavery Society*, 1850, p. 50.

[71] *Western Citizen*, Dec. 17, 1850, and Jan. 28, 1851.

[72] *Tenth Annual Report of the American and Foreign Anti-Slavery Society*, pp. 49–50.

[73] Chicagoans elected fifteen delegates to this meeting (*Western Citizen*, Feb. 5, April 5, 1850).

[74] Goodell, *Slavery and Anti-Slavery*, p. 209.

[75] *Western Citizen*, March 18, 1851.

This committee summoned such a convention to meet in Chicago on July 3, 1851.[76] Blanchard explained "to the Christian Public" in the columns of the *Western Citizen* that it would be open to all who desired to disfellowship slavery supporters from all denominations. That the forthcoming assembly was regarded in conservative circles as a serious threat is revealed by the gathering under the leadership of President Sturtevant of Illinois College of a forestalling convention that was held in Chicago two weeks before the Christian Anti-Slavery Convention. The former body devoted most of its time to defending the older mission organizations, provoking Blanchard to an attack on Sturtevant and his gathering.[77]

"Fanatics and enemies of the country," asserted the secular newspapers in describing the two hundred and fifty men who attended this Christian Anti-Slavery Convention.[78] One hundred and thirty of them were from Illinois, and sixty of these were Congregationalists; others were there from all over the Northeast and Middle West, but the largest delegation by far from outside of Illinois was the group from Ohio, which included Asa Mahan and C. G. Finney of Oberlin.[79] John G. Fee of Kentucky [80] stopped at Galesburg on his way to this gathering to address the Knox students during Commencement Week regarding his work of establishing anti-slavery churches in Kentucky. One of the Knox College seniors at that commencement, James Scott Davis, also attended the Chicago convention. Flavel Bascom, pastor of the Galesburg church, though not present, sent a letter that was read to the assembly.

Blanchard was elected president of the convention. He also served as chairman of the committee of three (Fee was another member) to inquire into slavery connections of home missionary

[76] *Ibid.*, March 25, 1851. Blanchard was now deeply involved in this movement. He had started in Galesburg a little periodical, *Christian Era*, and was preparing a series of essays on American slavery and the American churches; in October, 1851, he delivered a series of lectures on this theme in Cleveland, Ohio.

[77] *Ibid.*, June 3 and 17, 1851.

[78] Cole, *The Era of the Civil War*, pp. 223–24.

[79] *Western Citizen*, July 8, 1851.

[80] Goodell, *Slavery and Anti-Slavery*, p. 492.

organizations; the committee recommended that by correspondence or by the visit of agents those churches in the West
which were supported by home missionary bodies be asked if
they wanted to be subsidized by organizations that were allied
to slaveholding churches. A further convention to carry out
this idea was suggested.[81]

SLAVERY WIDENS THE GAP BETWEEN
CONGREGATIONALISM AND THE NEW SCHOOL

The growing gap between Congregationalists and New
School Presbyterians in Illinois was measured in 1851 by their
divergent actions on the American Board and the A.H.M.S.;
while the Congregational state association strongly criticized
these groups for slavery connections, the Presbyterian Synod
of Peoria, covering most of that part of Illinois touched by
Congregationalism, found nothing to condemn in those benevolent bodies.[82] This was only one of several aspects of the
slavery question in which abolitionists were increasingly disappointed by the New School Presbyterians, for they still admitted
slaveholders to their fellowship and had not ruled as a denomination that slaveholding was a bar to communion. Though
the New School called itself an anti-slavery church, unlike the
Old School which made no such pretension, yet, according to
the radicals, it was still "under the influence of the slave power,
that controls both Church and State." [83]

Blanchard maintained that since the schism of 1838 the
slaveholding membership of the New School had grown from
a negligible representation in its first General Assembly until
it tainted twenty presbyteries with fifteen to twenty thousand
members in slaveholding states, "all walking in Christian fellow-

[81] *Western Citizen,* July 8, 15, 22, 1851.
[82] "Records of the Peoria Synod," Oct., 1851, p. 128.
[83] *Thirteenth Annual Report of the American and Foreign Anti-Slavery Society,*
1853, p. 81. For example, the New School General Assembly in 1852 refused to
take action requested by two memorials which wanted the synods of Missouri,
Kentucky, Mississippi, Virginia, Tennessee, and East Tennessee cited to appear
before the next General Assembly on charges of "holding sentiments and coun-
tenancing practices on the subject of slavery, in opposition to the declarations
of the General Assembly" (*ibid.,* p. 67).

ship with slaveholders." Instead of fulfilling the "fervent prayer
and strong hope" that it might become an anti-slavery body, it
had become more intent on denominational success [84] and had
used the "peculiar machinery of Presbyterian polity . . . to
cripple and harass the opposers of slavery." [85]

Facts substantially sustained this accusation that New School
Presbyterians had lost much of their zeal for abolition and for
a more liberal church polity,[86] a zeal which had once clearly
distinguished them from the Old School. Though agitation
continued both within as well as from without the denomination for cutting off all churches with slaveholders, the crucial
legislation was avoided by the General Assembly, and some of
the members who once impatiently urged such radical action
had with the years become less insistent on discipline that
would, in effect, reduce the size of their sect. The Peoria Synod
continued to affirm anti-slavery principles, yet it took no action, and now spoke out less vehemently than in its earliest
sessions.[87] The Knox Presbytery, which through its representation to the General Assembly had been prominent in this agitation during the early forties, and which in 1844 had even discussed separation from the General Assembly on this principle,
had nonetheless remained within the fold. Indeed its most
prominent member, George Washington Gale, reflected in his
own career a definite cooling off on the related problems of
abolition and denominational polity. In 1837 he had professed
indifference to most of the Presbyterian system, but in 1850
he published his conviction that the time for being lax about
matters of denominational government was past, and that it
would be better if New School Presbyterians stayed close to

[84] Goodell, *Slavery and Anti-Slavery*, p. 162.
[85] *Thirteenth Annual Report of the American and Foreign Anti-Slavery Society*,
1853, p. 87.
[86] The New School at first had limited the power of its General Assembly and
made it essentially an "advisory council" that met triennially instead of annually, but the full authority of the General Assembly and yearly meetings were
resumed in 1849 (Muelder, "Jacksonian Democracy in Church Organization,"
pp. 268–73).
[87] Affirmations of the Peoria Synod on slavery may be reviewed in the "Records" for Oct. 13, 1843, Oct. 8, 1846, June 8, 1848, Oct. 14, 1856.

their peculiar polity and deviated neither to left nor to right.[88] He also changed on slavery, the alteration being noted by one of the early benefactors of Knox College whose contributions to that institution had been attracted by its anti-slavery stand.[89] In 1848 Gale had been a member of the committee of the Peoria Synod which brought in resolutions to the effect that it wished to take such action as would clear it "of all participation in the sin and guilt of slavery," and therefore asked the General Assembly to relieve the denomination from any such relation to the practice of holding slaves as "can fairly be regarded as implying approbation of it." [90] But in 1853 he was chairman of the committee which brought in what was decidedly the weakest resolution on slavery that the synod ever adopted.[91] The petition of 1848, if fulfilled, might have split the church; that of 1853 was merely an expression of strong disapproval.

What caused the change in Gale is not demonstrable of plain proof. It may have been in part his coming to old age; it may have been his personal estrangement from Blanchard, whose volatility may well have made Gale uneasy and whose younger, vigorous leadership may well have excited Gale's envy. It may have been partly the influence of his third wife, whom he married in 1847. She was an Old School Presbyterian before her marriage, and her slavery opinions were such that she was admitted into the Galesburg church only after a special committee headed by Blanchard had investigated her case.[92] Moreover, about 1850, Gale became interested in the project of a Presbyterian theological seminary which he hoped to have connected with Knox College. Far from being strictly anti-slavery, the seminary plan anticipated representation of certain Southern presbyteries on its board.[93] That Gale became concerned about the damaging effects to the college of Blanchard's radicalism is apparent from a bitter dispute occurring in the board of

---

[88] Galesburg *News Letter*, Oct. 10, 1850.

[89] J. P. Williston to Southwick Davis, July 27, 1857, Galesburg *Free Democrat*, Aug. 6, 1857.

[90] "Records of the Peoria Synod," June 10, 1848.   [91] *Ibid.*, Oct., 1853.

[92] "Records of the First Church," Book B, pp. 75–76.

[93] *Rights of Congregationalists in Knox College*, pp. 27, 81.

trustees at this time. In this controversy Blanchard opposed the advancement of Gale's eldest son, another possible source of estrangement between the chief founder of the college and its present president.

Though the abolitionists could not force the New School General Assembly to take the desired disciplinary measures, they could commit a serious attrition upon the New School membership to the gain of the Congregational communion, with which so many of the Western churches already had dual connections. Disgusted with a polity that would not stand firmly for anti-slavery principles, many Presbyterians were by the fifties converted to Congregationalism.[94] Already in December, 1848, Blanchard wrote to Gale: "I am aware that this is a difficult subject for you to consider dispassionately. Constitutional Presbyterians are everywhere, in the United States, becoming Congregationalists, and a generous mind feels all its pride and strength of will committed to a declining cause which it approves." [95] The change from one denomination to the other was made mainly by individuals, such as Blanchard's own shift on moving from Cincinnati to Galesburg in 1846, or by single churches that changed their polity or divided into parts, one of which became Congregational.[96] Sometimes, however, the anti-slavery defection was by larger aggregates, such as the action in the Ottawa Presbytery of Illinois where in 1850 four of its ministers, having a temporary majority, voted to withdraw from connection with the General Assembly over the slavery issue.[97] By 1852 a loyal supporter of the Presbyterian polity

[94] *Thirteenth Annual Report of the American and Foreign Anti-Slavery Society,* 1853, p. 87.

[95] Blanchard to Gale, Dec. 11, 1848, *Report on Knox College, 1861,* p. 49.

[96] Such as the First Congregational Church in Chicago, which "colonized" in 1851 out of the New School Third Presbyterian Church over the slavery question; or the similar formation of the Plymouth Congregational Church in Chicago out of the First Presbyterian Church in 1852 (Bascom, "Autobiography," p. 174).

[97] "Records of the Peoria Synod," Oct., 1850, pp. 97, 103, 106 ff. Two of these men, Chauncey Cook and Calvin Bushnell, were former acquaintances of Gale in the Burned-over District and former colleagues of his in the early abolitionist agitation in Illinois. They may be said to illustrate the continuing influence of the Great Revival in that part of Illinois. A similar action was taken by the Oswego Presbytery of New York, which in 1852 refused to send commissioners

from Illinois warned that failure to take decisive action was particularly disliked in the West and that if it was not done then he "could assure the Assembly that church after church, on our list now, will not be found there another year." [98] When such warnings went unheeded there were so many withdrawals from the Knox and Peoria presbyteries that the two were "reduced to the shadow of one," while prosperous Congregational associations developed in the same area.[99]

The opening of the fifties was marked in Illinois by an attempt to free New School Presbyterians from the guilt with which their denominational organization associated them by uniting them through a special state ecclesiastical organization with the Congregationalists. The idea of such an organic union had been promoted in the Galesburg locality since at least 1846, when on the occasion of the ceremony installing Kellogg as pastor of the Galesburg church, several of the brethren discussed the uniting of the Knox Presbytery with the Central Association "in a sort of convention, so there should be one and not two bodies," [100] and this suggestion was actually presented to the Peoria Synod by the Knox Presbytery that same year.[101] Late in 1850, from the same general source, there went out a call to officers and members of the New School Presbyterian and Congregational churches in the state of Illinois to consider union in one ecclesiastical organization. Though other benefits from such action were cited in the call, it was declared that "above all, it will deliver those of us who are Presbyterians, from our ecclesiastical connection with slave-holders, through

---

to the General Assembly (*Thirteenth Annual Report of the American and Foreign Anti-Slavery Society,* 1853, p. 68).

[98] *Thirteenth Annual Report of the American and Foreign Anti-Slavery Society,* pp. 70 and 78 ff. For Presbyterian testimony that failure to purge the A.H.M.S. of its slavery connections caused the New School to lose communicants to Congregationalism, see *Home Missions and Slavery,* pp. 4-5, 44-45.

[99] Churchill Scrapbook No. 1, Galesburg Public Library.

[100] Samuel G. Wright, "Journal," Feb. 9, 1846. Even earlier, in 1842, the Congregational Union of Fox River discussed a convention that should meet in Chicago "to consult with reference to the proposal of union of Congregational and Presbyterian churches" of northern Illinois (New York *Evangelist,* April 14, 1842).

[101] *History of the Presbytery of Peoria and Its Churches, from 1828 to 1888, by a Committee of the Presbytery,* p. 61.

the General Assembly, and enable us to withdraw Christian fellowship from them without incurring the charge of violating an ecclesiastical Constitution by so doing." The convention was to meet at Peoria, November 21, 1850.[102] Heading the list of ministers and laymen who signed the call was the Reverend Flavel Bascom of Galesburg. Two other ministers with direct Knox connections signing the call were Samuel Guild Wright and Levi Spencer. The call, in fact, had originated with members of the Central Association, the district organization of Congregational churches in the region around Galesburg. A year previously Bascom and Blanchard had talked about such action, and Blanchard corresponded with several persons about it, including his old Cincinnati acquaintance, J. B. Walker, editor of the *Herald of the Prairies* of Chicago. Blanchard advertised his endorsement by an article in the *Western Citizen* which emphasized the need for freeing New School Presbyterians from their slavery-tainted General Assembly. If need be he would be willing for Illinois Congregationalists to give up their state association to make union with New School Presbyterians possible.[103]

This proposal for union was not successful; indeed a large segment of the New School denomination was now strongly on the defensive against Congregationalism in general and Blanchard in particular. In May of 1851 the *Christian Observer* of Philadelphia made the charge that "first and foremost in the assault upon Presbyterianism at the West marches President Blanchard," and during the furor this accusation created, a leading Presbyterian in Illinois claimed the privilege of publishing evidence in the *Herald of the Prairies* that the Knox College president was indeed exerting his influence "to oppose the Presbyterian Church of the Northwest." Though trustees of the college and officers of the Galesburg church, significantly not all of them, hurried into print with denials of this sweeping accusation against their leader,[104] they could hardly deny that he

---

[102] *Western Citizen*, Nov. 12, 1850.   [103] *Ibid.*, Jan. 21, 1851.
[104] *Herald of the Prairies*, June 13 and 27, July 11, 1849; Knox College, "Trustees' Minutes," June 27, 1848; "Separate Session Records of the First Church of Galesburg" (MSS), May 28, June 2, 1849.

had provoked the charge; indeed that same month he used the leading columns of the *Western Citizen* again to attack the New School General Assembly for its pro-slavery connections.[105]

While the religious press was discussing Blanchard's hostility to Presbyterianism in the West, the denominational tension split the Galesburg church itself. In May of 1851 the stricter Presbyterians in Galesburg, led by Gale himself, withdrew from the original colony congregation to form a church with purely Presbyterian polity. In personnel these schismatics coincided with a party in the college board of trustees that was contending with Blanchard at this same time. The new church was called the Second Presbyterian.[106]

The Congregationalists and New School Presbyterians who remained with the mother church of Galesburg were now free to push as hard as they pleased for radical action against slavery on the part of the Presbyterian government. During the same month as the local schism the General Association of Congregationalists for Illinois was held at this church, and the discussions indicated that "nearly all seemed decided in the opinion of the necessity of an absolute and speedy divorce of the churches from all bodies in any way connected with the system" of slavery.[107] For some time this original Galesburg church kept its Presbyterian ties but continued to worry the presbytery to which it belonged. Finally, in the spring of 1853 the Galesburg First Church indicated that it would not send delegates to the Knox Presbytery until it was clear that that tribunal would "forsake the Assembly unless the Assembly forsakes slavery." Though relations were temporarily continued when hopes were raised that strong action was to be taken, in 1855 the church, following the recommendations of a committee headed by Blanchard, found the action unsatisfactory

---

[105] *Western Citizen*, May 6, 1851. This article was in the form of a letter to Philo Carpenter, whose church, the Third Presbyterian of Chicago, had been disciplined for taking action against the General Assembly. Carpenter made a gift to Knox College this same year.

[106] Muelder, "Congregationalists and Presbyterians in the Early History of the Galesburg Churches," *Papers in Illinois History and Transactions for the Year 1937*, pp. 53–70.

[107] *Knoxiana*, June, 1851.

and suspended all relations with the presbytery while it was in union "with a General Assembly, in which slaveholders are in fellowship." In April, 1856, the church was erased from the presbyterial rolls, and the original Galesburg church, now wholly free from slavery relations, was left only with Congregational connections. That it prospered during all this radicalism is revealed by the fact that in 1855 overcrowding resulted in an amicable withdrawal of a daughter church formed in that same year, significantly on a wholly Congregational basis.[108]

BLANCHARD'S ATTACK ON THE MISSIONARY SOCIETIES

Even Congregationalists were disturbed by Blanchard's relentless criticism of the American Board and the American Home Missionary Society. These two bodies had been criticized by radicals such as Weld and the Tappans for at least a decade,[109] and already in 1843 Oberlin men who opposed support of missions with slaveholders had founded the Western Evangelical Association.[110] In his debate with Rice in 1845 Blanchard expressed deep disappointment that the American Board tolerated slavery. He explained this shortcoming as due to the corrupting prestige of pro-slavery men in Eastern social and commercial circles, but he was then convinced that the influence of the New England clergy would shortly bring the board to bold action against slavery.[111] The following July, at the first general meeting of Congregationalists in the West, at Michigan City, Indiana, he was appointed chairman of the committee to report on the relations of the American Home Missionary Society to Congregational churches in the West. The report of this committee qualified its endorsement of the A.H.M.S. by stating that it "should plant or sustain no churches in slaveholding states, upon the principle of tolerating slaveholding in the members, but use all just efforts to extend a slavery-expelling gospel throughout our states." [112]

---

[108] Muelder, *Church History in a Puritan Colony*, Lectures IV and V.
[109] Weld to Lewis Tappan, Sept. 23, 1842, and note, *Weld Letters*, II, 942.
[110] Fletcher, *History of Oberlin*, I, 257–59.
[111] Blanchard and Rice, *Debate*, pp. 458–59.
[112] *Minutes of the Western Congregational Convention*, p. 11.

The following month it became particularly imperative to reform the American Board and the A.H.M.S., if abolitionists were to remain loyal to them, for a rival body was established under auspices that were very attractive to anti-slavery radicals. This new benevolent agency was the American Missionary *Association,* which united the earlier society founded by Oberlin men with a Committee for the West Indies that had been working among Jamaica freedmen since about 1837, and with the Union Missionary Society that sustained missions among freedmen in Mendi, Africa. The integration of these three organizations into one was promoted by the Tappans and allied to their American and Foreign Anti-Slavery Society.[113] The growth of the association in the West was fostered by Oberlin College, for its secretaries were Oberlin men, as were nine tenths of its workers down to the Civil War.[114] The community in Illinois most likely to be attracted into the orbit of such a body was that connected with Knox College, and by the summer of 1848 a recent Knox graduate worked as an agent of the American Missionary Association in central Illinois.[115]

Blanchard first tried to reform the older mission organizations, and the month following the organization of the American Missionary Association he decided to attend the next meeting of the American Board at Buffalo and to plead for purging of its slavery connections. To that end he exploited the advantage that one of the board's corporate members was Samuel Williston, whose family had taken a philanthropic interest in Knox College. Blanchard, in revealing his intentions to Williston, frankly stated, "I am anxious that your opinions as to what is proper and necessary to be done against slavery etc. etc. should become somewhat more decided and in the estimation of some, perhaps—somewhat more radical." By correspondence and personal visits Blanchard gradually persuaded this member of the board to exert his influence for strict anti-slavery action, and though Williston himself did not attend the board's meetings (he was handicapped by ex-

[113] Tappan, *Life of Arthur Tappan,* pp. 308–9, 317, 322–24; Beard, *A Crusade of Brotherhood,* chapter 1.
[114] Fletcher, *History of Oberlin,* I, 257–59. [115] *Western Citizen,* July 11, 1848.

tremely poor eyesight), Blanchard traveled East to the sessions of 1847, 1848, and 1849 at Williston's expense and assumed more or less the role of Williston's "agent and representative." [116]

Until at least 1850 Blanchard labored faithfully to clear the "great and sacred reputation" of the American Board [117] from the evil fact that it had slaveholders in its Indian missions and that in these missions slaves were hired from their masters to do the work around the houses, thus propagating a "slaveholding Christianity." [118] He warned that its doubtful stand on slavery was losing the board support in the West. An example cited by Blanchard was the debate in 1847 in the literary society of Knox College whether that group should make its contribution to the board. He also stated that he knew ministers in Illinois, Michigan, New York, and Ohio who had for two or three years taken no collections for foreign missions because members of their congregations would object to the board's fellowship with slavery.[119]

In one of his requests to Williston for traveling expenses to the American Board, Blanchard described his role in the West: "I honestly doubt whether there will be one man there who knows so well as I do what the reasonable anti-slavery Christians in the West require and expect of the Board." [120] This was no vain boast, and certainly the operators of the American and Foreign Anti-Slavery Society regarded Blanchard as the spokesman on this issue of the "churches of the Great West." [121] Williston himself cautioned Blanchard about alienating the West from the board.[122] And when that body at one of its meetings tried to keep one of Blanchard's provocative motions out

[116] Blanchard to Williston, Oct. 3, 1846; Dec. 2, 1847; Feb. 17, Sept. 14 and 28, Dec. 9, 1848; Feb. 22, April 29, 1849, Williston Papers.

[117] Blanchard to S. Williston, Feb. 17, 1848, Williston Papers.

[118] Blanchard to Williston, Dec. 2, 1847, Williston Papers; Whipple, *Relation of the American Board of Commissioners for Foreign Missions to Slavery*, pp. 57–58.

[119] Blanchard to S. Williston, Dec. 2, 1847, Williston Papers.

[120] *Ibid.*

[121] *Ninth Annual Report of the American and Foreign Anti-Slavery Society*, 1849, pp. 35–36.

[122] Blanchard to S. Williston, Feb. 17, 1848, Williston Papers.

of its minutes, both Lyman Beecher and his son Edward came to his support with the warning that if Blanchard's statements were not recorded the Western churches would "wheel away from them in companies and platoons." [123] The *Western Citizen* and the *Herald of the Prairies,* both of Chicago, provided their anti-slavery subscribers continuous and full accounts of Blanchard's arguments before the board, and counted on him "to exert all the powers of his eloquence and intellect to induce the Board to let go of slavery." [124]

The American Board of Commissioners for Foreign Missions was the special target of Blanchard because it was the very oldest foreign missionary society in the United States and had great prestige. It had "engrossed the affections of the churches more extensively than any other religious organization in this country," and its influence on the churches and the other benevolent societies that had been formed later had done more than any other, so Blanchard alleged, "to paralyze efforts for emancipation, and strengthen American Slavery." [125] Blanchard also corresponded, spoke, and published in his campaign to urge home missions, Bible, tract, and Sunday School societies to do justice to the American Negroes.[126] All these bodies failed to carry their religious services to the slave himself, and under the American Home Missionary Society an increasing number of churches with slaveholding members were being subsidized.[127]

By 1849 Blanchard was plainly losing hope that the older missionary societies would really take decisive action,[128] and it was evident that he was ready to turn to separate anti-slavery organizations. The Central Congregational Association in Illinois in October of 1849 issued a lengthy condemnation of the American Board that had been composed by a committee

[123] E. P. Chambers, "Reminiscences of Dr. Blanchard," Galesburg *Republican Register,* May 28, 1892; *Western Citizen,* Oct. 3, 1848.

[124] *Western Citizen,* April 11, 1848.

[125] *Thirteenth Annual Report of the American and Foreign Anti-Slavery Society,* 1853, pp. 115–17.

[126] Blanchard to S. Williston, Dec. 9, 1848, Williston Papers.

[127] Blanchard to S. Williston, May 7, 1849, Williston Papers; *Western Citizen,* Oct. 3, 1848.

[128] Blanchard to S. Williston, Feb. 22, April 29, May 7, 1849, Williston Papers.

of which Blanchard was chairman. This document, which pointed out that an effort of eight years to get the board clear of slavery had not yet succeeded, was published by Gamaliel Bailey, a former confederate of Blanchard in Cincinnati who was now in Washington, D.C., editing the *National Era*, perhaps the most influential anti-slavery periodical in the Northwest.[129] The General Association of Illinois in the spring of 1850 also expressed its continued dissatisfaction with both the board and the A.H.M.S. and asked them to be speedy in acting against slavery.[130] Blanchard wrote to the secretary of the American Home Missionary Society in September, 1850: "I think you must allow that I have 'possessed my soul in patience' tolerably well." A few days previously he had been made an officer of a Western Anti-Slavery Home and Foreign Missionary Society, and though this was done without his foreknowledge he was "resolved to follow" where the principles of this new anti-slavery organization would lead, even though he recognized that this prejudiced his relations to the A.H.M.S.[131] Though in June of 1851 he still preferred that the older boards and societies would be reformed rather than to join new ones that were altogether correct in their attitude to slavery,[132] that fall he publicly indentified himself with the latter procedure by delivering the "annual discourse" before the American Missionary Association and by endorsing its purpose to "divorce Christ's religion from . . . American slavery." [133]

The Christian Anti-Slavery Convention in Chicago, July, 1851, at which Blanchard had taken the leading role, adopted the suggestion of a committee headed by Blanchard that a special convention be held to set up machinery by which churches in the Northwest could withdraw from home missionary bodies that were allied to slaveholding churches.[134]

---

[129] *Tenth Annual Report of the American and Foreign Anti-Slavery Society*, 1850, pp. 55–57, which incorporated this document. The *Northwestern Gazetteer* of Galesburg on October 4, 1849, had regretted the failure of the American Board to divorce itself from slavery.

[130] *Western Citizen*, June 11, 1850.

[131] Blanchard to Milton Badger, Sept. 18, 1850, A.H.M.S. Papers.

[132] *Western Citizen*, March 25 and June 3, 1851.

[133] *Ibid.*, Oct. 7, 1851.   [134] *Ibid.*, July 22, 1851.

On September 4, 1851, a call for such a convention was sent out from Chicago to form a free mission organization for the Northwest. A second call for the same purpose was issued in March, 1852, over the signature of five men including the Reverend Flavel Bascom of the Galesburg church.[135] As a consequence a general meeting of the "friends of free missions, and the opposers of slave-holding fellowship in the Northwest" met on July 7 and 8, 1852, in Chicago, to perfect the organization and to "take further action in relation to the Anti-Slavery cause, and the purification of the Church from the abomination of slavery." The constitution that was framed was like that of the American Missionary Association, except that the labors of the new organization were to be confined "to the diffusion of an anti-slavery gospel in our land." [136] The address Blanchard delivered to this assembly received the distinction of being quoted at length in the next annual report of the American and Foreign Anti-Slavery Society.[137]

SECTIONALISM IN THE CONGREGATIONAL CHURCHES
AND THE ABANDONMENT OF THE PLAN OF UNION

Among the Congregationalists of the West the contention over slavery in missionary bodies and concerning relations with New School Presbyterians evoked a sectional self-consciousness. This feeling was characterized by anxiety about the status of Western Congregationalism, by agitation for separation from the Presbyterians, and by a more radical stand on the slavery issue than seemed expedient to the Eastern Congregationalists. General expression of this sectional self-consciousness first occurred in the Western Congregational Convention held at Michigan City, Indiana, in 1846.[138] The direct impulse for this meeting came from a small group of Congregationalists who met separately during a recess of a Presbyterian and Congre-

---

[135] *Ibid.*, June 29, 1852.
[136] *Thirteenth Annual Report of the American and Foreign Anti-Slavery Society*, 1853, pp. 122–23.
[137] *Ibid.*, pp. 115–17.
[138] *Minutes of the Western Congregational Convention Held in Michigan City, Indiana, July 30–August 3, 1846, with an Introductory Note by One of Its Secretaries and an Appendix* (New York, 1878).

gational convention in Detroit, Michigan, in June, 1845. These men were disturbed by the derogatory attitude manifest toward Congregationalism and agreed that Congregationalists should have a convention of their own. The following September they presented the matter to the General Association of Congregationalists of Michigan, which then issued a call for a convention the following summer which should consult on the conditions and wants of Western Congregational churches.[139] Accordingly on July 30, 1846, forty-eight delegates assembled at Michigan City, Indiana. The bulk of them came from Michigan and Illinois, with a dozen others arriving from Ohio, Indiana, Wisconsin, and Iowa, and with four representing the Northeast. They discussed the adaptation of Congregationalism to Western conditions, the regrettable abandonment of Congregationalism by ministers coming to the West, the "sprinkling" of a heresy called "modern perfectionism" in some Western churches, and the duty of preserving the Congregational form of church government. Derogatory reports on the Plan of Union culminated in resolutions that called for its nullification, that proposed that no new churches should be organized under it, and that suggested that Congregational churches in the Plan of Union should speedily withdraw from it where this could be done without injury.

The slavery issue was directly related to this move to free Congregationalism from its compromises with Presbyterianism. The convention asserted that the "spread of genuine Congregationalism" was an "effectual method of promoting the work of emancipation" because "our denomination differs from every other of the larger branches of the church in the land, in that her principles and the providence of God have kept her so clear from this sin of slaveholding." [140] A similar affirmation appeared in the report on the American Home Missionary Society; the convention declared that "as the Congregational form of church government cannot be administered in the churches composed of slaveholders and slaves, it is the judgment of this Convention that the American Home Missionary

[139] *Ibid.*, pp. 3–6.   [140] *Ibid.*, p. 23.

Society should plant or sustain no churches in slaveholding states, upon the principle of tolerating slaveholding in the members, but use all just efforts to extend a slavery expelling gospel throughout our states." [141] In this action we may discern the leadership of Blanchard, who was chairman of the committee on the American Home Missionary Society. His prominence in the gathering was attested by other events, such as his selection as one of the two vice-presidents and his success in procuring the singular endorsement of Knox College,[142] an achievement likely facilitated by the circumstance that the president of the convention, J. J. Miter, had been for three years associated with the college-colony.

While the convention had brought the men of the Western section closer together, and while it had accented a sectional difference with the South, it had results that eventually diminished the sectional differentiation of Eastern from Western Congregationalists. The discussions at Michigan City awakened attention in the East, stimulated a mutual interest in Congregationalism, and led to an improved understanding that culminated in the first national convention of the denomination at Albany, New York,[143] an event that marked the start of a movement to overcome the extreme localization of the denomination through the establishment of a permanent national organization.

Blanchard played a significant part in bridging the distance between a Western convention in 1846 and a national convention in 1852. As previously noted, he was active in promoting a national religious convention on the slavery question in Chicago in July, 1851, which though composed of men from several sects was largely Congregational and New School in character, and which though largely Western in membership had some Eastern men in it. During the succeeding summer he had also broached to the Willistons the thought of such a con-

---

[141] *Ibid.*, p. 11.   [142] *Ibid.*, pp. 9–10, 38.
[143] *Ibid.*, pp. 48–49; G. S. F. Savage, "Reminiscences of the Then and the Now," *In Commemoration of the Fiftieth Anniversary of the Organization of the General Congregational Association of Illinois* (Ottawa, Illinois, 1894), pp. 75–76; Flavel Bascom, "Past and Future of Congregationalism in Illinois," Illinois Society of Church History, Congregational, *Historical Statement and Papers*, p. 80.

vention to meet in Vermont. However, to his mind the need for this second convention was obviated by the action of the New York Congregationalists in calling for a national Congregational convention at Albany. Though he may have exaggerated his share in this action of the New York state association, there is no doubt that Blanchard's part was very important. He attended the state association in September, 1851, as corresponding delegate from the Illinois General Association, which had appointed him to this position at its session in Galesburg the preceding May.[144] Upon his appearance in the General Association of New York he was honored by an invitation to preach to them and by his choice as one of the two ministers to administer sacred communion to the brethren. This state organization, which had the previous year evinced a special concern over institutions of the Congregational order in the West,[145] had on its schedule of business a proposal from one of the district associations in New York that a special convention of New England and New York Congregationalists be called together to form a "Financial Congregational Convention for the United States." [146] This and a number of other concerns probably influenced New Yorkers to call a national Congregational assembly, but according to Blanchard it was the outgrowth primarily of a lively debate in this session of the New York General Association on the relation of home missions to slavery. Subsequently there was a difference of opinion as to whether the slavery issue was the main or only one of the principal purposes for sending out the call,[147] but there can be little doubt that the former was Blanchard's belief or intention, for on the day following the action of the New York association he gave that interpretation in a letter to J. P. Williston.[148] In his narrative

[144] "Minutes of the General Congregational Association of Illinois," May 15, 1851 (MS).

[145] *Minutes of the General Association of New York*, Paris Hill, N.Y., Aug. 22, 1850.

[146] *Minutes of the General Association of New York*, Brooklyn, N.Y., Sept. 3, 1851.

[147] *Proceedings of the General Convention of Congregational Ministers and Delegates, Albany, N.Y., 1852*, pp. 87, 90.

[148] Blanchard to J. P. Williston, Brooklyn, Sept. 6, 1851, Williston Papers.

to Williston, Blanchard told how "incidentally" a debate sprang up on the issue of slavery in home missions, in which "I, of course, took part." The chairman, "an inveterate Dutchman, equal to Walter the doubter in Knickerbocker," interrupted Blanchard to state that the association "were listening to the discussion with pain" and asked the speaker to "be short." Far from being rebuffed, Blanchard rebuked the chairman for attempting "to oppress one side of the debate by representing it as odious and unwelcome to the body." The editor of the *Independent* intervened, saying, "We can easily settle the question," and moved that "President Blanchard be requested to proceed." When the chairman hesitated, "Question" was called from the floor, and when put to a vote the motion passed without dissent. Whereupon the chairman left the chair, declaring he could not with propriety keep it, and another took his place and Blanchard finished his speech.

Beyond any expectation of Blanchard "the zeal of the brethren" was so prompt that they not only resolved in favor of a National Congregational Convention but appointed a committee to call one; "just such a convention as we held in Chicago as far as slavery is concerned!" Blanchard himself drew the resolution defining the convention and, according to his letter to Williston, "made the terms of it general so as to include the Presbyterian question as well as that of slavery, but slavery is to be the leading and engrossing topic of it." [149]

Though others differed with Blanchard's view or intention that slavery was to be the main subject of the national gathering, he did succeed, with the backing of Western delegates, in making it the most controversial topic in the convention that gathered at Albany, October 5, 1852. It was attended by 462 Congregational ministers and laymen from all the Northern states. Though only 13 percent of them came from west of New York and Pennsylvania, these were accorded an equal share of the officers chosen by the convention.[150] All the topics of discus-

[149] *Ibid.*
[150] *Proceedings of the General Convention of Congregational Ministers and Delegates, Albany, N.Y., 1852,* pp. 1–7.

sion were primarily related to problems rising out of the West, and the actions of the convention without exception dealt with Western concerns. These included a vote of confidence in the genuineness of Western Congregationalism, the establishment of a new denominational board to facilitate church construction in the West, and, most important of all, the decision to abrogate at the urging of the West that Plan of Union which the Eastern Congregationalists more than a half century before had made with the Presbyterians. It was agreed that the Presbyterians used that covenant unfairly, for, as one Yankee preacher expressed it, they had "ranged over our fat pastures, and borne away the fleeces from our flocks; they have milked our Congregational cows, but they have made nothing but Presbyterian butter and cheese." [151]

Western self-consciousness frequently expressed itself in the debates. Blanchard's was the most vigorous utterance of a frontier point of view in the convention,[152] and came near to saying that the West had its own terms on which union with the East might depend. As the leading spokesman for the West, he came to Albany with the prestige of the office of moderator of the Illinois General Association,[153] leading an Illinois delegation of twelve, four of whom were like himself associated with Knox College and Galesburg. When the convention selected a committee consisting of one delegate from each state present to report on the American Home Missionary Society, Blanchard was chosen for Illinois.

The conferences of this committee evoked the most protracted, stubborn, and contentious controversy in a convention which otherwise seemed consistently intent on harmony. The chairman, the venerable Absalom Peters (even Blanchard called him "Father"), who had led in the founding of the American Home Missionary Society and had for many years served as its secretary, hoped that the quarrelsome problem of slavery in missions could be avoided. He found, however, that

[151] *Ibid.*, pp. 69–71. [152] *Ibid.*, pp. 13–14, 56, 63–65.
[153] "Minutes of the General Congregational Association of Illinois," May, 1852 (MS).

the Western members of the committee insisted that the convention make some utterance on this issue, and when the committee could not agree on how strong this statement should be, the argument was carried to the floor of the convention. Here Peters led off the debate with a plea that the delegates consider the subject with "great calmness," observing:

There are two ways of letting our light shine. One is to light a candle and put it on a candle-stick, and let it light everything in the room and burn only the material of which it is composed. Another is to light torches and firebrands, and throw them broadcast through the country, as if we were in sport.

He concluded with the hope that there would not be a protracted debate, "for we have not the slightest prospect of converting each other on the subject of slavery now." His last sentence clearly pointed to the most likely source of argument. "Who is now ready to be converted from his position? Brother Blanchard is not, and I am not." [154]

Blanchard immediately followed with an argument for the most extreme statement on missionary work in slave soil. He was utterly dissatisfied with the proposal that the A.H.M.S. support only such ministers who would "endeavor, with simplicity of purpose and with a wise discretion in their ministry, so to preach the gospel" that it should have the effect of "mitigating the oppressions of slavery and leading to its ultimate abolition." Taking such ground, Blanchard declared, would set the anti-slavery movement back half a century, for slavery was not just an evil to be "mitigated" but "sin to be repented of." Therefore he spoke for a statement which would insist that no slaveholders ought to be admitted into Christian churches and that any church which recognized slaveholders as members should not receive aid from the A.H.M.S. In effect this meant that any minister who served a church that did not reject slaveholders would receive no support. Other speakers on this issue reflected on the disintegrating effects of the controversy and evinced their concern over Western warnings of withdrawal

[154] *Proceedings of the General Convention of Congregational Ministers and Delegates, Albany, N.Y., 1852*, pp. 15, 21, 77–90.

from the A.H.M.S. unless it was purged of its connections with churches with a slaveholding membership. Finally it was possible to compromise "unanimously" on a statement that aid should be given only to churches in slave territory if the minister preached an anti-slavery gospel and was permitted to do so.[155] Even then it was not certain that the West was satisfied, for in the closing ceremonies of the convention, three Western men, concluding with Blanchard, warned that though the convention had been a great boon to East-West relations and that though an acceptable compromise had been reached on slavery, this would not suffice to keep the West loyal to the A.H.M.S. unless it acted as the convention had declared.[156]

In fact, for several years the American Home Missionary Society steadily lost much of its following in Illinois to the radical American Missionary Association. By 1855 Blanchard had become one of the five vice-presidents of this missionary organization.[157] That year the Congregationalists of Illinois organized an auxiliary of the association, and Flavel Bascom of the Galesburg church became its general agent,[158] presenting it to the churches, superintending its collections, and overseeing its disbursements. Within a year, however, he could in good conscience relinquish this responsibility, for the American Home Missionary Society had then finally "freed itself from all responsible relations to slave-holding by resolving no longer to furnish aid to any church having slave-holders." Those who had been alienated from the A.H.M.S. and become patrons of the A.M.A. "could now return to their first love." The general responsibility for helping feeble churches now returned to the older body, while the association specialized rather on work among Negroes and anti-slavery missions in pro-slavery territory.[159]

After the Albany convention of 1852 the American Home

[155] The two extreme and the compromise forms of the resolution are found in *ibid.*, pp. 21 and 77.
[156] *Ibid.*, pp. 92–93.
[157] Tappan, *History of the American Missionary Association,* flyleaf.
[158] Spinka, *History of the Illinois Congregational Churches,* p. 125.
[159] Bascom, "Autobiography," pp. 209–12.

Missionary Society remained as the only important link between the Congregationalists and the Presbyterians. Though this society did eventually make itself acceptable to the anti-slavery radicals in the former denomination, many members of the latter were by that time already aspiring toward separate mission agencies of their own,[160] and the copartnership in missions that had begun in brotherhood degenerated toward a bickering bitterness.[161] That the complete disentanglement of the two religious bodies could not be effected without injury was nowhere to be more painfully apparent than at Knox College.

[160] "Minutes of the Peoria Synod" (MSS), 1853–55, more particularly, Oct. 12, 1855.

[161] For example, *Congregational Herald,* Dec. 1, 1859.

❧ XVI ❧

Anti-Slavery Colonies along the Border

And the King of the South shall be moved with choler, and shall
come forth and fight with him, even with the King of the North;
and at the time of the end shall the King of the South push at
him, and the King of the North shall come against him like a
whirlwind, with chariots, and with horsemen, and many ships,
and he shall enter into countries and shall overflow and pass over.
Dan. XI:11, 40.[1]

THE DOCTRINE THAT SLAVEHOLDING was a sin led
to a Sabbath night in October, 1859, when John Brown ordered, "Men, get on your arms, we will proceed to the Ferry."
Among the eighteen members of the "Provisional Army" who
set out, with rifles concealed under their coats, were three
former students from Oberlin [2] and Knox. Their presence followed a kind of historical logic for, spiritually, the march on
which Brown ordered them had its earlier sanction in the anti-
slavery crusade generated by the Great Revival. If the fagots
these zealots brought along were ignited, it would be from
the fires of Oneida that had been so faithfully fed at places
like Oberlin and Knox. It is remarkable how often the route
of Brown and his men from Kansas to Virginia crossed the
trail of colonies with Oneida antecedents. Returning east
across Iowa, Brown delayed at Tabor, a daughter colony of
Oberlin, and again at a colony founded by and named for

[1] Roy, *Kansas, Her Struggle and Her Defense. A Discourse Preached in the
Plymouth Congregational Church of Chicago, Sabbath Afternoon, June 1, 1856,
by the Pastor, Rev. J. E. Roy.* Published by vote of the church, Chicago, 1856.
This was the text used by Roy, graduate of Knox College, 1848.
[2] Fletcher, *History of Oberlin*, I, 414.

Josiah Bushnell Grinnell, a former Oneida Institute student, who for the party of the Kansas fighter found food, lodging, rail transportation, cash, and a public prayer "in behalf of the whole company for His great mercy, and protecting care, with prayers for a continuance of those blessings." [3] Farther east, in Oneida County itself, Brown was the guest of Gerrit Smith, a former patron of Oneida Institute, and heard him say at a public meeting, tears welling in his eyes, "If I were asked to point out—I will say it in his presence—to point out the man in all the world I think most truly a Christian, I would point out John Brown." [4]

Brown's traveling companion on this eastern section of his campaign to raise supplies and money for his invasion of the South was Jeremiah Anderson, who had been a student at the Knox Academy in 1851–52, coming there at the age of eighteen with a brother and a sister from Yellow Springs, Iowa.[5] After an unhappy attempt at preparation for the ministry and some time spent working in a sawmill, he went to Kansas and joined the contest for free soil. During the fighting with "bloody ruffians" from Missouri, he was twice arrested and once imprisoned by pro-slavery men; another time he barely escaped. As a lieutenant in a free-state military company he was involved in an attack on a troop of United States cavalry, and later participated in a shooting scrape in which a United States deputy marshal was shot in the head, "which done him up just right." He joined John Brown's band and accompanied it on a raid into Missouri liberating slaves; and in the late spring of 1859 became Brown's traveling companion in the East. The older man became very warmly attached to Jeremiah, and this pair, with two of Brown's sons, comprised the advance party that

[3] Warren, *John Brown, the Making of a Martyr*, pp. 308–9.
[4] *Ibid.*, pp. 312–13.
[5] Milton L. Comstock, the principal of the Knox Academy, had formerly conducted the Jefferson Academy in Yellow Springs. There were eight other students at Knox at this time attending from Des Moines County, Iowa. In 1852 the Jefferson Academy was reorganized as the Yellow Springs Collegiate Institute; Anderson was in attendance there in 1854 but got along poorly because of his heterodoxy; Merrill, *Yellow Spring and Huron*, pp. 68–69, 356–59; Gue, *History of Iowa*, II, 6–7.

established a base of operations on a farm near Harper's Ferry.[6] Late in September, Anderson wrote from this location to a brother in Iowa that "cries for help go out to the universe daily and hourly" for "millions of fellow beings."

Whose duty is it to help them. Is it yours, is it mine? It is every man's; but how few who dare to answer this call . . . in a manner that will make this land of Liberty and Equality shake to the center? If my life is sacrificed, it can't be lost in a better cause.[7]

Anderson stood by Brown in the Engine House at Harper's Ferry to the last and fell with bayonet stabs in his chest and stomach. He was dragged, vomiting gore, to the flagged walk outdoors, where he died in agony, reviled by the bystanders. His body was hauled off as a subject for dissection by medical students.[8]

As the news from the Virginia valley spread through the nation, the Union trembled wtih thrills of horror, exultation, anger, and fear, and shivered throughout the autumn till John Brown was executed. Most Northerners deplored or denounced Brown's unlawful violence, but not a few shared Emerson's dictum that he made the "gallows glorious like the cross." In the South the deeds of Brown's men confirmed the extravagantly evil words for many years spoken about abolitionists and intensified the fear of schemes for slave insurrections. Westward, across the Virginia Mountains, in the foothills of Kentucky ran the rumor that Sharpes rifles were being shipped to a company of abolitionist incendiaries at Berea. A company of some sixty Kentuckians rode into the town and called upon the ministers and teachers who had recently started a college there and forced them to leave homes and property and take refuge in Ohio.[9] Thus ended, even as John Brown's body moldered through its first month, the effort to plant in Kentucky a reforming college-colony like Oberlin and Knox,[10]

[6] Hinton, *John Brown and His Men*, pp. 238–39, 542–48; Villard, *John Brown* pp. 681–82; Karsner, *John Brown, Terrible "Saint,"* pp. 259–61.
[7] Hinton, *John Brown and His Men*, p. 548.　　　[8] *Ibid.*, pp. 309–10.
[9] *Congregational Herald*, Jan. 19, Feb. 23, 1860; Galesburg *Semi-Weekly Free Democrat*, Jan. 13, 1860.
[10] Fletcher, *History of Oberlin*, I, 213.

which had hoped to do peacefully what Brown had attempted violently.

The Berea colony in its relations to Oberlin and Knox (as in other features such as manual labor education and its financial support) faithfully resumed the methods and ideals of the original abolitionist crusade. The events that led to its founding recapitulated the religious arguments that had distressed American Christianity ever since the thirties. Its leading founder was John Gregg Fee, a Kentuckian who had come to Cincinnati to prepare for the ministry in 1842, the same year that Blanchard had, without success, proposed to a convention of Western Congregationalists and Presbyterians in that city that ministers going into the South should be instructed to establish anti-slavery churches.[11] Fee was converted to abolitionism at Lane Seminary and dedicated himself to anti-slavery evangelism in his own state.[12] The elaborate marking and glossing (in Fee's handwriting) of his copy of the Blanchard-Rice debate [13] in Cincinnati show that he owed much to Blanchard for his doctrine on the sin of slavery. On that principle, as in his belief in no fellowship with slaveholders and his break with New School Presbyterians and the American Home Missionary Society, Fee's career agreed exactly with the church politics of Blanchard.[14] Likewise the latter continued to advocate the Kentucky anti-slavery mission, and after he removed to Illinois he did not lose his interest in Fee's career.[15]

Fee's sermons, lectures, prayers, and tracts,[16] despite persecution, had some success in far eastern counties along the Ohio River, where he organized two anti-slavery churches. With the encouragement of the anti-slavery politician, Cassius M. Clay, he extended his labors farther into the interior to Madi-

---

[11] New York *Evangelist*, June 23, 1842, p. 196.

[12] Fee, *Autobiography*, chapters 1 and 2.   [13] In the Berea College Library.

[14] Fee, *Autobiography*, chapter 2; Rogers, *Birth of Berea College*, chapters 3 and 4.

[15] *Western Citizen*, Oct. 6, 1846; Oct. 3, 1848.

[16] Fee, *The Sinfulness of Slaveholding Shown by Appeals to Reason and Scripture;* also *Non-Fellowship with Slaveholders the Duty of Christians,* written in 1849 and originally published partly in the Louisville *Examiner* and the *National Era.*

son County, where the hill country touches on the blue grass. He became convinced that he should evangelize this new field more intensively, but disliked to neglect the churches already started along the Ohio River. "Just at this time," Fee asserts in his autobiography, James Scott Davis, a young man from both Knox and Oberlin, expressed his willingness to undertake this unpopular ministry.[17]

Davis belonged to the family of pioneer printers and newspaper proprietors from Peoria that had become more and more closely associated with the Galesburg colony in abolitionist activity, until the Davises moved their printing business to Galesburg, where several sons attended the college. At the Commencement of 1851, when James Scott Davis was graduated, Fee participated in the exercises, expressing to the Knox students his conviction that the sin of slavery could be eradicated by the extension of true Christianity and expounding his belief that this could be done by establishing thoroughly anti-slavery churches south of the Ohio River.[18] At this time Fee was on his way to Chicago to attend a convention of those who promoted the practice of cutting off slaveholders from religious fellowship. Blanchard was elected president of this gathering, which was also attended by Mahan and Finney from Oberlin. Davis, who also went to this convention, may very well have accompanied Blanchard and Fee on their trip from Galesburg, and must certainly have been impressed with Fee's work, for it was the concern of a special committee of three on home missions, of which Blanchard was chairman and Fee a member, which reported that Fee's activity in Kentucky was the right kind of mission work in the South.[19] At this time, Davis, after talking to the Reverend John Keep in Chicago, changed his mind about attending a theological seminary in New York and chose to enroll at Oberlin because of its "high ground on all reforms," especially the anti-slavery sentiments held by those who had charge of the institution. Keep also encouraged Davis to expect work in the

[17] Fee, *Autobiography*, pp. 89–90.   [18] *Knoxiana*, Aug., 1851, p. 62.
[19] *Western Citizen*, July 15 and July 22, 1851.

Oberlin printing office [20]—for which his family had given him ample training.

In the fall of 1854, having finished at Oberlin, Davis assumed the pastorate of Fee's churches in northeastern Kentucky. Fortunately for the historian he retained the journalistic habits of the Davises and frequently supplied the *Free Democrat* of Galesburg, operated by his brother, and also the *Congregational Herald* of Chicago with correspondence describing his Kentucky adventures. At the time he began his mission, there was much hope that the movement for "free churches" (those barring slaveholders) would succeed. It was estimated that there were about twenty such congregations in the state, and special stress was being placed on creating more of these on a nonsectarian or "Union" basis.[21] Soon after Davis arrived in the field, three or four other helpers from Oberlin began to give their vacations to this cause and eventually were committed to it full time.[22] They were supported wholly or partly, as in Davis's case, by the American Missionary Association, which was dominated by Oberlin men. The expansion of their preaching and teaching was encouraging. In the fall of 1855 Davis even made an excursion into western Virginia and found a good many church people of anti-slavery sentiments who needed only free-church leadership to join the crusade.[23] Though hopeful, the mission always remained an unpopular and sometimes a hazardous undertaking. The same fall that Davis arrived in Kentucky, a colporteur traveling for the American Missionary Association in the same neighborhood was jailed on suspicion of aiding fugitive slaves, and though released was forced by vigilantes to leave the state.[24] There were times when Davis was so menaced by threats that while he was preaching one of his deacons sat in front of the pulpit with a loaded gun in his hand.[25]

[20] James Scott Davis to Henry Cowles, Chicago, Illinois, Sept. 17, 1851, Cowles Papers, Oberlin College Library.
[21] Galesburg *Free Democrat*, Sept. 14 and Nov. 16, 1854.
[22] Fee, *Autobiography*, chapter 4.
[23] Galesburg *Free Democrat*, Feb. 21, 1856.
[24] *Ibid.*, Nov. 30, 1854.   [25] Rogers, *Birth of Berea College*, pp. 36–37.

The climax to this Kentucky anti-slavery campaign was the founding of Berea College. After several starts at other schools, two of which were burned down by incendiaries and one broken up by a mob, the abolitionists decided to fall back on Fee's headquarters in Berea, where they could count on the protective influence of Cassius M. Clay.[26] To direct this school they summoned J. A. R. Rogers, a brother-in-law of Davis, who at the time was pastor of a new Congregational church at Roseville, Illinois, where he had been ordained in 1856, in a ceremony mainly conducted by Edward Beecher and two other clergymen associated with Knox College, which was only twenty-five miles away.[27] Rogers was a graduate of both the literary and the theological departments of Oberlin and had some teaching experience there and in New York. At a Congregational meeting in Galesburg a discussion about the struggles in Kentucky stirred him to so deep an interest that he secured a release from his Roseville congregation and went to consult with his brother-in-law Davis.[28] While helping the latter in church work and looking for a school site in that part of the mission field, Rogers received a letter from Fee urging that he establish a school in Berea. In April, 1858, Rogers moved his family to Berea and got the school under way. The following September Fee and Rogers summoned Davis and another missionary to come to Berea to consult with Madison County men on starting a college. The constitution they drew up and adopted was closely modeled after that of Oberlin; it was especially characterized by absence of a color line and sectarianism.[29]

While steps were being taken to secure a charter for Berea College, Fee went east to raise money from the same sources which a generation before had helped finance Oneida Institute, Lane, and Oberlin; the Tappans and Gerrit Smith were again interested.[30] At Lewis Tappan's suggestion, Henry

[26] Fee, *Autobiography*, chapter 4.
[27] Galesburg *Free Democrat*, March 27, 1856.
[28] Rogers, *Birth of Berea College*, chapter 5.
[29] *Ibid.*, chapter 6; Fee, *Autobiography*, chapter 6.
[30] Fee, *Autobiography*, chapter 6; *Berea College Catalogue*, 1867, pp. 25–26;

Ward Beecher opened his church in Brooklyn for Fee to present his plea for Berea to the Eastern public. This church was notorious for its support of the free-soil fighters in Kansas; Sharpes rifles were in some places called "Beecher's Bibles"; and "Osowatomie" (John) Brown had visited Beecher during the preceding summer. Fee made his appeal for Berea while the country was at fever heat about Brown's raid at Harper's Ferry, and his anti-slavery utterances in Beecher's church were, under the circumstances, readily twisted into wild reports about mysterious shipments of guns into eastern Kentucky and then to warnings about being "murdered in cold blood." A mass meeting in Madison County in December, 1859, sent a "committee" of armed riders to expel Fee and his "gang of followers"; they were given ten days to leave.[31] When Davis sent to the *Congregational Herald* this story about the exiling of the anti-slavery colony at Berea, he hoped that elsewhere the work might go on, but mob anger and fear also struck against the other mission stations; two of the missionaries had their heads and beards shaved and their heads and faces tarred.[32] Davis himself was ordered by a "committee" to be out of the state in a week.[33] Thus the whole "Kentucky force" of the American Missionary Association was driven out.[34]

Davis with his wife and their two babies found temporary refuge with some of the other exiles in Cincinnati; by early March he was in Galesburg, a hero home with kinsfolk and neighbors, schoolmates and former teachers. From the pulpit of the original colony church he related how the apostles of anti-slavery Christianity had been driven out of Kentucky, and his audience contributed a substantial sum for "relief of the Kentucky exiles." [35] In June Davis had a reunion in Chicago with a dozen Kentuckians who had stood by him "when at

Harlow, *Gerrit Smith*, p. 232. When Berea reopened after the war, J. P. Williston, anti-slavery patron for Knox and Oberlin, gave it generous support.

[31] *Congregational Herald*, Jan. 19 and Feb. 16, 1860; Galesburg *Semi-Weekly Free Democrat*, Jan. 13, 1860.

[32] Roy, *Pilgrim Letters*, pp. 20–21.

[33] *Congregational Herald*, Feb. 16, 1860.   [34] Roy, *Pilgrim Letters*, p. 20.

[35] Galesburg *Semi-Weekly Free Democrat*, March 9, March 13, April 17, 1860.

a moments notice he had to fly from his home," [36] and he served with them as a member of the Kentucky delegation to the Republican convention, though unlike the other delegates he could not be listed on the roster with a specific residence.[37]

For most of 1860 Davis lectured in the Northwest on anti-slavery work in Kentucky, making propaganda out of his past adventures,[38] though as early as March, 1860, he had located a new field for anti-slavery preaching, in Pope County, Illinois, just across the river from Kentucky, where a former colleague, who had been expelled from Kentucky already in 1855, had been settled for four years.[39] In this Little Egypt, where animosity to abolitionism and to Yankees was nearly as rampant as over the Ohio, the American Missionary Association had been laboring for some time to overcome the earlier neglect of the less militant American Home Missionary Society. Davis started missionary work in this field in the fall of 1860. He was soon busy promoting the "Christian colony" at Hoyleton and became pastor of its Congregational church,[40] the southern-most of that sect in Illinois. This settlement, which was adver-tised in Knox County as a "religious and anti-slavery colony," [41] had started in 1857 on lands bought from the Illinois Central Railroad, under the leadership of Blanchard's brother-in-law, Avery Bent, who for three years had been on the Knox faculty.[42] When Davis arrived a seminary building was already under construction. To this "Yankee" outpost other prominent Gales-burg colonists also were attracted, including a physician and Davis's brother, Southwick, newspaperman and printer.[43]

The mob action against the Kentucky missionaries and other acts of violence were used by some Northerners to justify the crimes of John Brown. Davis himself, though calling Brown

[36] Correspondence of Mary Brown Davis, Oquawka *Spectator*, May, 31, 1860.

[37] *Proceedings of the Republican National Convention. Held at Chicago, May 16th, 17th, and 18th, 1860. Press and Tribune Documents for 1860.* No. 3, p. 43.

[38] Norton, *History of the Presbyterian Church in Illinois,* I, 666–67.

[39] *Congregational Herald,* April 12, 1860.

[40] *Ibid.,* Nov. 29, 1860; Jan. 10, March 28, 1861.

[41] Knoxville *Republican,* June 3, 1857.

[42] Gates, *The Illinois Central Railroad and Its Colonization Work,* p. 229.

[43] Townsley, *Pilgrim Maid,* pp. 62–63, 93–96; letters of M. B. Davis to Oquawka *Spectator,* Jan. 9 and 30, 1862.

a "good man," told the people of Galesburg that there was
no scriptural warrant for this method of "propagating reforms"
and deplored the consequences of Brown's deeds on peaceful
evangelism in the South.[44] This was a reasonably calm statement compared to the utterances of some of the firebrands of
the fifties, such as Joseph E. Roy, another Knox graduate also
affiliated with the American Missionary Association. On the
evening of Brown's hanging, Roy, who visited with Brown in
Chicago the summer before the Harper's Ferry raid, held a
"rousing" memorial service in the prominent Chicago church
of which he was pastor.[45] Already in 1856 Roy had preached
and published a sermon in which he asked if there had ever
been "any achievement of liberty that did not suck its life
from the blood of conscientious heroes?" There was, he told
his congregation, "a moral force in Sharpes rifles," and proph-
esied civil war in a sermon on the text from an apocalyptic
passage in the Old Testament that stands at the head of this
chapter.[46]

Emphasis on the anti-slavery purpose of home missions had
thoroughly permeated Knox College during the years when
both Davis and Roy were students. Indeed Roy was one of the
founders of a student literary society which in 1847 expressed
reluctance to contribute to the regular mission organizations
because they were not anti-slavery,[47] and a schoolmate who
graduated that year spent the summer of 1848 serving in west-
central Illinois as an agent of the recently organized American

[44] Galesburg *Semi-Weekly Free Democrat*, March 9 and 13, 1860. Several shades
of approval blended with disapproval of John Brown in Galesburg. One citizen
wanted the community to close down business for an hour at noon, to toll the
bells, and to wear mourning, as a demonstration honoring Brown on the day he
was executed. This was not done, but the Negroes held a memorial service in
the African Methodist Church, in which some of the leaders of the town participated. The editorials of the local *Free Democrat* deprecated any effort to
"elevate" Brown to the "dignity of a martyr." This last opinion reflects the
desire of a Republican Party organ to free itself from any complicity with
Radical Abolitionists. The editor regarded Brown as a "monomaniac," crazed by
the murder of his son and by destruction of his property in Kansas by "Missouri
ruffians" (Galesburg *Free Democrat*, Oct. 22, 29, Nov. 22, Dec. 3, 1859).

[45] Barton, *Joseph Edwin Roy*, pp. 15–22.

[46] Roy, *Kansas, Her Struggle and Her Defense.*

[47] Blanchard to S. Williston, Dec. 2, 1847, Williston Papers.

Missionary Association,[48] which was distinguished by its particular attention to work among Negroes and by its invasion of pro-slavery communities with abolitionist tracts and sermons. In 1850 Roy went east to Union Theological Seminary with another Knox graduate, Charles Finney Martin, who had served as principal of Knox Academy the preceding year, and when the two young men discovered that all other missionary magazines were received and distributed at the seminary except for the organ of the A.M.A., they took it upon themselves to circulate it regularly.[49] During his last six months at the seminary, Roy ministered to a Negro congregation in New York.[50]

Upon completion of his theological training Roy accepted a commission from the A.M.A. and returned west, where in short order he married a Galesburg girl, received a master's degree from Knox College, and in September, 1853, took charge of a church at Brimfield, about thirty miles from Galesburg. During his first year at Brimfield an academy was established which, according to Roy, was a "child of Knox—all four of the teachers being disciples of our cheerful and vigorous dame." [51] After two years in this locality, Roy was called to the pulpit of the Plymouth Church of Chicago, which in 1853 had been organized as an anti-slavery church. Roy soon made this the most notoriously abolitionist church in the city. In 1857 Roy spent a few weeks in Kansas at the main scene of direct hostilities between anti-slavery and pro-slavery combatants. He went there in September to settle the affairs of a brother who had died from the after effects of his imprisonment for fighting in the free-state forces of "General" James Henry Lane. While in Kansas Roy was asked by "Governor" Charles Robinson to accompany him on a political campaign in which the free-state men hoped to capture control of the legislature, which up to then they had repudiated as "bogus" even though backed by federal authority. Roy joined Robinson and T. J. Marsh, treasurer of the New England Emigrant Aid

[48] *Western Citizen*, July 11, 1848.   [49] Barton, *Joseph Edwin Roy*, p. 25.
[50] *Ibid.*, p. 13.   [51] Galesburg *Free Democrat*, June 29, 1854.

Company, and for three weeks this team toured the settlements, "lecturing day by day, the statesman talking politics and the churchman preaching abolitionism." When they got back to the anti-slavery headquarters at Lawrence, they were given a reception at an open-air meeting in which "General" Lane pleased Roy mightily by introducing him as "the fighting preacher; them's the sort we love." [52]

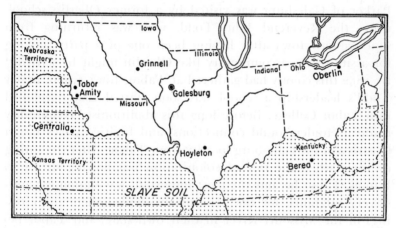

Colonies with Oneida, Oberlin, or Knox Antecedents
in the 1850s

The college community of Galesburg was particularly interested in the struggle for Kansas because of the deliberate colonization of the territory with anti-slavery settlers. Most of the colonies which migrated to Kansas during the fifties were prompted by the publicity and example of the New England Emigrant Aid Company, founded in 1854, and undoubtedly the three colonies that originated in the neighborhood of Galesburg were to some extent stimulated by this general movement. However, the colonies that derived from this particular location may be traced to the college-colony schemes that had been so common in the thirties and that were so successfully exemplified in the notable cases of Oberlin and Knox. There is direct testimony from a contemporary resident of Galesburg

[52] Roy, *Pilgrim Letters*, Lawrence, Kansas, Sept. 28, 1857.

that during the fifties the "success of the Galesburg colony in founding and endowing a College, the effect of the College in promoting the growth and prosperity of the community, awakened great zeal for college building in all that region." [53]

The lines of origin of at least three anti-slavery college settlements in Iowa during the fifties can be traced back to Oberlin and Knox. In November of 1848, the Reverend Lucius Parker of Galesburg was visited by a former Oberlin schoolmate, the Reverend John Todd, who was returning from southwestern Iowa after having been one of a party looking for a site where a community like Oberlin might be settled.[54] By 1852 this colony had gathered at Tabor, Iowa, where under Todd's leadership a school was soon started that developed into Tabor College. Before long this abolitionists' community made its underground connections, and fugitive slaves began to arrive in the Galesburg locality from Tabor. After the spring of 1856, when the tide of colonization was flowing strong to Kansas, Tabor became the most important way-station for anti-slavery migrants, for the Missourians denied them the crossings of the Missouri River in their own state, and Tabor became the refuge and strong outpost for a new route that avoided slave soil by running across Iowa.[55]

Tabor colony plainly exemplified how the idea of the college-colony of reform principles had persisted from the thirties. In October of 1851 an officer of the Western College Society reported to the annual meeting of that body that there was a renewed interest in schemes such as those that had resulted in Oberlin and Knox. These two colleges he cited as striking illustrations of successful "Christian colonies" that had been started in "good faith" with religious and educational purposes. Nevertheless, he reminded the members of the society that the earlier experience of the thirties had not in general been happy, for such schemes had most often worked badly and did not weather the hard times of the late thirties. The Western College Society had become suspicious of plans to establish

[53] Bascom, "Autobiography," MS, pp. 201-2.
[54] Todd, *Early Settlement and Growth of Western Iowa*, p. 78.
[55] *Ibid.*, pp. 115-34.

colleges by settlement on cheap land whose rising values would endow the college, for often the commercial motive was likely to be central in the enterprise; even if it was not, the college was subjected to all the "uncertainties and disastrous fluctuations of ordinary commercial enterprises." [56] These doubts about college-colonies were not, however, shared by the Reverend Josiah Bushnell Grinnell, who in Eastern papers during the early fifties advocated cooperative and organized emigration as against "isolated" individual migration. Grinnell was a prominent abolitionist minister who was at this time doing some journalistic work for Horace Greeley, from whom he received the now famous directive, "Go West, young man, go West." Grinnell recognized that there had been many "sordid grasping" attempts at organized emigration that had failed, but Oberlin and Knox, he noted, had proved that "devoted men" could successfully combine a land purchase and a colony in the founding of a college.[57]

Grinnell's own career had roots in the same soil that nourished the beginnings of Oberlin and Knox, for he had attended Oneida Institute and spoke proudly of the radical reforming influence that it had sent broadening throughout the land.[58] It is significant that in his own colony planting Grinnell picked up certain frayed or broken ends of strands of the reform banner of the thirties under which Knox and Oberlin had been planted. Originally Grinnell hoped to establish a colony in Missouri and in September, 1853, visited a tract of land near Marion College, to which his wife's family had donated funds in expectation that it would enhance the value of lands they owned in the vicinity. This had been one of the manual labor colleges founded in the thirties, whose beginnings had interlaced with that of Knox, but its leaders had been expelled to Illinois because of their anti-slavery principles and the school degenerated to extinction. Only after some difficulty could Grinnell locate the "campus," and when he did he found what to him was dreary evidence of the withering effect of

[56] Kirk, *The Church and the College*, p. 9.
[57] Grinnell, *Men and Events of Forty Years*, pp. 84–90.   [58] *Ibid.*, pp. 29–33.

slavery;[59] as he entered the deserted brick building, great numbers of frightened doves flew out of the open windows of the upper story, and a flock of sheep rushed out of the lower story.[60] Determined not to locate on slave territory, Grinnell discovered an opportunity to establish a colony on land in east-central Iowa along an extension of the Rock Island Railroad that was being projected west to the Missouri River. The town of Grinnell that began here in 1854 had speculative, ideological, and financial features analogous to those of Knox and Oberlin.[61] The community quickly became an important anti-slavery center and its founder probably the most notorious abolitionist in the state. When its school was started in 1856, a radical from Oberlin became principal.[62] Three years later this institution was merged with Iowa College, an older college whose beginnings can be traced by way of Davenport and Denmark, Iowa, to men who had participated in the religious and reforming crusade on the frontier of western Illinois and southeastern Iowa in the 1830s. The character of Iowa College was revealed in its effort, shortly before it removed to Grinnell, to procure as president Jonathan Blanchard, who had recently resigned from Knox College under circumstances underlining his radicalism.[63]

What Grinnell owed to Oneida for its founder, what Tabor owed to Oberlin for the Reverend John Todd, the colony of Amity owed to Knox for the Reverend Benjamin F. Haskins. This pioneer belonged to one of the families from the Burned-over District that had settled in Galesburg; he was graduated from Knox College in 1849 and became a preacher of the Wesleyan denomination that had split off from the main

---

[59] Payne, *Josiah Bushnell Grinnell*, p. 28.

[60] Grinnell, *Men and Events of Forty Years*, pp. 391–92.

[61] As in the case of Knox, the "Yankee" element was dominant in the settlement. Among other similarities, land was reserved to finance a school; land titles were to be void if liquor were sold on the premises; and, significantly, when the college faced a serious emergency in 1862 it found substantial assistance, as had Knox two decades earlier, in the philanthropy of the Willistons (Payne, *Josiah Bushnell Grinnell*, pp. 29–53; Grinnell, *Men and Events of Forty Years*, pp. 336–37).

[62] Payne, *Josiah Bushnell Grinnell*, pp. 51–52; Nollen, *Grinnell College*, pp. 57–58.

[63] Nollen, *Grinnell College*, pp. 1–62.

body of Methodism because it tolerated slaveholding. Already in 1853 Haskins had promoted the formation of a college-colony such as the one in which he had been reared to manhood. A circular was issued calling on Christians to establish in Iowa or Minnesota a colony "for religious and educational purposes." Like the original Knox scheme it proposed that government land should be bought and the subscribers paid off with land at the value of $5.00 an acre; the profit should be put into an educational fund for a college that was to be "religious and strictly anti-slavery in character." The examples of Oberlin and Knox were cited as encouraging for the success of this plan and "worthy of imitation." [64]

Though a committee of three, including Haskins, was appointed in March of 1854 to explore Iowa for a suitable site, actual search for land was delayed for about a year, apparently because the nation-wide excitement over the slavery contest in Kansas deflected attention in that direction. In the fall of 1854 Haskins became editor of the Galesburg *Free Democrat,* an anti-slavery paper founded early that same year and deeply involved in the political activities growing out of the Kansas-Nebraska Bill.[65] The proprietor of this paper at this time, William J. Woods, was Haskins's right-hand man in the promotion of a colony.[66] The duties of Haskins and Woods for the *Free Democrat* may have been partly responsible for delaying the settlement of a new community, though the paper was also useful in advertising the venture. Early in the spring of 1855 an article appeared in the *Free Democrat* describing the work of the New England Emigrant Aid Company and the "large companies of immigrants in all parts of the Union . . . . preparing to move to Kansas." This news was followed by the announcement:

Measures are on foot to establish a college in Kansas on the plan of Knox College. A large amount of money has been subscribed for this purpose, and in a short time we may be able to announce to

[64] *History of Page County, Iowa,* pp. 600–1.

[65] Galesburg *Free Democrat,* Nov. 30, Dec. 21, 1854.

[66] The first meeting of those friendly to the plan was held in Woods's home in Galesburg. Woods had been appointed with Haskins to the first exploring committee.

our readers that a sufficient amount has been subscribed to establish
it upon a firm foundation. For the gratification and consolation of
our Southern friends, we would state that the school will be in the
hands of thorough-going anti-slavery men—men who don't care a
straw for the Fugitive Slave Law, and who hide the outcast and feed
and clothe him.[67]

This revived excitement in Galesburg over a colony reflected
a series of events that had occurred since late in the winter.
Early in February those interested in the project had reorganized as the "Western Industrial and Scientific Association," [68]
and on March 1 published a new prospectus for their enterprise
in the *Free Democrat*. Within a week Haskins had relinquished
the responsibilities of editing the paper and was free to serve as
one of the agents of the association.[69] Though he continued to
be the leading spirit of the company,[70] he now shared prominence with one of the most widely known abolitionists in Illinois, John Cross, who had been elected president of the association and who also acted as one of its agents.[71]

Cross was the only man in the roster of officers of the association who did not live in Galesburg, but he was well known
there for he had been closely associated with the founders of the
town during their early abolitionist activities, when he had resided for a time in Knox County. Since his release from the
Knox County jail in 1843, when he and several Galesburg men
were unsuccessfully prosecuted for harboring fugitive slaves,
Cross had resided in northern Illinois. At "Temperance Hill"
(Cross also called it "Theoka") in Lee County his home became
a notorious headquarters for promoting abolitionism and a
strategic station on the Underground Railroad.[72] In 1848 Cross

[67] Galesburg *Free Democrat*, March 22, 1855.
[68] *History of Page County, Iowa*, p. 601.
[69] Galesburg *Free Democrat*, March 8, 1855.
[70] Sellen, *Review of Galesburg*, p. 50.
[71] Galesburg *Free Democrat*, March 1, 1855. Identification of the *Free Democrat*
with the colony project still was apparent in that Woods, who was treasurer of
the association, remained proprietor of the paper until August, 1856; also, George
Davis of Galesburg, who was corresponding secretary of the association, was
traveling agent of the paper until after April, 1856.
[72] Stevens, *History of Lee County*, I, 381–82; *Recollections of the Pioneers of
Lee County*, pp. 108–9, 230–31.

was president of the state convention of the Liberty Party.[73] These anti-slavery activities as well as his religious associations continued to bring him into contact with his friends in Galesburg,[74] so that he was quite at home when his role as a leader in the proposed colony brought him to that town in 1855.[75]

At a meeting in the *Free Democrat* office in April, 1855, a new exploring committee of three, including Haskins, was sent out to explore Kansas, northern Missouri, and southern Iowa for a colony site, and by early May they were in the field.[76] Though the area of choice was broad, it is evident from the notices in the *Free Democrat* and their relation to the Kansas news that it was anticipated at this time that the colony would go to Kansas. Certainly this was Haskins's own expectation, for he took his family with him that spring to Kansas,[77] and his address was given that summer as Lawrence, Kansas. The exploring committee reported to the stockholders in a meeting held in the *Free Democrat* office on August 8, 1855, giving an account of its travels in the territory under consideration, and each member stated his preference for location of the colony. The meeting agreed on a location in Iowa, and a committee of five, including Woods and Cross, was appointed to select and enter lands for the association, to plot part of them into town lots, and to appraise these for the selection of the shareholders. The meeting adjourned to November 7, when the land selection was to be made.[78]

The Location Committee was on its way to Iowa by early September[79] and was back on time to report to the stockholders in a meeting held in the mother church of Galesburg. The members announced that a location had been made in Page

---

[73] *Western Citizen*, Feb. 15, 1848.

[74] Cross was at Farmington when the General Congregational Association for Illinois was formed; he met Galesburg men at Geneseo when the Liberty Party convention for the sixth congressional district was held in June, 1848 (*Western Citizen*, July 4, 1848); with Blanchard he was prominent in the attempt made in 1851 to revive a state anti-slavery society (*ibid.*, June 21, 1851, March 23, 1852).

[75] He participated in the Knox College Commencement of June, 1855 (Galesburg *Free Democrat*, July 5, 1855).

[76] *History of Page County, Iowa*, p. 601; Galesburg *Free Democrat*, May 3, 1855.

[77] Galesburg *Free Democrat*, June 7, 1855.

[78] *Ibid.*, Aug. 16, 1855.   [79] *Ibid.*, Sept. 13, 1855.

County, Iowa, in an unsettled township directly on the Missouri border, in the far corner of the state that was near Kansas. It was reported that articles of incorporation were already recorded and the college named Amity.[80] The necessary business arrangements were made to carry out the work of the committee, such as election of college trustees, and soon after the winter was over the first settlers got under way. The colony out of a colony had been born; a history of Galesburg published in 1857 boasted that because of Amity College "the great West will be indebted to Galesburg for another amply endowed Institution of Learning." [81]

In 1858, while the Amity settlement was still gathering, the colonists were visited by a party from the next county. These visitors came from the Oberlin colony at Tabor and included the Reverend John Todd. He was impressed with the fact that though many were still living in tents and other temporary shelters and the chilly autumn weather already warned the settlers of winter, they found time every evening for religious services, to assist in which the leader from Tabor remained for a week. He found here a community much to his liking, for they "were as a body active in reforms, warm advocates of temperance, anti-slavery and anti-secret societies." [82] Since Amity was so close to the Missouri border and near to Kansas it was a useful station for fugitives from Kansas violence as well as for runaway slaves. The most remarkable anti-slavery exploit of the Amity settlers was a raid conducted sixty miles into Missouri to rescue the family of a fugitive Negro. Four white men on horseback and a fifth with team and wagon accompanied the runaway and rode across the border to haul fifteen slaves by night to free soil. Two others who could not be crowded into the wagon came along at the same time by riding the fine white

[80] *Ibid.*, Nov. 15, 1855.

[81] Sellen, *Review of Galesburg*, p. 50. A member of the Knox graduating class of 1857, Wm. T. Nelson, was in 1860 a professor at Amity College (*Nineteenth Annual Catalogue of Knox College, 1860*, p. 24). It is interesting to note that the plan of Amity so closely followed that of the original Knox as to propose the inclusion of manual labor, which at Knox had been abandoned by the early fifties.

[82] Todd, *Early Settlement and Growth of Western Iowa*, pp. 169–73.

stallion that their master had imported from France. All the escaped Negroes were successfully sped away along the Underground Railroad.[83] The Missouri border was jittery with threats of counterraids by Missourians when the Civil War broke out, and "border guards" were formed in Amity and other communities to protect Iowa soil. These "border guards" invaded Missouri several times in 1861 and 1862 to aid pro-Union persons or communities in northern Missouri who were threatened by or fearful of secessionists. On these expeditions the Iowa guards tended to be rather rough with Confederate sympathizers they encountered.[84]

Were its earlier antecedents not known, the Amity colony might easily be attributed only to the widespread interest in Kansas that was stimulated by the New England Emigrant Aid Company organized in 1854. The plans of the latter combined philanthropy and profits for subscribers, appealed for self-sacrificing migrants who would risk something to oppose slavery, and aimed to overcome the disadvantages of individual migration by providing leadership and capital for early establishment of churches, schools, and presses.[85] This program was quite familiar both to Oberlin and to Knox. Indeed, J. P. Williston, a generous supporter of both those schools, was one of the directors of the Emigrant Aid Company.[86] Similar Kansas aid societies appeared throughout the North, one being organized for Ohio at Oberlin under the leadership of Oberlin faculty members.[87] Though no such special organization was formed in Galesburg, that community was well represented in the migration to Kansas. It was particularly close to the trail leading to Kansas after the spring of 1856, when the hostility of Missourians turned free-soil migrants north to travel across Iowa from west-central Illinois. In June of 1856 the wife of the editor of the Kansas anti-slavery paper, *Herald of Freedom*, addressed a

---

[83] Clark T. Smith, "Boyhood Recollections Connected with the Early History of Amity, Iowa, now Known as College Springs," Santa Barbara, California, Oct. 13, 1921, MS in Knox College Library.

[84] Bruce E. Mahan, "Home Guards," *The Palimpsest*, V (June, 1924), 189–233.

[85] Thayer, *A History of the Kansas Crusade*, pp. 24–30.

[86] *Ibid.*, p. 53.   [87] *Ibid.*, p. 177.

meeting at which over $200 was raised in behalf of her husband, who was under indictment and being prosecuted by the pro-slavery government of the Kansas Territory.[88] The next month the editor of the *Kansas Free State* visited the town and at a meeting raised $82 toward the replacing of the press that ruffians from Missouri had destroyed at Lawrence.[89] The following September "General" Samuel Pomeroy of the free-state forces in Kansas spoke at a Galesburg meeting.[90] Another visitor picked up from Knox College and President Blanchard ideas about founding a Congregational college in Topeka which, significantly, also received a substantial contribution from J. P. Williston.[91] Perhaps the most important person from Galesburg in Kansas affairs during the fifties was C. H. Noteware, an elementary school teacher who in 1858 became the first superintendent of common schools in the territory.[92]

In February of 1857 the *Free Democrat* announced the planning of a colony to go to Kansas and called a meeting of those interested.[93] The announcements did not identify the sponsors of this enterprise; they may have referred to either of two companies that set out for Kansas within the next eighteen months. One of these was a Swedish group that had their promotion of a Kansas colony well under way by the beginning of the summer of 1857. Among the Swedes of Henry, Bureau, and Knox counties who were involved in this effort several factors favored the formation of a colony; many of the Swedes in that area had recently come to America under the influence of the famous Bishop Hill colony in Henry County, which, however turbulent its history, had made a most successful settlement; organized migration, Swedish leaders realized, facilitated use of the im-

---

[88] Galesburg *Free Democrat,* June 26, 1856.
[89] *Ibid.,* July 17, 1856.   [90] *Ibid.,* Sept. 18, 1856.
[91] Hickman, "Lincoln College, Forerunner of Washburne Municipal University," *Kansas Historical Quarterly,* XVIII (Feb., 1950), 20–54
[92] Milton Comstock, "Reminiscences," MS, Knox College Library; Oquawka *Spectator,* April 2, 1858; *Kansas Historical Collections,* V, 480, and XVI, 658. C. H. Noteware paid the tuition at Knox Academy for a sister and one other girl, of undetermined relationship to him, from 1853 to 1856 (Blotter Book B, MS). The C. N. Noteware who was in attendance at Knox from 1847 to 1849 presumably also came from this family.
[93] Galesburg *Free Democrat,* Feb. 5 and 12, 1857.

migrants' language and helped to preserve their religion better than individual migration. The initiator and leader of the venture, Dr. C. H. Gran, lived in Andover, Illinois, a Yankee colony of the thirties which faltered in its development and was overwhelmed by Swedish arrivals in the forties who transformed Andover into one of the leading Swedish communities of the fifties. The most important propagandist for Gran's colony was the Reverend T. N. Hasselquist, pastor of the Swedish churches in Galesburg and Knoxville, who was becoming the foremost figure in Swedish religious circles. Through the pages of the *Hemlandet*, the Swedish paper he had recently established in Galesburg, Hasselquist advertised and endorsed the plan for a colony to Kansas; a four-page supplement published in July, 1857, portrayed the religious, educational, and economic advantages of the scheme. Hasselquist's support for this colony was a departure from his previous preference for settlement in Minnesota. How much he was moved at this time by his antislavery sentiments to endorse a Kansas colony is not clear, though it is true that he was actively engaged in recruiting Swedes for the new Republican Party. Hasselquist was also in very close contact with the abolitionists at Knox College, who strongly influenced him in some rather radical reforming notions.[94]

A Kansas meeting was held in Hasselquist's church in September, 1857, and was attended by many who had come a considerable distance to discuss the plan for a colony. After a preliminary journey to Kansas that fall, Gran was ready in the spring of 1858 to lead a group from St. Louis to a site on the Saline River. Only a few were on hand to join him, some having gone on ahead in their impatience to get to the good lands that were reported available. Only about a dozen people were with Gran when he laid out the townsite of Granville, and the project failed for lack of sufficient strength. The long-run significance of the attempt is the occasion it offered to boost Swedish

[94] The Gran colony is described in Lindquist, "The Swedes in Kansas before the Civil War," *Kansas Historical Quarterly*, XIX (Aug., 1951), 254–68. For material on Hasselquist, see Ander, *Hasselquist*, pp. 24, 34, 157–59, 159–206.

interest in Kansas settlement, for during the late fifties several Swedish families went to the territory independently. Though the census as late as 1860 listed only about one hundred twenty Swedish settlers, a remarkably large number of these had resided in Galesburg or its near vicinity.[95] The kind of influence exerted on Swedish-Americans by that neighborhood is illustrated by the case of John Rosenquist, who had gone to Kansas as early as 1855. In 1854 Rosenquist stood one afternoon in the crowd around the courthouse in Knoxville that had come to hear Stephen A. Douglas, the politician who beyond all others was associated with the Kansas question. Excitement in the crowd was heightened by the fact that Dr. Blanchard, the president of Knox College, undertook to answer Douglas. During the latter part of the Senator's speech Blanchard interrupted by waving his hand to the crowd and calling for three cheers for a Douglas opponent. The crowd became more and more heated and unruly, until as Rosenquist later described it to his daughter, "all about him on the edges of the crowd . . . began a series of smaller discussions," and the "outskirts soon became a wriggling mass of arms, legs and human forms, a dozen deep." [96] The Kansas argument tended toward such disorder throughout the fifties!

While the Gran venture failed from feebleness, another group moved to Kansas that same summer in strength and with high hopes of success. This was a "colony of idealists from Galesburg" who had formed a somewhat "utopian society" [97] called the Home Association and who boasted by November, 1858, that about two hundred families were engaged in their enterprise. Every voter in it was "Republican to the back-

[95] These early Swedish settlers from Galesburg and Knox County were the vanguard of Swedish migration in Kansas, being followed by colonies of that nationality from Galesburg and Chicago which in the next dozen years were chiefly responsible for the Swedish settlements in central Kansas; see Dergin, "The Swedish Settlements in Central Kansas," *Collections of the Kansas Historical Society*, XI (1910), 19.

[96] Godsey, "The Early Settlement and Raid on the Upper Neosha," *Collections of the Kansas Historical Society*, XVI (1925), 451–63; Galesburg *Free Democrat*, Oct. 12, 26, 1854; Knoxville *Journal*, Oct. 17, 1854.

[97] Wells, "Abijah Wells," *Collections of the Kansas Historical Society*, XIV, 81. The utopian characteristics are also emphasized by an article on Judge Albert H. Horton in the *Horton Headlight Commercial* (Kansas), Oct. 23, 1924.

bone." [98] In Nemaha County, at a site about fifty miles from Atchison, they purchased an entire township, all of which was to be encompassed by one fence so as to protect the property of the pioneers until their private fences were built. Only actual settlers were allowed to buy farms in Home Township, and only actual residents were to be officers in the association. It was "expected" that "every man was to produce the necessities for his own table," and to make this possible for those whose vocation was not farming, part of the land was surveyed into ten-acre "mechanics plots." Nine school districts were laid out, and in the middle of the township, where the village of Centralia was staked out, a college was planned which by 1861 was actually operating.[99]

"Come and see a portion of bleeding Kansas transformed into a blooming garden," said a circular of the Home Association. In February, 1860, the president of the association told his former townsmen back in Galesburg that about one hundred farms had already been sold; [100] and it really seemed that this might be a new Eden as hundreds of people flocked to the new settlement and the town of Centralia sprang up as if by magic.[101] But 1860 was to be no year for gardens in Kansas, for in some parts scarcely a drop of rain fell for thirteen months; not a single roasting ear grew on the corn and cattle and hogs drifted away.[102] When harvest time came some families had not seen a garden vegetable since the year before.[103]

Early in September, 1860, the Reverend Daniel Foster from Centralia came to Galesburg and told a meeting about the destitution resulting from the protracted drought, describing the suffering in Kansas generally and particularly at Centralia, where so many of the famine sufferers were former citizens of

[98] Galesburg *Free Democrat*, Nov., 1858; an early reference to this group is apparently made in the Knoxville *Republican*, March 24, 1858.

[99] Tennal, *History of Nemaha County, Kansas*, p. 112; *Private Laws of Kansas Territory, 1859;* Seneca (Kansas) *Weekly Courier*, July 7, 1876; article by Abijah Wells in Topeka *Commonwealth*, March 23, 1881; *Second Annual Report of the Superintendent of Public Instruction*, Dec. 31, 1861.

[100] Galesburg *Free Democrat*, Feb. 24, 1860.

[101] Topeka *Commonwealth*, March 23, 1881.

[102] *Collections of the Kansas Historical Society*, XVI, 610.

[103] Galesburg *Free Democrat*, Nov. 20, 1860.

Galesburg. Immediately a committee was appointed to raise money and gather produce, and before the end of October 350 bushels of potatoes had been collected at Galesburg and Knoxville and sent to Atchison, one third being delivered to a former Galesburg resident who was chairman of the relief committee at Centralia and the rest assigned to ministers in Osage County and at Lawrence. A letter from the free-soil leader, Samuel Pomeroy, declared that these supplies were the first to arrive in the stricken area, and Galesburg and Knox County took pride in continuing to outdo the rest of the country in this relief work. Before winter fell six carloads of food had been sent, and the large contributions to many parts of Kansas continued, with pledges for delivery in the spring.[104]

During the half-dozen years when these several colonizing activities received so much support from the locality centering at Galesburg, that town itself was still very small but booming. In 1850 the population was less than 800; when the first talk about the Amity colony occurred it had increased to a little less than 1,400; in 1855, when the railroad reached Galesburg, the population had grown to nearly 3,000, and by the time the Gran colony and Home Association were formed it was approaching 6,000.[105] On the one hand it seems remarkable that so many resources were available both for internal growth and for expansion; on the other hand it is obvious that the prosperous example of the college-colony of Galesburg was itself an encouragement to colonial ventures.

What is most certain is that the campus and the town still generated a zeal for reform that supplied a surplus of spiritual energies for new ventures against evil.

[104] Galesburg *Semi-Weekly Free Democrat*, Sept. 7 and 11, Oct. 26, Nov. 20, Dec. 4, 1860. Though Centralia was thus saved from starvation, it soon began to fall apart from its own internal tensions, which reached a climax in what for years was known as the "Centralia Riot" of March 10, 1862. The rioting, for which sixteen were indicted, was a culmination of "private jealousies and sectarian prejudices." Although those indicted were acquitted, this regrettable incident marked the beginning of the process by which the organization went to pieces. Disgusted members moved on to new homes or returned whence they came. A good many of the houses in Centralia were moved away, some to Seneca, some to the railroad a mile farther south when it came through in the seventies, and others were torn down.

[105] Sellen, *Review of Galesburg*, p. 34.

PART FIVE

The Ripe and Bitter Fruit of Success

❧ XVII ❧

A College Town under "the Sun of Reform"

> Fanatic named, and fool, yet well content
> So he could be the nearer to God's heart,
> And feel its solemn pulses sending blood
> Through all the widespread veins of endless good.[1]

"PLACE YOUR SONS and daughters in this institution," advised the abolitionist editor of the *Western Citizen* in one of his many expressions of approval of Knox College. The reputation of the school, advertised in this as in many other places as a radical anti-slavery school, affected the character of its student body, for conservative families would be likely to avoid such an institution. Hardly any of the students came from counties lying south of a line through Quincy and Bloomington, an area first settled by Southerners. By far the greater part of those attending the academy, preparatory department, female seminary, and college came from the country lying north and west of the Illinois River and extending as far north as Galena and Chicago to the upper corners of the state. In general this area lay in that part of Illinois with communities of Yankee antecedents, and conformed more closely to the location of Congregational than of Presbyterian churches. There were occasional students from each of the states and territories of the Old Northwest and from Pennsylvania, Massachusetts, and Vermont, but the only considerable number outside of Illinois were from Iowa and New York. Students appeared consistently from southeastern Iowa; the peak of their arrivals occurred during the late forties and

[1] James Russell Lowell, "Sonnet: Wendell Phillips."

early fifties, after which the decrease in their number may be accounted for by the development of local institutions on the Iowa frontier. Though the coming of these Iowans can be explained by the geographical factor, the circumstance that the next largest out-of-state representation was from New York indicates the continuity of the ties of Galesburg with its place of origin.[2]

Many of the students came from households that had special notoriety in the anti-slavery crusade. James H. Warren, graduate '47, had lived in the home of Owen Lovejoy at Princeton and had there been prepared for college by that prominent anti-slavery preacher and politician, brother of the most famous of the abolitionist martyrs.[3] From the home of the preacher who led the abolitionist communities clustered in Putnam County came C. Wardlaw Dickey, graduate '49. James Scott Davis, graduate '51, could tell his classmates how he was hit over the head with a cane by ruffians in Peoria when he tried to go to the assistance of his father who was being beaten up for the alleged offense of objectionable contributions to the *Western Citizen*. Joseph E. Roy, graduate '48, as a youth in Ohio had seen a mob break up a meeting being addressed by one of the Lane Rebels, and while he walked home with his mother and the lecturer they had been pelted by eggs filled with tar. At Knox, Roy's sister could proudly wear a coat that her mother had made over from the one she had worn on that occasion, after the tar spots had been cut out of the fabric.[4] Stephen V. White, graduate '54, came from a family in Jersey County, Illinois, who were driven out of North Carolina when the father, a Quaker, refused to do police duty during the panic over slave insurrections at the time of the Nat Turner rebellion.[5] Isaac Mahan, graduate '53, was a nephew of John B. Mahan, who had been a central figure in one of the major episodes

---

[2] These conclusions are based on the tallying of all the students listed in the catalogues to 1860, each student and his home locality being tallied each year that he attended.

[3] Milton L. Comstock, "Life of Rev. James Warren," MS, Knox College Library.

[4] Barton, *Joseph Edwin Roy*, pp. 20–25.

[5] Churchill, Scrapbook No. 2; *Coup d'Etat* (Knox College), June, 1887.

in the early history of the Underground Railroad in Ohio, in the formation of which he had been closely associated with Levi Coffin. In 1838 this uncle of Isaac's was surrendered by the governor of Ohio to the jurisdiction of Kentucky, which desired to try him for abducting a slave, and although a Methodist minister, he was put into manacles and carried off. The episode attracted national attention[6] and became a political issue in Ohio, where it contributed to the defeat of the governor at the next election.[7] After the litigation costs took all of the minister's property, his brother, Isaac's father, sold his farm to assist him and then moved to McLean County, Illinois, in 1842; the persecuted man was to follow his kin when free, but died before he was able to do so. In the new settlement the Mahans were so plagued by their neighbors that they found it expedient to leave the Methodist church to which the elder Mahan belonged. The pastor of the Congregational church in Bloomington, Levi Spencer, a Knox colony protégé, organized the first anti-slavery society in the part of the county where the Mahans lived.[8]

That there are no contemporary references in the records to the presence of Negro students may be as much mute evidence of the absence of a color line as of the absence of Negroes.[9] There certainly was contemporary emphasis on the absence of any discrimination against Negroes. The State Female Anti-Slavery Society must have had Knox College in mind when it planned to educate Negroes in Galesburg. In 1846, while visiting in Virginia, Mary Brown Davis of Peoria recommended Knox College to a free Negro who planned to go north for an education.[10] The accident of research that resulted in uncovering one Negro student would suggest that there may have been others who still remain unknown. The one identified is none other than

[6] *Birney Letters*, I, 475–76.

[7] McMaster, *A History of the People of the United States from the Revolution to the Civil War*, VI, 499–500.

[8] Erastus Mahan, "Friends of Liberty on the Mackinaw," *Transactions of the McLean Historical Society*, I (1899), 396–404.

[9] The faculty minutes, for example, mention scholarship aid to Revels but make no reference to race or color ("Faculty Minutes," MSS, March 20, 1857).

[10] *Western Citizen*, Sept. 29, 1846.

Hiram Revels, who later succeeded as a Reconstruction senator to the place that had been occupied before secession by Jefferson Davis. Revels attended Knox College in 1856–57,[11] though he must have been an advanced student, for he had previously had schooling in a Quaker seminary in Union County, Indiana, in a Negro seminary in Drake County, Ohio, and then had studied theology at Oxford, Ohio.[12]

Until the mid-fifties students coming to Galesburg found that the same men who conducted the college also directed the affairs of the two most important churches and dominated the secular life of the town, for a large part of the property and much of the business was in the hands of the trustees and officers of the college. Thrust high above the houses and shops and the modest two-story college buildings was the ninety-foot steeple of the original colony church. Its auditorium, eighty feet long and sixty feet wide, was for a time the very largest in the west-central part of Illinois; and it was here that during the antebellum years the townspeople usually held their political meetings, heard lyceum lecturers, enjoyed such music programs and dramatic entertainment as seemed fitting, and observed the college commencements. Like the high school gymnasium of a small town in Illinois today, it was the biggest building investment of the village, and like the excitement of the present-day basketball season the recurrent religious revivals were the most dependable source of diversion during the gray, confining months of winter. Some of the secular interests that might have competed with the college and the churches for influence in

[11] The college *Catalogue* for this year lists one W. R. Revels, but this must be a typographical error for there are entries for Hiram Revels in the "Tuition Records," September, 1856, to April, 1857, on the following dates: November 13, 1856, and February 5, 1857, pp. 28 and 39. "The Session Record of the Old School Presbyterian Church" (MS) (Galesburg), p. 21, lists: "Mrs. Phebe Ann Revels (colored) received on certificate from the Haynes Colored Presbyterian Church of St. Louis, Missouri, in January, 1857"; page 26, May 28, 1857, of the same record reads that she, "having returned to St. Louis," requested a letter of dismission. A scrapbook kept by Professor Churchill refers to her as the wife of Hiram Revels, later "U.S. Senator from Mississippi who filled out the term of Jefferson Davis."

[12] A manuscript autobiography of Revels either dictated to or composed by Revels's eldest daughter. It was discovered by the author of this study in the possession of Revels's son-in-law, Horace R. Cayton, of Seattle, Washington; it is now in the Library of Congress.

the town were still largely absent, for the county seat, with its particular gathering of lawyers and politicians and its periodic distractions during court sessions, was still located at Knoxville, not far from and yet outside the immediate neighborhood. Merchandising, other than local retail business, and transportation were still largely focused at the two river ports, Oquawka on the Mississippi and Peoria on the Illinois, with both of which Galesburg was connected by stage.

There is a tradition about one of the stage drivers from Peoria, that when he arrived at the outskirts of Galesburg, he leaned over and warned his passengers, "You better put away them cards, and hide your flasks, and keep from swearing if you kin; this is Galesburg, the pious teetotal abolition town." [13] The discipline that maintained such sobriety was to a considerable extent ecclesiastical in origin. Both the First Church and its Presbyterian daughter used the withholding of fellowship to censure and to punish their communicants; to enforce the Sabbath; to admonish the profane, the violent, and the slanderous; to arbitrate disputes; to look into family troubles; and to sober the intemperate. In this last they were helped by the circumstance that the college had deeded its lands to colonists on the condition that no intoxicating liquors would be made or sold.[14]

Important factors in the sobriety and seriousness that characterized life on the Knox campus until the eve of the Civil War were the maturity of the students and the length of time they were associated with the school as students. The faculty minutes for 1848 list the age of most of the college students; of the eight seniors and juniors listed, the age twenty-three years is the mean, mode, and median; of the forty-nine college students of all four classes whose ages are listed, one was twenty-seven, one was twenty-six, five were twenty-five, six were twenty-four, and seven were twenty-three. During the next half-dozen years the faculty records give only the ages of freshmen; for three of these years the average age, as in 1848, was twenty; the other three

[13] Calkins, *They Broke the Prairie*, pp. 162–63. The author is greatly indebted to Calkins for his lively description of Galesburg during the forties and fifties.
[14] Muelder, *Church History in a Puritan Colony*, pp. 40–41.

years the average was at least eighteen and a half.[15] One cause of the comparative maturity of these students was interruption of their course of study for a year or more to work or teach. As a result of such intermissions and of the pre-college studies that many did in the academy or preparatory department, the typical student did not complete his course of study until five or six years after he had entered; and attendance during a span of seven, eight, or nine years was more common than attendance during four years.[16] Vocational plans of many of these students were reflected in the religious life on the campus, for by 1860 one fourth of the college alumni were ministers, missionaries, or theological students.[17]

The severity of the regime under which these students lived is revealed in the faculty disciplinary actions, which are recorded with a relish of detail that corresponds to the protracted attention given to them. Yet it is not until the fall of 1859 that we have references to a genuine student prank such as those which today at once distress and delight faculty disciplinary committees. The burning, in November, 1859, of one of the college outhouses, with the ringing of the fire alarm in town and the rousing of the fire company,[18] was a kind of disturbance very unlike the rather restrained, calculated, of even solemn offenses which had previously provoked faculty intervention: the "free thinking" student who insisted on holding meetings of his own at hours when more regular religious services required student attendance; [19] the student who sold the same copy of Thucydides to two purchasers; the student who damaged stovepipes in the rooms; the student who got married; the students who hanged a faculty member in effigy; [20] the three students who had to be told that "attendance at dance school" was

[15] "Faculty Minutes," 1848–56.

[16] These data were compiled from the *Alumni Directory, 1927.*

[17] The *Catalogue* for 1860 listed the vocations of college alumni.

[18] "Faculty Minutes," Nov. 30, 1859.

[19] Students were required to come to daily religious exercises at the college and on Sunday to be present at church services twice, attendance at the latter being checked by faculty members.

[20] A disappointing omission from the "Minutes" is the identity of the faculty member. On this occasion the faculty ordered that each student should be examined in the presence of the faculty (May, 1853).

"inconsistent with duties of studies in term time"; the nine seniors who in the spring of 1856 attended a "soiree at Mrs. Flagg's" after permission had been refused them to be excused from the rule that a student was not allowed to leave his room except one night a week to attend a literary meeting and one night to attend the Friday evening young people's prayer meeting. The incident that most graphically reveals the puritanic code for campus life occurred on Christmas Eve of 1851, when some students tried to prevent classes from meeting the next day by removing the bell, stealing the keys to the recitation rooms, and locking the doors after having fastened back the window catches with plugs. A two-day Christmas holiday was specifically refused in 1856, and it was not until 1859 that such a recess was granted, and then only to accommodate the three-day sessions of a state teachers' association.[21]

The students were well aware that their college was a "burning focus of anti-slavery principles,"[22] or, to use the phrase of a feminist lecturer who visited there, that in Galesburg one walked under "the sun of reform."[23] This theme of "reform" in its various aspects recurred over and over again in the student debates, orations, and literary publications. Such activities centered in the literary societies that dominated campus life during most of the nineteenth century. The first of these, the Adelphi, was organized in 1846, its membership being open to any college student but being divided into the Delteans and the Theteans each year to supply forensic groups. This more or less artificial division became unnecessary in 1849 when a rival society, the Gnothautii, was formed, and thereafter membership in the societies was elective, selective, and competitive. From the first these societies had their "medals" or "badges" or "ribbons," and soon each had a room in one of the college buildings that was regarded as its "hall," to the furnishing of which more and more attention was given. The extraordinary formal impression given by the printed programs of public meetings of these societies and by the com-

---

[21] "Faculty Minutes," 1848–60.

[22] *Knoxiana* (a student monthly printed in Galesburg), July, 1852, p. 28.

[23] Galesburg *Free Democrat*, April 10, 1856.

plete and careful minutes of their business sessions undoubtedly is somewhat misleading, for one of the early Adelphi bylaws provided, "There shall be no smoking of tobacco in the
Adelphi Room or spitting on the floor, walls, or furniture."

In the main the evidence suggests that the societies were
most seriously concerned about what they regarded as the critical issues of the day. The topics for debate tell us much about
what these were: capital punishment, free homesteads for
settlers, the need for a new translation of the Bible, the controverted justice of the Mexican War, the Mormons, tax-sup-
ported common schools, the new constitution of Illinois. Other
topics were more particularly debatable among anti-slavery
groups: should a minister of the gospel take active part in
politics and be elected to civil office? were the races of mankind
intellectually equal? could one vote for a slaveholder for office
without incurring guilt? [24]

Occasionally the literary societies offered a diverting varia-
tion from the diet of debate by presenting a discourse in the
form of a "conference" or "colloquy" on some historical,
literary, or political theme. Only the very first of these, that
presented at the Commencement in 1846, has been preserved.
This "conference" was only in the most rudimentary sense a
dramatic piece, each of the "characters" speaking from the
point of view of one of the professions, but it marks the beginning of a rather rapid evolution in dramatic presentation,
revealed in the plans and programs of later "conferences." For
the colloquy on "Phrenology," presented at the Commencement of 1848, the Adelphi hired a "mechanic" to build a
"stage"; by 1851 they also needed a "dressing room" and a
curtain that would "raise and fall." Terms such as "scene"
and "dramatis personae" were used by 1848, and in 1853 the
performance was frankly described as a "play in Two Acts."
This was as far, however, as the students indulged in the follies
of the theater. Apparently the performances remained essen-

[24] These particular topics are selected from those appearing in manuscript
minutes and records of the Adelphi Society, 1846–56.

tially what they purported to be, conferences, mutual discourse, with some dramatic embellishment. It was exceptional in these student-composed and -directed entertainments to focus on that aspect of a topic which lent itself most obviously to dramatic treatment, as when Mormonism was presented in a "conference" about the "Danite Band," or as when slavery was dealt with in a colloquy on "The Runaway," acted by some eight different characters, such as slaveholders, overseers, Negroes, abolitionists, commissioners, etc.[25] More often the drama depended on the setting in which the discourse was presented, such as a "Boarding House in Washington City," [26] or a "Bar," which was used in the first scene to contrast in the second with a "National Reform Convention." [27] A colloquy written by members of the preparatory class in 1852 "was a representation of a conclave of Anti-Reform Presbyterians," in which each member felt that his particular occupation or social interests were suffering from the encroachments of reformers and that they had to devise ways and means to stay the "heresies." [28] A very elaborate performance such as the "Historical Conference" of June, 1850, with many "historical" characters, evidently presented considerable pageantry in some of the seven scenes, but it ended in a contemporary setting with current anti-slavery heroes such as "John P. Hale" and "Frederick Douglass" on the platform.[29]

Though most of these student compositions have been lost, their flavor undoubtedly is present in the essays, orations, and other contributions to the two magazines, *Knoxiana* and *Oak Leaf*, published by the Adelphi and Gnothautii, respectively, during most of the fifties. It is significant how often these literary pieces turned to the issue of slavery. A speech on the Hungarian rebel-patriot, Kossuth, gave the speaker occasion to hope that America might "remove that only evil which

---

[25] *Knoxiana*, Jan., 1852, p. 143. This last colloquy was presented by the students of the Academy. All the others mentioned are taken from the "Minutes" of the Adelphi and their printed programs.

[26] Adelphi "Minutes," 1847.   [27] *Ibid.*, 1850.

[28] *Knoxiana*, Jan., 1852.   [29] Adelphi "Minutes," 1850.

so disgracefully mars our claim as the asylum of Earth's oppressed population." A debate—"Is Patriotism a Christian Virtue?"—brought out the following negative argument:

With the word liberty on his lips, Henry Clay is holding man, created in God's own image, and every whit by nature as free as he is, in bondage. While Daniel Webster is toiling from rising until the going down of the sun, to frame and execute a law which will ever be a stain as dark as night, on the fair escutcheon of American liberty, and help to perpetuate the bondage of the sixth of our whole population.[30]

A discourse on "Social Improvement" concluded by saying:

Slavery with all its attending evils is fast gaining upon and surrounding us, and the day may be in reverse, when the despised and enslaved sons of Ethiopa, shall have become so numerous, and mighty, and shall have been taught so well in our schools of oppression, as to subject us to a bondage to which compared to that of Egypt or Babylon were but a shadow.[31]

A "Vision of the Future" composed in 1857 showed how bitter was the feeling over the disorders in Kansas, the brutal beating of Senator Sumner, the Dred Scott case, the Democratic regime of Buchanan, and other evidences of pro-slavery ascendancy. This piece presented the United States corrupted by slavery, a country "wholly destitute of churches and schoolhouses" and with "here and there a dilapidated mill" standing in the stead of "busy manufactures." It foretold of "LEGISLATION A FARCE" by a congress filled with "bloated, savage, ill-looking men, lounging about in the greatest disorder, smoking, swearing, abusing each other, and then drinking together at the bar. . . . Fighting with all sorts of weapons, sometimes after a formal challenge, but oftener by sudden attack." Next was the premonition of "CIVIL WAR," and at the last a foreboding of "DESPOTISM." [32]

Of course at Knox one did not need to be one of the campus rebels to indulge in such radicalism, since it was native in the community, and in the college such ideas were faithfully nurtured. The students heard the college president devote most

[30] *Knoxiana*, Jan., 1852. [31] *Ibid.*, July, 1852.
[32] *Ibid.*, July, 1857, pp. 241–45.

of his baccalaureate address of 1856 to the subject of slavery, telling the seniors that it was the mission of educated Americans "to establish justice . . . , to repress outrage . . . , to take away oppression," and that slavery had "no foundation in law, and is no part of our civil government, anymore than other existing crimes and vices." [33] The faculty at that time still included Gale, Losey, and Grant, whose association with anti-slavery principles went back to their days as teachers in Oneida Institute when the abolitionist crusade was launched. The two most important additions to that nucleus of the Knox faculty were George Churchill, who had been reared in the colony itself, and another graduate of Knox, Milton L. Comstock, from Burlington, Iowa, whose anti-slavery sentiments had early been demonstrated by his affiliation with the Wesleyans, a sect that seceded from the larger denomination of Methodists when it had failed to purge itself of slavery.[34] For a time in the mid-fifties the teaching staff also included one of the famous Beecher family, Charles Beecher, who before becoming the popular teacher of elocution and music at Knox College had been pastor of a Free Presbyterian Church in Newark, New Jersey, where his anti-slavery views separated him and his church from the fellowship of the other churches in the city. In 1851 he published a sermon on the Fugitive Slave Law, *The Duty of Disobedience to Wicked Laws.*[35]

More than his other brothers or his sisters, Charles had much in common with Edward Beecher, who in 1855 had become the first pastor of the First Congregational Church, which was organized by some of the members of the overcrowded original colony church. This Beecher had earned his spurs in the opening battles of the abolitionists' conflict while president of Illinois College; he had been a leader in the convention organizing the Illinois Anti-Slavery Society in 1837; he had stood by Lovejoy to the very eve of his martyrdom and had written

[33] Blanchard, *Baccalaureate Address before the Senior Class of Knox College,* June 22, 1856.

[34] Galesburg *Evening Mail,* Nov. 9, 1906.

[35] Stowe, *Saints, Sinners, and Beechers,* chapter 22. References to Charles Beecher occur in the trustees' records and in the student periodicals for 1856 and 1857.

a little book describing his friend's death in the cause of a free press. The first contact of the Galesburg settlers with him was at the first annual meeting of the state anti-slavery society in 1838. After he left Illinois College in 1842 and returned to the East, that school became much more cautious on the slavery issue. He now came back west to Galesburg from one of the leading churches in New England, in the parsonage of which his sister wrote parts of *Uncle Tom's Cabin,* some of the material for which had been supplied by her brother Charles.[36] One of Edward's first concerns in Galesburg was the building of a church for his congregation a half block from the mother church and immediately adjacent to the college campus. Hardly had the structure been completed when it was severely damaged in a tornado. To assist his brother in raising money for the reconstruction, Henry Ward Beecher (of "Beecher's Rifles" and the notoriously anti-slavery Plymouth Church of Brooklyn) announced a series of six lectures in Illinois, two in Chicago, one each in Quincy and Aurora, and two in Galesburg during April, 1859. Over $1,300 was raised in this way.[37] Edward Beecher immediately became one of the foremost figures in the community and an active participant in the affairs of the college.

In addition to the numerous abolitionist teachers and preachers who resided there, Galesburg frequently was host to other anti-slavery speakers who visited for one purpose or another, such as the Reverend James H. Dickey from Hennepin and the Reverend Owen Lovejoy of Princeton, who served on the board of examiners,[38] and the Reverend Horatio Foote of Quincy, who was a member of the board of trustees.[39] Galesburg was a natural stopover or gathering place for anti-slavery notables, who might deliver one or more speeches during their stay, men like John Gregg Fee from Kentucky or the

[36] *Ibid.,* p. 338.
[37] Galesburg *Semi-Weekly Free Democrat,* April 13, 20, 23, 1859.
[38] "Trustees' Records," Book A, pp. 175, 196; Scrapbook No. 2, in Galesburg Public Library; *Knoxiana,* July, 1853.
[39] Foote, *An Address Delivered before the Missionary Association of Knox College, Sabbath Afternoon, June 20, 1852.*

crusaders for free soil in Kansas. The availability of such men facilitated the development, by the literary societies, of lecture programs. This student activity had begun when the Adelphi in 1846 sought a speaker for their first public anniversary celebration. It is significant that both that year and the next their first choice for speakers should have been such outstanding radicals as Owen Lovejoy and the Reverend J. B. Walker of Chicago. Soon a full-fledged public lecture course was being conducted by the two student societies, and the faculty found it necessary to curb their competitive zeal by limiting them to twelve speakers each year and by insisting that the two groups alternate in operating a yearly lyceum.

By the academic year of 1855–56 the program sponsored by the Adelphi included not only such local talent as Blanchard and Beecher but also an excellent schedule of such imported lecturers with anti-slavery reputations as the Reverend John Pierpont.[40] The lyceum of 1856–57, which was conducted by the rival society, Gnothautii, had strong speakers of national anti-slavery reputations such as Wendell Phillips, John P. Hale, Elihu Burrit, Cassius M. Clay, and Theodore Parker. Burrit was the author of a pamphlet on the peaceful abolition of slavery, Clay was an anti-slavery proponent in the unfriendly environment of Kentucky, Hale was Free Soil candidate for president in 1852 and member of the United States Senate and made a political address in Galesburg in addition to his scheduled lecture for the lyceum a few weeks later. From a letter written by Parker to Hale we have a vivid account of the impression the Galesburg and other Western audiences made on an itinerant lecturer from the East:

What a country is out here! Between this place and Chicago is not a hill fifteen feet high, no undulations, only little ripples of land in this great sea of earth. There are few trees. . . . The rapid growth of population too, seems fabulous, a miracle. Thus seven years ago, Galesburg had six hundred inhabitants; now about seven thousand.

Quantity is immense out here. Bulk is the word to describe it: quality will come later. Quantity is the great burly brother; quality

[40] Ralph Waldo Emerson was scheduled; whether he actually came is not certain (*Knoxiana*, May, 1856).

the nice, dainty little sister; but both the same father and mother. Babies! why, they are universal: babies in all the moods and tenses, babies indicative, subjunctive, potential, imperative, and also infinitive; babies present, imperfect, perfect, pluperfect, and in all the first (or obvious) and second (or potential) future; babies in the taverns, in the lecture rooms, in the meeting houses; in the cars, babies. Here they are stationary; there locomotive. I no more expect to see a woman without a baby than a man without tobacco. They are not only an "institution," but also a nuisance.[41]

Parker might have noticed another trait, of his Galesburg auditors at least, and that was their astounding endurance of speeches, for in the late fifties still another organization in Galesburg was bringing in lecturers. This was the Galesburg Young Men's Literary and Library Association, the nucleus of which consisted of men from the college.[42] Other lecturers in Galesburg during the two or three years before the Civil War included Horace Greeley [43] and Thomas Hart Benton, who spoke on preserving the Union.[44] The veteran anti-slavery congressman, Joshua R. Giddings, lectured twice for the Adelphi in February, 1860, on John Brown's raid.[45] The noted Negro orator, Frederick Douglass, must have spent over a week in town early in 1859, for he is known to have lectured on three different days during that period.[46] His brother who was with him at that time was back for a lecture a year later; [47] Mrs. Mary E. Webb, "sometimes called the Colored Siddens," read "The Christian Slave," a drama by Harriet Beecher Stowe, and also parts of *Uncle Tom's Cabin* in the original colony church in March, 1856; [48] and another Negro woman, Mrs. Wells, a former slave, spoke at Beecher's church in 1860, the returns to be used to help buy the freedom of her mother, two sisters, and four nieces.[49]

[41] Frothingham, *Theodore Parker*, pp. 307–8.
[42] See the list of officers: Galesburg *Semi-Weekly Free Democrat*, March 26, 1859.
[43] Before the Gnothautii; *ibid.*, Dec. 29, 1858.
[44] Galesburg *Free Democrat*, April 23, 1857.
[45] *Ibid.*, Feb. 13, Feb. 28, 1860.
[46] Galesburg *Semi-Weekly Free Democrat*, Feb. 23, 1859.
[47] *Ibid.*, May 11, 1860.   [48] Galesburg *Free Democrat*, March 13, 1856.
[49] Galesburg *Semi-Weekly Free Democrat*, Nov. 13, 1860.

In addition to being the locale of intensive anti-slavery indoctrination by these numerous and varied forensic events, Galesburg was also the site of a vigorous anti-slavery press and exerted an influence upon public opinion far beyond the limits of campus and town. The very first newspapers, established in 1848 and 1849,[50] were described in 1857 as "neutral in politics," but one of them, the *Northwestern Gazetteer,* may have been anti-slavery in its moral principles. Though not enough issues of this paper remain to determine this fact, the editor, Southwick Davis (Knox '46), by family connections and from what is known about his other activities would have inclined toward such a position. It is known that he supported Blanchard in the trustees' controversy of 1849 and 1850. Both the first two papers were short-lived. The *Western Freeman,* which was published in Galesburg during 1853 by W. J. Lane, was definitely anti-slavery; in a list of papers approved by the American and Foreign Anti-Slavery Society, it was one of only two outside of Chicago for the entire state.[51] In December, 1853, this paper was purchased by Southwick Davis,[52] and early the next year continued as a very strong anti-slavery paper under the title *Free Democrat.* It was conducted by Davis for almost a year, and after that, under the control of others, remained a very useful organ of the Republican Party well into the sixties. Its political role will become apparent in a subsequent chapter.

Another anti-slavery paper issued in Galesburg during the fifties was the special venture of President Blanchard and was known as the *Christian Era.* Actual copies of it have not been found, but several references to it and quotations from it indicate its existence, though for how long is also unknown. In his own brief autobiography Blanchard merely states that it was

[50] Sellen, in his *Review of Galesburg* (1857), states that the *Northwestern Gazetteer* began in the latter part of 1849 and that the *Knox Intelligencer* was first published "on or about the first of January, 1849." There is a reference, however, to the "Knox Intelligencer, Galesburg," in the *Western Citizen,* July 4, 1848.

[51] *Thirteenth Annual Report of the American and Foreign Anti-Slavery Society,* 1853, pp. 132-33.

[52] Knoxville *Journal,* Dec. 13, 1853; Oquawka *Spectator,* Dec. 14, 1853.

a periodical leaflet devoted to reform purposes and that he began to publish it while president of Knox College.[53] In the *Western Citizen* of March 18, 1851, he called attention to "the number of our little, '*Christian Era*,' just out this week," and revealed that it was all "devoted to anti-slavery reform," especially of religious bodies that would not cast out slavery.[54]

Possibly the most important newspaper originating from Galesburg at this time was in the Swedish language. By 1850 the Yankee town found itself near the main concentration of Swedish immigrants, whose rapidly increasing arrival made Illinois by that year and throughout the succeeding decade foremost among the states in the number of Swedish settlers and the home of one third of the total number in the nation. Within Illinois, since the middle forties, Knox and Henry counties and adjacent areas at the upper end of the Military Tract had received the Scandinavian newcomers in greater numbers than any other part of the state, and it was here that many of their pioneer adaptations to American life were made. Already in 1848 Blanchard had expressed to the secretary of the American Home Missionary Society his concern over how rapidly the Swedes were multiplying in the next county north of Galesburg, where the Bishop Hill colony not only had gathered a considerable settlement of pietistic communists but also advertised the region to many other Swedes with more conventional religious practices. Blanchard, who reported in alarm that the "prophet Johnson" at Bishop Hill rivaled even Joseph Smith "in evil, even murder," expressed hope that it would be possible to find "a sort of Lutheran Swedish minister . . . who would devote himself to building up a community of Protestant Swedes away from Johnson so that refugees from the prophet could find regular religious exercises elsewhere." [55] By 1850 the A.H.M.S. had awarded support to the Reverend Lars Paul Esbjörn, who became the "father" of the Swedish Lutheran church in America. Though Esbjörn became a member of the Central Congregational Association in Illinois and was responsible to it, he was not required to become a Con-

[53] Blanchard, "My Life Work," *Sermons and Addresses.*
[54] *Western Citizen*, March 18, 1851.
[55] Blanchard to Milton Badger, Jan. 31, 1848, A.H.M.S. Papers.

gregationalist and freely labored as a Lutheran missionary in the field of west-central Illinois, where the originally Yankee colonies of Andover and Galesburg were the sites of his most important Swedish congregations.[56] A letter which Esbjörn wrote in 1850 to a friend in Sweden shows how completely he had learned to use the evangelical apparatus of his Yankee friends in Galesburg. He had learned to insist on a "conversion" as an experience requisite for full status as a church member, he had yoked together the sins of intemperance and of slavery, and he stressed particularly the principle which Blanchard emphasized, that there should be no fellowship with those who failed to treat slaveholding as a sin. Very likely Blanchard is the "anti-slavery hero" about whom he writes and for whom he desires to procure a piece of anti-slavery propaganda on the elimination of slavery in Sweden through the influence of the Christian church.[57]

In 1852 the Galesburg Lutheran church issued a call to a minister in Sweden, Tufve Nilsson Hasselquist. As an excellent biography makes evident, Hasselquist soon was more than a local pastor of the Galesburg parish; he quickly "became an outstanding preacher who looked upon all the Swedes in America as composing his field of labor." [58] Like his predecessor, Esbjörn, soon after he arrived Hasselquist petitioned for and received aid from the A.H.M.S. This exemplifies how early he had common interests with Blanchard, Gale, and the Beechers, who must have been happy over his preaching against the drunkenness, swearing, and immorality among the non-Yankee settlers whom the building of a railroad was attracting into the community.[59] Hasselquist soon expressed a strong admiration for these Congregationalists and Presbyterians whose congregations were "strong in what a congregation is to be strong, in labor for Christ's sake and firmness in the confession and conversations." [60] He came to share with the leaders in Galesburg not only their Puritanism of manners and morals

[56] Olson, *The Swedish Element in Illinois*, pp. 61–65.
[57] L. P. Esbjörn to P. Wieselgren, Andover, Illinois, May 23, 1850, in Gunner Westin, ed., *Emigranterna och Kyrkan*, pp. 42–45.
[58] Ander, *Hasselquist*, pp. 8–10.   [59] *Ibid.*, pp. 13–25.
[60] Hasselquist to the A.H.M.S., Feb. 3, 1854, in Westin, ed., *Emigranterna och Kyrkan*, pp. 70–73.

but also their radicalism on several of the reform movements of the day. Already in June, 1854, he gave a talk at an anti-secret society meeting which he attended with President Blanchard, Professors Grant and Churchill of Knox College, and ministers Flavel Bascom and Lucius Parker.[61] What is more important is to observe him supplementing his political education by attending, with these men, an anti-Nebraska meeting at the old colony church in June, 1856, and being chosen as vice-president.[62]

Great significance must be attached to the circumstance that the first newspaper printed in the language of the Swedish immigrants was established in Galesburg by an editor who was in close communication with its abolitionist leaders, and who already in his native land had evinced a pietism and disposition for reform that qualified him for a cordial reception in the Yankee town. Hasselquist's paper, which bore the title *Hemlandet, Det Gamla och Det Nya,* made its first appearance on January 3, 1855, the plan being that it should be both religious and political in tone.[63] An old German press which he bought in the East did not arrive on time and the first numbers were printed on the press of the Knoxville *Journal* in Roman type which only a few Swedes could read. And so curious did the Swedish words look to the natives that a specimen paragraph was reprinted in the Knoxville paper.[64]

From the first the *Hemlandet* asserted that slavery was contrary to the spirit of the Bible, described the suffering of slaves, and taught that slavery was attended with degrading, impoverishing, and tyrannical social and economic consequences. The *Hemlandet* came to devote more and more of its space to political questions, until it was decided to establish an entirely religious paper called *Ratta Hemlandet.* By printing them on alternate weeks the Swedes would in effect have a weekly paper. In May, 1855, the circulation of the *Hemlandet* was already 800 and was widely distributed, not only throughout Illinois but also to about two hundred subscribers beyond. In estimat-

---

[61] Galesburg *Free Democrat,* June, 1854.   [62] *Ibid.,* June 5, 1856.
[63] Ander, *Hasselquist,* p. 27.
[64] *Ibid.,* p. 28; Knoxville *Journal,* Jan. 9, 1855.

ing its influence, moreover, it must be pointed out that its readers exceeded its subscribers; seven families in one New York community, for example, read the same copy. It continued to be published under Hasselquist's editorship in Galesburg into the year 1858, when it became an official denominational organ and moved to Chicago.[65]

Swedes before 1856 would appear to have inclined to the Democratic Party, and several attempts were made to secure support for that political viewpoint from the *Hemlandet,* but Hasselquist, within a year after the paper had started, repudiated the Democrats even though they had been friendly to foreigners. He recognized the Republican Party as the only true anti-slavery party. Through the *Hemlandet* he campaigned energetically for Fremont in 1856, and thereafter consistently supported the same party. The *Hemlandet* became an "openly partisan political newspaper" in which "the Democratic Party was constantly associated with corruption and dishonesty." During the Lincoln-Douglas debates he urged his countrymen to become naturalized in order that they might vote for the Republican candidate. A contemporary of his maintained that Hasselquist and his paper did more than any other agency in forming the political opinion of the Swedes in America, who between 1852 and the Civil War changed from Democrats to rock-ribbed Republicans.[66]

An anti-slavery press in the Swedish language continued in Galesburg even after the *Hemlandet* moved to Chicago in 1858. In September of that same year a Swedish society in Galesburg announced that it had purchased a press and would shortly issue *Den Frihetsvännen, the Friend of Freedom.*[67] This paper ran until 1861.[68] Its anti-slavery quality was manifest in that it was proscribed in a number of the Southern states. One subscriber wrote to the editor to ask that the paper stop coming, for his life had been threatened.[69]

Whatever the affinity of men like Hasselquist for the original

[65] Ander, *Hasselquist,* pp. 29–30, 152–59, 203–24, 239.   [66] *Ibid.,* pp. 154–60.
[67] Galesburg *Free Democrat,* Sept. 4, 1858.   [68] Ander, *Hasselquist,* p. 239.
[69] Galesburg *Free Democrat,* Oct. 23, 1860.

ideals of the founders of Galesburg, they could not undo the profound social changes occurring there; nor could they check the growth and transformation of the Yankee college village into a railroad town with a heterogeneous population of varied American stocks and of foreigners. The founders had lived long enough to see the environs of the campus (as they had existed for over a score of years) undergo a transition beyond their control. Within less than six months after the railroad arrived, Mary Brown Davis (who from Peoria had closely followed the settling of the colony, had lived there for a time herself, and had experienced its life at firsthand and through her student sons) made this observation about "that beautiful seat of science, learning, poetry, and song":

It is still beautiful, the muses still linger there, science still holds a mighty sway—but the iron chain which now unites it to the outer world has brought in a flood of business, and Galesburg is no longer the exclusive haunt of poesy and song. The profane oath, the rude jest, and even the besotted inebriate may now be seen and heard in that hitherto quiet village.[70]

At the very end of the decade, as briefly intimated above, faculty disciplinary records reflect a change in kind of student spirit. A hint of what was to come occurred in the spring of 1857, when on the motion of one of the sons of Edward Beecher the Adelphi challenged the Gnothautii to three games of football. This would have been an unprecedented extension of the competition of the two societies, which had been confined to histrionic feats and forensic meetings, and the proposed athletic contest was reconsidered a week later and given up.[71] But that a change in college affairs was under way is betrayed in 1858 by a new kind of faculty resolution that students be admonished to "play" further from the college buildings and make less noise in the halls. In May of that year it was reported that the students were playing cards! [72]

Indeed at this very time the faculty and the trustees were convulsed in a stubborn contest in which the original reforming character of the college was at stake. The threatened change

[70] Oquawka *Spectator*, March 20, 1855.
[71] Adelphi "Minutes," April 8, 1857.   [72] "Faculty Minutes," 1858.

in the college involved the issue of student fraternities. The founding of Knox had originated in the time when and a place where opposition to secret societies was one of the main planks of religious reform. Political anti-Masonry had been coeval with the abolitionist, revivalist, and temperance excitements of the Burned-over District. As a consequence the town of Galesburg in its early years and the First Church had been opposed in principle to secret societies. When the students first formed the Adelphi society they for a short time had followed the model of student organizations elsewhere and had based it upon the principle of secrecy; but, according to one of its earliest members, when Blanchard came to Knox College "we laid aside our silly secrets, and arranged a new society, open to the sun, to the light of every good thing." [73] According to Joseph E. Roy, this action was initiated by the students, not by any direct influence of Blanchard, who, like the colonists of Galesburg, had strong convictions against secret societies. But by 1854 another influence was affecting the students, for the faculty adopted a rule that "membership in any secret society was not a sufficient reason for permitting the absence of any student during study hours." [74] This rule apparently applied to some off-the-campus fraternal body, but five years later some student high-jinks led to the uncovering on the campus itself of a secret society, either "Phi Beta" or "Rho Beta," of seventeen members whose sessions of jollification and even conviviality contrasted with the programs of edification and solemnity provided by the literary societies.[75] That such a matter should have come up at all for faculty attention showed that the college was changing in character, and has a significant parallel with events in the board of trustees that had recently effected a revolution in the college administration.

[73] J. E. Roy to J. Blanchard, Jan. 19, 1891, in the *Christian Cynosure*, Jan. 29, 1891.
[74] "Faculty Minutes," Sept. 6, 1854.   [75] *Ibid.*, Nov. 30, 1859, and following.

❧ XVIII ❧

A College in Politics

The cords that bind the States together are not only many, but
various in character. Some are spiritual or ecclesiastical; some
political, others social. . . . The strongest of those of a spiritual
and ecclesiastical nature, consisted in the unity of the great religious denominations, all of which originally embraced the whole
Union. . . . The strongest cord of a political character, consists
of the many and powerful ties that have held together the two
great parties which have with some modifications, existed from
the beginning of the Government. They extended to every portion
of the Union, and strongly contributed to hold all its parts together. But this powerful cord has fared no better than the
spiritual.[1]

DURING THE FORTIES the Galesburg colony had provided leaders that pushed the slavery issue into the field of
political conflict in Illinois; during the fifties it continued the
fight in one of the most important salients of party warfare
in the state. The decade opened with the heated controversy
provoked by the Fugitive Slave Law, which the Yankees around
Knox College, notorious for their Underground Railroad activities, could certainly not ignore and probably would not
obey. On October 30, 1850, at a meeting held in the colony
church, vehement hostility to the new law was expressed; the
Reverend Flavel Bascom, pastor of the church, in an eloquent
speech against the statute proclaimed that man owed first
obedience to the "higher law" of God. President Blanchard
also made an address. A committee of five (G. W. Gale head-

[1] The last speech of John C. Calhoun, read for him to the Senate, March 4,
1850.

ing the list, and two other professors at Knox College, Grant and Losey, serving with him) was appointed to call a public meeting at which the matter should receive further consideration. Another committee was appointed to present memorials to Congress for the amendment or repeal of the law.[2]

At nearby Knoxville, where it was boasted that there was only one "imported case" of "Fugitive Slave Law Fever," [3] the Knoxville *Journal*, which had vaunted its neutrality in politics,[4] was provoked to oppose the principles pronounced in Galesburg. The editor declared that he could no longer refrain from public utterance on the issue when there were meetings "held in our county" at which it was "agreed that we must not conform to the law, although it is constitutional, because, forsooth, it conflicts with what we may choose to call a 'higher law.'" Knox County, he affirmed, would not countenance disobedience to the law.[5] A bitter and protracted controversy with the *Northwestern Gazetteer* of Galesburg ensued, the Knoxville paper replying to the vehement righteousness of its opponent with the calm statement that the latter's stand was treasonable.[6]

State-wide advertisement was given to the rebellious spirit of the Galesburg abolitionists when the *Western Citizen* gave practically its whole first page to a "Letter from President Blanchard to the Honorable Stephen A. Douglas" on the Fugitive Slave Law. Blanchard asked the senator the question: "Is it ever the right and duty of a people to Disobey a Statute of their Legislative?" In his powerful affirmative Blanchard not only used the moral "higher law" argument but also took the legal ground that the new federal law was unconstitutional because it violated the rights of the Negro. This article was the most extensive and in many respects the best of those published during this controversy in the *Western Citizen*.[7]

As the campaign of 1852 approached, the people of Galesburg girded themselves for a contest. A mass meeting of "friends of the slave" was held in Knoxville, May 6, 1852, at

[2] Knoxville *Journal*, Nov. 12, 1850.
[3] *Ibid.*, Dec. 3, 1850.
[4] *Ibid.*, Oct. 8, 1850.
[5] *Ibid.*, Nov. 12, 1850.
[6] *Ibid.*, Nov. 19, Nov. 26, Dec. 3, 1850.
[7] *Western Citizen*, Nov. 19, 1850.

which the Fugitive Slave Law was roundly denounced and the Whig and Democratic parties repudiated. Organizations were set up to select proper anti-slavery candidates and "vigilance committees" appointed to oversee the campaign in the various townships. It signifies the affinity in Galesburg of ecclesiastical with political radicalism that this same meeting denounced religious fellowship with slaveholders.[8] Professor Innes Grant of Knox College, one of the two "vigilance committee" members for Galesburg Township, presented to the mother church of the colony resolutions to the effect that no Christian could vote for any man sustaining the Fugitive Slave Law, or for any man who did not subscribe to "the Higher Law" in opposition to "human law," and that no Christian could vote for any man accepting the platforms of the two great political parties.[9] President Blanchard of Knox College himself took an active part in the campaign for the anti-slavery party.[10] At least two anti-slavery political mass meetings were held in Galesburg in September, and in October the Free Democrats held a convention in Victoria, Knox County, to select a candidate for the nineteenth senatorial district.[11] In the November election the only precinct in the county giving a plurality to the Free Democrats was the Galesburg precinct, and it cast one third of the anti-slavery votes in the county.[12]

It was in 1854 that the anti-slavery voters in Galesburg tasted the sweets of victory at the polls for the first time. The year was full of fireworks that began when Douglas dropped a bombshell into Illinois politics, as well as throughout the nation, with his report in the Senate on the Kansas-Nebraska territory. This report, if adopted, would supersede the Missouri Compromise of 1820. Douglas announced his intention to introduce the bill on January 4, 1854. In dramatic sequence there appeared the next day the first issue of the Galesburg *Free Democrat*, avowedly an organ for the anti-slavery politicians, edited by Southwick Davis, who the previous fall had

---

[8] Knoxville *Journal*, May 18, 1852.
[9] "First Church Record Book," MS, July 31, 1852, Book B, p. 136.
[10] Oquawka *Spectator*, Sept. 1, 1853.   [11] *Ibid.*, Oct. 19, 1852.
[12] Again in 1853 in an election involving only county officers Galesburg precinct furnished a third of the anti-slavery vote.

been a candidate for county surveyor on the Free Soil ticket.[13] He came from the family of printers and journalists whose connections with Galesburg have been noted at several points in this study; indeed, his brother, R. McKee Davis, now served as agent for the *Free Democrat* in Chicago [14] and his mother served as weekly correspondent from that city. This paper succeeded and took over the subscription list of the *Western Freeman,* which had been the none-too-regular organ of the Free Soil Party in this section of the country since May, 1853.[15]

The *Free Democrat* did much for the cause throughout the 1854 campaign. As late as July, 1855, its proprietor described his paper as the only "thorough going anti-slavery paper" in the entire congressional district.[16] The first issue frankly stated: "Our present enterprise is undertaken under the auspices of the FREE DEMOCRATIC PARTY of Central Illinois. . . . The platform upon which it will stand is that adopted by the Free Democratic Party of the United States at its National Convention in Pittsburg, in its main and principle features." That Davis regarded it primarily as a campaign organ is suggested by the fact that he gave up his editorship of it as soon as the 1854 campaign was over.[17]

[13] Oquawka *Spectator,* Nov. 15, 1853.

[14] Galesburg *Free Democrat,* June 29, 1854.

[15] The editor was W. J. Lane of Galesburg and it was printed by S. Gustavus Cowan, who had transferred to it his *News Letter* subscription list (Knoxville *Journal,* May 21, 1853). The *News Letter* was a Galesburg paper which in 1850 was being published by Messrs. Fish, Lanphere, and Gale, who represented in their political opinions the three leading political parties: Whig, Democrat, and Free Soil. It planned then to avoid politics (Oquawka *Spectator,* Aug. 7, 1850).

[16] Galesburg *Free Democrat,* July 12, 1855.

[17] To avoid complicating the pages of the text with changes of the personnel of the paper throughout the fifties, these changes may be summarized here:

a. Nov. 30, 1854: Davis and co-publisher, W. H. Holcomb, announce that they will give up the paper to Wm. J. Woods and Ben F. Haskins but that it will continue to be an anti-slavery paper.

b. Dec., 1854: Haskins's salutatory as editor.

c. March 8, 1855: C. J. Sellon succeeds Haskins as editor.

d. Aug. 2, 1855: C. J. Sellon succeeds W. J. Woods as publisher.

e. Dec. 11, 1855: W. J. Woods becomes publisher again and announces that he is negotiating with Southwick Davis to become editor again.

f. Aug. 21, 1856: W. J. Woods announces he has sold proprietorship to J. H. Sherman. Sellon is editor.

g. June 4, 1857: Sellon ceases to be editor; apparently Sherman is to be proprietor and also editor.

h. For a while after March 17, 1857, the *Free Democrat* was a daily paper.

The initial number of the new publication asserted that the "cause of political opposition to slavery in the central part of our State has suffered from want of organization," and called for a meeting in the original colony church of all those in the surrounding counties resolved to vote against "slave ascendancy." The date, January 17, was selected with regard to the fact that this was "the second day of the winter examination of several departments of Knox College, when there are always a large number of strangers in town." It had been determined that the "two objects will in no wise interfere," and the speaker at the meeting was the president of Knox College. At this Free Democratic meeting, of which Davis was secretary and his newspaper partner, W. H. Holcomb, president, and a Monmouth man vice-president, measures were taken to buy the press on which the *Free Democrat* was printed. A central committee of Free Democrats was appointed to act for Knox County, and resolutions were adopted to effect a general organization of the Military Tract.[18]

A month later [19] a meeting of all those opposed to the repeal of the Missouri Compromise and to the entry of slavery into Nebraska [20] was held in the same church. The events of this meeting reveal a movement toward agreement of political opinion in the community and indicate that within less than six weeks after Douglas's startling action there was apparent in Galesburg that movement toward anti-slavery cooperation regardless of former party lines which came so strongly to characterize this year's politics throughout the state, and which culminated eventually in the new Republican Party.[21] Though Blanchard and the elder Gale had a tiff in which they aired their differences regarding the slavery connections of a certain Presbyterian theological seminary, they agreed in their denunciation of Douglas and the proposed treatment of Nebraska.[22] Furthermore William Selden Gale, an active Whig leader in Galesburg, who as late as the preceding October had

---

[18] Galesburg *Free Democrat*, Jan. 25, 1854.   [19] *Ibid.*, Feb. 16, 1854.
[20] *Ibid.*, Feb. 9, 1854.   [21] Cole, *The Era of the Civil War*, pp. 127–28.
[22] Galesburg *Free Democrat*, Feb. 16, 1854.

been nominated for judge by the Whigs of Knox County,[23] not only spoke on the inviolability of the Compromise of 1820 but also was appointed to serve with Southwick Davis and Silas Willard on the committee which brought in resolutions that a remonstrance to Congress be prepared on the Nebraska Bill, and that the Illinois legislature ought to protest against it. The editor of the *Free Democrat* declared that during a dozen years' residence in Galesburg he had never seen so large a political meeting, nor one "in which so much harmony and unanimity of purpose was manifested." [24] The committee of five appointed to draw up the congressional remonstrance included three trustees of Knox College, one of whom, Nehemiah Losey, was also a professor in that institution.

During the spring other anti-Nebraska meetings were held in nearby Victoria, Knoxville,[25] and Farmington.[26] The students at Knox College held a meeting in the "East Building" of the campus and adopted resolutions against Douglas and the violation of the Missouri Compromise. Seventy-five student signatures were secured for a petition embodying these resolutions, which was sent to James Knox and by him presented in the United States House of Representatives.[27]

It signifies shifting political affiliations that six Democrats and six Whigs in September endorsed a call for a mass meeting of all those opposed to the repeal of the Missouri Compromise.[28] Later in the month another call for such an assembly "to meet without distinction of party" was signed by eighty persons including William Selden Gale and four Knox trustees, J. G. Sanborn, R. J. Bunce, C. S. Colton, and James Bull.[29] An editorial in the *Free Democrat* promised that at this meeting "will be found Abolitionists and Free Soilers—the Whigs and the Democrats—burying all past differences—disregarding all party names—uniting in one common cause—to the rescue

[23] Knoxville *Journal*, Oct. 25, 1853.
[24] Galesburg *Free Democrat*, Feb. 16, 1854.
[25] Knoxville *Journal*, March 7, 1854.   [26] *Ibid.*, April 18, 1854.
[27] Galesburg *Free Democrat*, March 2, March 23, 1854.
[28] *Ibid.*, Sept. 7, Sept. 14, 1854.   [29] *Ibid.*, Sept. 21, 1854.

of imperiled liberty," [30] a prediction which was fulfilled. So large a crowd convened that it had to remove from the county courthouse to the Knoxville public square; the editor of the Knoxville *Journal* conceded that it was to his knowledge the largest public meeting ever held in Knoxville.[31] Out of it came what was called the "People's Ticket." [32] James Knox, a Knox College trustee, was nominated for Congress, Samuel W. Brown for the legislature, and four delegates elected to a state convention, two of them being William Selden Gale and John G. Sanborn, a Knox trustee.[33]

The columns of the *Free Democrat,* the speeches made at the anti-Nebraska meetings, and the resolutions adopted at these meetings were full of denunciations of Senator Douglas. In October, on a tour to repair the damage done to his political fences, he came to Knoxville. The day before his scheduled appearance, a notice signed by "Many Citizens" announced in the *Free Democrat* that some one was going to reply to him; [34] and the "some one" proved to be Blanchard. The Knoxville *Journal* declared that this mass meeting, which had attracted "men of all parties," was greater than the gathering of "any previous day upon any occasion." It was an exciting event. Douglas spoke for one hour; then President Blanchard "occupied one and a half hours in reply to the Judge." [35] Blanchard later credited himself with having shown "the humbuggery of popular sovereignty carried out by Democracy," and at one point "turned to Mr. Douglas and remarked that he then had the pleasure of bowing to the *sole* and *absolute embodiment* of that doctrine. It had no other existence." Blanchard, referring to the fact that both Douglas and he were natives of Vermont, declared that the Senator, by becoming the instrument of slave power, was recreant to principles he had been taught in childhood.[36] The Knox students present felt that their president had "mopped the earth" with his opponent.

[30] *Ibid.,* Oct. 5, 1854.   [31] Knoxville *Journal,* Oct. 3, 1854.
[32] Galesburg *Free Democrat,* Oct. 5, 1854.
[33] *Ibid.;* Knoxville *Journal,* Oct. 3, 1854.
[34] Galesburg *Free Democrat,* Oct. 12, 1854.
[35] Knoxville *Journal,* Oct. 17, 1854.
[36] Galesburg *Semi-Weekly Free Democrat,* Sept. 4, 1858.

One of them long afterwards, toward the end of a long political career, still believed that Douglas had never been arraigned with such energy and bitterness, "never, probably, in all his life . . . . so held up to scorn and so relentlessly assailed." [37] Following Blanchard, Douglas concluded with another hour and a half speech, in which he made the intemperance of his adversary the main subject of his reply. There was a good deal of disturbance at the meeting. Blanchard himself interrupted the Douglas speech to wave his hand to the crowd and propose three cheers for James Knox, the People's Party candidate for Congress,[38] and during the latter part of the address, when Douglas referred to the Knox Know-Nothing Party, "there was much excitement and warm feelings," [39] which developed into some fighting.

On another big campaign day in Galesburg the anti-slavery orators J. R. Giddings of Ohio and Ichabod Codding spoke in the afternoon and evening to large crowds on the steps and within the lecture room of the mother church. Then came polling day. Led by James Knox, candidate for Congress, the People's Party won an easy victory in the county; the vote was 1,647 to 924 for his nearest opponent. Galesburg precinct, now grown to the largest voting precinct in the county, gave him 332 of these votes, which was more than a 6 to 1 majority over his opponent.[40]

The campaign of 1854 had clearly demonstrated that in Galesburg and Knox County the Kansas–Nebraska issue was breaking up the old Whig Party and even thinning the Democratic ranks. In 1855 and 1856 many men continued to seek new party bonds with which definitely to bind themselves. One of the new affiliations available to voters was the Know-Nothing Party, but because of its secrecy this was from the outset unacceptable to a large body of the Galesburg colony. These members derived from New York not far from the scene of the alleged Masonic murder of William Morgan, and many of the charter members and later adherents of the colony had

[37] Carr, *The Illini*, pp. 165–66.   [38] Galesburg *Free Democrat*, Oct. 26, 1854.
[39] Knoxville *Journal*, Oct. 17, 1854.   [40] *Ibid.*, Nov. 14, 1854.

strong anti-secret society convictions. President Blanchard was definitely opposed to the Knox-Nothings as a "secret order" despite the argument that they might give help to the anti-slavery cause.[41]

The truth was that the anti-slavery stand of quite a number of the Galesburgers was so extreme that it could hardly be adopted by any party whose platform would be acceptable to a majority of the nation. In May, 1855, fifteen men, including Blanchard, Professor Grant of Knox College, and George Davis, signed a call for a meeting of all those who believed slavery the "sum of all villainies" whether in church or state, and that it "is in conflict with the Bible and the Constitution . . . and cannot be legalized by any enactment." To the meeting were invited all who were "disposed to act promptly for its entire abolition." [42] It was hardly to be hoped to organize a victorious anti-slavery political society on these extreme principles.[43]

Nevertheless during 1855 the new, more moderate, "Republican" organization captured important followers in Galesburg. In June, 1855, the *Free Democrat* came out for the Republican Party and urged an early county organization.[44] This stand by the paper was retained when it changed hands the following December.[45] It took several attempts, however, to get the new party definitely established. Either very late in March or very early in April, 1856, a meeting was held in the original colony church. This session adjourned itself to April 8.[46] Though only a small number met, and decided not to organize till there was better attendance, a committee was appointed to arrange the next meeting, the list being headed by Blanchard. On April 24, 1856, the *Free Democrat* announced a meeting for May 10 in the county seat to elect four delegates to the Republican state convention as well as to do other necessary business.[47] The meeting, which filled the courthouse, formed a Republican organization for the county and elected the state convention delegates.

By this time Blanchard had so fully committed himself to

[41] Galesburg *Free Democrat*, March 8, 1855.   [42] *Ibid.*, May 10, 1855.
[43] *Ibid.*, May 17, 1855.   [44] *Ibid.*, June 7, 1855.   [45] *Ibid.*, Dec. 11, 1855.
[46] *Ibid.*, April 3, 1856.   [47] *Ibid.*, April 24, 1856.

the new party as to assume the privilege of nominating a presidential candidate for it. The *Free Democrat,* on May 8, 1856, printed a letter from him stating the reasons why he was satisfied that Governor Chase of Ohio ought to be placed in nomination by the Republicans. He cited not only Chase's personal attributes such as "ability and integrity as a politician" and his "positive and known antecedents," but also such practical factors as "the confidence of the mass" in him and the fact that though a "declared Democrat and friend of the foreign population," the "Know Nothing Lodges" of Ohio had placed his name on their ticket. Blanchard declared that Chase had done more and was able to do more for the Republican movement than any other man, not excepting Governor Seward. The "Pierce party," Blanchard declared, "rely on organization and ignorance," and would present an unknown name for candidate. The Republicans, who must rely on principle and "enthusiasm," must not present a name "without antecedents." "Let us first know what we are doing and then do it with our might." [48] Blanchard's preference for Chase over other aspirants to the presidential nomination undoubtedly was based on their personal friendship which had been formed during Blanchard's years in Cincinnati when both were interested in the beginnings of the Liberty Party. This personal factor undoubtedly strengthened the particular appeal that Chase had made to the abolitionists in Galesburg because of his leadership in forcing the anti-slavery cause against Douglas in the early arguments over the Kansas-Nebraska Bill and because he more than any other Republican politician of the first rank in the Northwest was definitely a radical anti-slavery man. [49] The Galesburg *Free Democrat* during most of its first year (1854) had run a quotation from Chase at its masthead. Already in February, 1854, Blanchard had particularly lauded Chase at the first of the great anti-Nebraska meetings in Galesburg,[50] and the students at Knox had soon after singled out

[48] *Ibid.,* May 8, 1856.   [49] Craven, *The Coming of the Civil War,* pp. 326–48.
[50] Galesburg *Free Democrat,* Feb. 16, 1854. This paper had, of course, printed the famous "Appeal" written by Chase and undersigned by other leading anti-slavery congressmen (*ibid.,* Feb. 9, 1854).

Chase for an expression of gratitude for his anti-slavery stand in politics.[51]

When the explorer John Fremont stampeded the Republican convention of 1856 and won the nomination instead of some tried and true anti-slavery leader, the abolitionists in Galesburg did not refuse their support. In July a large crowd of Republicans met at Knoxville to nominate a county Republican ticket as well as to ratify the national nomination of Fremont, and Blanchard was there and made one of the speeches.[52] On September 12 a "State Mass Convention" was held at Galesburg. The men elected as vice-presidents of the convention hailed from almost all the counties of the Military Tract. Speakers were there from Canton, Bloomington, Chicago, and Quincy, as well as Owen Lovejoy of Princeton, Governor Grimes of Ohio, and Governor Pomeroy of Kansas. Reports from partisan sources differed greatly as to estimates of the size of the crowd, but in any event it was a large meeting.[53] The Republicans, as Blanchard had asserted, certainly did have an important element of political power in their "enthusiasm":

At an early hour the delegations from the surrounding towns and country began to pour in, and by 10 o'clock the streets were literally blocked with teams. . . . The cars from Quincy, Burlington, and Chicago brought in thousands on thousands of enthusiastic freemen. The Delegation from Henderson was over a mile in length, and is deserving of more than a passing notice. It was decorated throughout its length with fine flags and banners, and brought in a wagon containing thirty-two young ladies representing the States and Kansas. . . . A splendid delegation also came in from Utah, Warren County. In this delegation there was a wagon containing thirteen young ladies, representing the thirteen original States. Each of the young ladies bore an appropriate banner. The Abingdon delegation came in fine style, headed by the Abingdon brass band. . . .

[51] *Ibid.*, March 2, 1854.

[52] *Ibid.*, July 17, 1856. This paper said the crowd numbered 2,000.

[53] The Knoxville *Journal* said 4,000, but the *Free Democrat* affirmed that not less than 20,000 were present (Galesburg *Free Democrat*, Sept. 18, 1856). According to the Burlington, Iowa, *Daily Hawk-eye and Telegraph*, Sept. 15, 1856, the Warren County delegation alone composed 1,500 people; "the train from Burlington was composed of fifteen cars and were densely crowded" and "trains from other directions were equally large, and equally incompetent to accommodate the mass of men who were anxious to be present."

We met people here from all parts of Illinois; and Iowa was well represented, especially "High Henry," the Banner County of that State. . . . We saw one banner from Iowa containing the inscription: "The first shriek for freedom!" The banner from Henry County, Iowa bore this inscription: "High Henry is good for 1,000 majority for Freedom!" But we have not time to speak particularly of the hundreds of banners displayed on the occasion.[54]

In the center of the Galesburg public square during the campaign a Fremont flag flew from a pole so tall that when it was to be cut down it was suggested that it might be given to some poor person for firewood.[55]

In October, 1856, Douglas spoke in Galesburg. He had a "very respectable audience," according to the third issue of the Knoxville *Republican*,[56] a new paper, the publication of which suggests a further weakening in the county seat of the resistance previously offered by that community to the political ideals of their Yankee neighbors in Galesburg. Theodore Parker, who was in Galesburg as a lecturer for the Knox College lyceum, heard Douglas speak and reported his impressions to his friend, Senator Hale:

I heard your opponent this afternoon, Douglas. He was considerably drunk, and made one of the most sophisticated and deceitful speeches I ever listened to. It was mere brutality in respect of morals, and sophistry of logic, and in the style and manner of a low blackguard. His enemies said he seldom or never did so ill. But there is a good deal of rough power in his evil face. I never saw him before.[57]

"Election day passed off muddily and under the influence of a snowstorm."[58] Fremont carried Knox County by a substantial majority, but almost one fourth of the vote came from the single precinct of Galesburg.[59] Though Fremont lost to Buchanan in the nation, his showing was more than good enough to encourage the new party to carry on. In 1858 the opportunity would offer itself to defeat Douglas in a senatorial contest which might also serve as a preliminary trial for the presidential race of 1860. Galesburg had earned and received

---

[54] Galesburg *Free Democrat,* Sept. 18, 1856.   [55] *Ibid.,* April 16, 1857.
[56] Knoxville *Republican,* Oct. 22, 1856.
[57] Frothingham, *Theodore Parker,* p. 448.
[58] *Knoxiana,* Dec., 1856, p. 59.   [59] Knoxville *Republican,* Nov. 12, 1856.

the distinction of being the scene for one of the crucial heats of that preliminary.

Lincoln, in 1858, campaigned with special intensity in the central and western part of the states.[60] While traveling on the railroad to various parts in that region he may very well have gone through Galesburg a number of times,[61] but only one such visit other than his debate with Douglas has been definitely ascertained. This occurred early in the campaign, on August 24, while he was on his way from Henry to Augusta. Arriving in Galesburg on the Peoria train at three-thirty in the afternoon, he stopped at the Bancroft House, where the crowd that gathered urged him to make a short speech.[62] Joseph Medill, who was traveling with Lincoln on this part of his itinerary (between the Ottawa and Freeport debates), remarked in a reminiscence of Lincoln that at this meeting in Galesburg he had an "immense audience."[63] Following the impromptu address the candidate's auditors accompanied him to the station, where he took the train for Augusta.[64]

Douglas also passed through Galesburg on a similar occasion about a month later. Unfortunately the only account of it is a satirical description contributed to the unfriendly Galesburg *Free Democrat,* from which it is impossible to tell just what the nature of his reception was.[65]

The precise reasons why Galesburg was selected as one of the sites for the seven debates between Lincoln and Douglas are not known. Douglas had suggested in reply to Lincoln's challenge that he would be willing to meet him in a joint discussion "at one prominent point in each Congressional District in the State, except the second and sixth districts, where we have both spoken."[66] One of the places mentioned was

[60] See the map following p. 210 in Angle, *Lincoln, 1854–1861.*
[61] It is very probable that it was while traveling on the line between Macomb and Freeport via Galesburg he formulated the famous questions to Douglas, which when put at Freeport reverberated so strongly in the South. For other possible occasions see *ibid.,* pp. 241–54.
[62] *Ibid.,* p. 243.   [63] Sparks, *The Lincoln-Douglas Debates of 1858,* p. 203.
[64] Angle, *Lincoln, 1854–1861,* p. 243.
[65] Galesburg *Free Democrat,* Oct. 4, 1858.
[66] Douglas to Lincoln, July 24, 1858, in Sparks, *The Lincoln-Douglas Debates of 1858,* p. 60.

Galesburg. It was rather west of the center of the fifth district, but lay in the heart of the Military Tract (then more obviously than now a definite geographical province of the state) and because of recent railroad construction was the most accessible point in that area. This railroad building, furthermore, had considerably boomed its significance as a population center. But even if these physical considerations were paramount in its selection, the fact still remained that for a score of years it had earned this distinction by keeping a light shining on the anti-slavery issue, which now the politicians no longer could hide under a bushel.

The Galesburg debate attracted the largest crowd in the series.[67] Not merely the neighboring villages, but Monmouth in Warren County and a group in Mercer County planned special delegations, and extra trains and fares were made available from Burlington, Iowa, and Peoria, Illinois. Eleven carloads came from Chicago. Unfortunately the twenty-four car train from Peoria was held up by a breakdown, and its 2,000 passengers did not arrive till late in the debate. All of the newspaper correspondents were agreed as to the gargantuan character of the assembly, most of them estimating that it approached 20,000. The Democratic *Missouri Republican* and other papers of the same persuasion charged that Republicans had gone to extraordinary pains in assembling their forces by "secret circulars" and by private letters, in order to make a strong showing, but boasted that nevertheless the Democrats outnumbered them two to one. With this calculation the Republicans vehemently disagreed.[68]

During the day and the night preceding the appointed day, October 7, it rained hard,[69] and throughout the day of the debate a strong northwest wind drove the cold fall air into every corner and under every skin, ripping emblems, tearing banners, and sending signs pell-mell all over town. It was such a day as not infrequently blows to tatters the floats of a Knox College

---

[67] The newspaper reports were in general agreement that the Galesburg crowd exceeded its predecessors. The subsequent debates at Quincy and Alton drew substantially smaller crowds; *ibid.*, pp. 378, 380, 387, 436, 496.
[68] *Ibid.*, pp. 329–30, 372–87.   [69] *Ibid.*, p. 378.

Homecoming parade and chills the ardor of returning alumni. At dawn the continued booming of cannon started the demonstrations.[70]

The first big event was the arrival of the Burlington train bringing Douglas and his party from Monmouth. Filling the string of eleven cars was a crowd of partisans from both sides coming from the west, to be followed by another that came over the same track two hours later. The Senator was met at the station by a procession headed by a band and three military companies. A short address of welcome was followed by the presentation from a Lombard College student of a banner beautifully worked by young women of the school, after which the candidate was escorted to the Bonney House. That establishment became the focus of the numerous Democratic delegations which constantly roused Douglas from whatever retirement the place might have offered him. Particularly prominent among the groups of his partisans were "two sets of ladies, each representing a State until the duplicate of States was complete." These women were "dressed in white, with banners representing the States of the Union and the territories, these last having the words, 'Popular Sovereignty' written on their banners." [71]

Lincoln came toward Galesburg from the county seat about noon. With him was the Republican delegation from Knoxville, which was met by a huge procession that moved out from Galesburg "with the military" to greet him. A cavalcade of a hundred ladies and gentlemen was the most striking feature of the combined Republican delegations, which in following their candidate into the city made a parade that even after marching past the Galesburg town square and crossing its own track had not yet brought its rear within the town limits.[72] Lincoln was accompanied to the home of Mr. Henry R. Sanderson, one of the early graduates of Knox College, where a reception speech was delivered by Thomas Gold Frost, a trustee of the same institution. At this point Miss Ada Hurd rode up to the head of the troop of riders and presented Lincoln with a handsomely embroidered banner inscribed as from the Re-

[70] *Ibid.*, p. 382.　　　[71] *Ibid.*, pp. 377–86.　　　[72] *Ibid.*, p. 379.

publican ladies of Galesburg. A group of Lombard College students, matching the action of their colleagues who had favored his opponent, gave Lincoln even another banner.

Both sides were amply supplied with signs and placards. The Galesburg *Free Democrat* was especially proud of those expressing Republican sentiments,[73] but the pro-Douglas St. Louis *Missouri Republican* (the confusion of nomenclature indicates the complicated political scene of the late fifties) regarded these exhibits of the Lincoln supporters as "dirty designs and beastly caricatures." [74] To one of these campaign devices one of Lincoln's most careful biographers assigns special significance. He remarks that at Galesburg we have "for the first time . . . a description of a campaign legend which played great and effective part in the contest"—a legend which was to be even a "stronger influence in electing Lincoln to the Presidency." The legend inscribed upon one of the Galesburg banners was: "SMALL-FISTED FARMERS, MUDSILLS OF SOCIETY, GREASY MECHANICS, FOR A. LINCOLN." This was a direct hit at a notorious remark made by a Southern senator who in defending slavery remarked that the unskilled toilers necessary to society were like the "mudsills" needed to furnish foundations for a structure erected in soggy ground.[75] Thus the Northern farmers and industrial workers were urged to feel themselves degraded by the black workers' slavery and aroused to slavery as a political issue.

The time for the debate was two o'clock. The speaking stand was erected at the east end of the chief building of Knox College where the wall would break the wind. The platform was gaily decorated with flags and streamers, and immediately above it was a great sign bearing the inscription "Knox College for Lincoln." Already at noon the crowd began to collect; for an hour before the debate was to begin, more than ten thousand people stood in the chilly wind waiting the arrival of the principals. In the meantime a pro-Lincoln speaker filled in the time. As the hour drew near, Lincoln and Douglas drove up

[73] See the long list, Galesburg *Free Democrat*, Oct. 9, 1858.
[74] Sparks, *The Lincoln-Douglas Debates of 1858*, p. 376.
[75] Beveridge, *Abraham Lincoln, 1809–1858*, II, 677–78.

side by side in two carriages accompanied by a large procession on horse and on foot.[76] James Knox, of Knoxville, acted as chairman of the debate and introduced the first speaker, Stephen A. Douglas.

Douglas opened the argument with a reference to his appearance in Knox County four years previously when he had defended his action on the Kansas-Nebraska Bill. To very many of his auditors that remark brought to mind his debate on that occasion with Jonathan Blanchard. Douglas continued with a review and defense of his political behavior since that event and an analysis of the political situation. He then proceeded to embarrass Lincoln by taking advantage of the close division of party power that had always existed in the region around Galesburg. "My friend Lincoln," he said, "finds it extremely difficult to manage a debate in the central part of the State, where there is a mixture of men from the North and the South." Reenforcing this point with quoted excerpts from Lincoln's previous speeches, he maintained that Lincoln posed as a bold abolitionist in northern Illinois but as an old Whig farther south.[77]

This charge Lincoln did not meet very effectively in his refutation,[78] and Douglas, immediately after he opened his rejoinder, put this particular barb deep into his rival again. "All I asked of him," said Douglas, "is that he should deliver the speech that he has made here today in Coles County instead of in old Knox." The excitement of the crowd reached its climax as Douglas pricked his opponent with this point. An uproar arose, and catcalls, groans, cheers, and other noises prevented the speaker from proceeding.[79] Douglas asked the crowd to give him the same respectful hearing they had given Lincoln, and the latter arose to say, "I hope that silence will be preserved." [80] Douglas's attack on him along this line worried Lincoln enough that he devoted a considerable part of his opening speech at the next debate in Quincy to counter it.[81]

[76] Galesburg *Free Democrat*, Oct. 9, 1858.
[77] Sparks, *The Lincoln-Douglas Debates of 1858*, pp. 339, 342.
[78] *Ibid.*, p. 348.   [79] *Ibid.*, p. 365.
[80] *Ibid.*, p. 366.   [81] *Ibid.*, pp. 397–400.

As Lincoln himself pointed out, much of what both he and Douglas had to say at Galesburg in this the fifth of the joint debates was not new. Nevertheless, as Beveridge points out, Lincoln brought out two new points at Galesburg. One was his contention that inability to proclaim a doctrine everywhere was no test of its truth. Republicans could not present their program in the South because of hostility to it, but neither could Douglas advocate his democracy in Russia.[82] Lincoln made one of the best hits of his speech when he suggested what had become true after the Freeport debate, that Douglas himself was becoming less popular in the South. According to the reporter, Lincoln's speech at this point was five times interrupted by the crowd: "Great Cheers and laughter"—"Loud cheers"—"Applause"—"Immense Cheering"—"Tremendous Applause." [83]

The second innovation made by Lincoln in this speech was his emphasis on the moral aspect of the slavery issue. It was true that he could not have discovered a community in Illinois more friendly than Galesburg to his forcing of this consideration into the argument. Douglas was probably provoked by this point especially to reassert vigorously in his rebuttal that Lincoln would not make the same speech farther south in the state. For good or ill, however, Lincoln made the point, and made it well. "Douglas," said Lincoln, "discards the idea that there is anything wrong in slavery." Hence came Douglas's vaunted indifference whether slavery was "voted up or down" just so that "popular sovereignty" was fulfilled. "Judge Douglas declares that if any community want slavery, they have a right to have it." Such an attitude Lincoln rebuked in some of the most forceful passages found in his campaign speeches. Twice in his Galesburg address did Lincoln deal with this problem. The second time he fell back for an effective quotation on Henry Clay, hero of many an old Whig in his audience. After repeating it, Lincoln paraphrased it in what is perhaps the best and most quoted passage from his Galesburg address: "He is

[82] Beveridge, *Abraham Lincoln, 1809–1858*, II, 678.
[83] Sparks, *The Lincoln-Douglas Debates of 1858*, p. 351.

blowing out the moral lights around us, when he contends that
whoever wants slaves has a right to hold them." [84]

The contest of the principals of the campaign was accompanied by a very intensive local campaign. In fact, at that time
the senatorial selection lay with the state legislators, and the
canvass for those and other local officers was inseparable from
the race for the greater prize. Probably the high point in the
Republican agitation within the limits of Galesburg was a
meeting at which Jonathan Blanchard spoke, at the request of
forty-six citizens who published a letter in the *Free Democrat*.[85]
The wings of that stormy petrel were partly clipped, for he had
lost his presidency of Knox following an acrimonious dispute
among trustees and alumni, but the great crowd which turned
out to hear him once more discuss the political issues of the
day applauded vigorously at his entrance, and upon his mounting the platform rose and gave him a great ovation. It had
been the ruthless self-righteousness of men such as he, after all,
which had forced the issue of slavery so that now even politicians like Lincoln and Douglas could no longer evade it. His
former colleague on the faculty, Professor Hurd, introduced
him. The radical educator and preacher rewarded his auditors
with an address exceeding two hours in length. He began with
the statement that he had never been able to find vital issues
distinguishing Whigs and Democrats, but now the issue between Republicans and Democrats was clear; it was "Slavery
and Slavery Extension." The succeeding discourse was not so
much a pro-Lincoln speech as a blistering anti-Douglas blast,
but it showed clearly that the crisis was causing the radical
abolitionists to find common cause with the more moderate
Republican Party.[86] Indeed, for a time in the summer there
was talk of Jonathan Blanchard being the Republican candidate for Congress. Two papers in the district gave him their
endorsement, but he almost immediately withdrew.[87]

As election day drew near partisan feelings in Galesburg became especially bitter. Newspaper evidences of this condition

[84] *Ibid.*, pp. 352–53, 360–62.   [85] Galesburg *Free Democrat*, Sept. 1, 1858.
[86] *Ibid.*, Sept. 4, 1858.
[87] Knoxville *Republican*, Aug. 4, Aug. 11, Aug. 18, 1858.

are numerous, and though their authenticity may not go un-
questioned, certain Republican accusations reveal the tenseness
of the situation. The pro-Douglas candidate for the legislature
was accused of advertising two hundred railroad construction
jobs near Macomb in order to get that many Swedes, who
were supposedly Republican voters, out of the district over
election day. Supporters of the same candidate, it was alleged,
had printed misleading facsimiles of Republican ballots, to be
used (in those days ballots were not publicly printed) to trick
the unwary into electing a legislator who would vote for
Douglas.[88]

Election day found the Galesburg region bogged down with
such mud and such incessant downpourings as were remarkable,
even for Illinois. "For days beforehand the rains began to
descend and the floods to come, and on that day the weather
gear was in good working order." Thus the *Free Democrat*
apologized for the disappointing Republican majority in the
county, saying that it had been almost an impossibility for the
farmers to get out to the polls. In Galesburg, however, there
was little cause for shame; the vote was 776 for Lincoln and 271
for Douglas, a three-to-one majority. Knox County went Republican by a vote of approximately 2,900 to 1,900.[89]

The platform of the Republican Party was apparently satisfy-
ing enough to the Galesburg radicals to win their support, but
their principles had been (and probably so far as convictions
were concerned remained) much more extreme than the moderate anti-slavery expressions of Lincoln and other relatively
recent Whigs who had joined the Republican ranks. There
were many men in Galesburg who for over twenty years had
been much more reckless in their opposition to the "peculiar
institution" of the South. For expediency's sake they perhaps
contented themselves with an indulgent smile when the *Free
Democrat* approved of the catcalls and hisses which had interrupted a local meeting when "Bob" Ingersoll designated the
Republicans as abolitionists.[90] The editor was right enough in

[88] Galesburg *Free Democrat*, Oct. 29, 1858.   [89] *Ibid.*, Nov. 3 and 10, 1858.
[90] *Ibid.*, Nov. 2, 1860.

denying that Republicans were abolitionists, but in Galesburg there were abolitionists in numbers who were now Republicans. For all of them the early spring of 1860 brought high hopes, for just north of Galesburg the town of Henderson, which for twenty-seven years had loyally adhered to the Democratic Party, elected a local Republican ticket for the first time.[91]

The excited interest with which Galesburg followed the nominations of 1860 is revealed by the fact that one of its citizens collected subscriptions in order that "telegraphic dispatches" of what happened at the Democratic convention in Charleston, South Carolina, would be received in the community.[92] When the Chicago Republican convention was held, the *Free Democrat* remarked that "the city is half emptied." "Those who thought they could not get away, as the time drew near became uneasy which grew into restlessness, seriously affecting business. One after another they yielded, put a change of linen into their carpet sacks, and as the train came steaming over the hill north of the city, the last man might be seen moving toward the depot with more haste than dignity."[93] When news of Lincoln's nomination reached Galesburg, the *Free Democrat* got out an extra, the distribution of which could be followed around town by the cheers that greeted the tidings that it carried.[94]

Knox College gave the Republican candidate its formal endorsement in an unprecedented manner. On June 29 the faculty voted that the honorary degree of Doctor of Laws be conferred upon Lincoln,[95] and presented its recommendation to the board of trustees on July 3. It was so ordered by the board.[96] Two days later this action was announced at the Commencement exercises and "elicited great applause from the audience."[97] The doctorate thus conferred upon Lincoln was the first ever granted by Knox College, not even a Doctor of Divinity hav-

[91] *Ibid.*, April 6, 1860.
[92] *Ibid.*, April 24, 1860.
[93] *Ibid.*, May 18, 1860.
[94] *Ibid.*, May 22, 1860.
[95] "Faculty Minutes," MSS.
[96] "Trustees' Minutes," MSS.
[97] Galesburg *Free Democrat*, July 6, 1860.

ing been created during nearly a quarter of a century of the college's existence.[98]

In August, 1860, a great Republican rally was held in Galesburg, which the Knoxville *Republican* asserted was attended by a crowd conservatively estimated at 20,000. The speaking stands were erected on an open space in front of the residence of George Washington Gale. There was a delegation of 700 from Macomb, a group of 1,800 from Quincy; thirty cars, it was said, had brought people in on the Peoria and Oquawka Railroad; and over the Knoxville Road alone, 2,000 wagons, it was estimated, had been driven into Galesburg.[99]

The Knox College students will probably never again see their campus committed so openly to a party's purpose as it had been during the last half-dozen years.[100] In October, 1860, it turned out a delegation of twenty students to attend the Republican demonstration at Rock Island, equipped with appropriate banners, mottoes, and other campaign paraphernalia. It was asserted that among the students at Knox College there were only two Douglas Democrats.[101]

The genius of the Galesburg colony had been to agitate the anti-slavery issue and to propagate it as a principle in religion and in politics. This was suited to the essentially academic character of the settlement. No Galesburg politician at this time reaped practical party profits of more than an ordinary sort by the emergence and success of the new party. None of Galesburg's soldiers in the war that followed became especially noted; the person that most nearly rose to fame in the conflict was a noncombatant, the nurse "Mother" Mary Bickerdyke.

Though this could not in the autumn of 1860 be clearly foreseen, the anti-slavery contest was reaching its conclusion as the fighting on the battlefields began. But in the little college town this eve of victory for the cause was one of mingled bit-

[98] Based upon a careful examination of the trustees' records.

[99] Knoxville *Republican*, Aug. 22, 1860.

[100] For examples of student expressions on politics see articles in *Knoxiana* and *Oak Leaf*. An especially good example is "Editor's Table," *Oak Leaf*, Jan., 1857, pp. 126–27.

[101] Galesburg *Semi-Weekly Free Democrat*, Oct. 12, 1860.

terness and exultation, for it was torn apart by its own internal strife. Even as its precious mission of emancipation neared completion, the zealot spirit that had carried it so far was tearing at the community itself and brought the career of the college as a reforming agency to an end.

Thereby hangs the last chapter of this tale.

❧ XIX ❧

Dissension Ends the "Martyr Age"

Sir, when a question of this kind seizes on the religious sentiments of mankind, and comes to be discussed in religious assemblies of the clergy and laity, there is always to be expected, or always to be feared, a great degree of excitement. . . . In all such disputes there will sometimes be found men with whom every thing is absolute; absolutely wrong, or absolutely right. . . . They are apt, too, to think that nothing is good but what is perfect and that there are no compromises or modifications to be made in consideration of difference of opinion or in deference to other men's judgment.[1]

COMMENCEMENT TIME OF 1857, twenty years after Knox was chartered, was a bitter time for Gale. He might have expected to be honored as the patriarch, as the chief founder and the longtime leader of the college; but instead the students of one of the literary societies voted that his picture should be taken down from the wall of the society room and "placed out of sight." The other society concurred in voting to support the seniors, all but one of whom were refusing to appear in the graduation exercises in protest against Gale's success in effecting the removal of Blanchard from the presidency. So many of the undergraduates declared that they did not intend to return to Knox the next fall that it seemed doubtful whether the student organizations would have the membership to carry on, and therefore they made preparations to wind up their affairs, such as the publication of their literary magazines, and elected special trustees to act as custodians of

[1] Daniel Webster, speech in the Senate, March 7, 1850.

their society effects. Having done this they adjourned *sine die*.[2]

It looked as if Knox College, having sown the wind, was reaping the whirlwind. Destruction of old political loyalties and religious fidelities had their price—the loss of former unity and harmony. The little world of Knox College echoed the clamor, debate, and partisanship of the greater world in its complaints, arguments, and factionalism. As the slavery issues disrupted Presbyterian-Congregational cooperation abroad, they progressively strained and ruptured the denominational cohesion of the Galesburg colony, and for reasons which were not simply sectarian there came to be two parties, one led by Gale that was Presbyterian and the other by Blanchard that was Congregational.

Dissension in the college first came into the open in 1849 at the same time that Blanchard was charged in the national religious press with being "first and foremost in the assault upon Presbyterianism at the West." The opening shots were fired by the Gale party in a meeting of the trustees on April 27, 1849. Previous notices gave no indication of what was to happen, for the board had been called together by the "building committee" for a special session with no notice that other business such as the election of new board members would be discussed; in fact, several members of the board were never notified that the board would meet at all. Only fourteen of twenty-one trustees were present, but the supporters of Gale had a bare majority and they proceeded to elect Orville H. Browning of Quincy and William Selden Gale, son of the founder, to the board.[3] President Blanchard knew that if this election stood he "must roast over a slow fire from that date," [4] and in retaliation he tendered his resignation, to take effect after the ensuing Commencement. The president's utterances were severe and were interpreted by those not his friends as "threatening to injure the institution." James Knox, a prominent Whig politician from Knoxville, moved that the resigna-

---

[2] Minutes of the Adelphi and Gnothautii societies for June 24 and 25, 1857, MSS.

[3] Knox College, "Trustees' Minutes," MSS, April 27, June 26 and 27, 1849.

[4] Blanchard to S. P. Chase, June 30, 1849, Chase Papers, Library of Congress.

tion be accepted, but after "further remarks" by Blanchard "explanatory of his language," this motion was indefinitely postponed.[5]

The fat was now in the fire. At the June meeting, the fullest meeting of the board for sometime,[6] Blanchard was in the ascendancy. Browning did not appear, but Selden Gale, who did, was refused his seat by a motion which passed by Blanchard's casting vote. The question was raised as to the propriety of this refusal to honor the April elections, but the Blanchard majority ignored the question and proceeded to another election to fill vacancies on the board. At this point Gale and his minority (J. G. Sanborn, Losey, Ferris, Milton Kimball, James Bunce, James Bull, S. F. Dolbear, and W. S. Gale) withdrew, in order to arrest further business of the board by leaving it with what they asserted was no quorum. The residue, however, proceeded with business and elected six trustees to fill the alleged vacancies,[7] the men thus chosen being Norman Churchill, Silas Willard, A. S. Martin, and the Reverend L. H. Parker, all of the Galesburg settlement, and the Reverend G. F. Magoun of Galena and Moses Pettingil of Peoria.[8] It would seem to indicate some careful preparation that Magoun should have been at hand immediately to take his seat on the board.[9]

A legal battle which immediately followed involved questions about the charter, the status of trustees under the charter, and the technicalities of a quorum of the board. Browning, one of the leading attorneys of the state, advised W. S. Gale within two weeks that "there can be doubt of the illegality of the election" of the six new Blanchard men, and suggested *quo warranto* proceedings against them.[10] When action was taken against the six men in October they appeared by counsel, and

---

[5] Knox College "Trustees' Minutes"; Galesburg *Free Democrat*, Oct. 14, 1857.

[6] Horatio Foote attended for the second time since his election in 1845; Milton Kimball for the only time since his election in 1845; Butler made one of his rare appearances.

[7] Galesburg *Free Democrat*, Oct. 14, 1857.

[8] Burlington (Iowa) *Hawk-eye*, Aug. 2, 1849.

[9] Knox College, "Trustees' Minutes," June 27, 1849.

[10] O. H. Browning to W. S. Gale, July 12, 1849, transcript of letter in Knox College Library.

the case was continued until the April term of 1850.[11] Blanchard, on the other side, had immediately turned for legal advice to Salmon P. Chase of Cincinnati.

Chase and Browning offer an interesting contrast that illuminates some of the differences between the two parties on the college board during the next decade. In his request for Chase's "opinion and advice," Blanchard had said, "I have no claim on which I can claim this unless it is that since my coming to be president of Knox College I have honestly endeavored to act as I did in Cincinnati against the slave power." [12] Blanchard was not presumptuous in this expectation, for Chase had become famous for his willingness to take anti-slavery cases and had gone into politics with the Liberty and Free Soil parties. Blanchard had been associated with Chase in the beginnings of the Liberty Party in Ohio. It was typical of Chase that he honestly subordinated his politics to his strong anti-slavery principles. In contrast, Browning was a cautious and somewhat disappointed Whig politician, who disliked slavery but was just as much concerned that Negroes keep their place; he opposed emancipation and supported colonization as a means of getting rid of the Negro problem. Though he, like Chase, eventually found his way to high place in the Republican Party, he left the Whigs slowly and as he did helped to frame the Illinois Republican platform conservatively so as to accommodate "Old Whigs." Even when emancipation did come in 1862 he regarded it as a calamity.[13]

In view of their later prominent roles in the establishment of the Republican Party, a legal contest between Chase and Browning would have been interesting. Investigation, however, showed that all elections by the board except those at the very beginning of its history had been illegal and the way was thus cleared for a compromise by retracing the board's actions for

---

[11] Galesburg *Free Democrat*, Oct. 14, 1857.

[12] Blanchard to Chase, June 30, 1849, Chase Papers, Library of Congress.

[13] *Dictionary of American Biography*. Many direct expressions of Browning's beliefs and actions are set forth in his *Diary*, Illinois Historical Collections, Vol. XX.

several years back.[14] In March, 1850, it was agreed that Blanchard should recall his threatened resignation, that all trustee elections before April 27, 1849, should be confirmed and all those thereafter be voided, and that five new trustees should be elected.[15] This was done in such a way as to give each faction twelve votes, exclusive of Blanchard's vote as *ex officio* trustee.[16] It was agreed to preserve "an equilibrium or balance of power" which should give neither Presbyterians nor Congregationalists, the friends of Professor Gale nor those of President Blanchard, a decided preponderance.[17] Early in April the *quo warranto* action in the circuit court was formally dropped.[18]

The community had been deeply involved in the argument. Two newspapers (the first papers established in Galesburg at this time, 1849) had taken sides in the controversy, the *Knox Intelligencer* favoring Gale and the *Northwestern Gazetteer* supporting Blanchard. It was now hoped that the bitter contest, which had attracted wide attention,[19] was closed. As the Knoxville *Journal* remarked, the troubles had been so serious as to alarm the friends of the college for its future welfare, and these were rejoiced that "to all human appearance the Board is one again." [20]

As it proved this was only apparently true. Even a committee appointed by the colony church and headed by its new pastor,

[14] Galesburg *Free Democrat*, Oct., 1857; Bascom, "Autobiography," MS, pp. 196-97.

[15] Galesburg *Free Democrat*, Sept. 20, 1857.

[16] Scrutiny of the votes in the trustees' meetings shows that the Gale and Blanchard groups were composed as follows:

Of those about whose legal membership there was no question, Gale, Losey, and Sanborn were Gale men; and G. H. Wright, Chambers, and Simmons were Blanchard supporters; three for each side.

Of those whose previous elections were confirmed, the following were Gale men: Ferris, Bunce, Bull, Knox, Kimball, Dolbear; the following were supporters of Blanchard: Bascom, Holyoke, Butler, Farnham, Foote, Colton, Sanderson; Gale six, Blanchard seven.

Of the new trustees elected, Browning, Marcus Osborn and W. E. Withrow acted with the Gale men, while L. S. Stanley and S. G. Wright sided with Blanchard; three for Gale, two for Blanchard.

[17] Flavel Bascom, a trustee at the time, in Galesburg *Free Democrat*, Sept. 23, 1857.

[18] Knoxville *Journal*, April 10, 1850.

[19] *Western Citizen*, April 5, 1850.   [20] Knoxville *Journal*, April 10, 1850.

Reverend Flavel Bascom, to compose the personal quarrel between the principals was not entirely successful.[21] The local fussing was in fact immediately renewed by the church trial of C. W. Gilbert for the alleged harsh, ill-mannered, extravagant, and unbrotherly manner in which he had expressed hostility to Blanchard.[22] In the spring of 1851 the first permanent rupture in the colony occurred when Gale and his Presbyterian party withdrew from the mother church to establish one of their own with a strictly Presbyterian polity. All of the local college trustees who had supported Gale in the board's troubles of 1849 and 1850 followed him into this new church.[23]

The factors in the college and church troubles that came to a head at this time, while manifesting themselves along denominational lines, were also political and personal. Gale, as the leading founder of the community, naturally expected to be preeminent in its affairs; Blanchard on the other hand was by nature inclined to find the foreground and hardly disposed to subordinate himself, even though it might look as if he was trying to "thrust out of Knox College the counsels of the old men." [24] Gale undoubtedly resented Blanchard's opposition to the selection of Gale's son as trustee and treasurer.[25] But the greatest single personal factor was probably the conservative direction in which Gale's religious and political opinions had moved since sometime in the mid-forties. By 1850 he was certainly less liberal in his ideas about denominational connections, and though an anti-slavery man he was less aggressive in his espousal of abolitionist principles.[26]

---

[21] "Church Records," MSS, Book B, Sept. 2, 1850, pp. 120–22; Galesburg *Free Democrat*, Oct. 14, 1857.

[22] "Separate Sessions Records," First Church of Galesburg, MSS, pp. 33–42, 64.

[23] Muelder, *Church History in a Puritan Colony*, pp. 44–47, 65–66.

[24] Bascom, "Autobiography," pp. 195–96; Knox College, "Trustees' Minutes," June 27, 1849.

[25] George Churchill, Scrapbook. There were unsubstantiated hints of charges against Gale for misappropriation of funds ("Church Records," Book B, Sept. 2, 1850).

[26] J. P. Williston to Southwick Davis, July 27, 1857, Galesburg *Daily Free Democrat*, Aug. 6, 1857; Galesburg *Semi-Weekly Free Democrat*, Aug. 17, 1860; Blanchard to Gale, Dec. 11, 1848, *Report on Knox College, 1861*, p. 49; Muelder, "Congregationalists and Presbyterians in the Early History of the Galesburg

When the contest first came into the open in 1849 there was also direct evidence that civil politics played a part. Blanchard wrote Salmon P. Chase that Gale's party objected to Blanchard's work for the Free Soil Party, for during the presidential campaign of 1848 he had stood as candidate for presidential elector on that ticket. According to Blanchard, Gale was aided in his schemes by a "rabid Whig lawyer," already on the board, in order to elect "two more Whig lawyers" to the board. On the other hand, so boasted Blanchard, the six new trustees who had been elected by his supporters were "good, honest, upright Anti-Slavery men, everyone of whom, but one, I know, vote against slavery, and that one did not vote against Free Soil." [27]

At this time there were still many men of strong anti-slavery convictions who did not regard parties organized on an anti-slavery basis as the best means to achieve abolition of slavery. This was especially true of the Whigs, who were inclined to believe that the chief effect of the Liberty and Free Soil parties was to take away votes from the Whig candidates and thus to help Democrats win elections. During most of the forties the Whig Party had missed election victories around Galesburg by a margin less than the Liberty or Free Soil Party vote. This may well have increased the hostility to Blanchard of three key men in the college dispute: Selden Gale,[28] a Whig leader in Galesburg; O. H. Browning, a Whig leader from Quincy; [29] and the leading Whig in Knox County, James Knox. The last of these politicians was, apparently, the "rabid Whig lawyer" who did much of the parliamentary maneuvering against the college president.[30] It is significant that the trouble for Blanchard should have come to a head within less than a year after Knox had been elected to the board; he had been defeated for Congress in 1846 in a very close contest in which the Liberty vote in the district had been nearly one thousand,

Churches," *Papers in Illinois History and Transactions for the Year 1937*, pp. 53-71.
   [27] Blanchard to Chase, June 30, 1849, Chase Papers.
   [28] William Selden Gale, "Autobiography" (MS, Knox College Library), p. 2.
   [29] In 1848, when Blanchard was on the electoral slate for the Free Soil presidential candidate, Browning was on the electoral slate for the Whigs.
   [30] Knox College, "Trustees' Records," MSS, June 26, 1849.

which was between two and three times the margin that Knox needed to give him a majority over the Democratic victor.[31]

It is certainly true that Blanchard's party on the board and the six men whom they tried to elect to the board were much more aggressive abolitionists than the men of Gale's party. Blanchard's supporters included the Reverend John Waters, Matthew Chambers, Eli Farnham, William Holyoke, and Horatio Foote, and among those whom they tried to elect were the Reverend L. H. Parker and Moses Pettingil. A survey of the preceding pages will reveal that these men had been very active as abolitionists and had participated prominently in the Liberty and Free Soil parties. In these respects they had excelled every member of Gale's party (except for Gale himself until the middle forties). Of course Browning, Knox, and Selden Gale were to figure rather prominently in the new Republican Party late in the fifties, but the same could be said of hundreds of other politicians who were still being prudent in 1850.

For two or three years a formal peace was preserved among the trustees. Samuel Guild Wright, who was one of the trustees accepted under the compromise of 1850, and who as a conciliator in 1849 had personally criticized both Gale and Blanchard for their faults in the fuss, noted in his journal that the board meetings of 1851 and 1852 were harmonious.[32] Also during the height of the troubles of 1849 the colony church received as its new pastor Flavel Bascom, who now became an active member of the college board [33] and immediately assumed the role of keeper of the peace. He soon became chairman of

[31] The vote stood as follows: Democrats, 8,843; Whigs, 8,456; Liberty Party, 947 (Pease, *Illinois Election Returns*). Knox had been elected to the board of trustees on March 29, 1843, and was listed as a member of the board in the *Catalogue* for 1843. There is no evidence that he ever accepted the election; he attended no meetings; and on March, 1844, the board accepted his resignation. A Whig politician would have been embarrassed during the middle forties by public connections with an abolitionist college. It was not until January 27, 1848, that he was again elected to the board; he attended his first meeting June 27, 1848.

[32] Samuel G. Wright, "Journal," MS, July 2 and 9, 1849; June 30, 1851; June 14, 1852.

[33] He had been elected in 1845 but never attended a meeting until after becoming pastor of the Galesburg church.

the executive committee and for the next six years continued in
that responsibility, the burdens of which were all the more
trying because injudicious action might upset the delicate fac-
tional balance on the board.[34] In his role as arbiter Bascom
was not altogether neutral, for he was one of the most notorious abolitionists in Illinois, and though solidly connected
to Presbyterian [35] as well as Congregational organizations, he
was by the force of the slavery issue carried along with his
Galesburg church more and more in the direction of Congregationalism. Though he meant to be conscientiously an arbiter
of the board's difficulties, he realized that he allowed himself
to be drawn into its arguments on the more radical side. Later,
as an old man who had watched hundreds of communities take
root in the prairies and groves of Illinois, he became doubtful
about the colony method of settlement. Looking back over
his many years on the Illinois frontier he noted that though
the homogeneity of population in a colony had certain advantages, it also caused trouble, for it implied "an equality
in standing, which is very apt to beget a jealousy of each others
influence, in the management of affairs. Teachers, agents, and
all who are entrusted with any official responsibility, are almost
sure to be accused of wrong doing, and discord and strife are
almost inevitable." With all his disposition to be philosophical
about the disturbances in Galesburg, at the time they occurred
Bascom believed that the Gale party was to blame for continuing the unrest, for they "waited and watched and worked"
for the balance on the board to turn in their favor that they
might remove Blanchard. Hence, "though the volcano was
capped" in 1850, "its fires were still smoldering and rumbling
during the six years that followed." [36]

Blanchard was criticized by his enemies for using the college
as a "propagandist agency for the spread of the peculiar views
of the president." [37] Gale complained early in 1853 that the

[34] Bascom, "Autobiography," pp. 197–204.
[35] He was stated clerk of the Ottawa Presbytery in 1847, and of the Chicago
Presbytery in 1849.
[36] Bascom, "Autobiography," pp. 197–208.
[37] H. Curtis in the New York *Evangelist*, reprinted in the Galesburg *Free
Democrat*, Feb. 3, 1860.

Congregationalists made "pretensions to greater zeal for reforms" and that this attracted some to their membership, but "the best portion of the community was getting tired of those agitations that are full of sound and fury ending in nothing but harm to those most prominent and injury to the causes they advocate." [38] It was true that Blanchard had no compunctions about using the college as a sounding board for his ideas. Of these so many were distinctly radical and unpopular in character, and these so freely aired, that cautious persons feared for the reputation of the college. O. H. Browning and others alleged that there was "abroad a wide-spread distrust of the prudence of the President, and a dissatisfaction on account of his violent and partisan character, and that many were deterred from sending their sons to Knox College." [39]

A public performance by Blanchard early in 1854 revealed the continuing of his differences with Gale. The occasion was an Anti-Nebraska Bill meeting in Galesburg at which political differences that had divided many persons of anti-slavery opinions were submerged in mutual wrath against violations of the Compromise of 1820. Blanchard somewhat spoiled the harmony by "sparring on a side issue" with Gale. His subject was the "aggression" of the slavery forces in establishing at Galena a Presbyterian theological seminary "which so far as a printed constitution and the solemn votes of church judicatories go, allows every slave-holding Presbytery of Missouri in its particular connection to choose one trustee." Gale responded by admitting that he was a director of the seminary and that the institution was connected with New School presbyteries in Missouri, but he declared that these had "few private members" who owned slaves and no ministers guilty of that sin. Gale was very evidently irritated that Blanchard raised this point on this particular occasion.[40]

As if he had not made enemies enough, Blanchard pulled still another "cause" from his quiver of reform and sent his barbs flying against Masonic lodges and other secret societies. He had become nationally identified with the anti-secret so-

[38] Gale to Lockwood, Feb. 15, 1853, Calkins Papers, Knox College Library.
[39] Clipping from the Quincy *Whig* in Churchill Scrapbook No. 1.
[40] Galesburg *Free Democrat*, Feb. 16, 1854.

ciety crusade while in Cincinnati, but upon removing to Galesburg he found a majority of the community were "political anti-Masons," thus faithfully reflecting the anti-Masonic agitation that had arisen in the Burned-over District of New York. He therefore held his peace on the subject until secret organizations began to intrude themselves into the settlement.[41] About 1850 he renewed his attack, aroused especially by the activities of the Sons of Temperance, the secrecy evil of which he would not condone, however commendable the objectives of the fraternity. Beginning in the spring and on into the fall a series of articles in the Oquawka *Spectator* revealed the irritation which he provoked in central-western Illinois.[42] And in October of that year an article by him in the *Western Citizen* gave even wider circulation to his hostility to secret societies. His discourse on this subject before the state meeting of Congregationalists in June was printed in pamphlet form. In fairness to Blanchard it should be noted that the Congregationalists on this occasion had concurred by condemning the Sons of Temperance and secret organizations in general,[43] and that the Galesburg church that year and later refused these temperance crusaders the use of the church building and curtly snubbed them in public religious ceremonies.[44] Even in Galesburg, however, Blanchard's strict stand on this issue offended some of the citizenry and there was considerable local controversy.[45] The agitation over secret organizations in the midfifties had serious political implications because of the rise of a political party, called the Know-Nothing Party precisely because it surrounded itself in secrecy. Members of both older political parties were attracted to its membership, and politicians such as Browning eventually aimed to attract them from that allegiance to the Republican Party.[46]

[41] Galesburg *Semi-Weekly Free Democrat*, Nov. 5, 1859.
[42] Oquawka *Spectator*, May 7, June 12 and 19, July 3, Aug. 14, 21, and 28, Sept. 4, 1850.
[43] *Western Citizen*, Oct. 1, 1850.
[44] Knoxville *Journal*, Sept. 17, 1850; Nov. 7, 1854; Galesburg *Free Democrat*, June 22, 1854.
[45] Knoxville *Journal*, Oct. 15, 1850; Oquawka *Spectator*, June 12 and 19, July 3, and Sept. 4, 1850.
[46] Browning, *Diary*, p. 237.

Much of the internal tension on the college board of trustees was undoubtedly not apparent to the general public. Outwardly, in fact, the period from 1850 to 1857 was a time of great improvement and building during which the school enjoyed a prosperity it was not again to achieve until the closing decades of the century. For example, students, most of the faculty, and even trustees would probably not know how Blanchard outmaneuvered Gale in 1853 in the selection of a new principal for the Female Department. When this position became vacant, Blanchard wrote for help from the Willistons, the wealthy patrons of the college in the East, and warned them that Gale had a candidate with whom to fill the position and that it was important that a woman be secured "over whom Gale might exercise less influence to pervert her mind, as he tries to pervert other minds and poison them against me." [47] Evidently the Willistons obliged, for late in the summer of 1855 a woman whose traveling expenses from the East to Galesburg, amounting to $50, had been paid by J. P. Williston, arrived to become principal of the Female Department.[48]

Gale's most important supporter on the board throughout the fifties was O. H. Browning, the only one of the trustees whose election had been disputed between 1849 and 1850 who had later been confirmed in his membership by the compromise. He regularly attended board meetings, and his diary shows the closest kind of association with Gale, at whose home he always stayed while in town. When one recalls the Gale of the Great Revival in the twenties and the Gale of the early abolitionist crusade, it seems hardly plausible that during the fifties he could have been the intimate and collaborator of Browning. The latter was distinctly conservative both in religion and politics; in religion he preferred Old School Presbyterians; in politics he abhorred "ultraism" and "rash counsels." He had the flexible traits of a man who by 1856 was attempting to make a place in the Republican Party elastic enough to accommodate former Whigs and Democrats with Know-Nothings and foreigners.[49]

[47] Blanchard to S. Williston, July 5, 1853, Williston Papers.
[48] Eunice Hayward; see Blotter Book C, MS, Aug. 24, 1855.
[49] Browning, Diary, pp. 237, 407.

That Gale should be yoked with Browning reveals probably better than anything else the bitterness of his quarrel with Blanchard, or perhaps it reveals the tiredness of an old man who repudiated much of his own youth by saying he would have a minister "who will neither fight his political enemies nor run for Congress, one who will have less of politics in preaching, and more the unadulterated word of truth. . . . Party politics, ultraism of all sorts, and sectarian propagandizing have too long desecrated the pulpit and polluted the public mind." [50]

It was Browning who upset the balance in the board. Until 1853 the equilibrium had been fairly maintained, for when two Blanchard supporters left in 1851, one by death and the other by resignation, new trustees were chosen who put their weight on the same side.[51] However, in 1853 it was reported that Peter Butler, another Blanchard man, was no longer a resident of the state and a vacancy therefore existed on the board. For the next three years at each annual meeting there was discussion of this information, but though the vacancy was confirmed in 1855, no action was taken to fill it. Finally in June, 1856, the board voted to fill this gap in its membership, after agreeing that no man should be accepted until two thirds of the trustees would vote for the candidate named. Several men were proposed, but there was "great strife between New School Presbyterians and Congregationalists," and when voted upon, none of the nominees could be elected. Finally a "recess" of fifteen minutes was taken for "consultation," and when formal business resumed Browning proposed a Baptist and a fellow townsman from Quincy, the meat packer and banker, Caleb Pomeroy. Apparently the friends of Blanchard had been persuaded by Browning that Pomeroy would probably be neutral, for he was unanimously elected.[52] But it immediately became evident in succeeding meetings that Browning had introduced a faithful follower of his own faction;

[50] Letter from Gale in the *American Presbyterian and Genesee Evangelist,* quoted in Galesburg *Semi-Weekly Free Democrat,* Jan. 25, 1859.
[51] When G. H. Wright, who had supported Blanchard, died, William J. Phelps filled the vacancy and during the contests of the fifties stood by Blanchard. Upon William Holyoke's resignation, he was succeeded by his own son, William E. Holyoke.
[52] Knox College, "Trustees' Records," June 25, 1856; Browning, *Diary,* p. 242.

Blanchard had lost a seat on the board and no longer had a full half of the trustees on his side.

The showdown occurred at the next annual meeting in June, 1857, with a full board present in Williston Hall, and with an audience of students and townspeople gathered to watch the proceedings. Evidently there had been intimations of the impending fireworks, for Blanchard revealed in the course of the proceedings that one of the Gale partisans had already approached him with an offer of a year's salary if he would resign peacefully. The opening move of Blanchard's foes was the appointment of a committee of five to deal with the subject of contentions within the college. The report of this committee was a foregone conclusion, for Browning was chairman and he had James Knox and one other Gale supporter to give their faction control. The next morning this committee brought in a report that was worthy of the two lawyer-politicians: they suggested that the troubles in the college be ended by having Blanchard and Gale both give up their positions on the faculty, the one the presidency, the other his professorship. Of course this proposal was not as evenhanded as appeared at first glance, for it removed Blanchard as a relatively young man of undoubted ability not only from the faculty but also from his ex-officio place on the board, while in removing the aged Gale it dropped a teacher of declining quality from the faculty but left him on the board of trustees. Bascom, speaking for the minority of the committee, suggested that Gale alone resign. On the second day the debate and delaying tactics of Blanchard's friends continued the battle until late in the afternoon; then finally Browning's recommendation passed by a majority of one. Blanchard and Gale both resigned, and with the former now off the board the Gale faction had clear control.[53]

On the third day the fighting spoiled the Commencement exercises, at which Edward Beecher took up the cause in an address that spoke for the students and townspeople, who over-

[53] In addition to the "Trustees' Records," information on the proceedings is contained in Browning's *Diary*, pp. 290–92. Calkins, in his interesting account of the affair, presents many insights and sidelights to the action (*They Broke the Prairie*, pp. 184–87).

whelmingly favored Blanchard. After the exercises Blanchard's friends on the board resumed the battle. Taking advantage of the fact that C. M. Pomeroy, Browning's nominee to the board, had gone back to Quincy the night before, Bascom brought forward a proposition to employ Blanchard as president the ensuing year; but as Browning noted in his diary, "after a hard contest we defeated the proposition." [54]

On the campus, in the town, and beyond, the news of what had been done to Blanchard aroused angry protests. The fascinating story of this "Blanchard War" has been so well told by Calkins that there is no need to present the details again.[55] Nine of the ten graduating seniors refused to participate in the Commencement exercises; the majority of the students asked for and received dismissal from the school; [56] direct and indirect expressions of support for Blanchard came from by far the most of the alumni. A special *Student's Farewell* was published during the summer, attacking the Gale party and accusing Gale himself of "deception," "forgery," and "misrepresentation" and declaring that he was not and never had been "a competent scholar." His professorship, said these former students of his, had been a "disgrace to himself and to the institution" [57] Later still another student publication asserted:

All those who think for themselves, and are not biased by family relationships or a bigoted church organization, the great majority sympathize with and uphold the stand of the students, and the side of our President.[58]

But the battling in the board was not over. In August the fighting was resumed as the trustees met to consider how to fill the vacated faculty positions. The excitement was great, for the Gale forces were weakened by the absence of one of their men who was ill in Wisconsin and could not come to the meeting; this would leave them without the majority with which they had overidden the Blanchard group the preceding June. Browning arrived by train from Quincy at 9:00 the evening

[54] Browning, *Diary*, p. 292.   [55] Calkins, *They Broke the Prairie*, pp. 184–96.
[56] Galesburg *Free Democrat*, July 2, 1857.
[57] *Student's Farewell* (Galesburg, 1857).
[58] *Knox Collegiate Magazine*, Nov., 1857.

before and as usual stopped over at Gale's home. But soon he
and other members of the board gathered, despite the late
hour, at the home of the aged Ferris (he was to resign from the
board as soon as this campaign was over), to plan their course
of action. The next morning they were back again at Ferris's
at breakfast with the full contingent of the Gale-Browning
band, except for the ailing one in Wisconsin, and by 10:00 they
had agreed upon their defensive strategy. When the board
convened they were ready for the effort of Blanchard's friends,
now in a majority, to reelect him. To avert such an "outrage"
the Gale-Browning group refused formally to meet with the
Blanchard faction, who thus could not form a legal quorum
to do official business. Since the latter were bent on reinstating
the deposed president and would hear of nothing else, the best
that the two opposing camps could agree upon was to hold
what Browning carefully referred to as an "informal and un-
official meeting for the purpose of Conference." With only an
hour off for dinner the discussion continued throughout a hot
humid day until nearly night without accomplishing anything.[59] Thus the Blanchard party was thwarted by the same
parliamentary trick that had opened the feud between the two
groups in 1849. They could hardly be blamed when at another
meeting in October, Blanchard's men used the same means to
keep the Gale-Browning men from having a quorum.[60]

All that came out of these maneuvers by stubborn opponents
were some important committee actions. After the August
deadlock, the executive committee, which had not yet been
trimmed of a Blanchard majority and was still headed by Bascom, did continue Blanchard as acting president for one year.[61]
And an "informal" meeting agreed upon a committeee of three
"to correspond with gentlemen in reference to the Presidency." [62]

This situation protracted, widened, increased, and deepened

[59] Browning, *Diary,* pp. 295–96; Samuel G. Wright, "Journal," Aug. 17, 1857.
[60] Browning, *Diary,* p. 304.
[61] MS Report of the Executive Committee; Samuel G. Wright, "Journal," Aug.
17, 1857.
[62] Browning, *Diary,* p. 304.

the controversy. Parallel to the local parliamentary contests in Galesburg were verbal skirmishes in the press and discussions in the larger sectarian organizations that were interested in the college. Both sides were impelled to make public statements of their cause; that for one side was prepared by Browning; [63] that for the other was a protracted speaking campaign by Edward Beecher, who carried his denunciations of Gale, Browning, and their faction to several Illinois towns including Chicago and Quincy. At the latter place he engaged in an epithet-slinging contest with Browning.[64] This member of the Beecher clan, though still rather new to Galesburg, had "acted as counsel for Blanchard" during the crucial June trustees' meeting, at which, though not a member of the board, he appeared with Jefferson's *Manual* in hand.[65] Another Beecher, brother Charles, who was then teacher of elocution at Knox, was vainly suggested as sucessor to the faculty position vacated by Gale.[66] For weeks the columns of the *Free Democrat* were full of the acrimonious discussion. And for two years more the Congregationalists and Presbyterians charged and investigated and countercharged and published, their arguments resulting in three book-length publications.[67]

During the early stages of the dispute Williston warned that the college was threatened with loss of the "Liberal policy" that had previously distinguished it and was likely to become of a "narrow and highly conservative and anti-progressive character." [68] Such a warning had also been issued by Bascom as his answer to Browning's recommendation that both Blanchard and Gale be removed. Bascom reminded the trustees that Knox had been planned, established, and operated as a "peculiar" institution, not to be just like any other college, and that its distinguishing features were likely to be rubbed

---

[63] *Ibid.*, p. 296.   [64] Calkins, *They Broke the Prairie*, pp. 191–94.
[65] *Ibid.*, p. 185.   [66] Galesburg *Free Democrat*, Aug. 19, 1857.
[67] *Rights of Congregationalists in Knox College;* Bailey, *Knox College; Report on Knox College, 1861.* All three of these works have been frequently cited in this study, for in their combing over the early history of the college the authors of these polemics presented and preserved much documentary material that otherwise is now lost.
[68] J. P. Williston to N. H. Losey, July 2, 1857, *Report on Knox College, 1861.*

out by the reckless actions of the Gale-Browning group.[69] Possibly the distinctive reforming character of Knox College might have been saved if a truly neutral outsider could have succeeded Blanchard and brought unity to the contending groups. But there is no evidence that Gale would have been at all satisfied with such a solution. Certainly the Gale men on the committee appointed to correspond regarding a president made no protracted effort to find an able man who had not been involved in the contest directly or indirectly. Only S. G. Wright, the sole Blanchard man on the committee, made a persistent effort to seek such a candidate. But the other two met without him and entered into negotiations with the Reverend Harvey Curtis of Chicago, a Presbyterian who shared with the Gales a deep dislike of Blanchard, against whom he had been publicly opposed on the issues that separated the two denominations in the West; he was just the kind of candidate for the presidency who could not be acceptable to Blanchard's friends. Wright protested the recommendation of the majority of the committee, but Curtis was elected by exactly the same board members who had deposed Blanchard, over the opposition of exactly the same embittered minority who had tried to keep Blanchard.[70]

The contrast between Blanchard and the conservative, cautious man who became his successor had been presented to the public seven years previously in a journalistic joust between them in the columns of the *Western Citizen*. On May of 1851 the leading article, written by Blanchard, commended a New School Presbyterian church in Chicago for its action against the slavery connections of the General Assembly. Blanchard particularly attacked the presbytery which had disciplined the church for its action. The editor of the paper praised Blanchard for his article,[71] but Curtis replied at length a week later and defended the presbyterial procedure; of Blanchard

---

[69] Knox College, "Trustees' Records," June 23-25, 1857, MS copy of the minority report.

[70] *Ibid.*, April 30, 1858; Samuel G. Wright, "Journal," Nov. 8, 1857, May 7, 1858; Browning, *Diary*, pp. 322-23.

[71] *Western Citizen*, May 6, 1851.

he said: "He is in the habit of indiscriminate denunciation against everything and everybody that does not agree exactly with his notions." [72] In June Blanchard's answer to Curtis was again given the leading place in the weekly; he admitted Curtis's honesty but directly censored him for his weak attitude on ecclesiastical disfellowship of slavery-tainted churches.[73]

Curtis's inaugural address in June, 1858, made it clear that on slavery, as with other public issues, Knox College was now to adopt an inactive, passive, and neutral policy. The change is strikingly apparent when Curtis's discourse is compared with the very different pronouncement on questions of academic policy which had been published about the time that Blanchard had become president.

In the two quotations below are set significant portions of Curtis's speech and extracts from the discourse by Blanchard which Gale in 1845 had published to inform the friends and patrons of Knox College "what views and principles guide its President in the discharge of his duties."

My own settled convictions are, that the college is not the place, and this early stage of education is not the fitting time, in which to inculcate distinctive opinions on doubtful or contested points, either in religion or morals. As in intellectual, so in religious and moral matters, the college is the place in which to lay foundations. Let pupils be trained to a clear apprehension of their personal responsibility; let a high sense of honor be inculcated, and an inflexible regard for truth and right; let pure sentiments, and a quick and correct moral sense be cultivated; let the principles and practical teachings of the Word of God be made familiar to the mind; and then, super-added to this, let gentlemanly manners and a courteous deportment and address be formed; and withal a habit of independent thought, and bold, frank, manly utterance, so it be also kind and conciliatory; and we may safely leave the rest to time, and free individual action. . . . Teachers in public institutions may form their own opinions on every question of religion, or reform or politics; and may utter or publish those opinions at their discretion, in fitting ways and on appropriate occasions. But they should not compromise the character of the college by becoming propagandists of any individual or partisan peculiarities, nor should the college

[72] *Ibid.*, May 13, 1851.   [73] *Ibid.*, June 3, 1851.

chapel, or lecture or recitation rooms be misappropriated to the inculcation of any such peculiarities.[74]

Blanchard's sharply contrasting views had been stated as follows:

And it is scarcely a reproach on colleges, seminaries, and societies, to say they have been smitten with the common leprosy of the land; to say that our institutions for the instruction of young men have taught the great principles of morals feebly, and *"in the abstract,"* that they have shunned the very questions which duty to God and the good of mankind required them to discuss; that they have left their pupils with little or no zeal to carry out in practice the truths which they have inculcated in theory. . . . The mind of the church or of the student, is apt to follow that of their teachers. But the mind of the non-committalist teacher, instinctively shunning controverted truths, that is truths which meet the opposition because they conflict with the sinful ways of men—he will lead the minds of his hearers to contemplate distant sins, or sins universally decried; . . . . for the sins of the present generation are commonly "exciting subjects" and must be treated "in the abstract". . . .

If then, I am asked: "What ought our College and Seminary faculties to do for reform?"

With the utmost simplicity and directness, I reply:—

Those Faculties ought to lead their students, both by precept and example, to take the simple ground of opposition to prevailing sins, which truth demands, and to do their utmost, by prayer and instruction to infuse into the youth a zeal for reformation which will enable them to breast the after opposition which they will meet from the world. We want a martyr-age of Colleges and Seminaries, to send forth a host of young men, at the sound of whose goings the whole land shall tremble—men who will not rest while one way or practice in the community violates the law of God.[75]

Blanchard made one last scene before he left the stage at the Knox Commencement at which Curtis was inaugurated. At the conclusion of the new president's address he rose and asked the people to remain after the meeting to listen to a "few corrections" which he desired to make. Almost everyone but the Gale trustees did stay (and two of them did). Despite the handicap of a very bad cold Blanchard made, according to

[74] Curtis, *Inaugural Address,* pp. 12–13.
[75] Blanchard, "Public Men and Public Institutions of the Church," in *A Brief History of Knox College,* by Rev. G. W. Gale, 1845.

Wright, a very effective speech, denying that the founders of Knox ever designed to have a school that was Calvinistic in doctrine or Presbyterian in church government. Blanchard assumed that Curtis was a "good man" who was deceived in regard to the facts, and that he would "not continue to be blind to them," but like the governors sent by the Democratic regime to Kansas Territory disposed to favor the pro-slavery side of the argument, he might "be sent for one purpose, but remain for another." According to Wright, Blanchard was "excessively cheered, the great audience seeming to be almost wholly carried by him." [76]

But popular disapproval notwithstanding, Gale and his men now had the kind of conservative president they wanted. By 1860 it was clear that the transfer from Blanchard to Curtis had "entirely changed the reformatory policy of the College which was inaugurated *at the first,* and which was ably and successfully maintained to the end of President Blanchard's connection with the College, for a strictly conservative policy." [77]

For about a year and a half following his surrender of the college presidency Blanchard remained at Galesburg. In the spring of 1859 he accepted a call to become pastor of the original colony church for a year.[78] Both before and after his assumption of the new pastorate he was called upon for addresses, speaking before the Teacher's Institute,[79] the Young Men's Association,[80] before other churches,[81] and delivering the Commencement address for the Knox Female Collegiate Department of January, 1859.[82] These calls upon his time and talents were significant evidence of the continued respect for him in Galesburg. Abroad he was also noticed; for it was announced that at the 1859 Commencement of Beloit College he and Owen Lovejoy, abolitionist congressman, were to be speakers.[83]

There is no indication whatsoever of an abatement of his

[76] Samuel G. Wright, "Journal," June 27, 1858.
[77] Galesburg *Semi-Weekly Free Democrat,* March 9, 1860.
[78] Galesburg *Free Democrat,* May 21, May 25, 1859.
[79] Galesburg *Semi-Weekly Free Democrat,* Nov. 13, 1858.
[80] *Ibid.,* Jan. 3, 1860.
[81] *Ibid.,* March 26, 1859.   [82] *Ibid.,* Jan. 22, 1859.   [83] *Ibid.,* May 28, 1859.

reformatory zeal. By a series of lectures and by a journalistic •
controversy he renewed his attack on secret societies.[84] For a
few weeks during the late summer of 1858 it looked as if civil
politics might take him up, for the Galesburg *Free Democrat*
and the Galva *Watchman* "hoisted the name of Jonathan Blanchard as their candidate for Congress" on the Republican
ticket. It is very doubtful whether any man with such a pen-
chant for unconcealed opinions and clear-cut issues and such
a host of enemies could ever have won a campaign. The Knoxville *Republican* editor declared that though he would support
him if nominated, Blanchard "is not our choice by a jugful." [85]
Blanchard in any event withdrew his candidacy in a few weeks
and endorsed the Republican holder of that office.[86]

During the middle of the winter of 1859-60 he closed his
pastoral term at the Galesburg First Church and accepted a
summons to the presidency of Wheaton College.[87] His passing
from Galesburg was symbolic of the change that had come over
the Yankee colony, now a quarter century old. The original
zeal for reform had quieted, the generation of the founders
was passing, and their successors were only a minority among
the many recent migrants brought by the new railroad construction. Galesburg had now become, as it remained, only
secondarily an educational community, and even less a reformatory colony.

[84] *Ibid.*, Nov. 5, Nov. 19, Nov. 30, 1859; Knoxville *Republican*, Nov. 30, 1859.
[85] Knoxville *Republican*, Aug. 4, 1858.   [86] *Ibid.*, Aug. 18, 1858.
[87] Galesburg *Semi-Weekly Free Democrat*, Dec. 29, 1859; Jan. 3, 1860.

Epilogue

PERENNIALLY IN THE FALL a college, reversing Nature, revives and renews its growth; in the spring it ripens, sheds the season's growth, and drops its fruit.

Often when the forest is greening, one tree remains gray, a bare wintry outline of a tree; but though deadened from wind damage, or disease, or drought, sometimes from the roots springs a fresh shoot that is part of the old and yet a new tree.

The strength of Knox College was dissipated by the quarrel within itself; important patrons sloughed away and students dropped off; soon the young men were drained away for Lincoln's army; and the community was distracted by the new burdens of the war years. For a decade at least the future was dubious; and when the school flourished again in the last quarter of the century, a rather different college was growing, one less committed to a cause or connected to a community and more concentrated upon its own campus affairs; one less concerned with molding men for a "martyr age" and more excited about forensic prizes won for the contest's sake by young men who would go to "Success" in business or law or to journalistic careers and a literary "Reputation." The college became a "good" educational institution, hardly to be distinguished from many others of the "liberal arts" colleges that had been seeded so thickly in the Great Valley.

Sometimes in an old woods in Illinois there is a tree still growing strong whose trunk long past was nearly broken. Of such a tree it is often said that while a sapling it was bent to point a trail in the wilderness.

Appendix

THE FOLLOWING ILLINOIS colonies are discussed in Chapter 7 and are annotated when reference is made to them:

Maryland Colony, Mt. Morris, Ogle County
Delavan Colony, Delavan, Tazewell County
Tremont Colony, Tremont, Tazewell County
Hampshire Colony, Princeton, Bureau County
Galesburg Colony, Galesburg, Knox County
Geneseo Colony, Geneseo, Henry County
New York Colony, Morristown, Henry County
La Grange Colony, Henry County
New York Association, Andover, Henry County
Connecticut Association, Wethersfield, Henry County
Lyndon Colony, Lyndon, Whiteside County
Lisbon Colony, Lisbon, Kendall County
Rockwell Colony, Rockwell, LaSalle County
Footes' Colony, Kishwaukee, Winnebago County

Other colonies which were studied but to which specific reference is not made elsewhere in the text are:

Lyons, Marshall County (Ford, *The History of Putnam and Marshall Counties,* pp. 123–24)
Como Colony, Whiteside County (Bent, *History of Whiteside County, Illinois,* pp. 243–49)
Providence Colony, Bureau County (Matson, *Reminiscences of Bureau County,* pp. 331–32)
Mackinaw Colony, Mackinaw, Tazewell County (Chapman and Co., *History of Tazewell County, Illinois*)
Hanover Colony, Metamora, Woodford County (*Past and Present of Woodford County,* pp. 234–35, 243–45, 273–74, 288–89)

Dale Colony, Hudson Colony, and Mount Hope Colony in McLean County (*History of McLean County, Illinois,* pp. 579–80, 603–64, 612)

Stonington Colony, Sangamon County (*Peoria Register and Northwestern Gazetteer,* June 20, 1838)

Fairview Colony, Fulton County (Chapman and Co., *History of Fulton County, Illinois,* pp. 623–29)

A "Company" from Metford, Connecticut ("Yankee Settlement"), and an unnamed colony in LaSalle County (Elmer Baldwin, *History of LaSalle County, Ill.,* pp. 296, 384–86)

"Yankee Settlement" (Hadley in Homer Township) and an unnamed colony in Will County (Stevens, *Past and Present of Will County,* pp. 77, 85; Maue, *History of Will County, Illinois,* I, 223–32. One of these may be the colony mentioned by Mary H. Porter, *Eliza Chappell Porter,* p. 120)

"Boston Colony," Geneva Township, Kane County (Wilcox, ed., *History of Kane County,* p. 703)

Bibliography

UNPUBLISHED MATERIAL [1]

Adelphi Society, Knox College. "Minutes," 1846–60. KCL.

Allan, James M. "Autobiography." See Bradley Papers.

American Home Missionary Society Papers. Hammond Library, Chicago Theological Seminary.

Avery, Seraphina Princess Phelps. "Canal Boat." KCL.

Bascom, Flavel. "Autobiography." Hammond Library, Chicago Theological Seminary.

Blanchard, Jonathan. "My Life Work." KCL.

Bradley Papers. This collection comprises papers in the possession of Mrs. Susan Bradley of Geneseo, Illinois, including a brief autobiography of her grandfather, James M. Allan, and a few letters of James and his brother William.

Calkins Papers. This collection comprises materials collected by Earnest Elmo Calkins for the writing of *They Broke the Prairie,* particularly an extensive correspondence in the pursuit of data for this history of Knox College and Galesburg. KCL.

Chambers, E. P. "Reminiscences of Early Days"; one of the papers of the now defunct Knox County Historical Society. KCL.

Chase, Salmon P. Papers. Library of Congress.

Churchill, George. Two scrapbooks, numbered I and II; also a MS, "Galesburg History." KCL.

Clipping Scrapbooks in the Galesburg Public Library.

Comstock, Milton L. "Life of Rev. James Warren." KCL.

Cowles, Henry. Papers. Oberlin College Library.

[1] Many of the sources used in this work are single items, such as letters, from the collection in the Memorabilia Department of the Knox College Library. Only when the manuscripts are unusually important or when they belong to some larger aggregation of papers are they listed below with a special heading. Manuscripts from the Knox College Library are identified by the abbreviation KCL.

DeNovo, Mrs. John (Jeanne Humphreys). "Mary Brown Davis, Journalist, Feminist, and Social Reformer." KCL.
Dillon, Merton L. "The Anti-Slavery Movement in Illinois: 1809–1844." Doctoral Dissertation, University of Michigan, 1951.
Dunn, E. M. "List of Donors to Knox College, 1836–1895." KCL.
Finney, Charles Grandison. Papers. Oberlin College Library.
First Presbyterian Church of Galesburg, Illinois:
    Minutes of the Society
    Records of the Church
    Separate Session Records. KCL.
First Congregational Church, Geneseo, Illinois. "Records of the First Orthodox Church in Geneseo, Illinois."
Gale, George Washington. Account Books. KCL.
—— "Autobiography." KCL.
Gale, William Selden. "Autobiography." KCL.
Galesburg Youth's Anti-Slavery Society. "Minutes," April 4, 1839. KCL.
General Congregational Association of Illinois. "Minutes," 1844–60. Hammond Library, Chicago Theological Seminary.
Gettemy, Charles Ferris. "A Memoir of Silvanus Ferris, 1773–1861." Boston, 1935. KCL.
Gnothautii Society. "Minutes." KCL.
Gould, Nahum. Diary. Hammond Library, Chicago Theological Seminary.
Gratz, Simon. Manuscripts. Historical Society of Pennsylvania.
Illinois Anti-Slavery Society. "Minutes," 1837–44. Chicago Historical Society.
Knox College:
    Old business records such as tuition records and
    "Blotter A," "Blotter B," and "Blotter C."
    Trustees' "Minutes," sometimes called "Records."
    Faculty "Minutes."
    "A Record of the Preparatory and Female Collegiate Department of Knox College." KCL.
Knox County Circuit Court Records, Book One. Knox County, Illinois, Courthouse.
Lamb, Wallace E. "George Washington Gale, Theologian and Educator." Dissertation for Doctorate of Education, Syracuse University, 1949.
Muelder, Hermann R. "Jacksonian Democracy in Church Organization." Doctoral Dissertation, University of Minnesota, 1933.
Old School Presbyterian Church of Galesburg. Session Record. KCL.
Peoria Synod. Records of the Peoria Synod of the Presbyterian Church, New School. KCL.

Porter, Jeremiah. "Journal," 1836–39. Chicago Historical Society.
Presbytery of Knox. "Records," 1839–44. KCL.
Revels, Hiram. "Autobiography." Library of Congress.
Smith, Clark T. "Boyhood Recollections Connected with the Early
   History of Amity, Iowa, Now Known as College Springs." Santa
   Barbara, California, October 13, 1921. KCL.
Smith, Gerrit. Papers. Syracuse University Library.
United States Census Returns of 1840 for Knox and Galesburg
   Townships, Knox County, Illinois. Photostatic copies, KCL.
West, Mary Allen. "How Galesburg Grew," MS dated May 23,
   1873, in Galesburg Public Library.
Wetmore, Isaac. Papers. KCL.
Williston Letters, transcript of letters by Jonathan Blanchard to
   Samuel and John P. Williston, received from G. R. Carpenter,
   New York City.
Wright, Samuel G. "Journal," 1839–60. KCL.

PUBLISHED WORKS

Allen, John W. "Slavery and Negro Servitude in Pope County,
   Illinois," *Journal of the Illinois State Historical Society*, XLII
   (1949), 411–23.
Alton *Observer*, 1836–37. Alton, Illinois.
Alton *Observer Extra*, "Proceedings of the Illinois Anti-Slavery Con-
   vention held at Upper Alton on the 26th, 27th, and 28th, October
   1837." Alton, Illinois, 1838.
American Annals of Education and Instruction, 1830–36. Boston,
   Mass.
American and Foreign Anti-Slavery Society. An Address to the Anti-
   Slavery Christians of the United States. New York, 1852.
—— Annual Report, ninth to thirteenth, 1849–53. New York.
American Anti-Slavery Society. Annual Report, first to sixth,
   1834–39. New York.
American Education Society. *Journal of the American Education
   Society*, 1834. Boston, Mass.
American Home Missionary Society. Annual Report, 1828–39. New
   York.
American Quarterly Register, 1829–43. Boston, Mass.
Ander, Oscar Fritiof. T. N. Hasselquist: The Career and Influence
   of a Swedish Clergyman, Journalist, and Educator. Rock Island,
   Illinois, 1931.
Anderson, L. F. "The Manual Labor School Movement," *Educa-
   tional Review*, XLVI (Nov., 1913), 369–86.
Angle, Paul M. Lincoln, 1854–1861: Being the Day-by-Day Activities
   of Abraham Lincoln from January 1, 1854, to March 4, 1861.
   Springfield, Illinois, 1933.

Asbury, Henry. Reminiscences of Quincy, Illinois. Quincy, Illinois, 1882.

Atkins, Glen, and Frederick L. Fagley. History of American Congregationalism. Boston, 1942.

Bailey, J. W. Knox College, by Whom Founded and Endowed. Chicago, 1860.

Baldwin, Elmer. History of LaSalle County, Illinois, and a Sketch of the Pioneer Settlers of Each Town to 1840. Chicago, 1877.

Baldwin, Theron. "Historical Sketch of the Society," Proceedings at the Quarter Century Anniversary of the Society for the Promotion of Collegiate and Theological Education at the West, Marietta, Ohio, November 7–10, 1868. New York, 1868.

Ballance, Charles. The History of Peoria. Peoria, Illinois, 1870.

Ballantine, W. G., ed. The Oberlin Jubilee, 1833–1883. Oberlin, Ohio, 1883.

Barnes, Gilbert H. The Anti-Slavery Impulse, 1830–1844. New York, 1933.

Barnhart, John H. "The Southern Influence in the Formation of Illinois," Journal of the Illinois State Historical Society, XXXII (1939), 358–78.

Barton, William E. Joseph Edwin Roy: A Faithful Servant of God and His Generation. Oak Park, Illinois, 1908.

Bascom, Flavel. A Discourse Delivered at the Funeral of Rev. Levi Spencer, Late Pastor of the Congregational Church, Peoria, Illinois, April 17, 1853. Peoria, Illinois, 1853.

—— A Historical Discourse: Commemorative of the Settlement of Galesburg. Galesburg, Illinois, 1866.

Bateman, Newton, and Paul Selby, eds. History of Kendall County by Special Authors and Contributors. 2 vols. Chicago, 1914.

Beard, Augustus Field. A Crusade of Brotherhood: A History of the American Missionary Association. Boston, 1909.

Beecher, Charles, ed. Autobiography of Lyman Beecher. 2 vols. New York, 1865.

Beecher, Edward. Narrative of Riots at Alton in Connection with the Death of Rev. Elijah P. Lovejoy. Alton, Illinois, 1838.

—— [Funeral] Sermon and Obituary [of Matthew Chambers]. n.p., 1869.

Beecher, Lyman. A Plea for the West. Cincinnati, 1835.

Bent, Charles. History of Whiteside County, Illinois. Morrison, Illinois, 1877.

Berea College. Catalogue, 1867. Berea, Kentucky.

Beveridge, Albert J. Abraham Lincoln, 1809–1858. 2 vols. New York, 1928.

Birney, James Gillespie. Letters of James Gillespie Birney, 1831–1857. Edited by Dwight L. Dumond. 2 vols. New York, 1938.

Birney, William. James G. Birney and His Times. New York, 1890.

Blanchard, Jonathan. Baccalaureate Address before the Senior Class of Knox College, June 22, 1856. Galesburg, Illinois, 1856.

—— Memoir of Rev. Levi Spencer: Successively Pastor of the Congregational Church at Canton, Bloomington, and Peoria, Illinois. Cincinnati, 1856.

—— Public Men and Public Institutions. Published with George Washington Gale, A Brief History of Knox College. Cincinnati, 1845.

—— Secret Societies: An Argument before the State Congregational Association Delivered in Two Discourses in the First Presbyterian Church in Galesburg, June 22, 1850. Chicago, 1851.

—— Sermon on Slaveholding: Preached by Appointment before the Synod of Cincinnati: at Their Late Stated Meeting at Mount Pleasant, Ohio, October 20, 1841. Cincinnati, 1842.

—— Sermons and Addresses. Chicago, 1892.

Blanchard, Jonathan, and Nathan Lewis Rice. A Debate on Slavery: Held in the City of Cincinnati on the First, Second, Third, and Sixth Days of October, 1845, upon the Question: Is Slavery in Itself Sinful, and the Relation between Master and Slave, a Sinful Relation? Cincinnati, 1846.

Blazer, D. N. "The History of the Underground Railroad of McDonough County, Illinois," *Journal of the Illinois State Historical Society*, XV (1922), 579–91.

Bonham, Jeriah. Fifty Years Recollections with Observations on Historical Events, Giving Sketches of Eminent Citizens—Their Lives and Public Services. Peoria, Illinois, 1883.

British and Foreign Anti-Slavery Society. Minutes of the General Anti-Slavery Convention Called by the Committee of the British and Foreign Anti-Slavery Society, Held in London on the 12th of June, 1840, and Continued by Adjournments to the 23rd of the Same Month. London, 1840.

—— Proceedings of the General Anti-Slavery Convention, Called by the Committee of the British and Foreign Anti-Slavery Society, and Held in London, from Tuesday, June 13th to Tuesday, June 20th, 1843. London, 1843.

—— Second Annual Report of the British and Foreign Anti-Slavery Society for the Abolition of Slavery and Slave Trade throughout the World; Presented to the General Meeting Held in Exeter Hall on Friday, May 14th, 1841. London, 1841.

—— Third Annual Report of the British and Foreign Anti-Slavery Society Held in Exeter Hall, on Friday, May 13th, 1842. London, 1842.

Brown, Ralph. Historical Geography of the United States. New York, 1948.

Browning, Orville H. Diary of Orville H. Browning, 1850–1865. Illinois Historical Collections, Vol. XX. Springfield, Illinois, 1925.

Buley, Roscoe C. The Old Northwest: Pioneer Period, 1815–1840. 2 vols. Indianapolis, 1950.

Burlington *Hawk-eye*, 1839–49. Burlington, Iowa.

Burt, John Spencer. Past and Present of Marshall and Putnam Counties, Illinois. Chicago, 1907.

Calkins, Earnest Elmo. They Broke the Prairie: Being Some Account of the Settlement of the Upper Mississippi Valley by Religious and Educational Pioneers, Told in Terms of One City, Galesburg, and of One College, Knox. New York, 1937.

Calkins, Earnest Elmo, ed. Log City Days: Two Narratives on the Settlement of Galesburg, Illinois. Galesburg, Illinois, 1937.

Carlson, Theodore L. The Illinois Military Tract: A Study of Land Occupation, Utilization and Tenure. Illinois Studies in the Social Sciences, University of Illinois Press. Urbana, Illinois, 1951.

Carmer, Carl. Dark Trees to the Wind: A Cycle of York State Years. New York, 1949.

Carr, Clark E. The Illini: A Story of the Prairies. Chicago, 1904.

Carriel, Mary Turner. The Life of Jonathan Baldwin Turner. Jacksonville, Illinois, 1911.

Chapman, Charles C., and Company, Publisher. History of Fulton County, Illinois. Peoria, Illinois, 1879.

—— History of Knox County, Illinois. Chicago, 1878.

—— History of Tazewell County, Illinois. Chicago, 1879.

—— Portrait and Biographical Album of Henry County, Illinois. Chicago, 1885.

—— Portrait and Biographical Album of Knox County, Illinois. Chicago, 1886.

Chicago *Democrat*, 1842. Chicago.

Chicago *Tribune*, 1866. Chicago.

Church, Charles A. History of Rockford and Winnebago County, Illinois. Rockford, Illinois, 1900.

Coates, Charles P. "From George Gale to Arthur Morgan," *Educational Review*, LXXII (1926), 53–55.

Colby, Lydia. "Historic Spots in Henry County," *Journal of the Illinois State Historical Society*, XXVIII (1936), 164–87.

Cole, Arthur. The Era of the Civil War, 1848–1870. Centennial History of Illinois, Vol. III. Springfield, 1919.

Collins, William H., and Cicero F. Perry. Past and Present of the City of Quincy and Adams County. Chicago, 1905.

Congregational Herald, 1859–61. Chicago.

Cooley, Verna. "Illinois and the Underground Railroad to Canada,"

Transactions of the Illinois State Historical Society, 1917, pp. 76–98.

Coup d'Etat, 1887. Knox College, Galesburg, Illinois.

Craven, Avery O. The Coming of the Civil War. New York, 1942.

Cross, Whitney R. The Burned-over District: The Social and Intellectual History of Enthusiastic Religion in Western New York, 1800–1850. Ithaca, New York, 1950.

Current, Richard Nelson. Old Thad Stevens: A Story of Ambition. Madison, Wisconsin, 1942.

Curtis, Harvey. Inaugural Address: The College—Its Mission, June 24, 1858. Chicago, 1858.

Delavan, 1837–1937: A Chronicle of 100 Years. Federal Writers Project. Delavan, Illinois, 1937.

Dergin, Alfred. "The Swedish Settlements in Central Kansas," *Collections of the Kansas Historical Society,* XI (1910), 19–46.

Dexter, Lewis A. "The Legend of William Lloyd Garrison," *Social Studies,* XXX (1939), 56–60.

Douglass, Trumann O. The Pilgrims of Iowa. Boston, 1911.

Drown, S. Dewitt. Drown's Record and Historical View of Peoria, from the Discovery by the French Jesuit Missionaries, in the Seventeenth Century, to the Present Time. Peoria, Illinois, 1850.

Eames, Charles M., ed. Historic Morgan County and Classic Jacksonville. Jacksonville, Illinois, 1885.

Eastman, Zebina. "History of the Anti-Slavery Agitation and the Growth of the Liberty and Republican Parties in the State of Illinois," in Rufus Blanchard, Discovery and Conquests of the Northwest with the History of Chicago, pp. 655–77. Chicago, 1879.

Ellsworth, Spencer. Records of the Olden Time, . . . Counties of Putnam and Marshall, Incidents and Reminiscences Connected Therewith. Lacon, Illinois, 1880.

Emery, S. Hopkins, ed. A Memorial of the Congregational Ministers and Churches of the Illinois Association on Completing a Quarter Century of Its History, Consisting of a Commemorative Discourse by Rev. William Carter, of Pittsfield, an Original Member, Delivered at Quincy, October 26, 1860. Quincy, Illinois, 1863.

Eversole, Mildred. "Canton College," *Journal of the Illinois State Historical Society,* XXXIV (1941), 334–43.

Fairchild, James H. Oberlin, the Colony and the College. Oberlin, 1883.

Fee, John Gregg. Autobiography of John G. Fee. Berea, Kentucky, 1891.

—— Non-Fellowship with Slaveholders the Duty of Christians. New York, 1855.

Fee, John Gregg. The Sinfulness of Slaveholding Shown by Appeals to Reason and Scripture. New York, 1851.

Finney, Charles Grandison. Memoirs of Charles G. Finney. New York, 1876.

First Church of Christ of Galesburg. Semi-Centennial Celebration of the Organization of the First Church of Christ of Galesburg. Galesburg, Illinois, 1887.

First Congregational Church of Peoria. Semi-Centennial of the Organization of the First Congregational Church of Peoria. Held on Sunday and Monday, December 21 and 22, 1884. Peoria, Illinois, 1884.

—— Seventy-Fifth Anniversary, First Congregational Church, Peoria, Illinois. Peoria, 1910.

First Presbyterian Church, Chicago. An Account of the Fiftieth Anniversary of the Organization of the First Presbyterian Church, Chicago. Chicago, 1883.

Fischer, Julia. Blessed Memories: Life of Mrs. Mary Blanchard, n.p., n.d.

Fletcher, Robert S. A History of Oberlin College from Its Foundation through the Civil War. 2 vols. Oberlin, Ohio, 1943.

—— "Oneida and Oberlin," Town Topics of the Mohawk Valley. Utica, New York, 1931.

Foote, Horatio. An Address Delivered before the Missionary Association of Knox College, Sabbath Afternoon, June 20, 1852. Quincy, Illinois, 1852.

Ford, Henry A. The History of Putnam and Marshall Counties, Embracing an Account of the Settlement, Early Progress, and Formation of Bureau, and Stark Counties. Lacon, Illinois, 1860.

Frothingham, Octavius B. Gerrit Smith: A Biography. New York, 1878.

—— Theodore Parker: A Biography. New York, 1874.

Gale, George Washington. Articles of Faith and Covenant of the Presbyterian Church in Galesburg. Galesburg, Illinois, 1849.

—— A Brief History of Knox College, Situated in Galesburgh, Knox County, Illinois. Cincinnati, 1845.

Galesburg Daily Mail, 1895. Galesburg, Illinois.

Galesburg Evening Mail, 1923. Galesburg, Illinois.

Galesburg Free Democrat, 1854–60. Galesburg, Illinois. Concurrent with this weekly the Semi-Weekly Free Democrat was also published in 1859–60.

Galesburg News Letter, 1850. Galesburg, Illinois.

Galesburg Republican Register, 1876, 1888, 1909, 1911. Galesburg, Illinois.

Galesburg *Weeks Review,* 1906. Galesburg, Illinois.

Gallaher, James. "Recollections of Dr. David Nelson," The Western Sketch Book. Boston, 1852.

Garretson, O. A. "Traveling on the Underground Railroad in Iowa," *Iowa Journal of History and Politics,* XXII (1924), 418–53.

Garrison, Wendell Phillips, and Francis Jackson. William Lloyd Garrison, the Story of His Life as Told by His Children. 2 vols. New York, 1885.

Gates, Paul Wallace. The Illinois Central Railroad and Its Colonization Work. Cambridge, Mass., 1934.

General Assembly of the Presbyterian Church. Minutes of the General Assembly of the Presbyterian Church in the United States of America from Its Organization A.D. 1789 to A.D. 1820, Inclusive. Philadelphia, 1847.

—— Minutes of the Presbyterian Church in the United States of America, 1820–1838. Philadelphia.

General Assembly of the Presbyterian Church, New School. Minutes of the General Assembly of the Presbyterian Church in the United States of America. With an Appendix. New York, 1838.

—— Minutes of the General Assembly of the Presbyterian Church in the United States of America, 1839, 1840, 1843, 1846, 1847, 1849, 1850. New York City, 1839–50.

General Association of New York. Minutes of the General Association of New York. Paris Hill, New York, 1850.

—— Minutes of the General Association of New York. Brooklyn, New York, 1851.

General Congregational Association of Illinois. In Commemoration of the Fiftieth Anniversary of the Organization of the General Congregational Association of Illinois. Ottawa, Illinois, 1894.

Genius of Liberty, 1841–42. Lowell, Illinois.

Genius of Universal Emancipation, 1839. Lowell, Illinois.

Godsey, Flora Rosenquist. "The Early Settlement and Raid on the Upper Neosah," Collections of the Kansas Historical Society, XVI (1925), 451–63.

Goodell, William. Slavery and Anti-Slavery: A History of the Great Struggle in Both Hemispheres, with a View of the Slavery Question in the United States. New York, 1855.

Green, Beriah. The Miscellaneous Writings of Beriah Green. Whitesboro, New York, 1841.

Grinnell, Josiah Bushnell. Men and Events of Forty Years: Autobiographical Reminiscences of an Active Career from 1850 to 1890. Boston, 1891.

Gue, Benjamin F. History of Iowa from the Earliest Times to the Beginning of the Twentieth Century. New York, 1903.

Haberkorn, Ruth E. "Owen Lovejoy in Princeton, Illinois," *Journal of the Illinois State Historical Society*, XXXVI (1943), 284–314.

Hammond, H. L. "The First Decade," in W. G. Ballantine, ed., The Oberlin Jubilee, 1833–1883. Oberlin, Ohio, 1883, pp. 192–206.

—— "The Gravel Debate: An Anti-Slavery Reminiscence," *Advance Supplement*, Chicago, Illinois, April 28, 1870.

Harlow, Ralph V. Gerrit Smith, Philanthropist and Reformer. New York, 1939.

Harris, N. Dwight. The History of Negro Servitude in Illinois and the Slavery Agitation in That State, 1719–1864. Chicago, 1905.

Heinl, Frank J. "Jacksonville and Morgan County, an Historical Review," *Journal of the Illinois State Historical Society*, XVIII (1925), 5–38.

Herald of the Prairies. Devoted to the Promotion of Practical Religion, the Maintenance of Essential Truth, and the Advancement of the Benevolent Enterprises of the Day, 1849. Chicago.

Hickman, Russel K. "Lincoln College, Forerunner of Washburne Municipal University," *Kansas Historical Quarterly*, XVIII (1950), 20–54.

Hicks, E. W. History of Kendall County, Illinois, from the Earliest Discoveries to the Present Time. Aurora, Illinois, 1877.

Hildner, Ernest G. "Colleges in Illinois One Hundred Years Ago," *Papers in Illinois History and Transactions for the Year 1942*, Illinois State Historical Society, pp. 19–31.

Hill, James Langdon. Rev. William Salter, D.D., 1821–1910: Minister of the Congregational Church and Society of Burlington, Iowa, 1846–1910. Des Moines, 1911.

Hinton, Richard. John Brown and His Men. New York, 1894.

History of McLean County, Illinois. Chicago, 1879.

History of Page County, Iowa. Des Moines, Iowa, Historical Co., 1880.

Hoffman, U. I. History of LaSalle County, Illinois. Chicago, 1906.

Holyoke, Samuel G. "A Historical Sketch," Galesburg *Republican Register*, July 7, 1911.

Home Missionary and American Pastors' Journal, 1831. New York.

Home Missions and Slavery: A Reprint of Several Articles, Recently Published in the Religious Journals; with an Appendix. New York, John A. Gray, Printer, 1857.

Hubbard, Anson M. "A Colony Settlement, Geneseo, Illinois, 1836–1837," *Journal of the Illinois State Historical Society*, XXIX (1937), 403–31.

Illinois Monthly Magazine Conducted by James Hall, 1830–31. Vandalia, Illinois.

Illinois Society of Church History, Congregational. Historical Statement and Papers. Chicago, 1895.

Jones, Pomroy. Annals and Recollections of Oneida County. Rome,
New York, 1851.

Jordan, Philip D. William Salter, Western Torchbearer. Oxford,
Ohio, 1939.

Karsner, David. John Brown, Terrible "Saint." New York, 1934.

Kellogg, Hiram H. Education for the People, an Inaugural Address
Delivered at Galesburg, February 2, 1842. Peoria, Illinois, 1842.

Kett, H. F., and Company Publisher. Henry County, Illinois, Its
Taxpayers and Voters; Containing also a Biographical Directory.
Chicago, 1877.

—— History of Winnebago County, Its Past and Present. Chicago,
1877.

—— Past and Present of LaSalle County, Illinois. Chicago, 1877.

—— The Voters and Taxpayers of Bureau County, Illinois. Chicago, 1877.

Kirk, Edward N. The Church and the College, an Address before
the Society for the Promotion of Collegiate and Theological Education at the West. Delivered in Park Street in Newark, N.J., October 30, 1851. Boston, 1851.

Kirkland, Mrs. C. M. Western Clearings. New York, 1846.

Knox College. Catalogue, 1841–65. Printed in Peoria and Galesburg.

Knox Collegiate Magazine, 1857. Knox College, Galesburg, Illinois.

Knoxiana, 1850–58. Knox College, Galesburg, Illinois.

Knoxville Journal, 1849–55. Knoxville, Illinois.

Knoxville Republican, 1856–61. Knoxville, Illinois.

Landon, Fred. "Benjamin Lundy in Illinois," Journal of the Illinois
State Historical Society, XXX (1940), 55–67.

Lane Seminary. Catalogue and History of the Foundation and Endowment of the Lane Theological Seminary. Cincinnati, 1848.

—— General Catalogue, 1829–99. Cincinnati, 1899.

Leeson, M. A. Documents and Biography Pertaining to the Settlement and Progress of Stark County, Illinois. Chicago, 1887.

Liberty Tree, 1843. Chicago.

Lindquist, Emory. "The Swedes in Kansas before the Civil War,"
Kansas Historical Quarterly, XIX (1951), 254–68.

Lovejoy, Joseph C., and Owen Lovejoy. Memoir of the Rev. Elijah
P. Lovejoy: Who Was Murdered in Defense of the Liberty of the
Press, at Alton, Illinois, Nov. 7, 1837. New York, 1838.

Lyman, Huntington. "Lane Seminary Rebels," in W. G. Ballantine,
ed., The Oberlin Jubilee, 1833–1883. Oberlin, Ohio, 1883.

McCulloch, David. History of Peoria County. 2 vols. Peoria, Illinois, 1902.

McKenzie, Clark. "Congregational Church at Toulon, Illinois, 1846–1921," *Journal of the Illinois State Historical Society*, XIII (1921), 504–37

McMaster, John Bach. A History of the People of the United States from the Revolution to the Civil War. Vol. VI. New York, 1914.

Magoun, George F. Asa Turner: A Home Missionary Patriarch and His Times. Boston, 1899.

Mahan, Asa. Autobiography, Intellectual, Moral and Spiritual. London, 1882.

Mahan, Erastus. "Friends of Liberty on the Mackinaw," *Transactions of the McLean County Historical Society*, I (1899), 396–404. Bloomington, Illinois.

Mars, Hiram. "Recollection of Half a Century," Galesburg *Republican Register*, June 19, 1909.

Martineau, Harriet. Retrospect of Western Travel. 2 vols. London, 1838.

Matson, R. Reminiscences of Bureau County, Illinois. Princeton, Illinois, 1872.

Maue, August. History of Will County, Illinois. Indianapolis, Indiana, 1928.

May, Samuel J. Some Recollections of Our Anti-Slavery Conflict. Boston, 1869.

Merkel, Benjamin G. "Abolition Aspects of Missouri's Anti-Slavery Controversy, 1819–1865," *Missouri Historical Review*, XLIV (1950), 232–53.

—— "The Underground Railroad and the Missouri Borders, 1840–1860," *Missouri Historical Review*, XXXVII (1943), 271–85.

Merrill, J. W. Yellow Spring and Huron: A Local History. Mediapolis, Iowa, 1897.

Minutes of the Western Congregational Convention Held in Michigan City, Indiana, July 30–August 3, 1846, with an Introductory Note by One of Its Secretaries and an Appendix. New York, 1878.

Missouri Republican, 1850–54. St. Louis, Missouri.

Moffat, Hugh R., and Thomas R. Rogers. History of Warren County. Chicago, 1903.

Montgomery, Hope. "My First Illinois Ancestor," *Journal of the Illinois State Historical Society*, XVII (1925), 608–9.

Muelder, Hermann R. Church History in a Puritan Colony of the Middle West. Galesburg, Illinois, 1937.

—— "Congregationalists and Presbyterians in the Early History of the Galesburg Churches," *Papers in Illinois History and Transactions for the Year 1937*. Illinois State Historical Society, 1938.

—— "Printer's Error in Call for Antislavery Convention," *Journal of the Illinois State Historical Society*, XLVII (1954), 321–22.

New England Anti-Slavery Convention. Proceedings of the New England Anti-Slavery Convention Held in Boston, May 24, 25, 26, 1836. Boston, 1836.

New York *Evangelist*, 1832–42. New York.

Niles' National Register, 1838. Washington, D.C.

Nollen, John Scholte. Grinnell College. Iowa City, Iowa, 1953.

Northwestern Gazetteer, 1849. Galesburg, Illinois.

Norton, A. T. History of the Presbyterian Church in the State of Illinois. 2 vols. St. Louis, 1879.

Oak Leaf, 1856–57. Knox College, Galesburg, Illinois.

Ohio Anti-Slavery Convention. Proceedings of the Ohio Anti-Slavery Convention Held at Putnam on the 22nd, 23rd, & 24th of April, 1835. Beaumont and Wallace, printers.

Olson, Ernst W. The Swedish Element in Illinois: Survey of the Past Seven Decades. Chicago, 1917.

Oneida Institute. First Report of the Trustees of Oneida Institute of Science and Industry, March, 1828. Utica, New York, 1828.

—— Second Report of the Trustees of Oneida Institute of Science and Industry, Whitestown, March 20, 1830. Utica, New York, 1830.

Oquawka *Spectator*, 1848–54. Oquawka, Illinois.

Past and Present of Woodford County. Chicago, 1878.

Payne, Charles E. Josiah Bushnell Grinnell. Iowa City, Iowa, 1938.

Pease, Theodore C. The Frontier State, 1818–1848. Centennial History of Illinois, Vol. II. Springfield, Illinois, 1918.

—— Illinois Election Returns, 1818–1848. Collections of the Illinois State Historical Library, Vol. XVIII. Springfield, Illinois, 1923.

Peck, John Mason. "Brief View of the Baptist Interest in Each of the United States," *American Quarterly Register*, 1842, pp. 42–58.

Peet, Stephen. History of the Presbyterian and Congregational Churches and Ministry in Wisconsin. Milwaukee, 1851.

Peoria *Democratic Press*, 1842–50. Peoria, Illinois.

Peoria *Register and Northwestern Gazetteer*, 1837–43. Peoria, Illinois.

Perry, Albert J., ed. History of Knox County, Illinois, Its Cities, Towns, and People. 2 vols. Chicago, 1912.

Pierce, Bessie L. A History of Chicago. 2 vols. New York, 1937–40.

Porter, Mary H. Eliza Chappell Porter: A Memoir. New York, 1892.

Portrait and Biographical Record of Winnebago and Boone Counties, Illinois. Chicago, 1892.

Presbytery of Peoria. History of the Presbytery of Peoria and Its

Churches, from 1828 to 1888 by a Committee of the Presbytery. Peoria, Illinois, 1888.

Prince, Ezra M. "The War with Mexico," *Transactions of McLean County Historical Society,* I (1899), 17–30.

Proceedings of the General Convention of Congregational Ministers and Delegates in the United States, Held at Albany, New York, on the 5th, 6th, 7th, and 8th of October, 1852. New York, 1852.

Proceedings of the Republican National Convention, Held at Chicago, May 16th, 17th, and 18th, 1860. Press and Tribune Documents for 1860. No. 3.

Proceedings of the Seventy-fifth Anniversary of the Congregational Church, Geneseo, Illinois, September 10, 11, 12, 13, 1911. Geneseo, Illinois, 1911.

Proceedings of the Triennial Convention of Ministers and Delegates in the Northwest, Held in Connection with the Chicago Theological Seminary at Chicago, October 20 and 21, 1858. Chicago, 1858.

Quarles, Benjamin. "Sources of Abolitionist Income," *Mississippi Valley Historical Review,* XXXII (1945), 63–76.

Rammelkamp, Charles Henry. Illinois College: A Centennial History, 1829–1839. New Haven, 1928.

—— "The Reverberations of the Slavery Conflict in a Pioneer College," *Mississippi Valley Historical Review,* XIV (1928), 447–61.

Recollections of the Pioneers of Lee County. Dixon, Illinois, 1893.

Report on Knox College. Presented to the General Association of Illinois, May 24, 1861. Quincy, Illinois, 1861.

Richardson, William, Jr. "Dr. David Nelson and His Times," *Journal of the Illinois State Historical Society,* XIII (1921), 433–63.

Richman, Irving G. John Brown among the Quakers, and other Sketches. Des Moines, Iowa, 1894.

Rights of Congregationalists in Knox College: Being the Report of a Committee of Investigation of the General Association of Illinois; with an Appendix. Chicago, 1859.

Robinson, Luther E., ed. Historical and Biographical Record of Monmouth and Warren County, Illinois. 2 vols. Chicago, 1927.

Rogers, John A. R. Birth of Berea College: A Story of Providence. Berea, Kentucky, 1933.

Roy, Joseph E. "Fifty Years of Home Missions," In Commemoration of the Fiftieth Anniversary of the Organization of the General Congregational Association of Illinois. Ottawa, Illinois, 1894.

—— Kansas, Her Struggle and Her Defense. A Discourse Preached in the Plymouth Congregational Church of Chicago, Sabbath Afternoon, June 1, 1856, by the Pastor, Rev. J. E. Roy. Chicago, 1856.

—— Memorial Addresses and Proceedings at the Thirtieth Anniversary of the Settlement of Geneseo, Illinois, November 19th and 20th, 1866. Chicago, 1867.

—— Memorial of the One Hundredth Birthday of John Roy. Privately printed, 1898.

—— Pilgrim Letters. Boston, 1888.

Sandburg, Carl. Abraham Lincoln: The War Years. 4 vols. New York, 1939.

Scammon, J. Young, ed. Reports of Cases Argued and Determined in the Supreme Court of the State of Illinois. Philadelphia, Boston, and Chicago, 1841–44.

Scott, E. C. Ministerial Directory of the Presbyterian Church, U.S., 1861–1941. Austin, Texas, 1942.

Scott, Franklin William. Newspapers and Periodicals of Illinois, 1814–1879. Illinois Historical Collections, Vol. VI. Springfield, Illinois, 1910.

Selby, Mrs. Paul. "Recollections of a Little Girl in the Forties with Apologies for a Somewhat Lengthy Sequel," *Journal of the Illinois State Historical Society,* XVI (1923), 157–83.

Sellen, C. J. Review of the Commerce, Manufactures, and the Public and the Private Improvements of Galesburg: Containing a Brief History of Knox College, and Sketches of the First Settlement of the Town. Galesburg, Illinois, 1857.

Shallenberger, E. H. Stark County and Its Pioneers. Cambridge, Illinois, 1876.

Shepphard, Thomas J. "An Abolition Center," *Ohio Archaeological and Historical Publications,* XIX (1910), 265–68.

Siebert, Wilbur H. The Underground Railroad from Slavery to Freedom. New York, 1898.

Smith, Bruce E. "Home Guards," *The Palimpsest,* V (1924), 189–233. Iowa City, Iowa.

Smith, Theodore Clark. The Liberty and Free Soil Parties of the Northwest. New York, 1897.

Society for the Promotion of Collegiate and Theological Education at the West. Annual Report, first to sixteenth, 1843–59. New York.

—— Proceedings at the Quarter Century Anniversary of the Society for the Promotion of Collegiate and Theological Education at the West, Marietta, Ohio, November 7–10, 1868. New York, 1868.

Sosey, Frank. "Palmyra and Its Historical Environment," *Missouri Historical Review,* XXIII (1929), 363–66.

Sparks, Edwin E. The Lincoln-Douglas Debates of 1858. Collections of the Illinois State Historical Library, Lincoln Series. Springfield, Illinois, 1908.

Spinka, Matthew, ed. History of the Illinois Congregational and Christian Churches. Chicago, 1944.

Staiger, C. Bruce. "Abolitionism and the Presbyterian Schism of 1837–1838," *Mississippi Valley Historical Review,* XXXVI (1949), 391–444.

Stanton, Henry B. Random Recollections. New York, 1887.

Stevens, Frank. History of Lee County. 2 vols. Chicago, 1914.

Stevens, W. Past and Present of Will County. Chicago, 1907.

Stowe, Lyman Beecher. Saints, Sinners, and Beechers. Indianapolis, 1934.

Sturtevant, Julian M. Autobiography. Chicago, 1896.

Sweet, William Warren, ed. The Baptists. Religion on the American Frontier, Vol. I. New York, 1931.

—— The Congregationalists. Religion on the American Frontier, Vol. III. Chicago, 1939.

—— The Presbyterians. Religion on the American Frontier, Vol. II. New York, 1936.

Tappan, Lewis. History of the American Missionary Association. New York, 1855.

—— Life of Arthur Tappan. New York, 1870.

Taylor, Elma Hulme. "A History of the First Congregational Church, Geneseo, Illinois," *Journal of the Illinois State Historical Society,* XX (1927), 112–27.

Taylor, Lathrop. "History of the Central Association," Illinois Society of Church History, Congregational, Historical Statement and Papers, pp. 91–96.

Tennal, Ralph. History of Nemaha County, Kansas. Lawrence, Kansas, 1916.

Thayer, Eli. A History of the Kansas Crusade, Its Friends and Foes. New York, 1889.

Thomas, Benjamin P. Theodore Weld, Crusader for Freedom. New Brunswick, N.J., 1950.

Thomas, Thomas Ebenezer. Correspondence of Thomas Ebenezer Thomas, Mainly Relating to the Anti-Slavery Conflict in Ohio, Especially in the Presbyterian Church. Edited by Alfred A. Thomas. n.p., 1909.

Thome, James A., and Horace Kimball. Emancipation in the West Indies: Six Months Tour of the West Indies in the Year 1837. New York, 1838.

Thompson, George. Prison Life and Reflections or a Narrative of the Arrest, Trial, Conviction, Imprisonment, Treatment, Observations, Reflections and Deliverance of Work, Burr and Thompson. Oberlin, Ohio, 1847.

Tisler, C. C. "Prudence Crandall, Abolitionist," *Journal of the Illinois State Historical Society,* XXXIII (1940), 203–6.

Todd, John. Early Settlement and Growth of Western Iowa: A Reminiscence. Des Moines, Iowa, 1906.

Townsley, Frances E. A Pilgrim Maid: The Self-Told Story of Frances E. Townsley. Butler, Indiana, 1908.

Tyler, Alice Felt. Freedom's Ferment: Phases of American Social History to 1860. Minneapolis, 1944.

Utica *Tribune,* 1904. Utica, New York.

Villard, Oswald Garrison. John Brown: A Biography, 1800–1859. New York, 1929.

Wager, Daniel E., ed. Our County and Its People—Oneida County (New York). Boston, 1896.

Warren, Robert Penn. John Brown, the Making of a Martyr. New York, 1929.

Way, Royal Bronson. The Rock River Valley, Its History, Traditions, Legends, and Charms. Chicago, 1926.

Weld, Theodore Dwight. Letters of Theodore Dwight Weld, Angelina Grimké Weld, and Sarah Grimké, 1822–1844. Edited by Gilbert H. Barnes and Dwight L. Dumond. 2 vols. New York, 1934.

Weld, Theodore Dwight, ed. American Slavery as It Is: Testimony of a Thousand Witnesses. New York, 1839.

Wells, Ira K. "Abjah Wells," *Collections of the Kansas Historical Society,* XIV (1918), 80–84.

Western Citizen, 1842–53. Chicago.

Western Monthly Magazine and Literary Journal, 1833–37. Cincinnati, Ohio.

Westin, Gunner, ed. Emigranterna och Kyrkan: Brev fran och till Svenskar, 1849–1892. Stockholm, 1932.

Whipple, Charles T. Relation of the American Board of Commissioners for Foreign Missions to Slavery. Boston, 1861.

"Whitestown Seminary, History of a Famous Educational Institution," Utica *Tribune,* Jan. 31, 1904. Utica, New York.

Whittier, John Greenleaf. "The Anti-Slavery Convention of 1833," *Old South Leaflets,* Vol. IV, No. 81. Boston.

Wilcox, John S., ed. History of Kane County. Chicago, 1904.

Williams, Wolcott B. A History of Olivet College, 1844–1900. Olivet, Michigan, 1901.

Wilson, Henry. History of the Rise and Fall of the Slave Power in America. 2 vols. Boston, 1872.

Woodley, Thomas Frederick. Great Leveler: The Life of Thaddeus Stevens. New York, 1937.

Wright, G. Frederick. Charles Grandison Finney. New York, 1893.

Wright, Luella. Peter Melendy: The Mind and the Soil. Iowa City, Iowa, 1943.

Index

Abolitionism: Allan family's attitude toward, 91, 93-95; Blanchard's contribution to, 221-37; in Burned-over District, 12; in colonies along North-South border, 302-26; in educational institutions, 1-3, 33-44, 52-61, 66, 238-59, 329-72; in Illinois, 84-114, 117-28, 129-55, 191-220, 268-77; importance of journalism in, 172-88 (*see also* Anti-slavery press); in Iowa, 139; Liberty Party and, 156-71; in Ohio, 93-94; religion and, 260-301; women in, 172-88; Yale Band and, 113-14; *see also* Anti-slavery societies

Adams, John Quincy, 166, 230

Adams, Ripley E., 161*n*

Adams, N.Y., 17, 20, 135

Adams County, Ill., 141*n*, 161*n*, 162*n*, 164, 166

"Address to the Anti-Slavery Christians of the United States," 278

Adelphi (literary society), 335-38, 341, 342, 348, 349

A.H.M.S., *see* American Home Missionary Society

Albany, N.Y., first national convention of Congregationalists in, 295-300

Allan, Irene B. (Mrs. William Allan), 181

Allan, James M. (father), 90, 91, 92

Allan, James M. (son), 91-93

Allan, William T., 53, 55, 91-98; in Illinois, 132, 143, 145-48, 172, 178, 180

Alton, Ill., 125-26, 127-28

Alton *Observer* (Lovejoy's newspaper), 118, 125, 132-33

American and Foreign Anti-Slavery Society, 11*n*, 144*n*, 278, 289

American Annals of Education (periodical), 30

American Anti-Slavery Society: agents of, 14, 63, 79; branches in Illinois, 117-28 (*see also* Illinois Anti-Slavery Society); internal dissension in, 144, 277; leaders in, 39-40, 59-61, 96, 137-38; organization of, 33; student delegate from Lane Seminary attends, 53-54

American Bible Society, 11*n*

American Board of Commissioners for Foreign Missions, 11*n*, 261, 279, 281, 288-301 *passim*

American Educational Society, 11*n*, 26, 31, 32, 262, 263

American Female Reform Society, 11*n*

American Home Missionary Society (A.H.M.S.), 11*n*, 48*n*; combined project of Congregational and Presbyterian churches, 254, 262, 263, 279, 281; work in Illinois, 72, 76, 77, 99, 102, 103, 111-14, in Iowa, 113, 139, in Missouri, 125

American Lyceum, 31, 32

American Missionary Association, 289, 292, 293, 300, 307

American Reform Tract and Book Society, 187

American School Agents Society, 32

American Seaman's Friend Society, 11*n*

American Slavery as It Is: Testimony of a Thousand Witnesses, 96

American Sunday School Union, 11*n*

American Temperance Society, 37

American Tract Society, 11*n*

Amity, Iowa, 316-20

Anderson, Jeremiah, 303-4

Andover, Ill., 107, 202, 323